Notes on the Folk-Lore of the Northern Counties of England and the Borders

William Henderson

Alpha Editions

This edition published in 2019

ISBN : 9789353920142

Design and Setting By
Alpha Editions
email - alphaedis@gmail.com

NOTES ON THE

FOLK-LORE

OF THE

NORTHERN COUNTIES OF ENGLAND AND THE BORDERS.

A NEW EDITION WITH MANY ADDITIONAL NOTES.

BY

WILLIAM HENDERSON,

AUTHOR OF "MY LIFE AS AN ANGLER."

"Our mothers' maids in our childhood . . . have so frayed us with bullbeggars, spirits, witches, urchins, elves, hags, fairies, satyrs, pans, faunes, sylvans, kit-with-the-candlestick (will-o'-the-wisp), tritons (kelpies), centaurs, dwarfs, giants, imps, calcars (assy-pods), conjurors, nymphs, changelings, incubus, Robin-Goodfellow (Brownies), the spoorey, the man in the oak, the hellwain, the firedrake (dead light), the Puckle, Tom Thumb, Hobgoblin, Tom Tumbler, Boneless, and such other bug-bears, that we are afraid of our own shadows."

REGINALD SCOTT.

LONDON:

PUBLISHED FOR THE FOLK-LORE SOCIETY BY

W. SATCHELL, PEYTON AND CO.,

12, TAVISTOCK STREET, COVENT GARDEN. W.C.

1879.

TO

THE MOST HONOURABLE

THE MARQUESS OF LONDONDERRY,

IN REMEMBRANCE OF MUCH KINDNESS

AND OF MANY PLEASANT HOURS SPENT TOGETHER,

THIS VOLUME IS, BY PERMISSION, INSCRIBED

WITH EVERY SENTIMENT OE RESPECT AND ESTEEM

BY

HIS LORDSHIP'S ATTACHED FRIEND,

WILLIAM HENDERSON.

The Council of the Folk-Lore Society, in issuing this work as one of the publications for the year 1879, desire to point ont to the Members that it is chiefly owing to the generous proposal of Mr. Henderson they are enabled to produce in the second year of the Society's existence a book so much appreciated hy the Folk-Lore student. The first edition, puhlished in 1866, has long since heen exhausted, and it is only very rarely that a second-hand copy is to he met with. Moreover, the Author has added some considerable and valuable notes obtained since the publication of the first edition; and these facts brought the book within the compass of the Society's Rules.

G. L. Gomme,

Hon. Secretary to the Folk-Lore Society,

Castelnau, Barnes London. S.W.

PREFACE TO THE FIRST EDITION.

THE AGE in which we live is remarkable, as in other points of view, so in this, that old habits and customs, old laws and sayings, old beliefs and superstitions, which have held their ground in the universal mind from the remotest antiquity, are fast fading away and perishing. We of the nineteenth century may congratulate ourselves on their disappearance; we may lament it, but the fact remains the same; and I for one will frankly acknowledge that I regret much which we are losing, that I would not have these vestiges of the past altogether effaced. It were pity that they should utterly pass away, and leave no trace behind. My heart as well as my imagination is too closely bound up with the sayings and doings which gave zest to the life of my forefathers, and so I became a Folk-Lore student before Folk-Lore came into vogue as a pursuit. And, as befitted a genuine North-countryman, my researches were chiefly made in the district between the Tweed and the Humber. Accordingly, when, on the 14th of May, 1861, I was called upon as President of the Durham Athenæum to deliver a lecture in my native city, I chose for my subject the Folk-Lore of that part of England, and through the kindness of a few friends, resident in the North, if not natives of it, who zealously aided my researches, I was enabled to lay before the members of the Athenæum a considerable collection of the stories, sayings, and superstitions of old Northumbria.

It was plain that the mine was one of great riches, and it was to some extent unworked. Strangely enough, the mention of North Country Folk-Lore in *Choice Notes*, reprinted from *Notes and Queries*, is exceedingly scanty and meagre; and though Brand's *Popular Antiquities* contains a fairer proportion of matter from this district, and there is a good deal that is interesting in Richardson's *Local Historian's Table Book*, much more clearly remained to be gathered up. But there was no time to lose. Old traditions were no longer firmly rooted in the popular mind, old customs were fast dying out, old sayings and household tales lingering only on the lips of grandsires and grandames; they had ceased to be the spontaneous expression of the thoughts and feelings of the mass of our peasantry. And this, I believe, from two causes: first, the more generally diffused education of the people, and the fresh subjects of thought supplied to them in consequence; and again, the migration of families which has taken place since the working of collieries and the extension of railways. Formerly, as our parish registers would show, families lived on for centuries in the same village or small town, sending out offshoots far or near, as circumstances might lead. Now whole families uproot themselves and move into other districts; and it has been found that when people are wrenched away from local associations, though they may carry their traditions with them, they fail to transmit them to their descendants.

Be this however as it may, I continued my researches, noting down carefully every morsel of Folk-Lore that came before me, and my reward has been far beyond my expectations. Besides many histories and sayings more or less noteworthy, I lighted on a treasure of exceeding value, which, through the kindness of my friend the Rev. R. O. Bromfield of Sprouston, I have been enabled to make my own. It was in fact a collection of Border customs, legends, and superstitions put together, about fifty years ago, by a young medical student of the name of Wilkie, residing at Bowden, near Eildon Hall; and this at the desire of Sir Walter Scott, for the purpose of being used by him in a projected work on the subject, which he never carried beyond two short essays on the Border Minstrelsy. Mr. Wilkie appears to have been a favourite and protégé of Sir Walter Scott, who procured him an appointment in India, where the young man died. The collection, although of great interest, was, as I received it, by no means in a fit state for publication. The contents were not arranged, there was a good deal of repetition, and the style was diffuse and wordy.

Meanwhile I had shown my lecture to the accomplished Editor of the *Monthly Packet*, whose interest in this and kindred subjects is well known, and whose varied and extensive reading renders her opinion peculiarly valuable. She expressed a wish that the lecture should be turned into an article for that magazine. This was done, and that article is the nucleus of this volume. To it I have annexed the numerous contributions which during upwards of five years I have received from a wide circle of friends, and with it I have incorporated the Wilkie MS. illustrating the whole, so far as I was able, by the Folk-Lore of other parts of the country, and in a measure of all Europe. But for the kindness of many valuable friends who have noted down whatever bore upon the subject, and communicated to me the result of their observations, the collection could never have been formed; and I desire to express my hearty thanks to all who have thus aided me in my task, especially to the Rev. J. C. Atkinson, Perpetual Curate of Danby; the Rev. J. Barmby, Principal of Hatfield Hall, University of Durham; the Rev. J. F. Bigge, Vicar of Stamfordham; the Rev. R. O. Bromfield, Sprouston; the Rev. J. Cundill, Incumbent of St. Margaret's Durham; the Rev. W. Greenwell, Rector of St. Mary in the South Bailey, Durham; the Rev. J. W. Hick, Incumbent of Byer's Green; the Rev. Canon Humble, St. Ninian's, Perth; the Rev. George Ornsby, Vicar of Fishlake; the Rev. James Raine, York, Secretary of the Surtees Society; the Rev. H. B. Tristram, Master of Greatham Hospital; the Rev. R. Webster, Vicar of Kelloe; the Author of *The Heir of Redclyffe*; Mr. J. R. Appleton, Durham; Mr. Henry Denny, Assistant Curator of the Museum of the Leeds Philosophical and Literary Society; Mr. H. Heaviside, Stockton-on-Tees; Mr. James Hardy, Old Cambus; Mr. John Holland, Sheffield; the late

F. H. Johnson, M.D. Sunderland; Mrs. Murray, Torquay; Mr. T. P. Teale, F.R.S. Leeds; Mr. George Markham Tweddell, Stokesley; Mr. F. J. Wharam, Durham; Mr. C. Waistall, Cotherstone; and Mr. W. Wilcox, Whitburn.

To my friend the Rev. George Ornsby I am under still further obligations for much valuable general assistance in my undertaking, and to the Rev. S. Baring-Gould for many notes of exceeding interest, and for much of the Introductory Chapter, including all the references to the Fathers and Schoolmen. The notes are dispersed throughout the work, and are distinguished by his initials. I must further add, that I have not pursued my labours single-handed, although it is the wish of my fellow-worker, who desires only to be designated by the initials S.W., that this volume comes out under my name alone. I cannot, however, in justice do less than state here that her share in the work has been fully equal to my own.

In comparing and classifying the subject-matter of this volume, I have chiefly used the following books: Brand's *Popular Antiquities*,—*Choice Notes from Notes and Queries: Folk-Lore*,—Kelly's *Indo-European Traditions*,—Thorpe's *Mythology and Popular Traditions of Scandinavia*,—and Richardson's *Local Historian's Table Book*.

Durham, 1866.

PREFATORY NOTICE TO THE SECOND EDITION.

At the close of the introductory chapter to the first edition of the following work, I expressed a wish which had grown and strengthened within me during its compilation—a wish that all such Folk-Lore as still existed in the remoter parts of our land should at once be gathered up, classified, and carefully preserved.

This was happily effected, after a lapse of some years, by the establishment, in 1878, of the Folk-Lore Society, which has for its object "the preservation and publication of popular Traditions, Legendary Ballads, Local Proverbial Sayings, Superstitions and Old Customs, and all subjects relating to them."

Meanwhile, much new matter bearing on the Folk-Lore of the North of England and the Borders was brought before me by the kindness of my personal friends, and of others who felt an interest in the subject. All this was carefully incorporated into the original work, and this spring I placed the whole in the hands of the Honorary Secretary of the Folk-Lore Society, offering it, should such a course be desired, for publication under the auspices of that Society.

The Council was pleased to accept my proposal, and hence the appearance of this volume under circumstances so gratifying to the Author.

I must next tender my grateful thanks to those among my earlier correspondents who have kindly communicated to me whatever fresh Folk-Lore has come under their notice, and also to the new friends who have come forward to impart to me the result of their observation and their researches. Among these latter I beg to particularise Henry Crombie, Esq. Woodville House, Isle of Man; Joseph Crawhall, Esq. Newcastle-on-Tyne; J. S. Crompton, Esq. Azerley Hall, Ripon; M. T. Culley, Esq. Coupland Castle, Northumberland; W. Dobson, Esq. Park Terrace, Fulwood Park, Preston; Mrs. Evans, Scremerston Vicarage, Northumberland; Colonel Johnson, The Deanery, Chester-le-Street; the Rev. W. De Lancey Lawson, Newland Vicarage, Gloucestershire; Professor Marecco, Newcastle-on-Tyne; G. A. Robinson, Esq. Hill House, Reeth, Yorkshire; the late Rev. G. Rooke, Vicar of Embleton; the late Thomas Sopworth, Esq. London; Mr. Joshua Stott, Perth; the Rev. Hugh Taylor, Wark, Hexham; T. C. Thompson, Esq. East Grinstead; the Rev. Morgan G. Watkins, Barnoldby-le-Beck Rectory, Great Grimsby; the Rev. T. H. Wilkinson, Moulsham Vicarage, Chelmsford; the Rev. T. P. Williamson, Little Brickhill, Bletchley; Mrs. Latham, Florence Villa, Torquay, to whom I elsewhere acknowledge my more than usual obligations; and Thomas Satchell, Esq. Downshire Hill House, Hampstead, who, with a most generous sacrifice of time and pains, has compiled the voluminous index which accompanies this edition of my work.

The pages of the present edition have further been enriched by references to Napier's *Folk-Lore of the West of Scotland;* Denny's *Folk-Lore of China;* Dobson's *Rambles by the Ribble;* and *Yorkshire Oddities*, by the Rev. S. Baring-Gould.

It only remains for me to add, that I feel it impossible for me sufficiently to express my obligations to my relative, Miss Susanna Warren, for much valuable assistance rendered to the work; indeed, ours must be understood to have been a joint labour.

Ashford Court, Ludlow,
July 1879.

CONTENTS.

INTRODUCTORY CHAPTER.

CHAPTER I.

LIFE AND DEATH OF MAN.

CHAPTER II.

DAYS AND SEASONS.

CHAPTER III.

Spells and Divinations.

CHAPTER IV.

Portents and Auguries.

CHAPTER V.

Charms and Spells.

CHAPTER VI.

Witchcraft.

CHAPTER VII.

Local Sprites.

CHAPTER VIII.

Worms or Dragons.

CHAPTER IX.

Occult Powers and Sympathies.

CHAPTER X.

Haunted Spots.

CHAPTER XI.

Dreams.

FOLK-LORE

OF

THE NORTHERN COUNTIES.

INTRODUCTORY CHAPTER.

IT is difficult, while living on the surface of society, so smooth, so rational, so commonplace, to realise what relics of a widely different past linger in its depths—relics of an extensive and deeply-rooted system of mythology, antedating in great measure Christianity itself. Yet so it is: in almost every part of our island we occasionally come across such bits of stubborn antiquity, but in the North of England they abound. The district between the Tweed and the Humber teems with Folk-Lore of a rich and varied character. Great part of the county of Durham is indeed spoiled (in an antiquarian point of view) by collieries; but it still contains some quiet villages far away from great thoroughfares, where strange tales are yet told and strange old customs practised; while the north and west of Northumberland, and the North and East Ridings of Yorkshire, abound with them.

Those who mix much among the lower orders, and have opportunities of inquiring closely into their beliefs, customs, and usages, will find in these remote places—nay, even in our towns and larger villages—a vast mass of superstition, holding its ground most tenaciously. On looking closely into this we discern, among much that is mythical and legendary in its character, and much that is the simple outgrowth of human fancy and imagination, a good deal of what is unquestionably heathenism in disguise. Archbishop Whately states this perhaps too broadly.

"It is," he says, "a marvel to many, and seems to them nearly incredible, that the Israelites should have gone after other gods, and yet the vulgar in most parts of Christendom are actually serving the gods of their heathen ancestors. But then they do not call them gods, but fairies or bogles, and they do not apply the word worship to their veneration of them, nor sacrifice to their offerings. And this slight change of name keeps most people in ignorance of a fact that is before their eyes."[1]

This is a strong statement, yet historical facts appear to bear it out. We know that as late as the seventeenth century undisguised idol-worship was to be found in Brittany, while down to the eighteenth it was common there for offerings of money, milk, and ears of corn to be made to the great Menhir, an obelisk once connected with Druidical worship. We know, too, that almost if not quite up to the present time, on holiday eves, the Norwegian peasant has offered cakes, sweet porridge, and libations of wort or buttermilk, on mounds consecrated to the invisible folk, and called bœttir mounds; and, as will be shown hereafter, well-nigh within the memory of man, beasts have been slain in sacrifice, at times of great extremity, in our own country; while the rites still in use for the dressing of wells at Buxton and Tissington in Derbyshire, and in other places throughout England and on the Borders, bear a singular resemblance to the Fontinalia of heathen Rome, when the nymphs of wells and fountains were honoured by flinging nosegays into the fountains and crowning the wells with garlands of flowers.

The question naturally arises, how is it that heathen beliefs and heathen observances still exist in a country which was christianized so many centuries ago? We may reply, with reference to the district especially under our consideration, that the stern mould of the northern mind is strong to retain images once deeply impressed upon it. And on the subject generally it may be observed that from the beginning the Church appears practically to have tolerated such parts of the old mythological system as she considered harmless, and to have permitted them to live on without check or rebuke. Thus the customs of the Lupercalia passed into those of St. Valentine's day, and, the Scandinavian

[1] *Miscellaneous Remains*, p. 274.

Yule coinciding with the Feast of the Nativity, the old Yule merrymakings and mummings continued in use without raising ecclesiastical censure. Thus the honour long given to persons and demigods was transferred to saints and martyrs. Thus, again, old sacred sites were taken possession of for the new faith. We often find Christian burial-grounds occupying the site of Pagan ones; and I myself have seen huge upright stones marking some place sacred in heathen eyes in close proximity to Christian churches.[1] In Sweden there was, at the first propagation of Christianity, a good deal of intermingling of truth and error. Heathen images were removed from the ancient oratories, and those of sacred beings set up in their places; still old associations proved sometimes too strong for the converts, and prayers to Thor and Freya were mixed with Christian orisons.

In judging the clergy of the day for their line of action in this and kindred matters we should in justice remember that they were taken from among the people, and consequently imbued with the same prejudices, feelings, and superstitions as those to whom they ministered. Nor must we forget that, like them, they were wholly unacquainted with the causes of natural phenomena. This universal ignorance of the laws of nature goes far to account for the widespread superstition which for ages pervaded all Europe, and which from local causes has taken so firm a grasp of some particular spots.

Perfectly unacquainted with the laws that govern the universe, the early Christians, like the Pagans and Neo-Platonists, made supernatural beings the special cause of all the phenomena of nature. They attributed to these beings, according to their beneficial or injurious effects, all atmospheric phenomena. According to them, angels watched over the different elements, and demons endeavoured to overthrow their power. From the struggle between them arose storms and whirlwinds, plagues and earthquakes. St. Clement of Alexandria refers all this to diabolical agency, and the same idea was perpetuated throughout the

[1] Thus, in Ireland, St. Patrick and his followers almost invariably selected the sacred sites of Paganism, and built their wooden churches under the shadow of the Round Towers—then as mysterious and inscrutable as they are to-day.

Middle Ages.[1] Hence it was that of old, storms were conjured to depart by the sign of the cross or the ringing of church bells, as indeed to this day Roman Catholics are wont to cross themselves during a thunderstorm.

From the first the Church, by the decrees of Councils and the voice of her chief Fathers and Doctors, condemned such superstition as she deemed worthy of notice; not however on the ground of folly, but of impiety. It is possible, therefore, that her denunciations might go towards confirming a belief in the whole fabric of superstition, as a real and powerful though forbidden thing. "Religion," said Lactantius, "is the cultus of the truth, superstition is that of the false." Among persons mentioned in the Apostolical Constitutions as unworthy of baptism are "magicians, enchanters, astrologers, diviners, magical charmers, idle and wandering beggars, makers of amulets and phylacteries, and such as dealt in heathenish lustrations, soothsayers and observers of signs and omens, interpreters of palpitations, observers of accidents in meeting others, making divinations therefrom as upon a blemish in the eye or in the feet, observers of the motions of birds or weazels, observers of voices and symbolical sounds. All these are to be examined and tried a considerable time whether they would relinquish their arts or not. If they did they might be received; if not they were to be rejected from baptism. Phylacteria were amulets made of riband with a text of scripture or some other charm of words written on them to cure diseases or to keep off danger—a piece of heathen superstition hard to cure. Clergymen who made such were condemned by the council of Laodicea, and the wearers ordered to be cast out of the Church. The council of Trullo decreed six years' penance for such offenders."—Bingham's *Antiquities*, book xi. chap. 5. "I omit other things that might make us weep," says St. Chrysostom.[2] "Your auguries, your omens, your superstitious observances, your casting of nativities, your signs, your amulets, your divinations, your incantations, your magical arts,—

[1] *St. Thomas Aquinas, Summ. Theolog. I. quæst.* lxxx. act 2. *St. Bonaventura, Comp. Theolog. veritat* ii. 26. *Albertus Magnus de Potentia Dæmonium.*

[2] Hom. X. on 1 Tim.

these are crying sins, enough to provoke the anger of God." "You may see a man washing himself from the pollution of a dead body; but from dead works, never. Again, spending much zeal in the pursuit of riches, and yet supposing the whole is undone by the crowing of a cock." "So darkened are they in their understanding, their soul is filled with all sorts of terrors. For instance: 'Such a person,' one will say, 'was the first to meet me as I was going out of doors to-day,' and of course a thousand ills must ensue. At another time, 'That wretch of a servant, in giving me my shoes, held out the left shoe first,'—terrible mishaps and mischief! 'I myself, in coming out, put my left leg foremost;' and here, too, is a token of misfortune. Then, as I go out, my right eye turns up from beneath—a sure sign of tears. Again, the women, when the reeds strike against the standards and ring, or when they themselves are scratched by the shuttle, turn this also into a sign. And again, when they strike the web with the shuttle, and do it with some vehemence, and then the reeds on the top sound, this again they make a sign; and ten thousand things besides as ridiculous. And so if an ass bray, or a cock crow, or a man sneeze, or whatever else happen, like men bound with ten thousand chains—they suspect everything, and are more enslaved than all the slaves in the world."[1]

A long list of popular superstitions was condemned by a council held in the eighth century at Leptines, in Hainault, under the title of *Indiculus superstitionum et paganarium.* Pope Gregory III. issued similar anathemas.[2] The *Capitularies* of Charlemagne aud his successors repeat the denunciation of them.

About the same date similar superstitions were rebuked in Scotland by the Abbot Cumeanus the Wise, in his tract *De mensura pœnitentiarum.* In the same century St. Eligius, Bishop of Noyon, preached against similar superstitions: "Above all, I implore you not to observe the sacrilegious customs of the pagans. Do not consult the gravers of talismans, nor diviners, nor sorcerers, nor enchanters, for any sickness whatsoever. . . .

[1] *St. Chrysost. Hom. XII. on Eph.* iv. 17. Compare also *St. Clem. Alex. Strom.* vii. 4, pp. 841-844. *St. Cyril of Jerus.* iv. 37. *St. Augustine, Enchiridion,* p. 134, *de Doct. Christ.* ii. 20, 21, &c.

[2] *Concil. ed. Labbe,* lib. vi. fol. 1476, 1482.

Do not take notice of auguries, or of sneezings; do not pay attention to the songs of the birds when you go abroad. Let no Christian pay regard to the particular day on which he leaves a house or enters it. Let no one perplex himself about the new moon or eclipses. Let no one do on the calends of January those forbidden, ridiculous, ancient, and disreputable things, such as dancing, or keeping open house all night, or getting drunk. Let no one on the feast of St. John, or any other saint, celebrate solstices by dances, carols, or diabolical chants; let no one invoke Neptune, Pluto, Diana, Minerva, or his genius ; let no one rest on the day of Jupiter, unless it fall on a saint's day; nor observe the month of May, nor any other season or day except the Lord's day. Let no one light torches along the highways and cross-roads; let no one tie notes to the neck of a man or some animal; let no one make lustrations or enchantments upon herbs, or make his cattle pass through a split tree, or through a hole made in the ground. Let no one utter loud cries when the moon is pale; let no one fear that something will happen to him at new moon; let no one believe in destiny of fortune, or the quadrature of the geniture, commonly called a nativity," &c. &c.

Four centuries later Burchard of Worms made a collection of denunciations of superstitions from the decrees of Councils and Popes, and the list is very remarkable. "Superstition is a vice opposed by excess to adoration and religion," said the illustrious Gerson; and in the provincial Council of York, in A.D. 1466, it was declared, with St. Thomas, that all superstition was idolatry.

On the whole, it certainly appears that the early and medieval Churches in their collective form, far from encouraging heathenish superstition, constantly protested against it. Individual clergy in remote districts may have taken a different line, as St. Patrick is said to have "engrafted Christianity on Paganism with so much skill that he won over the people to the Christian religion before they understood the exact difference between the two systems of belief."[1] At any rate, the old superstition lived on with marvellous vitality, and the Reformation, at least on the Continent and in Scotland, did little to check it. On the con-

[1] Dr. O'Donovan's *Four Masters*, p. 131.

trary, it would seem, that, when cut away from communion with the angelic world and saints departed, men's minds fastened the more readily upon a supernatural system of another order. Curiously enough, Martin Luther fell a prey to the grossest superstition. Witness the following extracts from his *Table Talk*, quoted in the Introduction to Thorpe's *Mythology*, vol. ii.:—

"Changelings (*Wechselbälge*) and Kielkropfs, Satan lays in the place of the genuine children, that people may be tormented with them. He often carries off young maidens into the water, has intercourse with them, and keeps them with him until they have been delivered, then lays such children in cradles, takes the genuine children out, and carries them away. But such changelings, it is said, do not live more than eighteen or twenty years." Again: "Eight years ago there was a changeling in Dessau, which I, Dr. Martin Luther, have both seen and touched: it was twelve years old, and had all its senses, so that people thought it was a proper child; but that mattered little, for it only ate, and that as much as any four ploughmen or thrashers, and when any one touched it, it screamed; when things in the house went wrong, so that any damage took place, it laughed and was merry; but if things went well it cried. Thereupon I said to the Prince of Anhalt, 'If I were prince or ruler here I would have this child thrown into the water, into the Moldau, that flows by Dessau, and would run the risk of being a homicide.' But the Elector of Saxony, who was then at Dessau, and the Prince of Anhalt, would not follow my advice. I then said they ought to cause a pater-noster to be said in the church, that God would take the devil away from them. This was done daily at Dessau, and the said changeling died two years after."

On at least one point the early Scotch and English Calvinistic divines showed the greatest credulity. It is notorious that they believed unhesitatingly in the existence of sorcery, and were ever ready to extend and enforce the legal penalties against it. "It is not to be denied," says Sir Walter Scott,[1] "that the Presbyterian ecclesiastics, who in Scotland were often appointed by the Privy Council commissioners for the trial of witchcraft, evinced a very extraordinary degree of credulity in such cases,

[1] *Demonology and Witchcraft*, letter viii.

and that the temporary superiority of the same sect in England was marked by enormous cruelties of this kind."

The notices, however, of the Folk-Lore of my fellow-countrymen which I have been able to collect during the last few years are widely varied in their origin. If some of them are unmistakeable relics of heathenism, some have their origin in the rites and customs of the unreformed Church, and some in the myths and historical traditions of our ancestors the Saxons and Danes; while others, again, appear to be the spontaneous growth of sensitive and imaginative minds, yearning for communion with a mysterious past and yet more mysterious future. They are varied, too, in their character; some breathing deep religious feeling, some full of light, graceful fancy, while some are gross, vulgar, even cruel superstitions. Let me add, that while recording them a conviction has deepened upon me that there are very, very many more incidents of a similar kind to be collected. Unless this be speedily done I firmly believe that many a singular usage and tradition will pass away from the land unnoted and unremembered. It would be very desirable if a scheme could be organised for systematically collecting and classifying the remnants of our Folk-Lore; but at least I would intreat all those in whose eyes the subject possesses any interest accurately to note down every old custom, observance, proverb, saying, or legend which comes before them.

CHAPTER I.

LIFE AND DEATH OF MAN.

Day of birth—Hour of birth—Border customs at the birth of a child—Unchristened ground—Unbaptized children at the mercy of fairies—Safeguards for the child—Folk-lore connected with baptism—Cutting of nails—The toom cradle—The child's first visit—The ash tree—Weeds and onfas'—Beads of peony root—The caul and veil—Folk-lore of childhood: Rain charms—Rainbow charms—Crow, snail, and nettle charms—Folk-lore of boyhood: School rites and customs—The riding of the stang—Confirmation—Days for marriage—Seasons for marriage—Marriage portents—Marriage customs: On the Borders—In Yorkshire—Throwing the shoe—Kissing the bride—The petting stone—Hot pots—Rubbing with pease-straw—Race for a ribbon—Portents of death—Whistling woman and crowing hen—Border presages—The wraith or waff—St. Mark's eve—Canffriddling—Saining a corpse—Death with the tide—Discovery of the drowned—Use of pigeons' or game-fowl feathers—Carrying the dead with the sun—The passing bell.

THROUGHOUT the Borders, and in the six northern counties of England, peculiar rites and customs are bound up with every stage of human life. To begin at the beginning—the nursery has there a Folk-Lore of its own. And, first, the future character and fortunes of the infant may be divined from the day of the week on which it was born. For, as the old rhyme runs—

Monday's child is fair of face,
Tuesday's child is full of grace,
Wednesday's child is full of woe,
And Thursday's child has far to go.

Friday's child is loving and giving,
And Saturday's child works hard for its living;
But the child that is born on the Sabbath-day
Is blithe and bonny, good and gay.

It is remarkable that these verses, which are still current in

Stockton and its neighbourhood, should be found also in the west of England. Mrs. Bray records them in her *Traditions of Devonshire* (vol. ii. p. 287), substituting "Christmas Day" for the "Sabbath Day," and "fair and wise" for "blithe and bonny," and says that they are in common use at Tavistock.

They do not correspond with the birth auguries in the *Universal Fortune-teller*, a book which has had, and indeed still has, a wide circulation among the lower orders of our countrymen.

Sunday—Great riches, long life, and happiness.

Monday—Unsuccessful, irresolute, easily imposed on, yet good-natured and obliging.

Tuesday—Passionate, implacable.

Wednesday—Studious, will excel in literature.

Thursday—Will attain riches and honour.

Friday—Of a strong constitution.

Saturday—An unlucky day—but the child may come to good.

"Sunday children" are in Yorkshire deemed secure from the malice of evil spirits. In Germany, too, they are held to be privileged beings, but I am not aware that their immunities are so clearly defined as they are in Sussex, where they are warranted against hanging and drowning.

"Sunday children" in Denmark have prerogatives by no means to be coveted. Witness the following narration from Thorpe's *Mythology*, vol. ii. p. 203: "In Fyen there was a woman who was born on a Sunday, and, like other Sunday's children, had the faculty of seeing much that was hidden from others. But, because of this property, she could not pass by the church at night without seeing a hearse or a spectre—the gift became a perfect burden to her. She therefore sought the advice of a man skilled in such matters, who directed her, whenever she saw a spectre, to say, 'Go to Heaven;' but when she met a hearse, 'Hang on.' Happening some time after to meet a hearse, she, through lapse of memory, cried out, 'Go to Heaven,' and straightway the hearse rose in the air, and vanished. Afterwards, meeting a spectre, she said to it, 'Hang on,' when the spectre clung round her neck, hung on her back, and drove her down into the earth before it. For three days her shrieks were heard before the spectre would put an end to her wretched life."

The hour of birth is also important, for children born during the hour after midnight have the power through life of seeing the spirits of the departed. Mrs. L——, a Yorkshire lady, informs me that she was very near being thus distinguished, but the clock had not struck twelve when she was born. When a child she mentioned this circumstance to an old servant, adding that mamma was sure her birthday was the 23rd, not the 24th, for she had inquired at the time. "Ay, ay," said the old woman, turning to the child's nurse, "mistress would be very anxious about *that*, for bairns born after midnight see more things than other folk."

The Wilkie MS. tells us that throughout the Border-land the birth of an infant is the signal for plenty of eating and drinking. Tea, duly qualified with brandy or whisky, and a profusion of shortbread and buns, are provided for all visitors, and it is very unlucky to allow anyone to leave the house without his share of these good things. But most important of all is the "shooten" or groaning cheese, from which the happy father must cut a "whang-o'luck" for the lassies of the company, taking care not to cut his own finger while so doing, since in that case the child would die before reaching manhood. The whang must be taken from the edge of the cheese, and divided into portions, one for each maiden. Should there be any to spare they may be distributed among the spinster friends of the family, but if the number should fall short the mistake cannot be rectified; there is no virtue in a second slice. The girls put these bits of cheese under their pillows, and ascribe to them the virtues of bridecake similarly treated.

Now it is plain that cake and a new cheese were formerly provided against the birth of a child both in England and Scotland, and the custom still extends as far south as the Humber. In the north of England, as soon as the happy event is over, the doctor cuts the cake and cheese, and all present partake of both, on pain of the poor baby growing up without personal charms. The cake which is in use on these occasions in Yorkshire is called pepper-cake, and somewhat resembles thick gingerbread. It is eaten with cheese and rich caudle, and all visitors to the house up to the baptism are invited to partake of it.[1] In Sweden the cake and cheese are got ready in good time; they are placed beside the bride in the bridal bed, in preparation for her first confinement.[2] In Oxfordshire the cake used to be cut first in the middle and gradually shaped to a ring, through which the child was passed on its christening-day. The Durham nurse reserves some cake and cheese, and when the infant is taken out to its christening she bestows them on the first person she meets of opposite sex to that of the child. I remember the perplexed face of a young undergraduate when at the baptism of one of my daughters the dole of cake and cheese was bestowed on him, and the late Canon Humble wrote thus on the subject: "I was once fortunate enough when a boy to receive the cake and cheese from a christening party going to St. Giles's church. I did not at once perceive what was meant when a great 'hunch' of cake and some cheese were thrust in my hand, so I drew back. The nurse, however, insisted on my taking them, and I did so, bestowing them afterwards on the first poor boy I met." A similar custom has I know but just died out in the Devonshire villages round Dartmoor, and in *Choice Notes, Folk-Lore*, we read of such a gift of bread and cheese in Somersetshire, and of a cake in Cornwall (page 147).

It is said in Yorkshire that a new-born infant should be laid first in the arms of a maiden before any one else touches it. Is this an outgrowth of the medieval belief that the Blessed Virgin was present at the birth of St. John the Baptist, and received him first in her arms?

It is thought unlucky on the Borders to tread on the graves of unbaptized children, or "unchristened ground" as they term it. The Wilkie MS. informs us of the special risk that is run. He who steps on the grave of a stillborn or unbaptized child, or of one who has been overlaid by its nurse, subjects himself to the fatal disease of the grave-merels, or grave-scab. This complaint comes on with trembling of the limbs and hard breathing, and at last the skin burns as if touched with hot iron. The following old verses elucidate this superstition:—

[1] Brand's *Pop. Ant.* ed. 1854, vol. ii. p. 71.

[2] Thorpe's *Mythology*, vol. ii. p. 109.

Woe to the babie that ne'er saw the sun,
  All alane and alane, oh!
His bodie shall lie in the kirk 'neath the rain,
  All alane and alane, oh!

His grave must be dug at the foot o' the wall,
  All alane and alane, oh!
And the foot that treadeth his body upon
  Shall have scab that will eat to the bane, oh!

And it ne'er will be cured by doctor on earth,
  Tho' every one should tent him, oh!
He shall tremble and die like the elf-shot eye,
  And return from whence he came, oh!

Powerless, however, as the faculty may be, there is a remedy for the grave-merels, though not of easy attainment. It lies in the wearing a sark, thus prepared. The lint must be grown in a field which shall be manured from a farmyard heap that has not been disturbed for forty years. It must be spun by old Habbitrot, that queen of spinsters, of whom more hereafter; it must be bleached by an honest bleacher, in an honest miller's milldam, and sewed by an honest tailor. On donning this mysterious vestment, the sufferer will at once regain his health and strength.[1]

It is curious to observe what a different feeling, with regard to stillborn children, may be met with in the South. We read in *Choice Notes* (p. 172) that one of the Commissioners of Devonport, after complaining of the charge made upon the parish for the interment of such children, said: "When I was a young man it was thought lucky to have a stillborn child put into any open grave, as it was considered a sure passport to heaven for the next person buried there." The late Canon Humble's experience is as follows: "When I was curate at Newburn, in Northumberland, the custom was to bring the coffin of an unbaptized babe with that of a full-grown person. The child's coffin was always laid on the other coffin towards the feet, and so rested while the service was said. There was generally a receptacle for it in the grave towards the feet, made by widening the grave at that

[1] In Sweden, if a person afflicted with an open sore walks over any grave, it will heal slowly or never.—Thorpe's *Mythology*, vol. ii. p. 110.

point." The same custom prevailed some years ago in the parish of Edmonton, near London. Possibly it has been very general.

In the southern counties of Scotland children are considered before baptism at the mercy of the fairies, who may carry them off at pleasure or inflict injury upon them. Hence, of course, it is unlucky to take unbaptized children on a journey—a belief which prevails throughout Northumberland, and indeed in many other parts of the country. Brand mentions this danger,[1] and says the Danish women guard their children during this period against evil spirits by placing in the cradle, or over the door, garlic, salt, bread, and steel in the form of some sharp instrument. "Something like this," he adds, "obtained in England;" and accordingly I am told that in the West Riding of Yorkshire "a child was kept safe while sleeping by hanging a carving knife from the head of the cradle with the point suspended near the infant's face." In Germany, the proper things to lay in the cradle are "orant" (which is translated into either horehound or snapdragon), blue marjoram, black cumin, a right shirt-sleeve, and a left stocking. The "Nickert" cannot then harm the child. The modern Greeks dread witchcraft at this period of their children's lives, and are careful not to leave them alone during their first eight days, within which period the Greek Church refuses to baptize them.[2]

In Scotland the little one's safeguard is held to lie in the juxtaposition of some article of dress belonging to its father. This was experienced by the wife of a shepherd near Selkirk. Soon after the birth of her first child, a fine boy, she was lying in bed with her baby by her side, when suddenly she became aware of a confused noise of talking and merry laughter in the "spence," or room. This, in fact, proceeded from the fairies, who were forming a child of wax as a substitute for the baby, which they were planning to steal away. The poor mother suspected as much, so in great alarm she seized her husband's waistcoat, which chanced to be lying at the foot of the bed, and flung it over herself and the child. The fairies set up a loud scream, calling out "Auld

[1] *Pop. Ant.* vol. ii. p. 73.

[2] Wright's *Literature of the Middle Ages*, vol. i. p. 291.

Luckie has cheated us o' our bairnie!" Soon afterwards the woman heard something fall down the lum (or chimney), and looking out she saw a waxen image of her baby, stuck full of pins, lying on the hearth. When her husband came home he made up a large fire and threw the fairy lump upon it; but, instead of burning, the thing flew up the chimney, and the house instantly resounded with shouts of joy and peals of laughter. Family affection must have been very strong when any trifle closely connected with the father was deemed a safeguard for the child,[1] a safeguard needed till its baptism shielded it from every evil or malicious sprite.

Our northern Folk-Lore is unanimous in bearing witness to the power of baptism. A clerical friend of mine, who once held a cure in Northumberland, tells me that it is there considered to affect a child physically as well as spiritually—a notion which I think prevails more or less through the whole country. I have heard old people in many places say of sickly infants, "Ah, there will be a change when he has been taken to church! Children never thrive till they have been christened." Another informs me that about five years ago an instance came under his notice of the healing power supposed to be wrought by baptism as regards the body. The infant child of a chimney-sweeper at Thorne, in the West Riding of Yorkshire, was in a very weak state of health, and appeared to be pining away. A neighbour looked in, and inquired if the child had been baptized. On an answer being given in the negative she gravely said, "I would try having it christened." The counsel was taken, and I believe with success. It is the custom in Northumberland to make the chrisom-child sleep the first night in the cap he wore at baptism. "Loud murmurs," says my friend, "arose against me early in my ministerial life for applying so much water that the cap had to be taken off and dried, whereas it should be left on till the next morning. I threw the blame on the modern caps, with their expanse of frilling, on which the good woman said that I was quite right; she had an

[1] A part of the father's clothes should be laid over a female child, and the mother's petticoat on a male child, to find favour with the opposite sex.—Thorpe's *Mythology*, vol. ii. p. 109.

old christening cap, the heirloom of a friend, which she could show me, of a very different make. Accordingly I examined the cap, which was evidently very old, and made with reference to affusion in baptism. It excluded forehead, ears, and chin, and apparently never had strings. I said that if a mother would bring her baby in such a cap I would undertake not to wet it."

In the North as in the South of England, nurses think it lucky for the child to cry at its baptism; they say that otherwise the baby shows that it is too good to live. Some, however, declare that this cry betokens the pangs of the new birth; some that it is the voice of the evil spirit as he is driven out by the baptismal water. As to the mother's churching, it is very "uncannie" for her to enter any other house before she goes to church; to do so would be to carry ill-luck with her. It is believed also that if she appears out-of-doors under these circumstances, and receives any insult or blows from her neighbours, she has no remedy at law. I am informed that old custom enjoins Irish women to stay at home till after their churching as rigidly as their English sisters. They have, however, their own way of evading it. They will pull a little thatch from their roof, or take a splinter of slate or tile off it, fasten this at the top of the bonnet, and go where they please, stoutly averring afterwards to the priest, or anyone else, that they had not gone from under their own roof.

A pleasant little custom is mentioned in the Wilkie MS.: the first child baptized by a minister after his appointment to a parish is to receive his Christian name. Through the North of England, if a boy and girl are brought together to the font, care must be taken that the former be christened first; else he is condemned to bear through life a smooth and beardless face, and, still worse, the young lady will surely be endowed with the ornament he lacks. This belief holds its ground in Durham, and extends as far north as the Orkney Islands.

One curious nursery practice exists both in the North and in the extreme West of England, that of leaving an infant's right hand unwashed; and the reason alleged is the same—that he may gather riches. The baby's nails must not be cut till he is a year old, for fear that he should grow up a thief, or, as they quaintly express it in Cleveland, "light-fingered." The mother must bite them off, if need be ; and in the West of Northumberland it is believed that if the first parings are buried under an ash tree the child will turn out a "top singer." The mention of the ash is curious, for has it not been from very ancient times a sacred tree, supplying in its sap the first nourishment to the Grecian hero, as now to the Celtic Highlander? Nay, according to Hesiod, Zeus made a third or brazen race of hard ash-wood—pugnacious and terrible;[1] as Yggdrasil, the cloud-tree of the Norseman, out of which he believed the first man was made, was an ash. Spenser speaks of this tree as being "for nothing ill," yet it has always been regarded as a special attractor of lightning, and mothers teach their children thus:—

Beware of an oak,
It draws the stroke.
Avoid an ash,
It courts the flash.
Creep under the thorn,
It will save you from harm.

The Norman peasant shows his confidence in the virtue of the thorn by constantly wearing a sprig of it in his cap, alleging as his reason that the Saviour's crown was woven of it. The maple, though "seldom inward sound itself," is thought in some parts of England to confer longevity on children if they are passed through its branches. In West Grinstead Park, Sussex, was an old maple much used for this purpose, and when a few years ago a rumour spread through the parish that it was about to be cut down, many petitions were made that it might be spared.

But to return. When the year of infancy is past, and baby's nails may safely be given up to the scissors, care must be taken not to cut them on a Sunday or Friday. Friday, of course, is an unlucky day, and as for Sunday the old rhyme says:—

Better a child had ne'er been born
Than cut his nails on a Sunday morn!

Another variation of the verse runs thus—

Friday hair, Sunday horn,
Better that child had ne'er been born!

[1] Grote's *History of Greece*, vol. i. chap. 2.

And yet another—

Sunday shaven, Sunday shorn,
Better hadst thou ne'er been born!

Or, at greater length—

Cut them on Monday, cut them for health,
Cut them ou Tuesday, cut them for wealth;
Cut them on Wednesday, cut them for news,
Cut them on Thursday, a pair of new shoes;
Cut them on Friday, cut them for sorrow,
Cut them on Saturday, a present to-morrow;
But he that on Sunday cuts his horn,
Better that he had never been born!

In Sussex they simply say "Cut your nails on Sunday morning, and you'll come to grief before Saturday night."

Again, the Cleveland nurses aver that it is very important for an infant to go up in the world before it goes down. Thus, if a child should be born in the top story of a house, for want of a flight of stairs, one of the gossips will take it in her arms, and mount a table, chair, or chest of drawers before she carries it down stairs. I have heard of a similar belief in the Channel Islands at the present day, and imagine it to have been formerly prevalent in every part of England.

The Wilkie MS. contains a caution against rocking a cradle when it is "toom," or empty, and cites on the subject the following fragment:

THE TOOM CRADLE.

Oh! rock not the cradle when the babie's not in,
For this by old women is counted a sin;
It's a crime so inhuman it may na' be forgi'en,
And they that wi' do it ha'e lost sight of heaven.

Such rocking maun bring on the babie disease,
Well may it grow fretty that none can it please,
Its crimson lip pale grows, its clear eye wax dim,
Its beauty grow pale, and its visage wax dim,

Its heart flutters fast, it breathes hard, then is gone,
To the fair land of heaven * * * *

The belief thus expressed holds its ground in the southern counties of Scotland. particularly in Selkirkshire. It crops out too in Holland, where rocking an empty cradle is affirmed to be injurious to the infant, and a prognostic of his death;[1] and in Sweden, where they say it makes the child noisy and given to crying.[2] Rocking the toom cradle is often deprecated in the counties of Durham and Yorkshire on another ground; it is said there to be ominous of another claimant for that place of rest.

In Sussex they express this notion in the couplet—

> If you rock the cradle empty,
> Then you shall have babies plenty.

And I am told of a village schoolmistress of that county who used to rate her scholars soundly if they ever touched her cradle. "There, leave the cradle alone," she would exclaim, "I've children enough already."

The proverb, "Soon teeth, soon toes," shows another portent of such an event. If baby's teeth come early there will soon be fresh toes, *i. e.* another baby. This belief extends to Sweden. "Leave off its caps on Sunday and it will not take cold," is a saying which will soon die out now babies have left off wearing caps at all.

Perhaps I may mention here a kindly northern custom, that in all sales, either under distraint for rent or common debt, the cradle should be left unsold, and remain the property of its original owner.[3] The late Canon Humble informed me that formerly a similar immunity attached to the corner cupboard, the place where the bread for the family was kept; at least it was the last thing sold under distraint. If a Northumbrian wishes to give you the idea of a man utterly and hopelessly ruined, he will say, "They have sold him up, corner cupboard and all." Are you curious to know the sex of the coming stranger? You must notice whether the old baby says papa or

[1] *Choice Notes*, p. 6.

[2] Thorpe's *Mythology*, vol. ii. p. 110.

[3] In the year 1848 the family house of the Nevilles, in the city of Durham, called the Bull's Head, from their cognizance probably, was pulled down to make way for the present Town Hall. In a garret of the mansion was discovered a highly ornamented cradle, in which, doubtless, the great barons of the North had been rocked in infancy. Unfortunately, it was destroyed by the workmen on the spot. There is something touching in the thought that the last relic in this city of a family so famed for deeds and for sufferings should be of such a domestic character. Probably the strong feeling alluded to in the text caused the cradle to be hidden when all the other furniture of this ancient house was dispersed.

mamma first; in the former case it will be a boy, in the latter a girl. If a child tooths first in its upper jaw, it is considered ominous of death in infancy.

Much importance attaches to the baby's first visit to another house, on which occasion it is expected that he should receive three things—an egg, salt, and white bread or cake; the egg a sacred emblem from the remotest antiquity, and the cake and salt things used alike in Jewish and in pagan sacrifices. Somewhat grotesquely they add in the East Riding of Yorkshire a fourth thing—a few matches to light the child on the way to heaven. These votive offerings must be pinned in the baby's clothes, and so brought home. I have heard an old woman in Durham speak of this as the child receiving alms. "He could not claim them before he was baptized," she said, "but now he is a Christian he has a right to go and ask alms of his fellow-Christians."[1] Near Leeds this ceremony is called "puddening."

Scotch nurses note with which hand a child first takes up a spoon to sup. If it be the left you may be sure that he will be an unlucky fellow all his life. So says the author of the Wilkie MS. He adds, that the women who live on the banks of the Ale and Teviot have a singular custom of wearing round their necks blue woollen threads or small cords till they wean their children. They do this for the purpose of averting ephemeral fevers, or, as they call them, "weeds and onfas." These threads are handed down from mother to daughter, and esteemed in proportion to their antiquity. "I possess," he says, "one of these myself, which was given me by a woman in the farm of Caverse, near Melrose, and I remarked that all the nursing mothers in that district wore a similar thread." Possibly these threads had originally received some blessing or charm. In Dundee people are accustomed to wear round the loins for the cure of lumbago a hank of yarn which has been charmed by a wise woman; and girls may be seen with single threads of the same round the head and temples as an infallible specific for tic-douloureux. I have not been able to learn the form of incantation. It is practised by Highlanders.

[1] Compare this with the Swedish saying, "You must not take an unbaptized child into anyone's house; it would bring misfortune there."

I am told that in Sussex a necklace of beads turned from the root of the peony is worn by children to prevent convulsions and assist the cutting of teeth. My informant[1] adds: "This piece of superstition is probably of very ancient date, for the peony is known to have been held in such high repute of old as to be accounted of divine origin, an emanation from the moon, endowed with the property of shining in the night, of chasing away evil spirits, and protecting the houses near which it grows. I know not whether there is association between this plant and the physician Peon, who healed the wounded gods."

In Durham when the first teeth come out, or indeed on the extraction of teeth subsequently, the cavity must be filled with salt, and the tooth burned while these words are repeated—

> Fire, fire, burn bone,
> God send me my tooth again.

My Sussex correspondent tells me of a young woman of that county who remonstrated against throwing away children's cast-teeth, declaring that, should they be found and gnawed by any animal, the child's new tooth would be like one of that animal. In proof of her assertion, she used to cite a certain old Master Simmons, who had a very large pig's tooth in his upper jaw, the sad consequence of his mother having by accident thrown one of his cast-teeth into the hog trough.

I do not know whether superstition ever interferes with the grown-up maiden's peeps in the looking-glass. Perhaps it would be as well if she did, but in Durham she strictly forbids boy or girl under a year old to look in one. Swedish maidens dare not look in the glass after dark, or by candlelight, lest they forfeit the goodwill of the other sex.[2] Several pieces of Swedish nursery folk-lore are recorded in this place, *e.g.*, a book must be placed under the head of a new-born child, that he may be quick at reading; so long as an infant is unnamed the fire must not be extinguished; nor must anyone pass between the fire and a suck-

[1] Mrs. Latham, formerly of Fittleworth, Sussex, who kindly placed in my hands her record of West Suffolk Folk-lore some time before it was published in vol. i. of the records of the Folk-Lore Society.

[2] Thorpe's *Mythology*, vol. ii. p. 108.

ing babe; nor, again, must anyone entering the house take a child in his hands, without previously having touched fire. Also a child must not be allowed to creep through a window, nor may anyone step over a child, or walk round a child that is sitting on the floor, or is in a carriage; for then it is believed that the little one will never grow bigger than it is.

The Wilkie MS. tells us that children born with a hallihoo (holy or fortunate hood) or caul around their heads are deemed lucky, but the caul must be preserved carefully; for should it be lost or thrown away the child will pine away, or even die. This superstition however is world-wide, and of such antiquity as to be reproved by St. Chrysostom, in several of his homilies. It still prevails in France, where its universality is attested by a proverbial expression: "Etre né coiffé" means to be prosperous and fortunate in everything. In our own country, seamen used to purchase cauls to save them from drowning; advocates, that they might thereby be endued with eloquence. Twenty guineas were asked for one in 1779, twelve pounds in 1813, six guineas in 1848. In this last case the caul was of some antiquity, and fifteen pounds had originally been given for it by a seaman who had carried it about with him for thirty years.[1] That this head-gear formed any link of affection between the child born with it and the mother I was quite unaware till I saw the following letter addressed to Dr. Paterson, of the Bridge of Allan, and by him kindly placed in my hands:—

DR. PATERSON, Glasgow, 1870.

Sir,—You will remember attending to my wife professionally at——, in the month of April, 1851, when my wife gave birth to a daughter, who was born with a very unusual accompaniment on her head resembling a crown, which you took away out of my house. I may here mention that I did not know of it for at least two months after, when I observed the mother's indifference and coolness towards the child which has continued ever since. Now I am not superstitious or led by any unnatural ideas, but why did you, a member and elder in the Free Church of Scotland, break the tenth commandment by coveting and carrying away out of your neighbour's house what did not belong to you? I know not what the consequences may be in your case (only I say may God forgive you), but I say it has been very serious in my case, and until you send back the said crown which you took off the girl's head back to me you shall get no peace from

[1] Brand's *Pop. Ant.* vol. iii. p. 114.

me. You may suppose this foolishness, but then the question arises, why did you covet and take it? Trusting you will give this document your serious consideration, and that I may hear from you soon enclosing my demand, I remain,

———.

Brand quotes from Willis's *Mount Tabor* (A.D. 1639) an account concerning "an extraordinary veile that covered my body at my coming into the world," which veil the author considered a sign of exceeding good fortune, "there being," he proudly adds, "not one child among many hundreds that are so born."

One other instance has however come to my own knowledge, and here, too, the happy mortal prided herself not a little on the distinction accorded to her. Within the last five years, in one of our northern cities, a servant was found by her mistress in a state of dejection, for which at first there seemed no assignable cause. After much questioning the lady elicited that her servant had been born with a veil over her head, which was now presaging evil to her. The veil, she said, had been carefully preserved by her mother, who had entrusted it to her on coming to woman's estate. It had been stretched and dried, and so had remained for many years. The girl kept it locked in her chest of drawers, and regularly consulted it as her oracle and adviser. If danger threatened her, the veil shrivelled up; if sickness, the veil became damp. When good fortune was at hand, the veil laid itself smoothly out; and if people at a distance were telling lies about her, the veil would rustle in its paper. Again the veil did not like her to cut her hair. If she did so it changed colour and became uneasy. The owner firmly believed that when she died the veil would disappear. She regarded it with mysterious awe, and only allowed her most intimate friends to know of its existence.

I am not aware that in the North of England popular superstition concerns itself with the birth of animals. In Sussex, however, it certainly does. Mr. T. C. Thompson, of East Grinstead, in that county, informs me that on hearing lately from one of his farm labourers that a favourite sow had just brought into the world a litter of stillborn pigs, the man added it was only what he had looked for. "Why so?" inquired the master. "Well, Sir," said the man, "you see this be the year the lions breed. They breeds every seven years, and when the lions breed the young pigs be still-born."

Childhood has its own Folk-lore all England over—its traditional beliefs and practices, couched most commonly in verses which attune the infant ear, and charm the infant imagination. The young northern is peculiarly favoured in these respects. Does he want to make a butterfly alight, he has only to repeat the following lines—

Le, la, let,
Ma bonnie pet;

and, if only he say them often enough, the charm never fails. Does rain threaten to spoil a holiday, let him chant out—

Rain, rain, go away,
Come another summer's day;
Rain, rain, pour down,
And come no more to our town;

or—

Rain, rain go away,
And come again on washing day;

or, more quaintly yet—

Rain, rain, go to Spain;
Fair weather come again:

and, *sooner or later*, the rain will depart. If there be a rainbow the juvenile devotee must look at it all the time. The Sunderland version runs thus—

Rain, rain, pour down
Not a drop in our town,
But a pint and a gill
All a-back of Building Hill.

Such rhymes are in use, I believe, in every nursery in England; but the following verse, though said to be popular in Berwickshire, is unknown elsewhere:—

Rainbow, rainbow, haud awa' hame,
A' yer bairns are dead but ane,
And it lies sick at yon grey stane,
And will be dead ere you win hame.
Gang owre the Drumaw and yont the lea,
And down by the side o' yonder sea;
Your bairn lies greeting like to dee,
And the big teardrop is in his e'e.

The Drumaw is a high hill skirting the sea in the east of Berwickshire. It was a bold flight of fancy to personify the rainbow, and endow him with a family of bairns; and the contrast is curious between the young Celt searching by the grey stone for the rainbow's bairn, with "the tear-drop in his e'e," and the Saxon boy running to catch the rainbow for the sake of the pot of gold at its foot.

The late Mr. Denham, a very careful collector of old sayings and old usages, says that he well remembers how he and his school-companions used, on the appearance of a rainbow, to place a couple of straws or twigs across on the ground, and, as they said, cross out the rainbow. The West Riding recipe for driving away a rainbow is, "Make a cross of two sticks and lay four pebbles on it, one at each end."

The crow-charm is perhaps universal in our island:—

Crow, crow, get out of my sight,
Or else I'll eat your liver and light;

as well as the snail-charm—

Snail, snail, put out your horn,
Or I'll kill your father and mother the morn;

though the latter more commonly runs in the South—

Snail, snail, come out of your hole,
Or else I'll beat you as black as a coal.

Our northern version is—

Snail, snail, put out your horn
Tell me what's the day t' morn.
To-day's the morn to shear the corn
Blaw bill buck thorn.

In Devonshire they have it—

Snail, snail, shoot out your horn,
  Father and mother are dead;
Brother and sister are in the back-yard,
  Begging for barley bread;

and in the South of Italy,

Snail, snail, put out your horn,
Your mother is laughing you to scorn
For she has a little son just born.

The ladybird is roused to activity by the cry of—

Ladybird, ladybird, fly away home,
Thy house is on fire, thy children all gone!

And during the nursery application of dock-leaves for a nettle-sting one of the following rhymes is sung:—

Nettle out, dock in,
Dock remove the nettle-sting;

Or,

In dock, out nettle,
Don't let the blood settle.

Or, again,

Nettle in, dock out,
Dock in, nettle out,
Nettle in, dock out,
Dock rub nettle out.

Or, lastly,

Docken in and nettle out,
Like an auld wife's dish-clout.

In the North of England children call, or used to call, thunder Rattley-bags, and to sing this couplet during a storm—

Rowley, Rowley, Rattley-bags,
Take the lasses and leave the lads.

Another quaint verse is connected with a game I have often played in my childhood—

Four-and-twenty tailors went to kill a snail,
The best man among them durst na touch his tail.
He put out his horns like a kiley cow,
Rin lads, flee lads, we're a' killed now!

The game of Sally Walker, in which song and dance are combined, is still played in the North of England. The following words were taken from the lips of some juvenile singers at Morpeth by Mr. Joseph Crawhall:—

Sally Walker, Sally Walker,
  Come spring time and love,
She's lamenting, she's lamenting,
  All for her young man.
Come choose to the east, come choose to the west,
Come choose the one that you love best.

(The couple kiss.)

Here's a couple got married together,
Father and mother they must agree;
Love each other like sister and brother,
I pray this couple to kiss together.

It is curious to discover that the village children of Devonshire find amusement in the same game. I transcribe the words sung at the school-feast of Chudleigh Knighton in that county, A.D. 1878, when "Sally Walker" seemed very popular. The first line is remarkable as apparently referring to some form of incantation—

Sally, Sally Walker, sprinkle water in the pan,
Rise Sally, rise Sally, and seek your young man,
Turn to the east and turn to the west
And choose the one that you love best.

(The pair kiss.)

Now you're married we wish you joy,
First a girl and then a boy,
Seven years after a son and a daughter,
So young lovers kiss together.

The following verses which accompany another game were communicated to me by Mr. Joseph Crawhall, but I well remember singing them with my young companions in my childhood. They are said to have been very popular on the Borders.

Dissy, dissy green grass,
Dissy, dissy duss,
Come all ye pretty fair maids
And dance along with us.

You shall have a duck, my dear,
And you shall have a drake,
And you shall have a nice young man,
To love you for your sake.

If this young man should chance to die
And leave the girl a widow,
The birds shall sing, the bells shall ring,
Clap all your hands together.

(Ending with a clapping of hands.)

Schools, too, have their superstitions and their legendary rites. One odd school-boy notion is that if the master's cane is nicked at the upper end, and a hair inserted, it will on its first use split to the very tip. In my own day, and perhaps at the present time, no boy would commit himself to the Wear without the precaution of an eel-skin tied round his left leg to save him from cramp. Well do I remember thus fortifying myself against danger before plunging into the stream. Another of our little superstitions was, that a horsehair kept in water would in due time turn into an eel; and many a time have we tried the experiment, ever attributing its failure to some adventitious circumstance, not to a fallacy in our belief. I am told that this mistake may be traced to the sudden appearance, after rain, of long hair-like worms in the deep holes left in clayey ground by horses' hoofs. There was no trace of such creatures before the holes were filled with rain-water; and, wondering how they could have arrived there, boys imagined them to be hairs, dropped from the horse's mane and tail, in course of transition into eels.

An odd expression was connected with the lending a knife among boys for the cutting up of a cake or other dainty. The borrower was asked to give it back *laughing, i. e.* with some of the good thing it was used to cut.

We had at our school an institution called "cobbing," which tells of rougher times than ours. A friend and schoolfellow of mine thus describes it:—

"When a cobbing match was called, all the boys rushed forward, and seized the unfortunate object of the match by the hair, repeating these lines:—

> All manner of men, under threescore and ten,
> Who don't come to this cobbing match,
> Shall be cobbed over and over again;
> By the high, by the low, by the wings of the crow—
> Salt-fish, regnum, buck, or a doe?

I spare you the details of the tortures named salt-fish and regnum; buck was a rap on the scull with the closed hand—doe a tug at the hair, dragging out many a lock. Those who bore no part in cobbing the victim were liable to be cobbed themselves; so were those who were so unlucky as not to be able to touch the hair of the victim, or who while repeating the verses neglected the prescribed rites, *i. e.* the standing on one leg, closing one eye, elevating the left thumb, and concealing the teeth."

The riding of the stang was not an act of such sheer barbarity, expressing as it did a sense of offended justice, and reserved as it was for occasions when the recognised code of honour was broken. But it was a horrible ordeal. I myself have more than once witnessed the ceremony in the cathedral churchyard of Durham, when, after a clamorous recitation of the culprit's misdeeds and a sound thrashing, the poor boy was finally bumped against a tombstone specially devoted to the purpose. But the riding of the stang is no mere piece of schoolboy Folk-Lore. It has been and still is widely practised among men. In old times, when law was less powerful than it now is for the repression of evil, the moral sense of the poorer classes, if outraged by witnessing some flagrant wrong, did not fail to find some way, coarse and rough perhaps, of expressing its instinctive feeling. Such was the riding of the stang, which set forth the public reprobation of certain disgraceful actions, *e. g.* sins against the seventh commandment, cruelty to women, especially the beating of wives by their husbands, unfaithfulness of workmen to their fellows when on strike, and dishonest tricks in trade. Originally the offender was himself compelled to ride, but, as law became stronger and the liberty of the subject was more respected, some young fellow of powerful lungs and obtuse sensibilities was selected as his deputy.

The custom is very ancient. Longstaffe, in his *History of Darlington*, says: "Eric, King of Norway, had to fly from the hatred of his people for inflicting this stigma on a celebrated Icelandic bard. It was then of a most tremendous character. The Goths erected a nidstaens, or pole of infamy, with the most dire imprecations against the guilty party, who was called niddering, or 'the infamous,' and was disqualified from giving evidence."

The riding of the stang has been practised from time immemorial in the towns and villages of the North of England, and is still resorted to on occasion of notorious scandal. A boy or young man is selected, placed on a ladder or pole, and carried shoulder height round the town, the people who accompany him having armed themselves with every homely instrument whence noise can be extracted—poker and tongs, kettles and frying-pans, old tin pots, and so forth. Amid the discordant sounds thus produced, and the yells, cheers, and derisive laughter of the mob, the procession moves to the house of him whose misdeeds evoked it. At his door the rider recites in doggrel verse the cause of the disturbance, beginning—

> Hey derry ! Hey derry ! Hey derry dan !
> It's neither for my cause nor your cause that I ride the stang,
> But its for . . . .

Or—

> I tinkle, O tinkle, O tang,
> It's not for my sake or your sake that I ride the stang,
> But it's for . . . .

The indictment is, of course, made as ludicrous as possible, and intermixed with coarse jests and mockery.

Recent instances of this mode of popular trial and punishment have come to my knowledge at Thirsk and Darlington. One such took place at Rawtenstall, near Preston, in August, 1870, on the beating of a woman by her husband, and was recorded in *The Preston Guardian*. Not many years ago the bride of a medical man at H——, in Yorkshire, being jealous of an old servant of her husband's, ran away to her father's house. Popular feeling was on her side. For several nights there was much excitement, and the stang was ridden thrice consecutively with a great deal of noise and confusion. The end of it was that the servant was dismissed, the bride returned, and the young couple settled down amicably at last. It may be added, that during the Napoleonic wars the riding of the stang was practised on crimps, those designing villains by whose treachery unfortunate sailors were betrayed to the press-gang.

It is interesting to compare the rough justice of our northern riding of the stang with the Haberfield Treiben of Upper Bavaria, a secret society dating from medieval times, for the denouncing and discouragement of sins of unchastity. The proceedings of the Haberfield Treiben somewhat resemble those of the Sacred Vehme, which, however, it has long survived. Its members are sworn to secrecy. They are numerous, and so distributed through every part of the country that nothing escapes their notice. At the close of autumn, when the nights are cold and dark, vague rumours may be heard in some Bavarian village of an approaching visit from the Haberfield Treiben. After a few days of anticipation the reality appears. A little before midnight, when all seemed quiet or asleep, a dreadful clang is suddenly heard of trumpets blowing, pottery broken, kettles and pans beaten together, mixed with irregular discharge of firearms. On rushing into the streets the frightened inhabitants find their village occupied by a band of men with blackened faces, all egress or ingress prevented by a regular chain of videttes round the place. The invaders promptly erect a platform in the market-place, chiefly of materials they have brought with them; then at a given signal torches are lighted, firearms discharged, horns blown, kettles beaten, and the opening of the tribunal proclaimed through a large speaking-trumpet. All this is done with astonishing rapidity, and such order and arrangement as to defy resistance.

The "act of accusation" is then read aloud by some peasant gifted with a powerful voice. It is written in verse, and makes mention of all the ill-doings of the inhabitants. They are handled pretty severely, with a mixture of broad humour.

The Haberfield Treiben has long been obnoxious both to the ecclesiastical and civil authorities. Indeed, the present Archbishop of Munich has at various periods issued pastoral letters threatening excommunication, but to little purpose. It is not easy to write down a long-cherished institution. So lately as October 20, 1866, preparation was made for performing the Haberfield Treiben at the town of Porenheim, between Munich and Innspruck. The Government, however, received information of it, and placed a body of gendarmerie in the town, who with the aid of the local militia attacked the "drivers" on their first appearance. A desperate fight ensued, which lasted an hour and a-half. One driver was killed, several wounded, and seven taken prisoners, on which the band dispersed and fled.

On November 2, the Archbishop pronounced the ban of the

Church against all persons favouring or taking part in the Haberfield Treiben. What the effect of this severe measure may be we cannot guess.

Before returning to Durham and its boys I will just mention that near Preston, in Yorkshire, popular displeasure against a wife-beater is shown by scattering chaff or straw in front of his house amid groans and cries of indignation.

I remember well that we schoolboys used to spit our faith when required to make asseveration on any matters we deemed important; and many a time have I given or received a challenge according to the following formula: "I say, Bill, will you fight Jack?"—"Yes." "Jack, will you fight Bill?"—"Yes." "Best cock, spit over my little finger." Jack and Bill both do so, and a pledge thus sealed is considered so sacred that no schoolboy would dare hang back from its fulfilment. Thus, fishwomen and hucksters generally spit upon the handsel, *i.e.* the first money they receive.

One schoolboy belief I remember attempting to verify, with a daring worthy of a better cause. It was a bold venture, and we laid our plans well and secretly, so that none but the actors knew anything about it. Providing ourselves with a black cat, from whose fur every white hair had been carefully abstracted, we assembled on a dark winter night in the cathedral churchyard, and grouped ourselves within a circle, marked on the grass. We were bent on raising the evil spirit, and meant instantly to present him with poor pussy as an offering. The senior of the party read the Lord's Prayer backwards, and repeated some cabalistic verses; but the adjuration was not responded to, which perhaps was something of a relief to the actors. It may be that this divination has prevailed among boys; is it hence that they are sometimes called young dare-devils?

May I be allowed to close the Folk-lore of boyhood with a couplet, which certainly crops up from the farmhouse—

All hands to work—then I'm but a boy.
All hands to meat—here I am a man.

In the Folk-lore of Presbyterian Scotland we find, of course, no mention of confirmation. Throughout England a preference is, I believe, universally felt for the touch of the bishop's right hand over the left. Thus, not long ago in Exeter a poor woman presented herself as a candidate for that rite to one of the clergy of that city, who remembered her having been confirmed three years before. On his taxing her with this she could not deny it, but pleaded that she had had the bishop's left hand then, and had been so uneasy ever since that she did want to try her luck again! In the North of England, however, this evil is more defined; the unfortunate recipients of the left hand are doomed on the spot to a life of single blessedness. A friend tells me of an old Yorkshire woman who came for confirmation a second, if not a third time, from a different motive. She had heard, she said, "it was good for the rheumatiz!"

To pass on to marriage, the nucleus of a vast store of Folk-Lore. The following rhymes show the importance of choosing an auspicious day for the ceremony; they express the popular belief of the county of Durham:—

Monday for wealth,
Tuesday for health,
Wednesday the best day of all;
Thursday for losses,
Friday for crosses,
And Saturday no luck at all.

This attribute of Thursday is curiously opposite to that which distinguishes it in Scandinavia, where, as Thor's day, it is regarded as an auspicious day for marrying. The English tradition coincides, however, with the German, where it is held unlucky to marry on Thursday, probably because Thor is partly identified there with the devil.[1]

As to Friday, a couple married on that day are doomed to lead a cat-and-dog life. But, indeed, a feeling is almost universal of the inauspiciousness of beginning any kind of work on this day, whether as the day of our Lord's crucifixion or that on which traditionally our first parents are said to have fallen.

[1] See Kelly's *Indo-European Tradition*, p. 293.

The unsuitableness of Lent for marrying and giving in marriage is bitterly expressed in the verse—

If you marry in Lent
You will live to repent.

But I fear that in point of fact the month of May is more avoided in Scotland than the season of Lent. The prejudice against marrying in May, which Lockhart calls a classical as well as a Scottish one, coming as it does direct from pagan Rome, was respected in his own marriage, Sir Walter Scott hurrying away from London that his daughter Sophia's wedding might take place before that inauspicious month commenced.

It is remarkable as showing the prevalence of this feeling to observe that during the year 1874 in the city of Glasgow the marriages in May were only 204, against 703 in June, the average of the eleven months, excluding May, being 441.[1] The ancient proverb still lives on the lips of the people of Scotland and the Borders—

Marry in May
Rue for aye.

The portents for good or evil which surround Border marriages are, as given in the Wilkie MS., numerous indeed. It is unlucky for swine to cross the path in front of a wedding party. Hence the old adage, "The swine's run through it." I believe this encounter is of ill omen to others beside marriage parties, especially before twelve o'clock. The presence of the bride's mother is inauspicious too. A wet day is also deemed unlucky, while a fine one is auspicious. Here, in fact, as all Christendom over—

Blest is the bride that the sun shines on!

Green, ever an ominous colour in the Lowlands of Scotland, must on no account be worn there at a wedding. The fairies, whose chosen colour it is, would resent the insult, and destroy the wearer. Whether on this account or any other I know not,

[1] Napier's *Folk-Lore of the West of Scotland*, p. 44.

but the notion of ill-luck in connection with it is wide-spread. I have heard of mothers in the South of England who absolutely forbade their daughters to wear anything of this colour, and who avoided it even in the furniture of their houses. Certainly the old couplets do run—

> Those dressed in blue
> Have lovers true;
> In green and white
> Forsaken qnite.

I dare say, too, in after days, Peter Bell's sixth wife thought her wedding dress inauspicious enough. And did she not

> put on her gown of green,
> And leave her mother at sixteen
> To follow Peter Bell?

At any rate nothing green must make its appearance at a Scotch marriage; kale and all other green vegetables are excluded from the wedding-dinner. With this exception, any good things in season may grace the board, and a pair of fowls must on no account be omitted. It is very important that the bride should receive the little bone called "hug-ma-close" (*anglice* "sidesman," or side-bone), for she who gets it on her wedding-day is sure to be happy in her husband.

To rub shoulders with the bride or bridegroom is deemed an augury of speedy marriage; and, again, she who receives from the bride a piece of cheese, cut by her before leaving the table, will be the next bride among the company.

Dinner over, the bride sticks her knife into the cheese, and all at table endeavour to seize it. He who succeeds without cutting his fingers in the struggle thereby ensures happiness in his married life. The knife is called "the best man's prize," since commonly the "best man" secures it. Should he fail to do so, he will indeed be unfortunate in his matrimonial views. The knife is, at any rate, a prize for male hands only; the maidens try to possess themselves of a "shaping" of the wedding-dress, for use in certain divinations regarding their future husbands. And the bride herself should wear something borrowed—for what reason I am not informed.

It should perhaps have been mentioned sooner, that, as the newly-married wife enters her new home on returning from kirk, one of the oldest inhabitants of the neighbourhood, who has been stationed on the threshold, throws a plateful of short-bread over her head, so that it falls outside. A scramble ensues, for it is deemed very fortunate to get a piece of the short-bread, and dreams of sweethearts attend its being placed under the pillow. A variation of this custom extends as far south as the East Riding of Yorkshire, where, on the bride's arrival at her father's door, a plate of cake is flung from an upper window upon the crowd below. An augury is then drawn from the fate which attends the plate; the more pieces it breaks into the better; if it reach the ground unbroken the omen is very unfavourable.

On this matter a clerical friend writes thus: "In my own case, on bringing my wife to her home in Scotland, the short-bread was thrown over her head, and a scramble ensued on the new carpet, which was thereby ruined. A soup ladle was put into my hands, together with the door-key, to imply that I was to be at once the master of the house and the bread-winner. My wife was required to hold the kitchen tongs and a bunch of keys, to indicate that her proper sphere was the fireside and her duties within doors.

The custom of passing bridecake through the wedding-ring, and placing it under the pillow, to dream upon, and that of throwing a shoe after the bride and bridegroom, are sometimes claimed as peculiarly northern. If so, they have travelled southwards very steadily, for they now prevail in every county in England. This last observance is usually said to be "for luck," but a writer in *Notes and Queries* (vol. vii. p. 411) suggests that it is rather a symbol of renunciation of all right in the bride by her father or guardian, and the transference of it to her husband. He quotes Ps. lx. 8, "Over Edom have I cast out my shoe," as meaning, "I have wholly cast it off;" and further illustrates the idea by a reference to Ruth iv. 7, 8. Ruth's kinsman, it will be remembered, refused to marry her, and to redeem her inheritance; therefore, "as it was the custom in Israel concerning redeeming and concerning changing that a man plucked off his shoe and delivered it to his neighbour," the kinsman plucked off his shoe, as a public renunciation of Ruth and of his own claim of pre-marriage. It may be inquired, however, whether there is any connexion between this custom and the usage of Swedish brides, to let a shoe slip off or drop a handkerchief, in the hope that the bridegroom, from politeness, will stoop to pick it up. If he does so it will be his lot to submit, *i.e.* to bend his back all through his married life. A good deal of Swedish bridal Folk-Lore points to the desire for mastery, *e.g.* the bride must endeavour to see her bridegroom before he sees her, to place her foot before his during the marriage ceremony, to sit down first in the bridal chair, and all that she may bear sway.[1]

The northern counties of England have, however, their own exclusively local wedding customs. I am informed by the Rev. J. Barmby, that a wedding in the Dales of Yorkshire is indeed a thing to see; that nothing can be imagined comparable to it in wildness and obstreperous mirth. The bride and bridegroom may possibly be a little subdued, but his friends are like men bereft of reason. They career round the bridal party like Arabs of the desert, galloping over ground on which, in cooler moments, they would hesitate even to walk a horse—shouting all the time, and firing volleys from the guns they carry with them. Next they will dash along the road in advance of the party, carrying the whisky-bottle, and compelling everyone they meet to pledge the newly-married-pair. "One can guess," he adds, "what the Border mosstroopers were by seeing the Dalesmen at a wedding." In the higher parts of Northumberland as well as on the other side of the Border the scene I am informed is, if possible, still more wild. In Northumberland the men of the party all start off from the church-door on horse-back, galloping like madmen through moss and over moor, till they reach the place where the wedding breakfast is to be held, and he who arrives first may claim a kiss of the bride. Such a wedding is called "a riding wedding," and the race to the young couple's new home after the marriage "running the braize, or brooze." In rural parts, too,

[1] Thorpe's *Mythology*, vol. ii. p. 108.

of the county of Durham, the bridal party is escorted to church by men armed with guns, which they fire again and again close to the ears of bride and bridesmaids, terrifying them sometimes not a little. At Guisborough, in Cleveland, I am told that these guns are fired over the heads of the newly-married couple all the way from church. There, too, it has been customary for the bridegroom to offer a handful of money together with the ring to the clergyman; out of this the fees were taken and the overplus returned.

A singular custom prevails at the village of Belford, in Northumberland, of making the bridal pair with their attendants leap over a stone placed in their path at the outside of the church porch. This is called the louping stone, or petting stone, and it is said on the spot that the bride must leave all her pets and humours behind her when she crosses it. At the neighbouring village of Embleton two stout young lads place a wooden bench across the door of the church porch, assist the bride and bridegroom and their friends to surmount the obstacle, and then look out for a donation from the bridegroom. Some think they see a symbol here of the obstacles that beset married life; but the Vicar of Embleton, who has kindly furnished me with this information, considers it to be connected with some superstition as to touching the threshold of the building or stumbling upon it. I am told, on the authority of no less a person than one of the bridesmaids, that in the year 1868, at a wedding in a High-Coquetdale family, "it was proposed to have a petted stone. A stick was therefore held by two groomsmen at the church door for the bride to jump over. Had she fallen or stumbled the worst auguries as to her temper would have been drawn." While Mr. Joseph Crawhall informs me that on June 5, 1873, entering the church of Bamburgh during a wedding, he witnessed the following scene: "The ceremony ended, on leaving the church, a three-legged stool, about a foot high, was placed at the churchyard gate, and covered with about two yards of carpet. The whole of the bridal party had separately to hop or jump over this stool, assisted on either side by a stalwart villager. I inquired the name of the custom, its reason, and so on. The reply was,

'It is the parting-stool, and is always used here;' but nothing appeared to be known about the origin or meaning of the ceremony."

Throughout Cleveland, he who gives the bride away claims the first kiss in right of his temporary paternity. One clerical friend of mine, however, declares that it is the privilege of the parson who ties the knot; and, though he will not aver that he has ever availed himself of it, he knows an old north-country clergyman who was reported so to do. Another tells me that a brother-priest, a stranger in the neighbourhood, after performing a marriage in a Yorkshire village, was surprised to see the party keep together as if expecting something more. "What are you waiting for?" he asked, at last. "Please, Sir," was the bridegroom's answer, "ye've no kissed Molly." And my old friend, the late Dr. Raine, used to relate how the Rev. Thomas Ebdon, Sacrist of the Cathedral and Vicar of Merrington, invariably kept up the custom when he performed the marriage ceremony, and this plainly as a matter of obligation, for he was one of the most shy and retiring of men. Nay, I can testify that within the last ten years, a fair lady from the county of Durham, who was married in the South of England, so undoubtedly reckoned upon the clerical salute, that, after waiting for it in vain, she boldly took the initiative and bestowed a kiss on the much-amazed South-country vicar.

In a certain old song, the bridegroom thus addresses the minister—

It's no very decent for you to be kissing,
It does not look weel wi' the black coat ava,
'Twould hae set you far better tae hae gi'en us your blessing
Than thus by such tricks to be breaking the law.
Dear Wattie, quo' Robin, it's just an old custom,
An the thing that is common should ne'er be ill ta'en,
For where ye are wrong, if ye had na a wished him
You should ha' been first. It's yoursel is to blame.[1]

The custom has, however, been very general, and it may possibly be a dim memorial of the *osculum pacis*, or the pre-

[1] Napier's *Folk-Lore of West Scotland*, p. 48.

sentation of the Pax to the newly-married pair. I am informed that in Ireland, some years back, it was customary for the clergyman to conclude the ceremony with the words, "kiss your wife," and occasionally the bridegroom was hard put-to to prevent one or other of his companions from intercepting the salute designed for himself.

A singular local custom still exists in the village of Whitburn, near Sunderland—that of sending what are called hot pots to church, to meet the bride and bridegroom on coming out. A gentleman of that place thus describes what took place at his own marriage last year: "After the vestry scene, the bridal party having formed in procession for leaving the church, we were stopped in the porch by a row of five or six women, ranged to our left hand, each holding a large mug with a cloth over it. These were in turn presented to me, and handed by me to my wife, who, after taking a sip, returned it to me. It was then passed to the next couple, and so on in the same form to all the party. The composition in these mugs was mostly, I am sorry to say, simply horrible; one or two were very fair, one very good. They are sent to the church by all classes, and are considered a great compliment. I have never heard of this custom elsewhere. Here it has existed beyond the memory of the oldest inhabitant, and an aged fisherwoman, who has been married some sixty-five years, tells me that at her wedding there were seventy hot pots."

Another old wedding usage seems confined to Yorkshire. In remote parts of that county it is the custom to pour a kettlefull of boiling water over the doorstep, just after the bride has left her old home; and they say that before it dries up another marriage is sure to be agreed on.

At Newcastle-on-Tyne sand is strewn on the pavement before a bridal party tread on it. Thus, the other day a friend of mine seeing a crowd at the corner of a street in that town, expressed his opinion that the volunteers were out. "No," said a bystander, "it's a wedding. Don't you see the sand on the pavement?" And, throughout the county, when a bride's "furnishings" are carried to her new home, ribbons are tied on the cart, and must be given to the first person who comes forward to meet the cart on its arrival at its destination.

In many of the rural parts of Cumberland the following curious practice exists. When the lover of a Cumbrian maiden proves unfaithful to her, she is, by way of consolation, rubbed with pease-straw by the neighbouring lads; and should a Cumbrian youth lose his sweetheart, through her marriage with his rival, the same sort of comfort is administered to him by the lasses of the village. This is illustrated by the following verse from an old Cumbrian ballad:—

> For Jock the young laird was new wedded,
> His auld sweetheart Jennie luik'd wae,
> While some were aw tittern and flytin
> The lads rubbed her down wi' pease-strae.

This reminds me of a custom very common among the school-boys in the neighbouring county of Durham, when, if a boy is so unlucky as to fall into trouble, and so weak as to show it by crying, he is quickly beset by his companions, who rub him down with their coat-sleeves, and that in such rough style as to make him forget past troubles in present discomfort.

It is unlucky for a woman to marry a man whose surname begins with the same letter as her own, for—

> If you change the name and not the letter,
> You change for the worse and not for the better.

When a younger daughter marries before her elder sisters, it is said that they must dance at her wedding without shoes.

A Yorkshire wedding is, by rights, wound up by a race for a ribbon. In Cleveland this ribbon is given by the bridegroom as he leaves the church, and all who choose run for it, in sight of the house where the wedding-feast is held. All the racers, winner and losers alike, are entitled to a glass of spirits each; and accordingly, as soon as the race is over, they present themselves at the house, and ask for their 'lowance without any particular invitation. At the village of Melsonby, near Darlington, and in the adjoining district, the bride was placed as winning-post, holding the ribbon in her hand, and the winner claimed a kiss on receiving it. I am told that on one occasion the bride, being a Methodist, refused, from conscientious scruples, to give the ribbon. There was much dissatisfaction through the place, and the youths revenged themselves after the traditional manner of punishing stingy brides. They fired the stithy at her; that is, they placed a charge of gunpowder in the stith, or anvil of the blacksmith's shop, and fired it as she passed on her way from church.

In the neighbourhood of Leeds, and I believe in the North of England generally, it is counted unlucky for a young woman to attend church when her banns are published; her children run the risk of being deaf and dumb. But there is no chance at all of a family unless, when she retires on the wedding-night, her bridesmaids lay her stockings across. Again, when a woman's hair grows in a low point on the forehead, it is supposed to presage widowhood, and is called a "widow's peak."

I may close our collection of bridal Folk-Lore by two little sayings rife in the county of Durham. The first of the bridal pair to go to sleep on the wedding-night will be the first to die; and the wife who loses her wedding ring incurs the loss of her husband's affection. The breaking of the ring forebodes death. This belief holds ground as far south as Essex, where, in 1857, a farmer's widow, on being visited after her husband's death, exclaimed, "Ah! I thought I should soon lose him, for I broke my ring the other day; and my sister, too, lost her husband after breaking her ring—it is a sure sign." An old woman of Barnoldby-la-Beck, Lincolnshire, whose husband died on the fiftieth anniversary of their wedding-day, told her vicar that she had known he would die before her. "Why so?" asked he. "Because when we were married at church he knelt down first at the altar, and they always say the one that kneels down first at the marriage will die first." At a Basque wedding the husband is bound to kneel down on a fold of his wife's dress.

The portents of death related in the Wilkie MS. are numerous indeed. Thus, he who meets a Border funeral is certain soon to die, unless he bares his head, turns, and accompanies the procession some distance. If the coffin is carried by bearers he must take a lift. This done, if he bows to the company, he may turn and go on his way without fear. Perhaps this belief was once more widely spread. I have been told of an old Sussex gentleman who would, at any inconvenience, avoid meeting a funeral. He has often been known, whether on foot or on horseback, to turn round and go straight home rather than pass one. As to following the funeral, I may be allowed to mention how rigidly it is enjoined in the Talmud. An Israelite is there commanded to follow every dead body that is carried out for burial among his people, the least allowable distance prescribed being four yards.

Again, if at a funeral the sun shines brightly on the face of one among the attendants, it marks him for the next to be laid in that churchyard; or if the sound of the "mools" falling on the coffin be heard by any person at a considerable distance from the spot it presages a death in that person's family.

A crowing hen is looked upon with fear and suspicion far and wide, I suppose as an intruder into the province of her mate. Old Francis Quarles makes her the type of wives who bear rule over their husbands:—

Ill thrives the hapless family that shows
A cock that's silent and a hen that crows.
I know not which live more unnatural lives,
Obeying husbands or commanding wives.

According to the Northamptonshire proverb,

A whistling woman and crowing hen,
Are neither fit for God nor men.

In Normandy they say, "Une poule qui chante le coq et une fille qui siffle, portent malheur dans la maison;" and in Cornwall, "A whistling woman and a crowing hen are the two unluckiest things under the sun."

The former delinquent is much dreaded on the coast of Yorkshire by the seafaring part of the population. A few years ago, when a party of friends were going on board a vessel at Scarborough, the captain astonished them by declining to allow one of them to enter it. "Not that young lady," he said, "she whistles." Curiously enough the vessel was lost on her next voyage; so, had the poor girl set foot on it, the misfortune would certainly have been ascribed to her. It is remarkable that no miner in Devonshire or Cornwall whistles underground, or allows others to do so. I have conversed with them about it, and do not gather that they think it unlucky, but unseemly and irreverent. All assure me that it is never done in a mine even by the youngest boy.

A crowing hen is counted on the Borders a forerunner of death. Thus, a few years ago, we are told, an old woman in the parish of East Kilbride heard one of her hens crow loudly on the top of a dyke before her house. She mentioned the circumstance to a neighbour, saying that no good would come of it, and accordingly her husband soon died. About a month afterwards she heard the creature again, and within a few days tidings reached her of the death of her only son. A week later the hen crowed once more, and the eldest daughter died. On this the old woman was roused to desperation; she seized the warning bird, wrung its neck, and burned it.

Mr. Wilkie records the following singular portent of death, which took place about seven years before it was related to him: "A farmer's wife, who resided on the banks of the Ale, near St. Boswell's, looking out at window, thought she saw a funeral approaching; and at once mentioned the circumstance to some neighbours, then with her in the house. They ran out to look, but came back and sat down again, saying she must be mistaken, for there was nothing of the kind to be seen; the woman felt restless, however, and out of spirits; she could not help going to the window again, and again she saw the funeral moving on. Her friends ran out-of-doors and looked along the road, but still could perceive nothing; a third time she went to the window, and exclaimed, 'It is fast coming on, and will soon be at the door.' No other person could discern anything; but within half an hour a confused noise was heard outside, and the farm-servants entered, bearing her husband's lifeless body. He had died suddenly, by a fall from his cart."[1]

The presages of death on the Border are very numerous, *e.g.* the sound of bells in the night, the chirping of crickets, lights of circular form seen in the air, when there is no fire or candle, the dead chack or death-watch, a call by night or day in the voice of some absent person, a gripe of the arm or leg by an invisible clay-cold hand, the howling of dogs before your house-door, hens bringing off a brood all hen-birds, or laying eggs with double yolks, the birth of lambs deformed or with superfluous limbs, the chirping of fish long after they have been taken out of the water, sounds as though the house were falling down, magpies flying round the house or preceding you on the way to church, ravens croaking on or near it, swords falling out of their scabbards—all these are tokens of approaching death; but the most fatal of all is for a man to see his own wraith walking to or from him at noon or before sunset.

Compare with the third of these death omens, "lights of a circular form seen in the air," the following account from Sussex: "They believe in that county that the death of sick persons is shown by the prognostic of 'shell-fire.' This is a sort of lambent flame, which seems to rise from the bodies of those who are ill, and to envelop the bed. A distant connexion of mine asserts that she saw this phenomenon in the case of two of her sisters who died of typhus fever, and gives, in attestation, the remark of one of the sufferers herself, who asked what the light was."

In Lancashire it is believed that to build, or even to rebuild, a house, is always fatal to some member of the family—generally to the one who may chiefly have advised or wished for the building or alteration. But to return to the most fatal of Border portents.

[1] With this Border portent compare the following narration:—"Dr. Abraham Vander Meer, an upright and zealous Reformer, relates in his *Memorabilia* that his grandmother while residing at the Hague, being one summer night unable to sleep, placed herself about four o'clock in the morning at the window, and there saw a coffin coming up the Spui Straab, but without anyone else seeming to notice it. It moved on until it stood up erect before a house, where it vanished in an open window. Before six weeks had expired every inmate of that house had died of the plague."—Thorpe's *Mythology*, vol. iii. p. 211.

The wraith is an apparition exactly like a living person, and its appearance, whether to that person or to another, is commonly thought an omen of death. These apparitions are called "fetches" throughout the sister island, in Cumberland "swarths," and in Yorkshire "waffs." Of waff I have two examples from the East Riding of Yorkshire. The first was narrated to the clergyman from whom I received it by an old man of Danby, in Cleveland, eighty-two years of age, and highly respectable as to character. Some years before, he was passing one evening by an uncle's house, and, seeing the glow of firelight streaming through the window, looked in. To his great surprise he saw his uncle, who had long been "bed-fast" in the room above, seated in his former place in the "neukin." He was astonished—still there could be no mistake; the form and features were those of his relation, and he further assured himself of the fact by a second look. He entered the house to obtain an explanation; but the room was dark, the seat empty, and the old man lying upstairs in his bed. But his uncle's death took place before long.

A second case of this kind is said to have happened, at Whitby, to a tradesman suffering from stone, and ordered to the hospital at York for an operation. Before he set out, the patient said it was in vain, he should not return alive; he had seen his own waff, and knew he should die during the operation, or after it. His belief was verified: the operation was performed, but he did not long survive it. Either he was ignorant how to avert the ill-consequences of the apparition or he lacked courage at the moment. Had he spoken to it all would have been well. Thus a native of Guisborough, on going into a shop at Whitby, saw his own "waff," and boldly addressed it thus: "What's thou doin' here? What's thou doin' here? Thou's after no good, I'll go bail! Get thy ways yom wi' thee. Get thy ways yom!" The result of his thus taking the initiative was perfectly satisfactory.

The Vicar of Stamfordham has kindly communicated to me two cases of "wraiths," or apparitions, from his parish. The first is of a poor woman, called Esther Morton, of Black Heddon, who went out gathering sticks on the ground of a neighbouring farmer. Looking up, she saw him before her, and turned quickly to get out of his way. Then she remembered he was ill in bed and could not possibly be there, so she went home much alarmed, and found he had just died.

Again, one William Elliott, of the same place, saw his neighbour Mary Brown cross the fold-yard and disappear in a straw-house. Knowing her to be very ill, he made instant inquiries, and discovered that she had died at the moment of his seeing her.

Mr. Robinson, of Hill House, Reeth, writes thus on the subject: "We have in Wensleydale frequent instances of second sight, the people so gifted foretelling the deaths of their neighbours. For instance, some years back a man told me that he had met Mr. —— (a respectable inhabitant of the next village, and then in perfect health) walking on the road; 'but,' added he 'it was nobbut his shadow, and I don't think he'll live long.' He died within a short time. This is only one instance of many."

These Yorkshire stories recall to my memory an incident in which the "waff" was no prophet of death, but an instrument for saving life. The musician Gluck, Piccini's rival in Paris about 100 years ago, made some stay in one of the Belgian cities —Ghent, I believe. While there he was accustomed to spend the evening with friends, and, returning late to his lodging, to let himself in with a key. One moonlight evening, while going home as usual, he observed before him a figure resembling himself. It took every turn through the streets which he was accustomed to take, and finally, on reaching the door, drew out a key, opened it, and entered. On this the musician turned round in some perturbation, went back to his friends, and begged to be taken in for the night. The next morning they accompanied him to his lodging, and found that the heavy wooden roof of Gluck's sleeping-room had fallen down in the night and covered the floor. It was plain that had he passed the night there he must have been killed.

My own county furnishes a story of a similar character, which was thus related by the late Canon Humble: "I have heard a Durham story of a farmer going home at night after having sold his corn, with a considerable sum of money in his pocket. After leaving the town—Darlington, I believe—he saw a person emerge from a lane and walk behind him at the distance of five or six paces. He stopped, so did the other. He walked on, and the double did the like, still keeping at the same distance as before. He came to a very lonely part of the road, the double joined him, and soon a whisper was distinctly heard from the hedge as of a man speaking to a companion. 'It's nae use, there's twa o' them.' The double continued with the farmer till the road became open and then disappeared. But for this intervention the latter would have been robbed, perhaps even murdered."

But to return to the omens in the Wilkie MS. Some of them are more or less remarked in every part of our island—such as the death-watch, the croaking raven, or the solitary magpie; nor is it matter of astonishment that when the mind is impressed by the awe of sickness and impending death in our household we are prone to notice and brood over sounds and sights which seem to connect themselves with our anxieties and sorrows. The howling of dogs is a widely-known death omen. We find it in every part of our island, in France and Germany, and even in Constantinople. A close observer, who has seen the omen given, and noted its fulfilment, describes the dog as very uneasy till it can get under the death-chamber. If the house stands within an inclosure, and it cannot get in, it will run round the premises, or pace up and down before them. If it succeeds in forcing an entry, it will stop under the window, howl horribly, finish with three tremendous barks, and hurry away. Mr. Kelly, who relates this,[1] adds that the dog is an attendant on the dead in the German as in the Aryan mythology, that dogs see ghosts, and that when Hela, the goddess of death, walks abroad, invisible to human eyes, she is seen by the dogs. Again, in the North of England the flight of jackdaws or swallows down the chimney is held to presage death, as well as the appearance of a trio of butterflies flying together. So does a winding-sheet, or piece of curled tallow in the candle, called in Scotland a "dead spale." Three raps given by no human hand are said also to give warn-

[1] *Indo-European Tradition and Folk-Lore*, p. 110.

ing of death. Such were heard a few years ago, at Windy Walls, near Stamfordham, in Northumberland, on the outside of a window-shutter, and the same night a man belonging to the house fell accidentally off a cart and was killed. An Albino mole presages the demise of the farmer on whose land it is found, and again, if thirteen persons sit down to eat together one of them will shortly die. This belief is widely spread, and doubtless originated in the remembrance of the thirteen who sat down at the last Paschal Supper, and of the fate of Judas.

Another death-omen is the crowing of a cock at dead of night. A lady in the East Riding of Yorkshire tells me that a few years ago, a cook, who had recently come to her from the north of that county, told her one morning, with tears in her eyes, that she should not be able to stay long in her place, for her sister was dead or dying. The mistress naturally concluded that the tidings had come by post that morning, but it turned out that such was not the case. The cock had crowed at midnight on two following nights, and as she had not heard from her sister for some time she was doubtless ill, if not already dead. Happily the good woman's fears were groundless, and she lived some time in my informant's service.

Again, the flying or hovering of birds around a house, and their resting on the window-sill, or tapping against the pane, portends death. This last belief is widely spread, and I cannot divest myself of the notion that there is a sympathy between us and the animal creation, which comes to view in times of sorrow. I am permitted to mention that the recent death of a clergyman of some eminence in the town of Hull was preceded by the flight of a pure white pigeon around the house, and its resting again and again on his window-sill. And the Vicar of Fishlake, in the West Riding, informs me that one of his parishioners mentioned the same portent to him; telling him, as an illustration, of a Primitive Methodist preacher, a very worthy man, who had fallen down dead in the pulpit soon after giving out his text. "And not many hours before," she went on, "I had seen a white pigeon light on a tree hard by, and I said to a neighbour I was sure summat were going to happen."

I have heard of the same belief in Suffolk, where an old woman expressed her dismay at having a robin come "weeping, weeping," as she called it, at her door, and related two instances in her own family in which it had been a warning of death.

The following list of death omens has been communicated to me from Sussex. It is interesting to compare them with our north-country portents. An unusual rattling of the church door, a heavy sound in a funeral bell, or the appearance of the ignis-fatuus or will-o'-the-wisp, the cry of the screech-owl or three caws of a carrion crow, are thought in that county to presage death. So is the breaking of a looking-glass, which they say in Denmark is a sign of utter ruin to the family in which it takes place. Again, if a dead body continues limp, and does not stiffen, another death will soon take place. And it is accounted unlucky to take the first snowdrop or primrose into a house, or blackthorn blossom, or broom in the month of May. My informant heard a Sussex cottager scold her child for taking a single snowdrop into the house, and, asking the reason, was told it was a death token, and looked "for all the world like a corpse in its shroud," and "that it kept itself quite close to the ground, seeming to belong more to the dead than the living." As for primroses, they used to be sought for to strew on graves and dress up corpses, and the black-thorn was thought to represent a strange commingling of life and death in its white flowers on the bare twigs unclothed with leaves. On a lady (the wife of the clergyman) entering a Sussex cottage with a branch of it in blossom, the poor woman snatched it out of her hand and flung it out of doors, saying, "How could you think, Ma'am, of bringing that death token into my house?" This belief extends to Germany, where the blackthorn is said to spring from the corpse of a heathen slain in battle. The broom was especially baleful if used for sweeping. I am told of an old Sussex gentleman who strictly forbade the use of green brooms during the month of May, and justified himself by repeating the adage—

If you sweep the house with broom in May,
You'll sweep the head of that house away.

The following form of divination seems purely Northumbrian. After a death has taken place in a family, the straw or chaff from the bed of the departed is taken into an open place and burned. Among its ashes the survivors look for a footprint, and that member of the family whose foot fits the impression will be the next to die.

Yorkshire, too, has its own manner of inquiring who will be taken from this world. Those who are curious to know about the death of their fellow-parishioners must keep watch in the church-porch on St. Mark's Eve for an hour on each side of midnight for three successive years. On the third year they will see the forms of those doomed to die within the twelvemonth passing one by one into the church. If the watcher fall asleep during his vigil he will die himself during the year. I have heard, however, of one case in which the intimation was given by the sight of the watcher's own form and features. It is that of an old woman at Scarborough, who kept St. Mark's vigil in the porch of St. Mary's in that town about eighty years ago. Figure after figure glided into the church, turning round to her as they went in, so that she recognised their familiar faces. At last a figure turned and gazed at her; she knew herself, screamed, and fell senseless to the ground. Her neighbours found her there in the morning, and carried her home, but she did not long survive the shock. An old man who recently died at Fishlake, in the West Riding of Yorkshire, was in the habit of keeping these vigils, and was in consequence an object of some dread to his neighbours. The old sexton at —— did so too, in order, it was said, to count the gains of the coming year. At the gates of Bramley church, Yorkshire, lived, some years ago, a man named Askew, son of a Baptist minister, who was reported always to keep St. Mark's watch. One year he let it transpire that he had seen the spirit of a neighbour called Lester, who, in consequence, would die during the twelvemonth. Mr. Lester, who was not in good health at the time, was much affected. He was then building a house, and he now arranged it with double doors, so that his widow might conveniently let half of it in case of his decease. He used to say that if he lived over the year he would shoot Askew; but he died before St. Mark's day came round again.

I have received a very remarkable story of an apparition on St. Mark's Eve, at Ford, Northumberland, which I give in the words of my informant, M. T. Culley, Esq. Coupland Castle: "Two men, both of whom my wife has seen, were ascending the hill at Ford alongside of the churchyard, having been surveying land. They had just turned into the Ford Road from, I think, Kimmerston Lane, when they saw the chancel door of the church open, and the rector, the Rev. —— Marsh, walk out in his surplice. It was the dusk of the evening, but there was a light around the figure, which enabled the men to see his features distinctly, and they afterwards asserted positively that there could be no doubt as to his identity. The figure advanced to a certain point in the churchyard and vanished. That night the rector was taken ill at Ford Castle, where he was dining, was carried home, died the following day, and was buried just were the figure had been observed to disappear."

I have heard of the rite in Cleveland too, and at Teesdale; at Sedbergh, in the West Riding of Yorkshire, the local belief is somewhat different. It is said there that the forms of those who will die during the year, preceded by the parish clerk, parade the churchyard on All Saints Eve. The clerk's daughter, named Barbara Butterwith, narrated this to my informant, the Rev. W. Delancey Lawson, and declared that she was going out to see the procession, but he dissuaded her from it, thinking that she might in some way get a panic.

Another mode of divining into futurity has also been resorted to in Yorkshire, called cauff-riddling, and was thus practised. The barn-doors must be set wide open, a riddle and some chaff must be procured, and those who wish to pry into the future must go into the barn at midnight, and in turn commence the process of riddling. Should the riddler be doomed to die during the year two persons will be seen passing by the open barn-doors carrying a coffin; in the other case nothing will be visible.

Not many years ago two men and a woman went to a barn near Malton, in Yorkshire, on St. Mark's Eve, to riddle cauff.

All the requisite observances were attended to; the men took their turns, but nothing was seen; then the woman began to riddle. Scarcely had the chaff begun to fall on the floor when all saw the ominous pair of coffin-bearers passing by. There was a moment's pause; the men rushed out to look, but all had disappeared; there was no living creature in sight. The woman died within the year. This story was related to my informant by one who knew the persons concerned, and spoke of them by name.

The rites accompanying the saining or blessing of a corpse in the Scottish Lowlands are given at some length in the Wilkie MS. They are as follows:

When a body has been washed and laid out, one of the oldest women present must light a candle, and wave it three times around the corpse. Then she must measure three handfuls of common salt into an earthenware plate, and lay it on the breast. Lastly, she arranges three "toom" or empty dishes on the hearth, as near as possible to the fire; and all the attendants going out of the room return into it backwards, repeating this "rhyme of saining:"

Thrice the torchie, thrice the saltie,
Thrice the dishies toom for "loffie" (*i. e.* praise),
These three times three ye must wave round
The corpse, until it sleep sound.
Sleep sound and wake nane,
Till to heaven the soul's gane.
If ye want that soul to dee
Fetch the torch frae th' Elleree;
Gin ye want that soul to live,
Between the dishes place a sieve,
An it sall have a fair, fair shrive.

This rite is called Dishaloof. Sometimes, as is named in the verses, a sieve is placed between the dishes, and she who is so fortunate as to place her hand in it is held to do most for the soul. If all miss the sieve, it augurs ill for the departed. Meanwhile all the windows in the house are opened, in order to give the soul free egress. The dishes are placed near the fire, from a notion that the soul resembles a flame, and hovers round the hearth for a certain period after death.

In some of the western counties, however, the dishes are set upon a table or "bunker" (as they call a long chest) close to the deathbed; and it is actually said that while the attendants sit with their hands in the dishes they "spae" or tell fortunes, sing songs, or repeat rhymes, in the middle of which the corpse, it is averred, has been known to rise frowning, and place its cold hand in one of the dishes, thus presaging death to her whose hand was in that dish already.

The Dishaloof so far over, the company join hands and dance round the dishes, singing this burden, "A dis, a dis, a dis, a green griss, a dis, a dis, a dis." Bread, cheese, and spirits are then placed on the table, and, when the company have partaken of them, they are at liberty to go home.

The candle for "saining" should be procured from a suspected witch or wizard, a seer or Elleree, or from a person with "schloof," or flat feet, "ringlit-eyed," that is with a great portion of white in the eye, or "lang-lipit," that is, with thick projecting lips; for all these persons are unlucky, and, in this affair, unlucky really means fortunate in the extreme. Unless the old mosstroopers are belied, they preferred for saining a torch made from the fat of a slaughtered enemy, or at least of a murdered man. The saining candle must be kept burning through the night, and the table covered with a cloth so long as the dead body remains in the house. Some people also make a point of turning the cat out-of-doors all the time.

The corpse must be watched till its burial by one of its kindred and a stranger, who may be relieved, when weary, by another relation and another stranger. In point of fact, however, they are seldom left to themselves. Neighbours assemble from a great distance to join them, and keep what is called "a sitting" while the sun is above the horizon, or after dark "a lykewake." These gatherings are common in North Wales also, but, whereas the Welsh pass the night in reading the Scriptures and singing Psalms, a strange sort of merriment seems to have characterised the Scotch "lykewake." Songs were sung and games played—Blind Harrie, for example, according to the old song of the "Humble Beggar:"

It happened ill, it happened worse,
It happened sae that he did dee,
And wha d'ye think war at the lykewake
But lads and lasses o' high degree?

Some were blithe and some were sad,
And some they played at Blind Harrie,
But suddenly uprose the auld carle,
"I rede ye gude folk tak tent o' me."

No doubt the custom of assembling neighbours and friends to keep watch in the house of death is ancient and wide-spread. The following injunction of Bishop Voysey (A.D. 1538) shows that it prevailed in the West of England: "Also that every curate . . . . especially within the archdeaconry of Cornwall, exhort effectuously their parishioners, that at the death of their friends they have no solemn nightwatches or drinkings."[1]

On the Borders games at cards are actually played on these occasions, the coffin, incredible as it may appear, being the card-table, while the round table on which the candle is placed may on no account be used. It is imperative that every watcher at a lykewake should touch the corpse with his hand, to keep him from dreaming of the dead, or brooding over any evil occurrence which may have taken place during the watch. For things do not always go right on these occasions. Thus tradition tells how once the corpse arose, sat upon the bed, and frowned dreadfully, though without speaking, an unseen hand having previously moved the plate of salt to the rack of the bed. It was plain that something essential had been omitted in the saining, or that the attendants had been performing some unhallowed rites. An old woman, eminent for her piety, was hastily summoned in this emergency. She came and found the room empty, the attendants having all fled in terror. Drawing her Bible from her pocket, the woman began to read it aloud, on which the corpse ceased to frown, and fell slowly back upon the bed. Closing her book, she prayed aloud; then covered the corpse, replaced the plate of salt upon its breast, and prayed again. All continuing still, she fetched water, washed her hands, and brought in the terrified

[1] Wilkins, vol. iii. p. 845.

attendants, who were huddled together round the door of the house, assuring them that if they abstained from evil amusements the devil would not molest them any more.

On another occasion it was reported, that, while hide-and-seek was going on at a lykewake, some young men took the dead body out of the coffin, and laid one of their number in its place to hide. Search being made for the youth, he was discovered in the coffin quite dead, but the corpse they had come to watch could nowhere be found. It was believed in the neighbourhood that it had been carried off by the fairies, and that the young man had been slain by the evil spirit.

A paper in Richardson's *Local Historian's Table Book* (vol. iii. p. 66) confirms and illustrates this account of a lykewake on the Borders. It adds a few particulars, the shrouding of the looking-glass, to intimate that all vanity, all care for earthly beauty, are over with the deceased, and the stopping and shrouding of the clock, to show that with him time is over; and it painfully evinces that the solemnity of the occasion did not preclude practical jokes, which appear to us profane and sacrilegious in the highest degree.

Some traces of these Scottish rites may be found in widely-separated parts of our island. I have seen the plate of salt on the breast of the dead in the North of England, and heard of its use in the Isle of Man, as well as in Wales, Hertfordshire, and Somersetshire. Probably its use has been very general, and this as an emblem of incorruption and eternity.

Sir Walter Scott considered that the word "sleete" in the chorus of the lykewake dirge was a corruption of "selt" or "salt:"

This ae night, this ae night,
  Every night and all,
Fire and sleete and candlelighte,
  And Christe receive thy sawle.

The custom of opening the door at the time of death is also widespread. I have heard of it as far south as Spain, and also in Germany. My readers cannot forget how, at the smuggler's death in the Kaim of Derncleugh, Meg Merrilies unbars the door, and lifts the latch, saying:

> Open lock, end strife,
> Come death, and pass life.

As to the touching of the corpse by those who come to look at it, this is still expected by the poor of Durham on the part of those who come to their house while a dead body is lying in it, in token that they wished no ill to the departed, and were in peace and amity with him.

No doubt this custom grew out of the belief, once universal among northern nations, that a corpse would bleed at the touch of the murderer. In King James the First's *Dæmonology* we read: "In a secret murder, if the dead carkasse be at any time thereafter handled by the murderer, it will gush out of blood, as if the blood were crying to Heaven for revenge of the murderer." And it is mentioned in a note to chap. v. of the *Fair Maid of Perth*, that this bleeding of a corpse was urged as an evidence of guilt in the High Court of Justiciary at Edinburgh as late as 1668.

The practice of covering or removing the looking-glass from the chamber of death extends into the northern counties of England, and this not only for the cause assigned above. The invisible world trenches closely upon the visible one in the chamber of death; and I believe that a dread is felt of some spiritual being imaging himself forth in the blank service of the mirror.[1]

I may here mention that in Denmark it is forbidden to bury a corpse in the clothes of a living person, lest as the clothes rot that person wastes away and perishes. It is said there, too, that one must not weep over the dying, still less allow tears to fall on them; it will hinder their resting in the grave.

[1] I suspect that the true reason for shrouding the looking-glass before a funeral is that given me in Warwickshire, that if you look into a mirror in the death chamber you will see the corpse looking over your shoulder. I have heard the same superstition in Devonshire. In the West Riding of Yorkshire there is a strong feeling against burying a woman with her rings or jewellery. A gentleman told me that when his mother died he was desirous of leaving on her hand her wedding-ring, but was reproved for the wish by the women who laid her out. "Ye mun no send her to God wi' her trinkets about her," they said.—S. B. G.

Throughout Northumberland when a married woman dies her head should be bound round with a black ribbon; for a spinster white is used.

It is a common belief along the east coast of England, from Northumberland to Kent, that deaths mostly occur during the falling of the tide. As Mr. Peggotty explained to David Copperfield by poor Barkis's bedside, "People can't die along the coast except when the tide's pretty nigh out. They can't be born unless it's pretty nigh in—not properly born till flood. He's agoing out with the tide—he's agoing out with the tide. It's ebb at half arter three, slack-water half-an-hour. If he lives till it turns he'll hold his own till past the flood, and go out with the next tide." And after many hours' watching, "it being low water, he went out with the tide." In some extracts which I have seen of old date from the parish register of Heslidon, near Hartlepool, the state of the tide at the time of death is named: "The xith daye of Maye, A.D. 1595, at vi. of ye clocke in the morninge, being full water, Mr. Henrye Mitford, of Hoolam, died at Newcastel, and was buried the xvi. daie, being Sondaie, at evening prayer; the hired preacher maid ye sermon." "The xvii. daie of Maie, at xii. of ye clock at noon, being lowe water, Mrs. Barbara Mitford died, and was buried the xviii. daie of Maie, at ix. of the clocke. Mr. Holsworth maid ye sermon." Indeed, the belief must be of some antiquity, and must have found its way inland, since Sir John Falstaff is recorded to have "parted even just between twelve and one, e'en at turning o' the tide." I cannot hear of it on the south or west coast of England. A friend suggests to me that there may be some slight foundation for this belief in the change of temperature, which undoubtedly does take place on the change of tide, and which may act on the flickering spark of life, extinguishing it as the ebbing sea recedes.

The obtuseness of feeling with regard to death shown in the Border Lykewake certainly extends southward. A friend tells me of two instances in Yorkshire where persons have had their coffins made some years before their death, and have used them to keep bread and cheese in. Such was certainly the custom of an old brother at Sherburn Hospital, who was well known to many of the inhabitants of Durham. I myself saw the coffin set up against the wall, and witnessed the old man opening it to take out a jug of milk, which he offered to the young lad who accompanied me. The Master of Sherburn Hospital informs me that this old brother was in his way a luxurious man, with a due regard for creature comforts; and that, having a decidedly Roman nose, he had caused a corresponding cavity to be made in the inside of the coffin-lid, for fear the projecting member should be inconvenienced. An old Yorkshire woman was, I am told, very explicit in the directions she gave about her coffin. She ordered two holes to be made in its lid, that when the devil came in at one hole to catch her she might slip out at the other.

A very singular belief prevails along the Borders, of which I find no mention in any book of Folk-Lore, though there is a passing allusion to it in Pennant's *Tour in Scotland:* "All fire is extinguished where a corpse is kept, and it is reckoned so ominous for a dog or cat to pass over it that the poor animal is killed without mercy." Two instances of this slaughter were recently related to the Rev. J. F. Bigge by an old Northumbrian hind. In one case, just as a funeral was about to leave the house, the cat jumped over the coffin, and no one would move till the cat was destroyed. In the other, as a funeral party were coming from a lonely house on a fell, carrying the coffin, because they could not procure a cart, they set it down to rest themselves, and a collie dog jumped over it. It was felt by all that the dog must be killed, without hesitation, before they proceeded further, and killed it was.

It is said, in the county of Durham, that the bodies of the drowned will float on the ninth day; and again, that if a gun be fired over a dead body lying at the bottom of the sea or river, the concussion will break the gall-bladder and cause the body to float. A friend informs me that he has seen this done twice at Stockton, but without success. He also tells me that a loaf weighted with quicksilver, if allowed to float on the water, is said to swim towards and stand over the place where the body lies. This is a very widely-spread belief. I have heard of it not only in several parts of England but in Ireland, and among the North American Indians. To its firm hold in the city of Durham I can myself bear witness. When a boy I have seen persons endeavouring to discover the corpses of the drowned in this manner in the River Wear, near to Stoker's Wall; and ten years ago the friends of one Christopher Lumley sought for his body in the Smallhope, near Lanchester, in the county of Durham, by the aid of a loaf of bread with a lighted candle in it. Indeed, the same means were practised in the autumn of the year 1860, within two miles of the city of Durham. A little child named Charles Colling fell into the Wear at Shincliffe, on the 21st of October in that year, and was drowned. His friends, after vainly trying the usual methods of finding the body, charged a loaf of bread with quicksilver, and floated it on the stream. Long and earnestly was its course watched, but all in vain; it floated onwards without pausing to mark the resting-place of the little child, and, though the body was ultimately recovered, it was by other means.

The old superstition, that no one can die in a bed containing the feathers of pigeons or game-fowl, can scarcely be called local, for we hear of it in many different parts of England. A Sussex Mrs. Gamp lately told the wife of her clergyman that never did she see any one die so hard as old Master Short, and at last she thought (though his daughter said there were none) that there must be game feathers in the bed. So she tried to pull it from under him, but he was a heavy man and she could not manage it alone, and there was no one with him but herself, and so she got a rope and tied it round him and pulled him by it off the bed, and he went off in a minute quite comfortable, just like a lamb. This old woman's belief holds its ground in the North, and in Yorkshire the same is said of cock's feathers. The Russian peasantry have a strong feeling, too, against using pigeon's feathers in beds. They consider it sacrilegious, the dove being the emblem of the Holy Spirit. Some Yorkshire people declare that no one can die easy on any bed, and will lay a dying man on the floor, to facilitate the departure of the soul. It is remarkable that this is also a Hindoo and Mohamedan custom. In

India the dying are always taken from their beds and laid on the ground, it being held that no one can die peaceably except when laid on "mother earth."

A singular circumstance has been related to me as having occurred a few years ago at a funeral, in the village of Stranton, near West Hartlepool.

The vicar was standing at the churchyard gate awaiting the arrival of the funeral party, when to his surprise the whole group, who had arrived within a few yards of him, suddenly wheeled round and made the circuit of the churchyard wall, thus traversing its west, north, and east boundaries, and making the distance some five or six times greater than was necessary. The vicar, astonished at the proceeding, asked the sexton the reason of so extraordinary a movement. The reply was as follows: "Why, ye wad no hae them carry the dead again the sun; the dead maun ay go wi' the sun."

This custom is doubtless an ancient British or Celtic one, and corresponds with the Highland usage of making the deazil, or walking three times round a person according to the course of the sun. Old Highlanders will still make the deazil around those to whom they wish well. To go round the person in the opposite direction, or "withershins," is an evil incantation, and brings ill fortune.

It is curious to compare this Yorkshire custom of carrying the dead with the sun to the Welsh usage mentioned by Pennant.[1] Speaking of Skir'og, in North Wales, he says: "When a corpse is carried to church from any part of the town the bearers take care to carry it so that the corpse may be on the right hand through the way, be it nearer, or be it less trouble to go on the other side, nor will they bring it through any other way than the north gate."[2]

It is a Northumbrian belief that three funerals constantly follow one another in quick succession, an opinion to which we

[1] Brand's *Pop. Ant.* vol. ii. p. 285.

[2] This prejudice existed very strongly in Iceland in ancient times. According to the *Vatnsdœla saga*, a woman, by going against the sun round a house and waving a cloth, brought down a landslip against the house (*Vatnsdœla*, s. c. 363;

may find a parallel in Durham, where it is a matter of common remark that if the cathedral bell tolls once it tolls thrice with little intermission, and in Sussex, where they say that if death enters a house he will not take leave of it till he has carried off three of its inmates. On this point a kind contributor writes: "It is believed in Rome that three cardinals always die in quick succession. On the death of one 'Eminentissimo' it is usual to hear discussions as to which of the Sacred College will be the second and the third. Reference to the Annuaria Pontifico will show that the deaths of the cardinals have so occurred in threes up to the latest time. Three thus died in the winter of 1866-7.' A Buckinghamshire variation is to this effect: If the clock strikes while the bell is tolling there will be another death within the week. A friend from that county informs me also, that, whereas it was a rule in her parish that the bell should only be tolled in the daytime, it was once heard by the clergyman at five o'clock on a winter's morning, and he accordingly sent to the church to have it stopped for two hours. The deceased person was a wealthy farmer, and his widow complained bitterly over the delay in the tolling. "It was so cruel in Mr. Y." she

Laudnama, iii. and p. 181). The date of this event was about A.D. 990. So a magical storm was laid (*Vatsn.* c. 47; and also Thorfin's *S. Karlsefnis*, c. 9, p. 11; *Droplavgar Sonar*, s. p. 10): "The hag did not lie down to sleep that night, she was so restless. The weather was cold without, a keen frost, and the sky clear. She went several times against the sun and round the house, set her face in all directions, and turned her nose up. And as she thus went about the weather began to change. There rose a dense fog, and after that an icy blast, and an avalanche broke off on the mountain-side, and the snow shot down on the farm of Berg, and twelve men died of it. The signs of the fall are visible now."—(*Gisla S. Surssonar*, p. 33.) Again: "The hag took her knife, and cut on the log runes, and smeared them with her blood, and chanted charms over them. Then she went many times against the sun round the log, and muttered many troll-like sayings. After that she had the log rolled down to the sea, and she said that it would be washed to Drangey, where it would work mischief to Grettir."—(*Gretla*, c. 81.) To go against the sun is "andsælis" in Icelandic. I have heard in Yorkshire that if you walk three times round the room against the sun at midnight, and in perfect darkness, and then look into the glass, you will see the devil's face leering out of it at you. Again, on All Souls Day (I believe), if two people walk round the room at midnight, and in darkness, going contrary ways, they will never meet; one of the two will have been spirited away —S. B. G.

said, "to keep the poor soul those hours a-waiting!" Now the "passing bell" was supposed in former times to serve two purposes: it called on all good Christians within hearing to pray for the departing spirit, and it scared away the evil spirits, who were watching to seize it, or at least to scare and terrify it. Evidently the widow thought that for want of these helps the progress of her husband's soul to its rest was impeded.

There is, I am informed, among old-fashioned families in Northumberland, a feeling that the death of an inmate is a token of the Divine wrath, and that this wrath rests on the house until after the visit of the parish clergyman, which is therefore anxiously looked for and much valued. A friend of mine well remembers, when a curate in Northumberland some twenty-four years ago, being told by a clergyman of that county that he had been frequently asked to "bless the house" after death had taken place in it.

CHAPTER II.

DAYS AND SEASONS.

Christmas—St. Stephen's Day—The Sword Dancers—Mummers—New Year's Eve—New Year's Day—The first foot—Shrove Tuesday—Passion Sunday—Palm Sunday—Good Friday—Easter Day—May Day—Ascension Day—Whitsun Day—Corpus Christi—The Harvest, Mell Supper, and Kern Baby—St. Agnes' Fast—St. Valentine's Day—April 1—First Cuckoo Day—The Borrowing Days—May 29th—St. Michael's Day—All Hallowe'en—St. Clement's Day—St. Andrew's Day—Epithets for the days of the week.

IF we pass on to days and seasons we shall find them marked in the North by time-honoured customs, unobserved for the most part elsewhere. Of course we must not look in Scotland for any distinctive note of Christmas, though I am informed that the observance of this festival is much increasing there. The shops of Edinburgh and Glasgow are now decorated with evergreens as gaily as those of any English town. Christmas-trees are common there, too, and mince-pies may be found on the tables even of strict Presbyterians. In the English Border-counties there is much to mark this blessed season. Yule-cakes are spread on our tables at Christmas tide, and the yule-log lights up our hearths as duly as does the ashen faggot in Devonshire.[1] In the city of Durham, and in many other northern towns, an old woman carries from house to house, on Christmas Eve, figures of the Virgin and Child, and shows them to the young people while she sings the old carol:

> God rest you, merry gentlemen, let nothing you dismay,
> Remember Christ our Saviour was born on Christmay Day,
> To save our souls from Satan's fold, which long had gone astray.
> And 'tis tidings of comfort and joy!

[1] A Devonshire friend informs me of the legend connected with this west-country observance. It is said that the Divine Infant at Bethlehem was first washed and dressed by a fire of ashwood.

We do not come to your house to beg nor to borrow,
But we do come to your house to sing away all sorrow;
The merry time of Christmas is drawing very near,
And 'tis tidings of comfort and joy !

We do not come to your house to beg for bread and cheese,
But we do come to your house to give us what you please ;
The merry time of Christmas is drawing very near,
And 'tis tidings of comfort and joy !

God bless the master of this house, the mistress also,
And all the little children that round the table go,
And all their kith and kindred, that travel far and near ;
And we wish you a merry Christmas and a happy New Year !

Children carry about these figures through the West Riding of Yorkshire in what they call milly-boxes, a corruption of "My Lady." The boxes are lined with spice, oranges, and sugar. They call this "going a-wassailing." The wassail-cup hymn there in use runs thus:

Here we come a-wassailing
Among the leaves so green,
Here we come a-wandering
So fair to be seen.

Chorus.

For it is Christmas time,
Strangers travel far and near.
So God bless you and send you
A happy New Year.

We are not daily beggars
That beg from door to door,
But we are neighbours' children,
Whom you have seen before.

Call up the butler of this house,
Put on his golden ring,
Let him bring us a glass of beer,
And the better we shall sing.

We have got a little purse,
Made of stretching leather skin,
We want a little o' your money
To line it well withiu.

Bring us out a table,
And spread it with a cloth.
Bring out a mouldy cheese,
Also your Christmas loaf.

Good master and mistress,
While you're sitting by the fire,
Pray think of us poor children,
Who are wandering in the mire.

Later in the evening, the streets of many a Northumbrian town (I use the word in its fullest meaning) echo the same carol, or the yet finer one "Christians awake, salute the happy morn!" In the West Riding the singers are dressed in the most fanciful attire, and are called "mummers." Throughout the district of Cleveland they carry about with them a "bessel cup," more properly a wassail cup, together with figures of the Virgin and Child, placed in a box and surrounded with such ornaments as they can collect. To send these singers away unrequited is to forfeit good luck for the year. No meat is eaten there on Christmas Eve, doubtless because it is a fast of the Church; the supper there consists of frumety, or wheat boiled in milk with spice and sugar, and of fruit tarts. At its close the yule-cake and cheese are cut and partaken of, while the master taps a fresh cask of ale. This cake and cheese are offered through the season to every visitor who calls. At Horbury, near Wakefield, and at Dewsbury, on Christmas Eve is rung the "devil's knell:" a hundred strokes, then a pause, then three strokes, three strokes, and three strokes again.

But to return to Cleveland. The yule-log (or clog) and yule candles are duly burned there on Christmas Eve, the carpenter supplying his customers with the former, the grocer with the latter. It would be most unlucky to light log or candle before the proper time. The whole season has a festive character, and visiting and card-playing are kept up throughout it. Christmas-boxes, however, are not common in Cleveland. New Year's Day is the time there for making presents, as in the eastern counties is St. Thomas's Day. The poor, and especially poor widows, go from house to house on this last day, asking for Christmas gifts. This custom prevails also in the West Riding of Yorkshire, where the widows ask and commonly receive at the farmers' houses a small measure of wheat, and they call it "going a Thomasing."

St. Stephen's Day in Cleveland, as indeed all England over, is devoted to hunting and shooting, it being held that the game-laws are not in force on that day; but I am not aware that the apple-trees are deliberately aimed at, as is the case in Devonshire, with the view of insuring a good crop of apples. A friend reminds me of the nursery rhyme which connects field-sports with this day:

> Three Welchmen went a-hunting
> All on St. Stephen's Day,

the point of the tale being that none of the three can quite make out what the moon is.

The old custom of hanging up a stocking to receive Christmas presents, a custom which the Pilgrim Fathers carried to America, and bequeathed, curiously enough, to their descendants, has not yet died out in the North of England. If any of my readers are Folk-Lore collectors they will divine my feelings on discovering in one of our northern capitals, among my own personal friends, a family in which, without the excuse of a child to be surprised and pleased, each member duly and deliberately hangs out her stocking on Christmas Eve to receive the kindly gifts of mother and sisters.

I may add, that throughout the parish of Whitbeck, in Cumberland, the country people breakfast early on Christmas Day on black pudding, a mess made of sheep's heart chopped with suet and sweet fruits.[1]

But a Christmas in the North would be quite incomplete without a visit from the sword-dancers, and this may yet be looked for in most of our towns from the Humber to the Cheviot Hills. There are some trifling local variations both in dance and song: the latter has altered with the times; the former is plainly a relic of the war-dances of our Danish and Saxon ancestors. I had an opportunity, A.D. 1866, of making inquiries into the mysteries of

[1] Hutchinson's *History of Cumberland*, vol. i. p. 555.

sword-dancing from a pitman of Houghton Colliery, Houghton-le-Spring, Joseph Brown by name, and will simply relate what I heard from him on the subject. He was well qualified to speak, having acted as sword dancer during the past twelve years, in company with eight other men, nine being the number always employed. Five are dancers, one a clothes-carrier, two clowns, and one a fiddler.

There are two sets of verses used near Durham, termed the old and new styles. The old verses are certainly of the date of a hundred years back; they were always used 'till about ten years ago, and are still sung in turn with the modern ones. They are as follows:

First Clown: It's a ramblin' here I've ta'en
The country for to see,
Five actors I have brought,
Yet better cannot be.

Now, my actors they are young,
And they've ne'er been out before,
But they'll do the best they can,
And the best can do no more.

Now the first that I call on
Is George, our noble king;
Long time he's been at wars,
Good tidings back he'll bring.

One of the sword-dancers here steps from the ring, in which all had been standing, and follows the first clown, holding his sword upright as he walks round the outside of the ring; and the first clown then sings:

The next that I call on,
He is a squire's son,
He's like to lose his love,
Because he is too young.

The squire's son steps forward and follows King George, and the first clown sings:

Little Foxey is the next,
With the orange and the blue,
And the debts he has paid off,
Both French and Spaniards too.

Little Foxey steps forward and follows the squire's son, and the clown sings:

Now the next that I call on
  Is the King of Sicily;
My daughter he shall have,
  And married they shall be.

The King of Sicily steps forward and follows Little Foxey, and the clown sings:

Now the next that I call on,
  He is a pitman bold;
He works all underground,
  To keep him from the cold.

The pitman follows the rest, and the clown sings again:

It's now you 've seen them all,
  Think o' them what ye will,
Though we'll stand back awhile
  Till they do try their skill.

Now fiddler then, take up thy fiddle,
  Play the lads their hearts' desire,
Or else we 'll break thy fiddle,
  And fling thee a' back o' the fire.

The five men then commence dancing round, with their swords all raised to the centre of the ring, till the first clown orders them to tie the points of their swords in "the knot." When this is done, and the five swords are knotted, the knot is held upright by one of the dancers, whom they call Alexander, or Alick. Alick then takes the sword from the knot, and, retaining it, gives the second dancer his sword; then the second dancer gives the third dancer his sword, the third dancer gives it to the fourth, and the fourth to the fifth.

The first clown, called the Tommy, is dressed in a chintz dress with a belt, a fox's head for a cap, and the skin hanging below his shoulders.

The second clown, called the Bessy, wears a woman's gown, which of late years has been well crinolined, and a beaver hat.

The five dancers have black breeches, with red stripes at the sides, white shirts decked with gay ribbons, and hats surmounted with streamers.

The verses given by Sir Cuthbert Sharpe, in the *Bishoprick Garland*, differ widely from both the old and new style of Durham verses. Probably his may be in use in Newcastle or Sunderland, for two of his characters are a sailor and a skipper.

The dance corresponds most remarkably with the account given by Olaus Magnus of the sword dance of the ancient Goths and Swedes.[1] Some such dance is still kept up in Gothland, with an allusion to the sacrifice to Odin, which formerly accompanied it. One of the company is clad in skin, and holds a wisp of straw in his mouth, cut sharp at the ends, to resemble a swine's bristles, and thus he personates the hog formerly sacrificed at Yule. Throughout Yorkshire, and formerly, indeed, all England over, the Christmas visitants are mummers disguised in finery of different sorts, with blackened faces or masks, and carrying with them an image of a white horse. This white horse appears at Christmas throughout the North of Germany with the "Hale Christ," "Knecht Rupert," or "San Claus," who brings the good children presents, but punishes the naughty ones.

In the Midland counties, people asking for Christmas-boxes on Christmas Eve drag about with them a horse's head and skin. I have seen this myself in the Forest of Dean. Mr. Baring Gould writes on the subject: "At Wakefield and Stanby the mummers enter a house, and if it be in a foul state they proceed to sweep the hearth, and clean the kitchen-range, humming all the time 'mum-m-m.' At Horbury they do no sweeping now, though I believe in old times they used to practise it. As far as I can judge there is generally one man in sailor's dress, the rest being women, or rather men in women's dress, but this is not universal. The Christmas-tup is another amusement. It is distinct from the white horse. I believe that the Christmas mummers represent the yule host, or wild hunt, and that the man of the party

[1] Brand's *Pop. Ant.* vol. i. p. 512.

is Wodin or Odin. The horse is evidently the white steed. Gleipmir, of the ancient god."

From Mr. Joseph Crawhall, of Newcastle, I have received the following song. It was given to him by a friend who called it a carol, and said that in his early days he used to sing it every Christmas with his sisters:

The first day of Christmas my true love sent to me
A partridge upon a pear tree.

The second day of Christmas my true love sent to me
Two turtle doves and a partridge upon a pear tree.

The third day of Christmas my true love sent to me
Three French hens, two turtle doves, &c. &c.

The fourth day of Christmas my true love sent to me
Four curley birds, three French hens, &c. &c.

The fifth day of Christmas my true love sent to me
Five gold rings, four curley birds, &c. &c.

The sixth day of Christmas my true love sent to me
Six geese laying, five golden rings, &c. &c.

The seventh day of Christmas my true love sent to me
Seven swans swimming, six geese laying, &c. &c.

The eighth day of Christmas my true love sent to me
Eight maids milking, seven swans swimming, &c. &c.

The ninth day of Christmas my true love sent to me
Nine drummers drumming, eight maids milking, &c. &c.

The tenth day of Christmay my true love sent to me
Ten pipers piping, nine drummers drumming, eight maids milking, seven swans swimming, six geese laying, five gold rings, four curley birds, three French hens, two turtle doves, and a partridge upon a pear tree.

Another version of this carol may be found in Halliwell's *Nursery Rhymes*, and one which recognises all the "twelve good days" of the Christmas feast. In its complete form it runs thus:

The twelfth day of Christmas my mother sent to me
Twelve bells a-ringing, eleven ladies spinning, ten ships a-sailing, nine lords a-leaping, eight ladies dancing, seven swans a-swimming, six geese a-laying, five gold rings, four canary birds, three French hens, two turtle doves, and a partridge upon a pear tree.

Holy Innocents Day is still called Childermas Day in and near Preston, and is considered an appropriate day for children's treats and parties.

New Year's Eve is one of the nights on which it is deemed highly unlucky in the Borders to let the fire out, the others being All Hallowe'en, Beltane or Midsummer Eve, and Christmas Eve. It is not easy to repair the mischief if once committed, for no one is willing on the following morning to give his neighbour a light, lest he should thus give away all his good luck for the season. And he who should steal fire unseen from his neighbour's hearth would fare no better for it, since fire thus taken is not counted holy.

It is curious to compare this statement of Mr. Wilkie with that given by Mr. Kelly respecting the "holy fires of the Germanic race," in his *Indo-European Traditions and Folk-Lore* (page 46). Mr. Kelly enumerates the Easter fires with those on St. John's Day, Michaelmas, Martinmas, and Christmas. It will be observed that in Scotland the Easter, Michaelmas, and Martinmas fires disappear, while that of All Hallowe'en takes their place. And, while in Scotland all care is taken to preserve the house-fire alight at these hallowed seasons, it has been the usage in Germany, and earlier still throughout all Christendom, to extinguish it and re-light it with holy fire, kindled by the priest with flint and steel in the churchyard.

Empty pockets or an empty cupboard on New Year's Eve portend a year of poverty. The poet Burns makes mention of this in an epistle to Colonel de Payster, from whom he borrowed a small sum at this season:

> To make the old year go out groaning
> And keep the new year from coming in moaning.

Indeed, on the Borders care is taken that no one enters a house empty-handed on New Year's Day. A visitor must bring in his hand some eatable; he will be doubly welcome if he carries in a hot stoup or "plotic." Everybody should wear a new dress on New Year's Day, and if its pockets contain money of every description they will be certain not to be empty throughout the year. The last glass of wine or spirits drained from the last bottle on New Year's Eve or Day is called the "lucky glass." It brings good fortune to whoever comes in for it, and if an unmarried person drinks it he will be the first to marry among the company. You must take note what is the Christian name of the first person you see of the opposite sex on New Year's Day: it will be that of the future husband or wife.

On New Year's Day much importance is attached to the first foot which crosses the threshold. That of a fair man is luckier than of a dark one, but (alas for the chivalry of the North!) should it be a woman's, some misfortune may certainly be looked for. The servant-girls are desirous that their "first foot" should be a lover, and sometimes they insure it by admitting him as soon as the New Year is rung in. They arrange, too, that he should bring something with him into the house, for, as the Lincolnshire rhyme runs:—

> Take out, and then take in,
> Bad luck will begin;
> Take in, then take out,
> Good luck comes about.

A friend tells me, that in the western part of the county of Durham he has known a man to be specially retained as "first-foot," or "Lucky-bird," as they call him in Yorkshire; his guerdon being a glass of spirits; but it was not necessary that he should be a bachelor. The man took care to be at the house by 5 o'clock in the morning, which insured his being the earliest visitor. This custom prevails through all our northern counties.

At Stamfordham, in Northumberland, the first-foot must be a bachelor. He generally brings in a shovelful of coals, but, unfortunately, whisky is coming into fashion as his offering. One inhabitant of the village, I scarcely know why, was considered a lucky "first-foot," and he always went in that capacity to the blacksmith's house hard by. One year some one else was, by accident, first-foot. This was considered an ill omen, and accordingly, during the following hay harvest, the house was broken open and half-a-sovereign stolen.[1] In some districts, however, special weight is attached to the "first-foot" being that of a person with a high-arched instep, a foot that "water runs under." A flat-footed person would bring great ill-luck for the coming year. The possessor of the lucky, *i.e.*, arched foot, whether male or female, will then be asked to come first to the home or to the room to awaken the sleepers.

It is recorded by Hospinian that formerly, in Rome, no one would suffer another to take fire out of his house on New Year's Day, or anything made of iron, or indeed would lend anything.[2] But I can bear witness that this idea has been more thoroughly worked out in the farmhouses of the county of Durham. It happened that, when a boy, I spent Christmas in one of those primitive secluded spots, which now, alas! have disappeared before the collieries which crowd and darken the land. I remember accompanying the mistress of the house to her kitchen on New Year's Eve, when she called together all her servants, and warned them, under pain of dismissal, not to allow anything to be carried out of the house on the following day, though they might bring in as much as they pleased. Acting on this order, all ashes, dish-washings, or potato-parings, and so forth, were retained in the house till the next day; while coals, potatoes, firewood, and bread were brought in as usual, the mistress keeping a sharp look-out on the fulfilment of her orders.

Now, we may see in this practice on the first day of the year a shadow of anxiety that the incomings of the ensuing twelvemonth should exceed the outgoings, or in other words that the year might be prosperous. Much of our Folk-Lore points to this craving for material prosperity: *e.g.*, the keeping the tip of a dried tongue in the pocket, that it may never be empty; or turning the money in it on the first sight of the new moon, or

[1] This holds good of the West Riding of Yorkshire. Doors are there chained up to prevent females from entering. A man in the town comes early to —— Parsonage, and bids the maids unbar and let him in, as he brings the new year to them.—S. B. G.

[2] Brand's *Pop. Ant.* vol. i. p. 13.

on first hearing the note of the cuckoo, to insure there being always plenty there—practices still common among us.[1]

The Cleveland New Year's greeting is very definite on this matter:—

> I wish you a merry Christmas,
> And a happy New Year,
> A pantry full of roast beef,
> And a barrel full of beer.

You may constantly hear the lads of that district calling it through their neighbour's keyholes early on New Year's morning. It is also recited by the children of the West Riding when they make their rounds soliciting New Year's gifts. There is much visiting at this season throughout the North of England, and much hospitality in the matter of rich cake and wine, but the name applied to this practice in Northumberland is singular. They call it "fadging," or "eating fadge."

Old people are careful to note how the wind blows on New Year's Eve, as they think it significant of the weather during the following season, according to the old rhymes:—

> If New Year's eve night wind blow south,
> It betokeneth warmth and growth;
> If west, much milk, and fish in the sea;
> If north, much cold and storms there will be;
> If east, the trees will bear much fruit;
> If north-east, flee it, man and brute.

Perhaps I may mention here two other weather prophecies. It is well known that "a green yule makes a fat kirk-yard," but the following couplet is of narrower circulation. It was communicated to me by a friend, who assures me that it is current in Buckinghamshire:—

> If the calends of January be smiling and gay,
> You'll have wintry weather till the calends of May.

It is curious to find that the word "calends" still lives on the

[1] In Sweden, if a grain of corn be found under the table when sweeping on a New Year's morn, there will be an abundant crop that year.

lips of the English peasantry. What idea it conveys to their minds I will not inquire. There is an old rhyme yet current which avers:

> If the sun shine out of Candlemas Day, of all days in the year,
> The shepherd had rather see his wife on the bier.

Or, according to another version—

> If the sun shines bright on Candlemas Day,
> The half of the winter's not yet away;

which corresponds with the Latin proverb—

> Si sol splendescat Maria purificante,
> Major erit glacies post festum quàm fuit ante.

The oak and ash, both sacred trees, and the ash in particular, the cloud-tree of the Norsemen, with sacred fountains springing from every root, still supply us with a weather prophecy. If the oak comes into leaf before the ash, expect a fine summer; if the ash is first, a wet one; or, as it runs in verse:

> If the oak's before the ash,
> You will only get a splash;
> If the ash precede the oak,
> You will surely have a soak.

It is customary in Scotland for children to go to the neighbouring houses on New Year's Eve, singing this verse:

> Rise, good wives, and shake your feathers,
> And dinna think that we are beggars;
> We're but bairns come out to play,
> Rise up and gie's your hogmaney.

Oat-cakes are given to them, on which they sing:

> We joyful wish you a good day,
> And thank ye for your hogmaney.

Now here we come upon a custom of great antiquity, and very widely spread, if, as Mr. Ingledew informs us in his *Ballads and Songs of Yorkshire*, Hagmena songs were formerly sung throughout England, Scotland, and France. He gives a fragment of that in use at Richmond, in Yorkshire:

> To-night it is the New Year's night, to-morrow is the day,
> And we are come for our right and for our ray,
> As we used to do in old King Henry's day.
> Sing, fellows, sing Hagman heigh!
>
> If you go to the bacon-flitch, cut me a good bit,
> Cut, cut and low, beware of your man;
> Cut, and cut round, beware of your thumb,
> That I and my merry men may have some.
> Sing, fellows, sing Hagman heigh!
>
> If you go to the black ark, bring me ten mark,
> Ten mark, ten pound, throw it down upon the ground,
> That I and my merry men may have some.
> Sing, fellows, sing Hagman heigh!

In Perth, and I believe in most towns in Scotland, Hogmenay songs are still in common use, the children beginning on St. Sylvester's night at six o'clock, and never ceasing till after ten, ringing at every bell and singing their songs as soon as the door is opened.

The dole of cakes causes New Year's Day to be called "cake day" on the Scottish borders, and the following Monday is known as Hansel Monday, because of the presents of money made on that day, and placed in the receiver's hands. It is named in the old formula of good wishes, "A happy New Year and a merry Hansel Monday." Scholars commonly give a hansel to their master or mistress on this day. The boy who gives the largest sum is called the king, and the girl the queen, and the king claims the right of demanding at least that day as a holiday.

Shrove Tuesday, though not observed in Scotland in its religious aspect, was marked up to a recent time by some curious customs. Foot-ball and cock-fighting were the great diversions on what was called Fastens Eve. A lady, to whom I am much indebted, writes thus on the subject: "My father-in law used often to speak of the cock-fights which regularly took place in all schools on that day. The master found the cocks, but the boys paid for them. There was a regular subscription for the purpose, each boy giving what was called a 'cock-penny.' The masters made a good profit out of the transaction, as they were entitled besides to claim all the runaway birds, which were called 'Fugees.'" This custom is mentioned by Brand, and he brings forward in proof of its extreme antiquity a petition of the date of 1355 from the scholars of the school of Ramera to their schoolmaster for a cock he owed them upon Shrove Tuesday to throw sticks at, according to the usual custom, for their sport and entertainment. I learn from a clergyman, formerly a scholar at the grammar-school of Sedbergh, in Yorkshire, that the master used to be entitled to 4½*d.* yearly from every boy on Shrove Tuesday to buy a fighting-cock. At Heversham, a village one mile from Milnthorpe, the cock-pit was in existence close to the school a few years ago.

The historian of Cumberland gives a detailed account of the manner in which Shrove Tuesday was formerly observed in a grammar-school of that county:—Till within the last twenty or thirty years it had been a custom, time out of mind, for the scholars of the free-school of Bromfield, about the beginning of Lent, or in the more expressive phraseology of the country, at Fastings Even, to bar out the master, *i.e.* to depose and exclude him from his school, and keep him out for three days. During the period of this expulsion, the doors of the citadel, the school, were strongly barricaded within; and the boys, who defended it like a besieged city, were armed in general with bur-tree or elder pop-guns. The master meanwhile made various efforts, both by force and stratagem, to regain his lost authority: if he succeeded heavy tasks were imposed, and the business of the school was resumed and submitted to; but it more commonly happened that he was repulsed and defeated. After three days' siege, terms of capitulation were proposed by the master and accepted by the boys. These terms were summed up in an old formula of Latin Leonine verses, stipulating what hours and times should, for the year ensuing, be allotted to study and what to relaxation and play. Securities were provided by each side for the due performance of these stipulations, and the paper was then solemnly signed by both master and scholars. The whole was concluded by a festivity, and a treat of cakes and ale, furnished by the scholars.

One of the articles always stipulated for and granted was the privilege of immediately celebrating certain games of long standing, viz. a foot-ball match and a cock-fight. Captains, as they were called, were then chosen to manage and preside over these games, one from that part of the parish which lay to the westward of the school, the other from the east. Cock and foot-ball players were sought for with great diligence. The party whose cocks won the most battles, was as victorious in the cock-pit; and the prize, a small silver bell, suspended to the button of the victor's hat, and worn for three successive Sundays. After the cock-fight was over, the football was thrown down in the churchyard: and the point then to be contested was, which party could carry it to the house of his respective captain; to Dundraw, perhaps, or to West Newton, a distance of two or three miles, every inch of which ground was disputed keenly. All the honour accruing to the conqueror at foot-ball was that of possessing the ball, Details of these matches were the general topics of conversation among the villagers, and were dwelt on with hardly less satisfaction than their ancestors enjoyed in relating their feats in the Border wars. These Bromfield sports were celebrated in indigenous songs, one verse only of one of them the writer happens to remember:—

At Scales great Tom Barwise gat the ba' in his hand,
And t' wives aw ran out, and shouted, and bann'd:
Tom Cowan then pulch'd, and flang him 'mang t' whins,
And he bledder'd, od-white te', tous broken my shins.

Other customs obtained in the neighbourhood of Blencogo. On the common, to the east of that village, not far from Ware-Brig (*i.e.* Waver Bridge), near a pretty large rock of granite, called St. Cuthbert's Stane, is a fine copious spring of remarkably pure and sweet water, which (probably from its having been anciently dedicated to the same St. Cuthbert) is called Helly-Well, *i.e.* Haly or Holy Well. It formerly was the custom for the youth of all the neighbouring villages to assemble at this well early in the afternoon of the second Sunday in May, and there to join in a variety of rural sports. It was the village wake, and took place here, it is possible, when the keeping of wakes and fairs in the churchyard was discontinued.—Hutchinson's *Hist. of Cumberland*, vol. ii. p. 322-3.

In the villages of the West Riding the streets may be seen on this day full of grown-up men and women playing "battledore and shuttle feathers."

Passion Sunday, the fifth in Lent, is called in the North Care, Carle, or Carling Sunday, the proper fare for that day being grey-peas steeped a night in water and then fried in butter. Formerly doles of these carlings were made to the poor; at present they are chiefly a treat to children. Boys have their pockets full of peas at this time, shooting them and flipping them about in frolic.

The use of palms on Palm Sunday has, for the most part I fear, passed away, except among Roman Catholics. The late Mr. Denham, however, in one of his tracts, printed in 1858, speaks of palm-crosses as relics still often to be seen in the hands of north-country children on Palm Sunday, and on cottage-walls through the rest of the year. And he quotes the proverb as still current, "He that hath not a palm in his hand on Palm Sunday must have his hand cut off." The Rev. G. Ornsby also relates that when he was a child palm-crosses were always made for Palm Sunday by the people in the Vale of Lanchester. The substitute for palm was the willow with its early catkins, which formed the extremities of the arms of the cross; they were tied together with blue or pink ribbon, disposed with bows here and there, and were often very tasteful and pretty. And I can myself bear witness to their constant use in the city of Durham about forty years ago. Many a time have I when a boy walked with my comrades to the river-bank, near Kepier Hospital, to gather palms; and many a cross have I made of them for Palm Sunday. We formed them like a St. Andrew's cross, with a tuft of catkins at each point, and bound them up with knots and bows of ribbon. In Yorkshire children mark the day differently; they get "pawne bottles," *i. e.* bottles containing a little sugar, and betake themselves to the springs and wells to fill their bottles, and suck at them all the afternoon.

To pass on to Good Friday. The Incumbent of Fishlake, a village in the south-east of Yorkshire, tells me that in that place, on Good Friday morning, at eight o'clock, instead of the usual bell being rung as on Sundays and other holydays, to give notice of Morning Service, the great bell of the church is solemnly tolled as for a death or funeral. This custom is very beautiful and suggestive, but I do not remember to have heard of it elsewhere. A friend, who passed his boyhood in the north of Durham, informs me that no blacksmith throughout that district would then drive a nail on that day; a remembrance of the awful purpose for which hammer and nails were used on the first Good Friday doubtless held them back.

I learn from a clergyman familiar with the North Riding of Yorkshire that great care is there taken not to disturb the earth in any way; it were impious to use spade, plough, or harrow. He remembers, when a boy, hearing of a villager, Charlie Marston by name, who shocked his neighbours by planting potatoes on Good Friday, but they never came up.

The popular feeling in Devonshire is very different. The poor there like to plant crops on Good Friday, especially to sow peas, saying they are sure to grow "goody," and it is thought a very lucky day for grafting, while in some part of the South of England (of the exact locality I am uninformed) they sow annuals on this day before the dawn, to make them come up double. A distinctive observance of Good Friday seems, however, to have once prevailed in that county, and so singular a one, that I trust its mention may not be deemed irrelevant. The rector of a country parish about fourteen miles from Exeter was startled one day by this inquiry, from a Sunday scholar, "Please, Sir, why do people break clomb (*i.e.* crockery) on Good Friday?" The question was rather puzzling to the rector, but he was a good deal struck by hearing afterwards that it is the custom in the island of Corfu for the inhabitants on that day to fling potsherds down a steep rock, uttering imprecations on the traitor Judas.

An old woman of the North Riding once asked a friend of mine whether it was wrong to wash on Good Friday. "I used to do so," she said, "and thought no harm of it, till once, when I was hanging out my clothes, a young woman passed by (a dressmaker she was, and a Methodist); and she reproved me, and told me this story. While our Lord Jesus was being led to Calvary they took Him past a woman who was washing, and the woman 'blirted' the thing she was washing in His face; on which He said, 'Cursed be every one who hereafter shall wash on this day!' And never again," added the old woman, "have I washed on Good Friday."

Now it is said in Cleveland that clothes washed and hung out to dry on Good Friday will become spotted with blood; but the Methodist girl's wild legend reminds me more of one which a relation of mine elicited from a poor Devonshire shoemaker. She was remonstrating with him for his indolence and want of spirit, when he astonished her by replying, "Dont'ee be hard on me. We shoemakers are a poor slobbering race, and so have been ever since the curse that Jesus Christ laid on us." "And what was that?" she asked. "Why," said he, "when they were carrying Him to the cross they passed a shoemaker's bench, and the man looked up and spat at Him; and the Lord turned and said, 'A poor slobbering fellow shalt thou be, and all shoemakers after thee,[1] for what thou hast done to Me.'"

In the Midland counties, bread and cakes made on Good Friday are thought to be preserved through the holiness of the day from becoming mouldy. I have heard of a cross-bun being kept for a year, and then soaked, warmed, and eaten with a relish, not being in the least mouldy. And throughout the whole of England we here and there find it maintained that such bread has great virtue either of healing or preserving life. The Sunderland wives see that their husbands take some to sea with them to avert shipwrecks. In Sussex it is, or has been,

[1] This curse is suggested, I presume, by the legend of the Wandering Jew; Cartaphilus or Ahasuerus, whichever was his name, having been a shoemaker, and cursed, it is said, by Our Lord, for refusing to allow Him to rest on the door-step of his shop.—S. B. G.

hung up in the cottages, and, when any illness breaks out in the family, a fragment is cut off, pounded, and given as medicine. Indeed, the superstition extends to America. In Florida it is held that three loaves baked on Good Friday and put into a heap of corn will prevent rats, mice, weevils, or worms from devouring it. In Suffolk, eggs laid on Good Friday are also kept with the greatest care by the farmers' wives, who maintain that they will never go bad, and that a piece of suoh an egg gives immediate relief to a person suffering from colic.

The question has often been asked why the large black beetle is called "clock" in the North of England. An answer has reached me from Ireland, which, as it bears upon this day, I will note here—"Sure it told Judas the time." On this account the Catholic peasantry in Ireland always crush beetles. I believe in Kent the creatures are called "the devil's coach-horses," and elsewhere "the devil's footmen."

All England over it is commonly said that one must put on something new on Easter Sunday, else the birds will spoil one's clothes, or, as it stands in verse,

> At Easter let your clothes be new,
> Or else, be sure, you will it rue.

The belief that the sun dances at its rising on Easter morning peeps out in many parts of Yorkshire, as well as in Durham and Northumberland. Here, again, there is a singular correspondence between the Folk-Lore of the North and the West. Devonshire maidens get up to see the sun rise on Easter morning, as duly as do their northern sisters, though what they look for is the Lamb and flag in the centre of the sun's disc. Poor women in the neighbourhood of Dartmoor have told me that they used, as girls, to go out in parties at sunrise to see the Lamb in the sun, and look at it through a darkened glass, and always some declared they saw it.

As to Easter eggs, they are as duly painted and gilded, and rolled on the greensward, throughout the North of England, as they are in Russia or Germany. They are also given as little offerings of goodwill by one person to another. I believe their use chiefly prevails throughout countries in communion with the Eastern church. The egg is an obvious symbol of the resurrection of life in apparent death. Throughout Yorkshire it is customary to hide the coloured eggs in little nests out of doors, and set the children to hunt after them, and see what eggs the "hares" have been laying. Another Eastern custom, and one, perhaps, better honoured in the breach than the observance, still lingers in Durham. In a Sunday-school there, a scanty attendance of girls on Easter Day was recently accounted for by their being "terrified" lest the boys should pull off their shoes. "To-morrow," it was added, "they may pull off the boys' caps." This frolic, whatever be its origin, seems to have extended into Yorkshire. At least, a friend tells me that she remembers, when a little girl, having her shoes pulled off one Easter on the sands at Redcar; and I have heard of a stout-hearted Yorkshire curate who used to go round his parish on Easter Sunday afternoon to collect the girls, and pioneer them safely to church and school. That was the time of danger, for the young men had no right to take their shoes till after Morning Service. I may add that in the West Riding "luking" (playing at knor and spell) begins at Easter,[1] and that near York tansy pudding used to be eaten on this festival in allusion to the bitter herbs at the Passover.

[1] In Lancashire it is customary for the lasses on Easter Monday to "heave" the lads, *i. e.* to lift them up from the ground in their arms. On Tuesday the lads heave the lasses.

A friend of mine, a native of Warrington, tells me that her Majesty's Inspector of Schools took it into his head to visit Warrington on Monday in Easter week. The lasses, seeing a timorous spectacled parson walking down the street, with one accord heaved him, and carried him in their arms through the town. My informant declares that the terror and agony of the poor inspector were something awful. The more he struggled the closer he was hugged, while an occasional smack from the lips of a vigorous mill-girl blanched his cheek, and made his rumpled hair stand on end. He firmly believed that his character and position were irretrievably ruined. On another Easter Monday one of my friends was lifted and kissed till he was black in the face by a party of leather-breeched coalpit women at, I think, Wednesbury. The same custom prevails in the Pyrenees, where I have been lifted by a party of stout Basque damsels. Another instance of this observance has been related to me. A number of convict women on their way to Australia were allowed one Easter Monday to come on deck for a little fresh air and change. The decks had previously been cleared,

Before passing on from Easter observances, let me mention one old custom still kept up at University College, Oxford, the most ancient college, I believe, in the University. A block, in the form of a long wooden pole decorated with flowers and evergreens, is placed outside the door of the hall, leaning against the wall of the buttery which is opposite. After dinner on Easter Day, the cook and his attendant, dressed in white paper caps and white jackets, take their stand on either side of the block, each bearing a pewter dish, one supporting a blunt chopping-axe from the kitchen, the other in readiness for the fees expected on the occasion. As the members of the college come out of the hall—first the master, then the fellows, and so on—each takes the axe, strikes the block with it, and then places in the proper dish the usual fee to the cook. This rite is called "chipping the block;" its origin is unexplained. The tradition among the undergraduates is that anyone who can chip the block in two (under the circumstances a physical impossibility) can lay claim to all the college estates, but the master and fellows dispute this.

The ancient observances on May Day, the Maypole and garlands, the May Queen, and the chimney-sweeper's pageant, have, I fear, passed away throughout the North as well as the South, except in some remote localities, or where special pains have been taken by the upper classes to keep up or to revive them. In Devonshire, the local custom, now almost extinct, is for the children to carry about dolls, as richly dressed as may be, in baskets of flowers, doubtless with reference originally to the Blessed Virgin, patroness of the month of May. On May Day morning in Edinburgh, not many years ago, everyone went up to the top of Arthur's Seat before sunrise to "meet the dew." In Perth they climbed Kinnoul Hill for the same purpose, with a lingering belief in the old saying—that those who wash their faces in May

and the chaplain was the only man within their reach. Making the most of their opportunity, they rushed upon him, and lifted him, bestowing the usual salutations all the time. His screams and cries for help were alarming, and at last they brought the captain to the spot, but unfortunately he was too much amused to interfere, and the play was played out in spite of the poor victim's intense alarm and disgust.—S. B. G.

dew will be beautiful all the year. A relic of the old observance seems to survive at Warboys, in Huntingdonshire, where certain poor of the parish are allowed to go into Warboys Wood on May Day morning to gather and bring away bundles of sticks.

Ascension Day appears unmarked in the North by any peculiar observances. I only learn that near York it was the custom, twenty years ago, for children to lay rushes or "seggs" on their doorsteps to mark the festival. The Rev. G. Ornsby suggests that this has probably arisen from the streets having been thus strewn before the procession on this festival in pre-Reformation times. He was once at Cologne on Ascension Day, and witnessed a most imposing procession, the streets having been strewn previously with fir branches and other green things.

On Whit-Sunday cheesecakes were formerly eaten in the county of Durham. At Whitby it is the custom on Midsummer Day to eat white cake and "kidgelled" (query whipped or cudgelled) cream, for which repast presents of cream are sent by the milkman to his customers. This custom is said to be as old as the time of the Danes.

In by-gone days the festival of Corpus Christi was the occasion in Durham of a "goodly procession" of the trades companies to the Abbey Church. "The Baley of the towne did call the occupations that was inhabitens within the towne, every occupation in his degree, to bring forth ther Banners, with all the lightes apperteyninge to these several Banners, and to repaire to the Abbey Church doure, every Banner to stand a rowe, according to his degree; on the west syde of the waye did all the Banners stand, and on the east syde did all the Torges stand." Then the Prior and convent came forth to meet them in their best copes with "S. Cuthbert's Banner and two goodly fair crosses. All entered the Abbey Church together, and Te Deum was solemnly sung and plaide of the orgaynes."[1] Nay, this Durham procession of the trades companies on Corpus Christi Day did, in a mutilated form, survive the Reformation, and linger on till about eighty years ago. The companies still repaired to the Cathedral and attended Divine Service. The

[1] *Rites and Monuments.* Surtees Society Publication.

banners of their respective trades were still to be seen; there was a band of music, and boys carried pieces of burning rope instead of torches. As the Prior of old, so the Dean of later days, accompanied the procession to the door of the Cathedral, but, whereas the Prior there dismissed them with his blessing, the Dean presented each warden with a pair of gloves.

But our most characteristic festive rejoicings accompany the harvest—the mell-supper and the kern-baby, usages which are by no means extinct among us. In the northern part of Northumberland the festival takes place at the end of the reaping, not of the ingathering; and an essay written about the year 1750, by the unhappy Eugene Aram, states that such was also the case in Yorkshire. When the sickle is laid down, and the last sheaf of golden corn set on end, it is said that they have "got the kern." The reapers announce the fact by loud shouting, and an image is at once hoisted on a pole, and given into the charge of the tallest and strongest man of the party. The image is crowned with wheat-ears and dressed up in gay finery, a white frock and coloured ribbons being its conventional attire. The whole group circle round this harvest-queen, or kern-baby, curtseying to her, and dancing and singing; and thus they proceed to the farmer's barn, where they set the image up on high, as the presiding goddess of their revels, and proceed to do justice to the harvest-supper.

Nor is this all. Each cottage must at harvest-time have its own household divinity, and, oaten cakes having formerly been the staple food of the North, these figures are commonly formed of oats. Such have I repeatedly seen in cottages on the Tweed side, elaborately decorated and enshrined at the top of the bink or dresser, with the family stock of big dishes ranged on either side. These, too, are kern-babies. There has been some controversy as to the derivation of the word "kern." To me it clearly seems to mean corn. I may mention, in support of this opinion, that in Cornwall an ill-saved harvest is said to be "ill kerned," and that throughout Devonshire the forming of the grain in the ear is called the "kerning" or "corning." I must add that throughout Northumberland, when the last cart of corn arrives at the stackyard gate, the driver leaves it standing there while he carries his whip to the mistress of the house, who must either drive in the load herself or give the man a glass of whisky to do it for her.

The mell-supper takes its name from the Norse "mele," corn. In Icelandic, "melr" is the Psamma-arenario, the wild corn of the sand-flats: melr also signifies sandy land. Both are derived from the same root, which means to grind to dust. It has come to be applied to corn because it can be made into meal—to sand, because it is pounded stone. As kept up till lately in my own county, the mell-supper is closely akin to the Northumbrian kern-feast. I am not too old to have taken part in more than one of them, and most thoroughly did I enjoy them. My recollection of a mell-doll is of a corn-sheaf stuck with flowers, and wrapped in such of the reapers' garments as could be spared. This, too, was carried to the scene of the harvest-supper amid music and dancing, and then master and servants sat down together to feast, on terms of perfect equality.

This feature of harvest festivities is common to all the northern districts, and springs from a grateful sense of the reapers' services at a peculiarly anxious time. As far south as Hertfordshire some of these observances have held their ground, and the last cart of wheat leaves the field decorated with oak boughs; but one part of the entertainment I connect especially with my own county. I well remember, not far from its cathedral town, helping to dress some young men who were to play the part of "guisers," and force their entrance into a mell-supper. Disguised they most effectually were—covered with masks, or blackened with burned cork past all recognition, and their dress the gayest motley imaginable. In apprehension of such invaders, the doors and windows of the barn or dancing-room were barricaded, and the whole building placed in a state of defence; but, whether through treachery within-doors or their own unassisted valour, the guisers did at last effect an entrance and claimed the privilege of conquerors.

Such scenes I often witnessed in my young days, and such I believe still to be enacted in many north-country farmhouses;

but who among the groups that dance before the kern-baby deem that they are treading in the steps of their old British ancestors, as, taught by their Roman conquerors, they danced and bowed before the goddess Ceres? Or, again, of those who at a later period in history paid the same votive honours to the Virgin Mary? Or, who, as they sit at the mell-supper, master and servant on equal terms, imagine that their festival had its origin, it may be, in the Jewish Feast of Tabernacles—it may be, in the Roman Saturnalia? "Thou shalt observe the feast of tabernacles seven days, after that thou hast gathered in thy corn and thy wine: and thou shalt rejoice in thy feast, thou and thy son, and thy daughter, and thy manservant, and thy maidservant, and the Levite, the stranger, and the fatherless, and the widow, that are within thy gates."[1]

A friend from Yorkshire tells me that the mell-doll is now unknown in the north of that county, but with mell-suppers and guisers he is quite familiar. The Yorkshire custom is, that, when in any farm the harvest is won, one of the reapers should mount a wall or bank, and proclaim as follows:

Blest be the day when Christ was born,
We've getten mell of (—'s) corn,
Weel bun and better shorn.
Huzza! huzza! huzza!

—every one then joining in the general cheer.[2]

In Cleveland, the mell-supper is still kept up, though with less ceremony than formerly. "Guising" was practised there thirty years ago, but is now discontinued. On forking the last sheaf in the harvest-field they shout in chorus:

Weel bun and better shorn,
Is master (—'s) corn;
We hev her, we hev her,
As fast as a feather.
Hip, hip, hurrah!

Among minor festivals, St. Agnes' Day is marked in our northern counties by a superstitious observance of its own, called

[1] Deut. xvi. 13, 14.

[2] Through Devonshire the reapers leave a bunch of corn, which they call a neck, to be afterwards tied up with ribbons and flowers, and hung in the barn.

St. Agnes' Fast, the same which has furnished Keats with a subject for his little poem, *The Eve of St. Agnes.* He recounts, in his own glowing yet chastened style, how all the wintry day Madeline's heart had brooded

> On love, and winged St. Agnes' saintly care,
> As she had heard old dames full many times declare.
>
> They told her how, upon St. Agnes' Eve,
> Young virgins might have visions of delight,
> And soft advisings from their loves receive,
> Upon the honeyed middle of the night,
> If ceremonies due they did aright;
> As supperless to bed they must retire,
> And couch supine their beauties, lily white;
> Nor look behind, nor sideways, but require
> Of Heaven, with upward eyes, for all that they desire.

St. Agnes' Fast is thus practised throughout Durham and Yorkshire. Two young girls, each desirous to dream about their future husbands, must abstain through the whole of St. Agnes' Eve from eating, drinking, or speaking, and must avoid even touching their lips with their fingers. At night they are to make together their "dumb cake," so called from the rigid silence which attends its manufacture. Its ingredients (flour, salt, water, &c.) must be supplied in equal proportions by the friends, who must also take equal shares in the baking and turn-

And they approach it, saying, as they cut each line of corn, "Wee day, wee day!" When the neck is cut there is shouting and halloing, and the reapers call out—

> We have ploughed, we have sowed,
> We have reaped, we have mowed,
> We have brought home every load,
> With a Hip, hip, hurrah!

Compare with these harvest customs those of Schaumberg-Lippe. When barley was cut there a tuft was left called "Waul roggen." In this was placed a stick adorned with flowers, called the "Waul staff;" and then the reapers bowed to it with hats off, shouting together thrice, "Waul, waul, waul!" Waul is a corruption of waud-wod, that is to say, Wustan or Woden. In like manner is *d* changed into *l* in the two German dialects—as, for instance, *meleein* for *medeein*. The Greek δάκρυ = lacrima, the Sanskrit *madhu* in Latin is *mel*. Wee-day is also a corruption of Wustan or Woden.—S. B. G.

ing of the cake, and in drawing it out of the oven. The mystic viand must next be divided into two equal portions, and each girl, taking her share, is to carry it upstairs, walking backwards all the time, and finally eat it and jump into bed. A damsel who duly fulfils all these conditions, and has also kept her thoughts all the day fixed on her ideal of a husband, may confidently expect to see her future partner in her dreams.

"Dumb cake" is, or has been, made as far south as Norfolk. A friend tells me that his mother when a girl with another young companion duly made their dumb cake in perfect silence, walked to their bed backwards, laid their stockings and garters crosswise, and their shoes "going and coming," and then sitting up in bed began to eat the cakes, which were small enough, having been made in thimbles. Still the lady in question could not get through it, owing to its excessive saltness, and with her mouth full of the compound she exclaimed, "I can't eat it!" This of course broke the spell, and her friend was much annoyed.

The prescribed formula is somewhat different in Northumberland. There a number of girls, after a day's silence and fasting, will boil eggs, one apiece, extract the yolk, fill the cavity with salt, and eat the egg, shell and all, and then walk backwards, uttering this invocation to the saint:

Sweet St. Agnes, work thy fast,
If ever I be to marry man,
Or man be to marry me,
I hope him this night to see.

Or,

Fair St. Agnes, play thy part,
And send to me my own sweetheart,
Not in his best or worst array,
But in the clothes of every day,
That to-morrow I may him ken,
From among all other men.

A raw red herring, swallowed bones and all, is said to be equally efficacious, and doubtless is very provocative of dreams and visions. Northumbrian swains sometimes adopt this plan to get a glimpse of their future wives.

A Yorkshire friend mentions another way in which St. Agnes' Fast might be broken, and the success of the charm utterly ruined—that is, by a kiss; and it was a constant trick of the young wags to come unawares upon a girl who was believed to be keeping St. Agnes' Fast, and break her fast by a salute.

We learn from the Wilkie MS. that the second of April shares on the Borders the character which the first bears all England over. There are two April-fool days there, or, as they call them, "gowk days." Unsuspecting people are then sent on bootless errands, and ridiculed for their pains. One such day has, I believe, usually sufficed us in England. To the full observance of this day in my native city, at the time of my boyhood, I can bear witness; having been duly sent, with many another urchin, to the chemist for a pennyworth of oil of hazel, and received it in another way than I looked for, from the stout hazel stick hidden behind the shopman's counter. Sometimes the victim is instructed to ask for "strap oil." This custom extends to Germany: in Berlin "crab's blood" or "gnat's fat" are the articles sent for.

But "hunting the gowk" is more fully carried out by sending the victim from place to place with a letter, in which the following couplet was written:

> The first and second of Aprile,
> Hound the gowk another mile.

I need hardly add that gowk is a local name for the cuckoo, of which bird our ancestors said:

> In April
> He opes his bill.

Now, according to White of Selborne, the 7th of April is the earliest day for hearing the cuckoo, the 26th the latest. Therefore, before the change of style, the 1st and 2nd of the month, now the 12th and 13th, were days on which it would probably be heard for the first time. In Sussex, April 14 is called "first cuckoo day," and is greeted with these couplets:

The cuckoo is a merry bird, sings as she flies.
She brings us good tidings and tells us no lies.
She picks up the dirt in the spring of the year,
And sucks little birds' eggs to make her voice clear.

The piece of slander in the last line is firmly believed by the Sussex peasant, who also maintains that the cuckoo is finally metamorphosed into a hawk,—an ancient fable refuted by Aristotle more than two thousand years ago. I have been accustomed in the North to the first half alone of this verse, in the following form:

The cuckoo is a bonnie bird,
She whistles as she flees,
She brings us all good tidings,
And never tells no lees.

But in truth rhymes about this bird abound through our whole island, and many portents are drawn from it. In some places children say:

Cuckoo, cherry tree,
Good bird, tell me
How many years before I dee?

and listen for an answer in the repetitions of the bird's cry. In Sweden the question is, "In how many years shall I be married?" It is considered lucky in Scotland to be walking when one first hears the cuckoo:

Gang and hear the gowk yell,
Sit and see the swallow flee,
See the foal before its mother's 'ee,
'T will a thriving year wi' thee.

But it is unlucky to have no money in your pocket, and you must without fail turn the money when you hear the bird for the first time in the season.

Sussex cottagers tell their children of a scolding old woman who has charge of all the cuckoos. In the early spring she fills her apron with them, and, if she is in a good humour, allows several to take flight, but if cross, only one or two. A poor woman complained not long ago to my informant of the ill-temper of the cuckoo keeper, who had only let one bird fly out of her apron, "and that 'ere bird is nothing to call a singer."

The Yorkshire farmers are not above taking a practical hint from the early or late arrival of the cuckoo. Their adage on the subject runs thus:

When cuckoo calls on the bare thorn,
Sell your cow and buy your corn.

St. Valentine's Eve has an observance of its own in the South of Scotland. The young people assemble and write the names of their acquaintances on slips of paper, placing those of the lads and lasses in separate bags apart. The maidens draw from the former, the young men from the latter, three times in succession, returning the names after the first and second times of drawing. If one person takes out the same name three times consecutively, it is without fail that of the future husband or wife. Thus, in Burns's song of Tam Glen the maiden sings:

Yestreen at the Valentine dealing,
  My heart to my mou gi'ed a sten,
For thrice I drew ane without failing,
  An' thrice it was written, Tam Glen.

In a Buckinghamshire village, to the present day, the boys go round for halfpence to every house, singing:

Good morrow to you, Valentine,
First 'tis yours and then 'tis mine,
I'll thank you for a Valentine.

Old people presage the weather of the coming season by that of the last three days of March, which they call the "borrowing days," and thus rhyme about:

March borrowed from April
Three days and they were ill;
The first o' them war wind an' weet,
The next o' them war snaw an' sleet,
The last o' them war wind an' rain,
Which gaed the silly puir ewes come toddling hame.

Brand[1] gives the verses somewhat differently:

March said to Aperill,
I see three hogs upon a hill;
But lend your first three days to me,
And I'll be bound to gar them dee.
The first it sall be wind an' weet,
The next it sall be snaw an' sleet,
The third it sall be sic a freeze,
Sall gar the birds stick to the trees.
But when the borrowed days were gane,
The three silly hogs came hirplin' hame.

A third variation, common in my native county, runs thus:

March borrowed of April
Three days, and they were ill:
The first was sleet, the second was snow,
The third was the worst day that ever did blow.

It is curious that in the country parts of Devonshire the same three days are called "blind days," and considered unlucky for sowing any kind of seed. And it is yet more remarkable that the Highlanders have their borrowed or borrowing days, but with them February borrows from January, and bribes him with three young sheep. These first three days of February, or Faiolteach, by Highland reckoning (that is, old style), occur between February 11 and 15. And it is accounted a most favourable prognostic for the ensuing year that they should be stormy and cold.[2]

Of the next month we have the following rhyme in Durham:

Aperill,
With his hack and his bill,
Sets a flower on every hill;

or, as it runs in Yorkshire,

April comes in with his hack and his bill,
And sets a flower on every hill.

[1] *Pop. Ant.* vol. ii. p. 42.

[2] See Mrs. Grant's *Superstitions of the Highlanders*, vol. ii. p. 217.

The 29th of May is marked in Fishlake and its neigbourhood as the close of the birds'-nesting season. The boys think it unlucky to take nests later, and religiously abstain from doing so.

There is an old saying in the North about St. Michael's Day: "So many days old the moon is on Michaelmas Day, so many floods after." I am not aware that the Irish custom of abstaining from blackberries after this day extends to the North of England, but I have come across it in Devonshire. The saying in Ireland is this: "At Michaelmas the devil puts his foot on the blackberries." On the Tweed side, although no mention is made of St. Michael's Day, yet it is held that late in the autumn the devil throws his club over the blackberries and renders them poisonous or at least unwholesome. The Rev. R. O. Bromfield informs me that a boy once related to him circumstantially that he had seen this done, and that the club had come thundering over an old dyke and among the brambles just beside him, effectually putting an end to his feast off their berries. In Sussex the 10th of October is fixed as the limit of blackberrying, and they say that the devil then goes round the country and spits on the bramble-bushes! Note that the 10th of October is "Old Michaelmas Day." It is also held in that county a dangerous thing to go out nutting on Sunday for fear of encountering the evil one, though he often comes to the nutters in friendly guise and holds down the branches for them to strip. The devil in his character of nut-gatherer has plainly taken hold of the popular imagination in Sussex, for a proverb is current there, "As black as the de'il's nutting-bag." In Yorkshire this festival is called "hipping day," from its connection with a confection of hips, the red berries of the wild rose.

How All-Hallowe'en is kept in Scotland, English readers well know from Burns's poem on the subject. It is an evening of mirth and hilarity, and many divinations into futurity take place during its mystic hours. The Wilkie MS. mentions some of these which are not named by Burns, but as they may also be practised on the eves of Christmas, New Year's Day, and Midsummer Day, they will be more properly ranged under the head of "Divinations into Futurity." Ordeal by fire and water are, however, peculiarly Hallowe'en sports. The latter consists in ducking for an apple in a tub of water with the mouth, the hands being clasped behind the back. In the former, a small rod of wood is suspended from the ceiling, with a lighted candle fixed at one end and an apple at the other. The stick is twirled round, and the company in turn try to catch the apple in their teeth, at the moment it passes before them. These sports are still practised in the neighbourhood of Durham. At Whitbeck, in Cumberland, it is said, that to whatever quarter a bull faces as he lies on All-Hallow Even, from thence the wind will blow during the greater part of the winter following.[1]

Another fiery ordeal consists in whirling before the face a lighted brand, singing the old verse,—

Dingle, dingle, dowsie, the cat's in the well;
The dog's awa' to Berwick, to buy a new hell.

One then observes the last sparks of fire, and augurs from them: many round spots mean money, a quick extinction loss of property, and so on.[2]

St. Clement's Day was formerly observed, in the North of England, by men going about to ask for drink, that they might make merry in the evening. In Staffordshire the boys now go from house to house on that day, but they only ask for apples, which are generally given them. Compare with this the custom formerly prevalent at Ripon Minster on or about St. Clement's Day. The choristers went round the church offering a rosy-cheeked apple with a sprig of box stuck into it to every one present, for which a small gratuity was expected and of course commonly given.

At the risk of being deemed discursive I cannot refrain from mentioning a Buckinghamshire custom, communicated to me by a friend. It was once universal among the lacemakers of that

[1] Hutchinson's *History of Cumberland*, vol. i. p. 555.

[2] On the 5th of November parkin, a sort of pepper-cake, made with treacle and ginger, is found in every house in the West Riding. As, however, the cake is eaten several days before the 5th, I have no doubt it originally formed part of the All-Hallows' feast. The Sunday within the octave of All Saints is called Parkin Sunday.—S. B. G.

county, but is fast becoming obsolete. St. Andrew is there considered the patron saint of lacemaking, possibly because the intersecting threads in their delicate fabric so frequently form his cross; at any rate, his day is kept as a festival by all who practise that handicraft. The cakes that are made in honour of it are called "T'andry cakes," a curious corruption of St. Andrew. Though this saint be the patron of Scotland, his day is now little heeded there. It was formerly kept by repasts of sheeps' heads, the old national dish, and the day was called Andermas.

The days of the week are distinguished in the North by certain epithets, taken in part from Church feasts or festivals, in part from some local circumstance. According to my memory they run thus—

> Collop Monday, Pancake Tuesday, Ash Wednesday,
> Bloody Thursday, Long Friday, Hey for Saturday afternoon;
> Hey for Sunday at twelve o'clock,
> When all the plum-pnddings jump out of the pot.

Another version is as follows—

> Black Monday, Bloody Tuesday, Sorrowful Wednesday,
> Joyful Thursday, Lang Friday 'll ne'er be done,
> Hey for Saturday afternoon,
> Hey for Sunday at two o'clock,
> When all the spice puddings come out of the pot.

CHAPTER III.

SPELLS AND DIVINATIONS.

With the Horse-knot—Three pails of Water—Holly-leaves—Yarrow—The Sark—The Willow Branch—Hair-snatching—Hemp-seed—A Glass Globe—A New-laid Egg—Wishing Chairs—Ring and Water—Palmistry.

THE Borderland is peculiarly rich in ways and means for getting a peep into futurity, especially as regards the all-important point of the future partner in wedded life. Some of these may be practised at any time, but most are restricted to All-Hallowe'en, Christmas Eve, New Year's Eve, and Beltane or Midsummer Eve.

The following rite seems of the former class. Let a youth or maiden pull from its stalk the flower of the "horse-knot," or *centaurea nigra*, cut the tops of the stamens with a pair of scissors, and lay the flower by in a secret place, where no human eye can see it. Let him think through the day, and dream through the night, of his sweetheart, and then, on looking at it the next day, if he find the stamens shot out to their former height, success will attend him in love; if not, he can only expect disappointment.[1]

The next rite, however, is restricted to the above-named eves. Let a Border maiden take three pails full of water, and place them on her bedroom floor; then pin to her night-dress, opposite to her heart, three leaves of green holly, and so retire to rest. She will be roused from her first sleep by three yells, as if from

In Berwickshire a similar divination is practised by means of "kemps," *i. e.* spikes of the ribwort plantain. Two spikes must be taken in full bloom, and, being bereft of every appearance of blow, they are wrapped in a dock-leaf and laid beneath a stone. One represents the lad, the other the lass. If next morn-

the throats of three bears; as these sounds die away they will be succeeded by as many horse-laughs, after which the form of her future husband will appear. If he is deeply attached to her, he will change the position of the water-pails; if not, he will pass out of the room without touching them. Tradition tells how, on one occasion, the lover who had been thus invoked, while moving the pails of water, let fall a rope with a noose at the end, which the young woman took up the next morning and laid in her press. She was married soon afterwards to the man whose form she had beheld, but within a fortnight of the marriage he hung himself with that very rope in a fit of intoxication.

The use of holly in this form of divination recalls a somewhat different use made of it in Northumberland. We hear there of he-holly and she-holly, according as it is with or without prickles, and the leaves of the she-holly are alone deemed proper for divination. These "smooth and unarmed" leaves, as Southey calls them, must be plucked, late on a Friday, by persons careful to preserve an unbroken silence from the time they go out to the next morning's dawn. The leaves must be collected in a three-cornered handkerchief, and on being brought home nine of them must be selected, tied with nine knots into the handkerchief, and placed beneath the pillow. Dreams worthy of all credit will attend this rite, though, if the old rhyme

ing the spikes appear in blossom then there will be "aye love between them twae." The same rite has been practised in Northamptonshire. Witness the following lines from Clare's *Shepherd's Calendar:*

> Or, trying simple charms and spells,
> Which rural superstition tells,
> They pull the little blossom threads
> From out the knotweed's button-heads,
> And put the husk with many a smile
> In their white bosoms for a while.
> Then if they guess aright the swain
> Their love's sweet fancies try to gain,
> 'Tis said that ere it lies an hour
> 'Twill blossom with a second flower,
> And from the bosom's handkerchief
> Bloom, as it ne'er had lost a leaf.

be trustworthy, so would be any dream dreamt on that night and repeated the next day; for—

> A Friday night's dream on a Saturday told,
> Is sure to come true if it's ever so old.[1]

Compare this with the analogous south-country charm which prevails, or has prevailed, from Sussex to Devonshire. A damsel must pluck some yarrow (*millefolium*) from a young man's grave, repeating these words:

> Yarrow, sweet yarrow, the first that I have found,
> In the name of Jesus Christ I pluck it from the ground.
> As Joseph loved sweet Mary, and took her for his dear,
> So in a dream this night, I hope, my true love will appear.

She must then sleep with the yarrow under her pillow.

On All Hallowe'en or New Year's Eve a Border maiden may wash her sark, and hang it over a chair to dry, taking care to tell no one what she is about. If she lie awake long enough, she will see the form of her future spouse enter the room and turn the sark. We are told of one young girl who, after fulfilling this rite, looked out of bed and saw a coffin behind the sark; it remained visible for some time and then disappeared. The girl rose up in agony and told her family what had occurred, and the next morning she heard of her lover's death. In another instance the young woman is said to have seen her lover at first, but his image quickly vanished, and was replaced by a coffin; she was shortly afterwards married to the man, but he soon died and left her a widow. I have heard of precisely the same practice in Ireland, and in the county of Sussex, where it seems to have been prevalent. I am told of one instance there in which a very tall man in black came in, turned the sark, and walked out again.

In Norfolk, this piece of divination was connected with St. Mark's or St. Agnes' Eve. It was resorted to some years ago by the servant of a house on Yarmouth Quay. She opened the doors and sat in silence to see the spectre enter, turn the shift, and go out again; but a sailor from one of the vessels on

[1] *Local Historian's Table Book*, vol. iii. p. 254.

the Quay learned what was going on, came in, tore the shift away, and vanished, to her no small alarm; and the first thing which attracted her sight the next morning was her shift hanging up on the mast of one of the vessels. A variation of the rite is prescribed in a pamphlet, which appears to have had a wide circulation among the lower orders of our country generally. It is called *The Universal Fortune Teller; being sure and certain directions for discovering the secrets of Futurity.* The printer's name is wanting, or has been obliterated, but it bears the date of Monmouth Court, Seven Dials. Oddly enough, the copy in my possession dropped from the pocket of a chorister on leaving Exeter College Chapel, Oxford, and was sent to me by one of the Fellows who picked it up. It prescribes the following charm for gaining sight of a future husband.

On Midsummer Eve, just at sunset, three, five, or seven young women are to go into a garden in which there is no other person, and each gather a sprig of red sage. Then going into a room by themselves, they must set a stool in the middle of the room, and on it a clean basin full of rose-water, into which the sprigs of sage are to be put. Lastly, tying a line across the room, each girl is to hang on it a clean shift, turned the wrong side outwards, and then all are to sit down in a row on the opposite side of the stool, as far off as may be, not speaking all the time, whatever they may see. Just after midnight the future husband of each one will take her sprig out of the water, and sprinkle her shift with it.

The same authority prescribes another mode of procedure. A young woman must sleep in a county different from that in which she usually resides, and, on going to bed, must knit the left garter about the right stocking, rehearsing the following verses, and at every comma knitting a knot:

> This knot I knit,
> To know the thing I know not yet,
> That I may see,
> The man that shall my husband be,
> How he goes, and what he wears,
> And what he does all days and years.

Accordingly, in a dream, he will appear with the insignia of his trade or profession.

Another mode of divination is by the willow wand. Let a maiden take a willow branch in her left hand, and, without being observed, slip out of the house and run three times round it, whispering all the time, "He that's to be my gude man come and grip the end o't." During the third run, the likeness of her future husband will appear and grasp the other end of the wand. A sword is sometimes used instead of a wand, but, in this case, it must be held in the right hand.

This spell somewhat resembles one by which German girls ascertain the colour of their future husband's hair. They call it hair-snatching, and practise it thus. Between the hours of eleven and twelve at night, on St. Andrew's Eve, a maiden must stand at the house-door, take hold of the latch, and say three times "Gentle love, if thou lovest me, show thyself." She must then quickly open the door wide enough to put out her hand, and make a rapid grasp out in the dark, and she will find in her hand a lock of her future husband's hair.[1] Belgian girls, who desire to see their husbands in a dream, lay their garters crosswise at the foot of the bed, and a looking-glass under their pillow; in this glass the image of their future husband will appear.[2]

A story is told in the Wilkie MS. of a young woman who, on waking one New Year's morning, found a sword lying at her bedside. Imagining that it had been used in the divinations of the previous evening, and carried away from its owner by some spirit who had been too rashly invoked, she took it up, and locked it in her chest. Those who find these swords or divining-rods do this, lest the spirits make them a means of temptation; at the same time, those who lose them are always restless till they can recover them. The young woman was afterwards married to a gentleman's servant, and in course of time became a mother. One day, soon after her infant's birth, she gave her husband the key of her chest, and begged him to give her some articles of clothing from

[1] Thorpe's *Mythology*, vol. iii. p. 145. [2] *Ibid.* p. 273.

it; he opened the chest, beheld the sword, recognised it as his own, seized it, and exclaiming, "This is my sword which has troubled me so long!" transfixed himself with it on the spot, to the consternation and horror of his poor wife.

The sowing of hemp-seed on All Hallowe'en, with a hope that the future husband or wife will appear to reap it, is a well-known Scottish observance. Burns describes how, in spite of Auld Grannie's warnings,

> Up gat fechtin Jamie Fleck,
> And he swoor by his conscience,
> That he could saw hemp-seed a peck,
> For it was a' but nonsense.

So the gudeman brought down the pock and gied him out a handful, and Jamie slipped away into the rick-yard,

> And every now and then he says,
> Hemp-seed I saw thee;
> And her that is to be my lass
> Come after me and draw thee
> As fast this night.

Nothing however seems to have come of it but an encounter with "grumphie" and the overthrow of the hero. I learn with surprise from Mr. H. Denny that this rite was practised as far south as Norfolk. St. Martin's night was the proper occasion for it, and he calls it a well-known custom. "I remember," he writes, "a young girl who was staying at my mother's house about fifty years since who wished to go through the ceremony a few minutes before 12 P.M. She accordingly went downstairs into the kitchen followed by me. In the centre was a round table, and around this she was to go at midnight with hemp-seed, repeating as she scattered her seed,

> Hemp-seed I sow, hemp-seed I grow,
> If you be my true love come after me and mow.

If the person intended to be evoked was to be the husband, he would appear behind the sower with a scythe in his hand to mow, and the sower must escape before the scythe reaches her, else some accident will happen. I remember as well as if it were only last night, just as I came downstairs in my night-clothes, the young woman came rushing upstairs in a great fright, and never did I get over the ground so quickly in my life as I did when I followed her. She thought she saw a figure coming after her."

A new-laid egg offers another means of diving into futurity. On New Year's Eve, perforate with a pin the small end of the egg, and let three drops of the white fall into a basin of water. They will diffuse themselves on the surface into fantastic shapes of trees, &c. From these the initiated will augur the fortunes of the egg-dropper, the character of his wife, number of his children, and so forth. This is still practised in Denmark, where also, as a variety, the girls will melt lead on New Year's Eve, and, pouring it into water, observe the next morning what form it has assumed. If it resembles a pair of scissors, she will inevitably marry a tailor; if a hammer, her husband will be a smith, and so on.

A Yorkshire schoolmaster tells me the following tale of fortune-telling in that county. He learnt it from the wife of an intimate friend, and gives it in her words: "My sister and I made it up one day to go to the fortune-telling woman, so we went the next Sunday afternoon, and found a good many young men and women there for the same purpose. When my turn came to go into the room (for each person was let in alone) the old creature bid me get into bed and then gave me something like a hen's egg made of glass. She covered me over with the bed-clothes and told me to look in the glass. Presently she asked me whether I saw anything. I said no, for there was nothing to be seen; but directly a light seemed to break out in the glass and I saw a row of three houses with a kind of shed at one end, and in a moment a man came out of the house next the shed, went past the other houses, and disappeared down a road. I noticed that he wore a blue coat and yellow buttons. Some three months afterwards my sister and I came here on a visit to an old friend of my father's; we had never been here before. On our first Sunday morning here we took a walk out of the village, and as we were returning I noticed a man coming out of a house. I seemed to know the place quite well, though I had never been there before. All at once I knew it was what I had seen in the glass egg—three houses, a shed, blue coat and brass buttons. I pulled my sister's arm and said, 'That's my husband,' while he turned down a road and walked out of our sight. We walked straight to our friend's house, and there we found the very man we had been talking about. He turned out to be a member of the same congregation as our friend, so we all went to chapel together, and in three months from that day I was married."

The maidens in Durham have their own way of testing their lovers' fidelity. They will take an apple-pip, and, naming the lover, put the pip in the fire. If it makes a noise as it bursts with the heat, she is assured of his affection; if it burns away silently, she will be convinced that he has no true regard for her.

As to wishing, we have wishing-chairs here and there through the country. There is one at Finchale Priory, near Durham; and he who seats himself in it, breathes a wish, and tells no one what it is, will receive it. But there is an easier mode of gaining what one desires. If you see a horseshoe, or piece of old iron, on your path, take it up, spit on it, and throw it over your left shoulder, framing your wish at the same time; keep the wish secret, and you will have it in time. Or, on meeting a piebald horse, utter your wish, and whatever it may be you will have it before the week is out.

In Cleveland, girls will resort to the following way of divining whether they will be married or no. Take a tumbler of "south running water," that is, water from a stream which flows southwards; borrow the wedding-ring of some gudewife, and suspend it by a hair of one's head over the glass of water, holding the hair between the finger and thumb. If the ring hit against the side of the glass the holder of it will die an old maid; if it turn quickly round she will be married once—if slowly, twice. This is practised in Durham "with a difference." A shilling is used instead of a ring, the hair is held between the first finger of each hand, joined vertically, and the name of the person beloved is pronounced. If the coin strikes three times against the rim of the tumbler, marriage is to ensue. If more frequently there will be a lengthy courtship and nothing more; if less frequently the affair will be broken off, and if there is no striking at all it will never come on. I have heard of this as far south as Sussex.

One of my correspondents writes thus respecting the practice of different arts of divination: "Six-and-thirty years ago divination certainly used to be practised in the North of England by servants in two or three ways, which have come under my notice. A nurse more than once told my fortune by palmistry. Nor was this mere amusement; she thought it would come true; and, however arbitrary the science might be, she had a uniform way of explaining similar lines in different hands. Thus if I remember rightly the line round the thumb had to do with money. If deep and well defined, riches were denoted; if slight and delicate, a moderate estate. If cut by other lines, heavy losses were indicated; if it was broken before it ran into the transverse line of the palm, ruin was shadowed forth. Of course there was a marriage line somewhere telling whether the lady was dark or fair, and another which prophesied the extent of her dower. The nurse used to speak of all this as if she much more than half-believed in her own predictions." *The Universal Fortune Teller*, still an authority in the North of England, is however fuller and more definite on this point. After dilating on the importance of the matter, the amount of knowledge to be gained, and its absolute certainty and truth, we read as follows:—

"There are five principal lines in the hand, viz.

"The Line of Life,

"The Line of Death,

"The Table Line,

"The Girdle of Venus,

"The Line of Fortune,

besides the Line of Saturn, the Liver Line, and some others which only serve to explain the principal Lines.

"The chief line on which the greatest stress is laid is the Line of Life, which generally takes its rise where the thumb-joint plays with the wrist on the inside, and runs in an oblique direction to the innermost joint of the little finger. If this line is crossed by other lines at or near the wrist, the person will meet with sickness in the beginning of life, and the degree of sickness will be proportioned to the size, length, and breadth of the intervening lines. If the Line of Life runs far and uninterrupted, the person will enjoy good health; and according to its length towards the outside of the forefinger you may judge if the person will live long, as the longer the line the longer the life.

"The next is the Line of Death, which separates the fleshy part of the hand, on the little-finger side, from the hollow of the hand, running in various directions in different people. If the Line of Death be short and runs even without being broken or divided, it shows that the person will enjoy length of days and not be subject to many maladies, but if it be interrupted it evidently shows that the person's life will be endangered by illness. If this line ends abruptly and with a broad point, it shows that the person will die suddenly; if it goes off in a tapering point, the last illness will be slow and consuming by degrees. If other lines run across it, the person will be of a weakly and infirm habit of body, often incapable of following any hard or laborious business.

"The Table Line originates with the Line of Life at the wrist, and runs through the hollow of the hand towards the middle finger. If broad and fair without being broken, it is a sure sign of a happy and comfortable life; if narrow and contracted, it is a sign of poverty and crosses in the world.

"The Girdle of Venus takes its course from the extremity of the innermost joint of the little finger, and forming a curve terminates between the fore and middle fingers.

"The Line of Fortune strikes from behind the ball or mount of the forefinger, across the palm or Line of Life, and loses itself in or near the fleshy part of the hand on the little-finger side. If it runs smooth, broad, and clear, the person will enjoy affluence through life and be prosperous in all his undertakings.

"The ball of the thumb is called the Mount of Venus, and there are lines in the fleshy parts around it which are governed by the various planets; the hollow of the hand is called the Place of Mars.

"Always observe to choose the left hand, because the heart and brain have more influence over it than the right hand."

CHAPTER IV.

PORTENTS AND AUGURIES.

On the Borders—In Durham—At Leeds—From the New Moon—Gift of a Knife—The Spilling of Salt—First Stone taken from a Church—First Corpse laid in a Churchyard—A Buried Charm—Auguries from Birds—Rooks—Swallows—Redbreast—Yellow Hammer—Wren—Bat—Raven—Magpie—Gabriel Hounds—Gabble Retchet—Wild Huntsman—Sneezing.

F portents and auguries we find large mention made in the Wilkie MS. The number of trifling circumstances held to presage good or evil is really astonishing. Thus, it is fortunate for the housewife if a brood of chickens turn out all cock birds; very fortunate if her cabbages grow double, *i.e.* with two shoots from one root; or "lucker," that is, with the leaves open instead of closing into a "stock" or heart; fortunate, too, if she meet with potatoes, gooseberries, &c. of an unusual shape, or with peas and beans more than the usual number in the pod; nine is the lucky number in Sussex. A pod containing only one pea is equally auspicious, and so is a four-leaved clover or an even ash-leaf. Witness the following lines from a privately-printed collection of North Country Folk-Lore:

> The even ash-leaf in my left hand,
> The first man I meet shall be my husband.
> The even ash-leaf in my glove,
> The first I meet shall be my love.
> The even ash-leaf in my breast,
> The first man I meet's whom I love best.
> The even ash-leaf in my hand,
> The first I meet shall be my man.

Even ash, even ash, I pluck thee,
This night my true love for to see;
Neither in his rick nor in his rear,
But in the clothes he does every day wear.
Find even ash or four-leaved clover,
An' you'll see your true love before the day's over.

A spider descending upon you from the roof is a token that you will soon have a legacy from a friend. Fuller, in his "Worthies," refers to this belief: "When a spider is found upon our clothes, we use to say, some money is coming towards us. The moral is this. Those who imitate the industry of that contemptible creature may, by God's blessing, weave themselves into wealth, and procure themselves a plentiful estate." In Ireland the saying is as follows: If a spider be found running over the dress or shawl of a woman the garment will soon be replaced by a new one.

On the other hand, the sudden loss of hair is a prognostic of the loss of children, health, or property. He who hears a loud stroke upon the table, as if by a wand or club, or three successive strokes, or the noise as of a bullet dropped upon the table, is a doomed man himself, or will soon hear of the death of a friend. Or, again, if a man dream that his teeth fall out, he will hear next day of the death of a friend, while a dream of fire prognosticates sorrow and pain. If you dream of a wedding you will hear of a death; if you dream of water you will hear of sickness.

A list of little superstitions of the same kind, still extant in the county of Durham, has been supplied to me by a careful observer.

Put on your left stocking inside out, it is lucky. Put on the right one so, it is unlucky. A bright spark in the candle betokens the coming of a letter; if it drops on the first shake, the letter is already in the post. If you find your friend burning three candles you may hail him Lord Mayor of London next year. In Germany, on the other hand, they say if there are three candles alight in the room one of the party must be a bride, *i.e.* a betrothed maiden.

It is counted lucky to carry in the pocket a crooked sixpence, or one with a hole in it, or the tip of a dried tongue. People with meeting eyebrows are thought fortunate fellows.[1] It is lucky to set a hen on an odd number of eggs; set her on even ones, and you will have no chickens. Again, if two persons wash their hands together in the same basin, they will be sure to fall out before bed-time. This is said all England over. A lady informs me that the belief held its ground when she was at school, and that it was necessary to avert the evil omen by "crossing the water" with the fore-finger. I have seen this done by a farmer's daughter in Devonshire. If a person's hair burn brightly when thrown into the fire it is a sign of longevity; the brighter the flame the longer the life. On the other hand, if it smoulder away, and refuse to burn, it is a sign of approaching death.[2] Among the lower orders in Ireland however it is held that human hair should never be burnt, only buried, because at the resurrection the former owner of the hair will come to seek it. Neither should it be thrown carelessly away lest some bird should find it and carry it off, causing the owner's head to ache all the time the bird was busy working the hair into its nest. "I knew how it would be," exclaimed a Sussex servant one day to her mistress, "when I saw that bird fly off with a bit of my hair in its beak, that flew out of the window this morning while I was dressing. I knew I should have a clapping headache, and so I have." If the nose itches it is a sign that you will be crossed, or vexed, or kissed by a fool; if the foot, it foretells that you will soon tread on strange ground. Itching of the right hand portends receiving

[1] This is curious, since in Icelandic sagas a man with meeting eyebrows is said to be *hamrammr*, or a kveldulfr, that is, a werewolf. Thus, Olaf Tvennubruni is spoken of in the *Landnama*, v. c. 10, as *hamrammr*, *i. e.* able to change his shape. His nickname signifies one with drooping brows, but in later Icelandic Folk-Lore the eyebrows growing over the nose is a token of a man being a werewolf. The same idea holds in Denmark (Thiele's *Danmarks Folke Sagn*, vol. ii. p. 279), also in Germany (Simrock's *Deutsche Sagen*, p. 467), whilst in Greece it is a sign that a man is a brukolak, or vampire.—S. B. G.

[2] It is deemed a sign of longevity in Devonshire if the hair grows down on the forehead and retreats up the head above the temples.

money; of the left hand, paying money; of the ear, hearing sudden news. If the right ear tingles, you are being spoken well of; if the left ear, some one is speaking ill of you. If you shiver, some one is walking over your future grave. If you find an ashleaf with an equal number of indentures on each side, you will meet a person of the same name with that of your future husband or wife. If you stumble upstairs (by accident) you will be married the same year; if you snuff out the candle you certainly will. So at least says one of my friends. Another professor of Folk-Lore informs me that both accidents are very unlucky, and who shall decide when doctors disagree? If you sing before breakfast you will cry before supper. If you put a button or hook into the wrong hole while dressing in the morning, some misfortune will occur during the day. A mole at the back of the neck marks out the bearer of it as in danger of hanging. The little white specks sometimes seen on the nails of the human hand are thus interpreted:—

On the thumb they presage gifts.

On the first finger they presage friends.

On the second finger they presage foes.

On the third finger they presage lovers to the young, else letters.

On the fourth finger they presage approaching journeys.

These are Durham sayings, but many of them are much wider in their range. The same may be said of the following, which were communicated by a friend at Leeds:—

If a snake crosses the path, it will rain.

If glowworms shine at night, it will soon rain.

Spring has not arrived till you can set your foot on twelve daisies.

March search, April try,
May will prove if you live or die.

If you take violets or primroses to a house in less quantity than a handful, all the owner's young chickens or ducks will die.

Before you kill anything it is necessary to wash your face.

Eat pancakes on Shrove Tuesday, and grey peas on Ash Wednesday, and you will have money in your pocket all the year round.

If you want to have extra good luck to your dairy, give your bunch of mistletoe to the first cow that calves after New Year's Day.

Turn the money in your pocket on the first sight of the new moon, and you will always have plenty there. Should your pocket be empty you can only avert the lady moon's displeasure by turning head over heels immediately.

Again, look at the first new moon of the year through a silk handkerchief which has never been washed. As many moons as you see through the handkerchief (the threads multiplying the vision), so many years will pass ere you are married. But it is very unlucky to see the new moon through a window-pane. A friend tells me she has known a maidservant shut her eyes when closing the shutters unless she should unexpectedly catch sight of it through the glass.

Throughout Northumberland this couplet is said and believed in:

> A Saturday's moon and a Sunday's prime
> Never brought good in any man's time.

Again, courtesy to the moon when first you see her after the change, and you will get a present before the moon is out. It must be done three times, and not through glass. This last is a Durham superstition. A Yorkshire lady informs me that in her childhood she was accustomed to repeat the following lines while looking at the first new moon of the year through a silk handkerchief:

> New moon, new moon, I hail thee,
> New moon, new moon, be kind to me,
> If I marry man or man marry me,
> Show me how many moons it will be.

Another variation of the practice runs thus: "At the first appearance of the first new moon of the year go out in the evening, and, standing over the spars of a gate or stile, and looking on the moon, repeat the following lines:

> All hail to thee moon, all hail to thee,
> I prythee, good moon, reveal to me
> This night who my husband shall be.

You will dream that night of your future husband." This rite is practised too in Sussex, where they say also that if you can catch a falling leaf you will have twelve months of happiness. A Yorkshire rhyme avers—

> The new moon's mist
> Is better than gold in a kist,

but does not specify wherefore.

Mr. Denham tells us that he once saw an old matron turn her apron to the new moon to insure good luck for the ensuing month. I may, perhaps, mention here, that apples are said to "shrump up" in Devonshire if picked when the moon is waning.

The May new moon is said in the South of England to have a share in curing scrofulous complaints. I have been told of a man residing near Chichester who has twice travelled into Dorsetshire with different members of his family to place them under a "cunning man" there. His charms were only potent in the month of May. And he required his patients to have their eyes fixed upon the new May moon while they received from his hands boxes of ointment made from herbs gathered when the moon was full. On the man's last visit he found more than 200 persons waiting to be charmed, who had sat up for several hours for fear of missing the right moment for looking at her.

A certain unluckiness is held all England over to attend a May kitten as well as a May baby. The latter will be sickly and difficult to rear; the former must be drowned without mercy; no good would come of rearing it; it would only bring snakes and slowworms into the house and never kill rat or mouse. Nay, it is averred that it would suck the breath of children and cause their death. On this point the Rev. Hugh Taylor writes: "My groom, a native of North Tyne, tells me no one would keep a May cat because it would lie on the children's faces and suffocate them. He said there were many cases of children in that neighbeurhood having lost their lives from this cause. He himself has a cat they are obliged to watch. If it is left alone in the house for a few minutes it is found lying on the baby's face. My housekeeper, a native of Chatton, in Northumberland, says that no one would keep a May cat because it sucks the breath of children and kills them, though indeed all cats seem to have this propensity. An instance occurred at Greenock on May 25 of the present year, when an infant of five months old, the child of a baker, was suffocated by a strange cat."

To return to the Borders. A maiden can scarcely do a worse thing there than boil a dish-clout in her crock. She will be sure, in consequence, to lose all her lovers; or, in Scotch phrase, she would "boil all her lads awa."

Thus in Durham, if you put milk in your tea before sugar, you lose your sweetheart.

If, on leaving your house, you see a black snail, seize it boldly by one of its horns and throw it over your left shoulder; you may then go on your way prosperously; but, if you fling it over your right shoulder, you will draw down ill-luck. This practice extends as far south as Lancashire. In Yorkshire it is unlucky to meet a white horse on leaving home; you must spit to avert misfortune.

Skir or kir-handed people, *i.e.* left-handed ones, are not safe for a traveller to meet on a Tuesday morning. On other days it is fortunate to meet them. Again, if you enter another man's house with your "skir" foot foremost, you draw down evil on its inhabitants. If, therefore, you have carelessly done so, you must avert the mischief by going out, and making your entrance a second time with the right foot foremost. I conclude that this little superstition once held its ground in the South, for Dr. Johnson is said to have entertained it, and to have left a house and re-entered it right foot foremost, if on the first occasion he had planted his left foot on the threshold.

If any person deemed auspicious meet a young tradesman who has just donned his apron, and say to him " Weel may ye brook (or dirty) your apron," the young man will be sure to do well in life.

It is unlucky for a traveller on Monday morning to meet a man with " schloof," or flat feet; but mischief may be averted by returning home, eating and drinking, and starting afresh on one's way.

If meat shrinks in the pot, it presages a downfall in life; but, if it swells to a large size, the master of the house will be prosperous in his undertakings.

To sweep the dust out of your house by the front door is to sweep away the good fortune of your family; it must be swept inwards, and carried out in a basket or shovel, and then no harm will follow.

If a quill be thrown over the house, and caught in a basin on the other side, it will turn to a silver spoon.

It is unlucky, after one has started on a journey, to be recalled and told of something previously forgotten; but the spell may be broken by asking for meat and drink, and partaking of it. This done, the journey may be resumed without fear. This little bit of superstition, too, has crept southwards into England. A clergyman from Yorkshire tells me that his grandfather, though anything but a weak man, would never turn back when he had once started on an expedition; he has been known to stand on horseback at the end of his grounds, shouting to the house for something that he had forgotten, rather than turn back for it.

Thus, in Sweden, one must not turn round when going on any business, for fear it turn out ill, nor may one look back when setting out on a journey.

Akin to this is the belief that it is unlucky to watch anyone out of sight; if you do so you will never see that person again.

Many north-country people would not, on any account, lend another a pin. They will say, " You may take one, but, mind, I do not give it." Akin to this is the objection, once universally felt, to giving a knife or other sharp implement; it would cut friendship or love. Thus Gay, in his *Shepherd's Week:*

But woe is me! Such presents luckless prove,
For knives, they tell me, always sever love.

I have heard in Durham of a schoolmaster who wished to reward one of his pupils with a knife, but dared not do so without receiving from the boy a penny, in order that the knife might be purchased, not given. This feeling extends to Denmark, if indeed the Danish settlers did not bring the belief into England. It was defied by a versifier of the last century (the Rev. Samuel Bishop, A.D. 1796), who presented a knife to his wife on her fifteenth wedding day, with a copy of verses so spirited and full of character that I cannot forbear transcribing them. They are taken from Locker's *Lyra Elegantiarum:*

A knife, dear girl, cuts love, they say,
Mere modish love perhaps it may;
For any tool of any kind
Can separate what was never joined;
The knife that cuts our love in two
Will have much tougher work to do—
Must cut your softness, worth, and spirit,
Down to the vulgar size of merit;
To level yours with common taste
Must cut a world of sense to waste;
And from your single beauty's store
Clip what would dizen out a score.
The selfsame blade from me must sever
Sensation, judgment, sight—for ever!
All memory of endearments past,
All hope of comforts long to last,
All that makes fourteen years with you
A summer—and a short one too—
All that affection feels and fears,
When hours without you seem like years.
Till that be done—and I'd as soon
Believe this knife would clip the moon,
Accept my present undeterred,
And leave their proverbs to the herd.
If in a kiss—delicious treat—
Your lips acknowledge the receipt,

Love, fond of such substantial fare,
And proud to play the glutton there,
All thoughts of cutting will disdain,
Save only—"cut and come again."

In the West Riding of Yorkshire it is thought sinful to burn evergreens which have been used for decorations; or, again, to point at the stars, or try to count them. Many, they say, have been struck dead for so doing. I believe that this idea extends to Durham. Neither must you collect hailstones. The impropriety of this is said to be shown thus—if you put them into a wine glass to melt, they will run through it, and make a slop underneath!

No one in the Borders will put on a new coat or dress without placing some money at once in the right-hand pocket. This insures the pocket being always full; but if, by mistake, it is put in the left-hand pocket, you will never have a penny so long as you wear the coat.

My native county supplies many conventional speeches proper to be made on first seeing one's friends in new clothes, *i.e.*, "There you go, and well you look." "May you have health to wear it, strength to tear it, and money to buy another." Those in use in our schools are less kindly in their character, especially as they are accompanied with actions to correspond:

A nip for new,
A bite for blue.

or,

A nip for new,
Two for blue;
Sixteen
For bottle green.

Among country people in Lancashire it is considered unfortunate to buy cattle without receiving back some small coin from the purchase-money "for luck." A farmer of fourscore years old told a friend that in early life he once bought a cow without thus receiving a gift from the purchase-money, but the animal was soon afterwards found dead in the field. During the remainder of his life, more than fifty years, he had taken care never to buy a cow or any other animal without seeing to the "gift again."

When you see the first lamb in the spring, note whether its head or tail is turned towards you. If the former, you will have plenty of meat to eat during the year; if the latter, look for nothing beyond milk and vegetables. As far south as Lancashire it is thought lucky to see the first lamb's head, and unlucky to see its tail.

It is reckoned unlucky in Lincolnshire to be bitten by a fox. A man at Barnoldby-le-beck fled lately from two foxes, alleging, by way of excuse, "You know, Sir, that if a man is bitten by a fox, he is sure to die within seven years."[1]

As to the spilling of salt, it is considered ominous in the North as elsewhere; the ill-luck can only be averted by throwing a pinch of it over the left shoulder; and he whose misplaced courtesy should lead him to offer to place salt on the plate of a northern, would probably be repelled with the words:

Help me to salt,
Help me to sorrow!

The ill luck may, however, be averted by a second help. It is thought unlucky through the North to turn a loaf upside down after helping oneself from it. Along the coast, they say, that for every loaf so turned a ship will be wrecked. If a loaf parts in the hand while you are cutting it, it bodes dissension in the family: you part man and wife.

In Aberdeenshire it is believed that whosoever pulls the first stone out of a church, although it is for a good purpose, and to make way for a new one, will come to a violent end. My informant, a clergyman of the Church in Scotland, knew a case in which no workman had courage to begin, although the new place of worship had been built. The agent of the estate pulled out the first stone, and after that the labourers proceeded without further demur. In the same place there was great difficulty in

[1] Communicated by the Rev. M. G. Watkins.

bringing the new churchyard into use. No one would be the first to bury his dead there, for it was believed that the first corpse laid there was a teind to the Evil One. At last a poor tramp who was found dead in the road was interred, after which there was no further difficulty. Precisely the same superstition exists in Devonshire. The churchyard round St. John's church, Bovey Tracey, South Devon, was long unused, the country people declaring that the devil would seize the first body laid in it. At last a stranger was buried there, the servant of a visitor in the parish, after which interments began at once to take place.[1]

In accordance with this belief, Mr. Baring Gould points out the following Yorkshire superstition: "It is said in that county that the first child baptized in a new font is sure to die—a reminiscence of the sacrifice which was used for the consecration of every dwelling and temple in heathen times, and of the pig or sheep killed and laid at the foundation of churches. When I was incumbent of Dalton a new church was built. A blacksmith in the village had seven daughters, after which a son was born, and he came to me a few days before the consecration of the new church to ask me to baptize his boy in the old temporary church and font. "Why, Joseph," said I, "if you will only wait till Thursday the boy can be baptized in the new font on the opening of the new church." "Thank you, Sir," said the blacksmith, with a wriggle, "but you see it's a lad, and we shu'd be sorry if he were to dee; na if t'had been a lass instead, why then you were welcome, for 'twouldn't ha' mattered a ha'penny. Lasses are ower mony and lads ower few wi' us."

On the site of an ancient monastery or hospital in Preston, tradition maintains that a church has sunk into the earth, and

[1] Thus, in Germany it is said that the first person who enters a new church becomes the property of the devil. At Aix-la-Chapelle is shown a rent in the door, which is thus accounted for. The church was ready for consecration, and before anyone entered it a dog was driven in. The devil in a rage seized the dog, and flew away with it, shivering the door. In various parts of Germany and in Norway a dog or a pig was buried in the churchyard as an offering to the devil. He is thus outwitted, and receives a beast instead of a man as his tribute. —S. B. G.

that the bells ring on Christmas Eve. This pretty legend may be compared with that of the bells of Bottreaux or Boscastle, on the north coast of Cornwall, which never reached that still "silent tower," the vessel that was freighted with them foundering at sea. The bells are said to be rung in oceans' caves by unseen hands, and the Cornish fisherman listens for their chimes on Sunday mornings.

Birds have always supplied numberless auguries. When rooks desert a rookery it foretells the downfall of the family on whose property it is. There is a Northumbrian saying, that the rooks deserted the rookery of Chipchase before the family of Reed left that place. On the other hand, the Wilkie MS. informs us, that, when rooks haunt a town or village, mortality is supposed to await its inhabitants, and if they feed in the street it shows a storm is near at hand.

The same authority tells us that it is a very good omen for swallows to take possession of a place, and build their nests around it; while it is unpropitious for them to forsake a place which they have once tenanted. Now the swallow, "God's fowl," the herald of spring, has been held a sacred bird by the whole Germanic race: it preserves the house on which it builds from fire and storms, and protects it from evil; while, in its turn, it is protected by the penalties which threaten the sacrilegious hand which should destroy it—the loss of dairy-produce, or continued rain for four weeks. In Yorkshire the punishment is not so defined, but it is considered certain to fall in one form or other. A farmer's wife near Hull told a friend of mine, Mrs. L., how some young men, sons of a banker in that town, had pulled down all the swallows' nests about a little farm which he possessed. "The bank broke soon after," she went on, "and, poor things, the family have had nought but trouble since!" This belief crops out in Sussex too, where they say that misfortune is sure to follow the taking of a swallow's nest, or killing a house cricket. In Perigord the swallow is the "messenger of life;" in some parts of France it shares with the wren the title of "poule de Dieu;" and among our own peasantry, those who say—

The robin and the wren
Are God Almighty's cock and hen;
Him that harries their nest,
Never shall his soul have rest,

add—

The martin and the swallow
Are God Almighty's bow and arrow;

or, as it runs in some of our midland counties,—

The martin and the swallow
Are God Almighty's birds to hollow.

The Lancashire version is—

The robin and wren
Are God's cock and hen.
The spink and the sparrow
Are the deil's bow and arrow.

Archbishop Whately tells us, however, that in Ireland the swallow is called the "devil's bird" by the vulgar, who hold that there is a certain hair on every one's head, which if a swallow can pick off, the man is doomed to eternal perdition. In Scotland, on the other hand, the pretty little yellow-hammer is called the "devil's bird," and a superstitious dislike to it extends as far south as Northumberland. My friend the vicar of Stamfordham tells me that when the boys of his parish find its nest they destroy it, saying:

Half a paddock, half a toad,
Half a drop of de'il's blood.
Horrid yellow yowling!

A cock crowing on the threshold or a humblebee entering a house are in Buckinghamshire deemed omens of a visitor. To turn the bee out is a most inhospitable action.

As to the robin redbreast, it is invested with a sacred character all Christendom over, though various reasons are assigned for it in different countries. In Brittany it is reverenced for an act of devotion to the Crucified Saviour, in extracting one thorn from

His crown, thus dyeing its own breast red; in Wales for daily bearing in its bill one drop of water to the place of torment, in order to extinguish its flames.

The Breton legend has been thus versified by the Rev. J. H. Abrahall:

Bearing His cross, while Christ passed forth forlorn,
His Godlike forehead by the mock crown torn,
A little bird took from that crown one thorn.

To soothe the dear Redeemer's throbbing head,
That bird did all she could: His blood, 'tis said,
Down dropping, dyed her tender bosom red.

Since then no wanton boy disturbs her nest,
Weazel nor wild-cat will her young molest—
All sacred deem that bird of ruddy breast.

Boys always respect its nest: they say in Cornwall,

Who hurts the robin or the wren
Will never prosper, sea or land.

But the penalty attached to such sacrilege in Devonshire is peculiar. A little boy in the neighbourhood of Dartmoor was heard to say that if you took a robin's nest all the "clomb" (*i. e.* crockery) in the house would break.

In Scotland, however, the song of the robin is thought to bode ill to the sick person who hears it, and a similar belief holds in Northamptonshire; where, indeed, the bird is counted a certain prophet of death, and is said to tap three times at the window of a dying person's room. Thus, again, at St. John's College, Hurstpierpoint, the boys maintain that when a death takes place a robin will enter the chapel, light upon the altar, and begin to sing.[1]

The wren generally shares in the reverence paid to the robin;

[1] Singularly enough, I saw this happen myself on one occasion. I happened to be in the chapel one evening at six o'clock, when a robin entered at the open circular east window in the temporary apse, and lighting on the altar began to chirp. A few minutes later the passing bell began to toll for a boy who had just died.—S. B. G.

thus the two birds are named together in the Pastorals of George Smith, A.D. 1770:—

I found a robin's nest within our shed,
And in the barn a wren her young ones bred;
I never take away their nest, nor try
To catch the old ones, lest a friend should die:
Dick took a wren's nest from his cottage side,
And ere a twelvemonth passed his mother died.

Nevertheless, at Christmas-tide boys are accustomed in Essex to kill wrens and carry them about in furze-bushes, from house to house, asking a present in these words:—

The wren, the wren, the king of the birds,
St. Stephen's Day was killed in the furze;
Although he be little his honour is great,
And so, good people, pray give us a treat.

It is remarkable that the custom extends to the Isle of Man, where the following verse is used:—

We hunted the wren for Robin the Bobbin,
We hunted the wren for Jack of the Can;
We hunted the wren for Robin the Bobbin,
We hunted the wren for every one.

And after making a circuit, and collecting what money they can, the boys lay the wren on a bier and bury it. The same usage has prevailed in Ireland and in France; it is a singular one, and has been thus explained. The bird had a sacred character among our Celtic ancestors, as among the Greeks. It was a bearer of celestial fire, and disputed with the eagle the kingship of the feathered creation. Early Christian teachers opposed the superstitious respect paid to the little creature, and their lessons were singularly embodied in this cruel persecution.[1]

The bawkie-bird, or bat, immortalised by Shakespear as "the delicate Ariel's" steed, is in Scotland connected with witchcraft.

[1] See Kelly's *Indo-European Tradition*, pp. 75-82

"If," says Mr. Wilkie, "the bat is observed, while flying, to rise, and then descend again earthwards, you may know that the witches' hour is come—the hour in which they have power over every human being who is not specially shielded from their influence."

The raven,[1] crow, and magpie,[2] are ominous birds on the Border, as elsewhere. A North-country servant thus accounted for the unluckiness of the magpie to her master, the late Canon Humble. "It was," the girl said, "the only bird which did not go into the Ark with Noah; it liked better to sit outside, jabbering over the drowned world." A yet quainter reason was given for it by the Durham lad, who said the magpie was a hybrid between the raven and the dove, and therefore, unlike every other bird and beast, had not been baptized in the waters of the Deluge. Yet, uncanny as the creature is, and mischievous too, there are parts of the Continent where no one dares kill it. An English traveller in Sweden once saw a flock of magpies greedily devouring the pig's food, and, having a gun with him, offered to shoot some. He did so, and the farmer thanked him heartily, but expressed his hopes that no harm might befall him in consequence.[3]

I received my first lesson respecting the portents to be drawn from magpies very early in life. Well do I remember, when a

[1] In Sweden the ravens which scream by night in forest swamps and wild moors are held to be the ghosts of murdered men, whose bodies have been hidden in those spots by their undetected murderers, and not had Christian burial. In Denmark the night raven is considered an exorcised spirit. There is a hole in its left wing, caused by the stake driven into the earth where a spirit has been exorcised. One must take care not to look up when the bird is flying overhead, for he who sees through the hole in its wing will become a night raven himself, and the night raven will be released. It is ever flying towards the east, in hopes of reaching the Holy Sepulchre, for when it arrives there it will get rest.—S. B. G.

[2] The magpie is considered in Sweden a downright witches' bird, belonging to the Evil One and the other powers of night. When the witches on Walpurgis night ride to the Blakulli, they go in the form of magpies. These birds moult in summer, and become bald about the neck; and then the countrypeople say they have been to the Blakulli and helped the Evil One to get his hay in, and that the yoke has rubbed their feathers off.—Thorpe's *Mythology*, vol. ii. p. 84.

[3] Archbishop Whately's *Remains*, p. 270.

boy of ten or twelve years old, driving an old lady in a pony-carriage to visit a friend in a secluded part of the county of Durham. Half our journey was made when, without a word of warning, the reins were suddenly snatched out of my hand, and the pony brought to a stand. Full of astonishment, I looked to my companion for some explanation of this assault on my independence, and saw her gazing with intense interest on a magpie then crossing the road. After a pause of some seconds she exclaimed, with a sigh, "Oh, the nasty bird! Turn back, turn back!" And back we turned, the old lady instructing me on the way home in the following verse, which certainly justified the course we had taken:

> One is sorrow, two mirth,
> Three a wedding, four a birth,
> Five heaven, six hell,
> Seven the de'il's ain sell.

I have since heard another rendering of the last couplet—

> Five a sickening, six a christening,
> Seven a dance, eight a lady going to France.

The first couplet, with some variations, is in universal use; but I think, on the whole, the magpie receives more notice in the North of England than elsewhere. One clerical friend informs me of a lady who pleads guilty to making a cross in the air when she sees a magpie crossing her path, by way of dispelling the ill-luck attending the bird; and another tells me how he himself invariably takes off his hat on catching sight of a single magpie, in the hope that by this polite attention he may avert the evil consequences attendant on the apparition. I have heard precisely the same thing of a man of education and good position in Yorkshire; and a lady of that county, Mrs. L——, tells me a curious instance of the good effects of attending to the magpie's warning. It relates to a gentleman with whom she was well acquainted, a county magistrate and a landowner. One day, in the year 1825, he was riding to York with the view of depositing his rents in Challoner's Bank, when a magpie flew across his path. He drew up his horse, paused a moment, and turned homewards, resolving to defer his journey till the next day. That day, however, the bank failed, and it only remained for the gentleman to congratulate himself on his prudent attention to the magpie's warning. From another Yorkshire lady I have received the following verse, which she informs me she used to repeat as a child on seeing this bird, making at the same time the sign of the cross:

> I cross the magpie,
> The magpie crosses me;
> Bad luck to the magpie,
> And good luck to me.

It is prudent also to look out at once for a crow, as the sight of that bird disperses the ill-luck which the magpie may have brought.

Now, all this is very curious when viewed in connection with ancient pagan mythology. Auguries drawn from the flight and action of birds formed a part of its complex system, from the days when Themistocles was assured of victory at Artemisium by the crowing of a cock, or Romulus claimed to be King of Rome from the appearance of vultures. The Greeks made a science of these auguries and their interpretation, and called it Ornithomancy. Is it not marvellous to find traces of such direct heathenism among even the upper classes of a country Christianised so many ages back? Eleven hundred years ago, efforts were made by doctors of the Church to root them out, but here they are still. We find Alcuin, who was born at York about A.D. 735, the friend of Charlemagne, and one of the glories of Anglo-Saxon times, writing thus to a bishop, evidently a Saxon one: "Prognostics also, and cries of birds, and sneezings, are altogether to be shunned, because they are of no force except to those who believe in them, so that it may happen unto them according to their faith. For it is permitted to the evil spirit, for the deceiving of persons who observe these things, to cause that in some degree prognostics should often foretell the truth." In another place Alcuin defines augurs as "those who pay attention to prognostics, and to the flight and voice of birds."

But to proceed. We can scarcely be surprised that lonely walks among the wild hills and cheerless moors of the North should be attended by superstitious fears, or that the strange unearthly cries, so like the yelping of dogs, uttered by wild fowl on their passage southwards, should engender a belief in a pack of spectral hounds. Wordsworth speaks of it in a sonnet, evidently connecting it with the German legend of the Wild Huntsman. He tells of a peasant, poor and aged, yet endowed—

With ample sovereignty of eye and ear;
Rich were his walks with supernatural cheer:
He the seven birds hath seen that never part,
Seen the seven whistlers on their nightly rounds,
And counted them! And oftentimes will start,
For overhead are sweeping Gabriel's hounds,
Doomed with their impious lord the flying hart
To chase for ever on aërial grounds.

In Devonshire the spectral pack is called the "Wisht hounds," a name which Mr. Kelly derives from Wodin's name, Wunsch, corrupted into "wisht." It has a huntsman there who guides his pack over the wild wastes of Dartmoor; but I cannot hear of such a being in my own neighbourhood. The Gabriel hounds, as they call them in Durham and some parts of Yorkshire, are described as monstrous human-headed dogs, who traverse the air, and are often heard though seldom seen. Sometimes they appear to hang over a house, and then death or calamity are sure to visit it. A Yorkshire friend informs me that when a child was burned to death in Sheffield, a few years ago, the neighbours immediately called to mind how the Gabriel hounds had passed above the house not long before. From another quarter I hear of a person who was hastily summoned one night to the sick-bed of a relative whose illness had suddenly assumed an alarming character. As he set out he heard the wild sound of the creatures above his head; they accompanied him the whole way, about a mile, then paused, and yelped loudly over the house. He entered it, and found that the patient had just breathed her last.

In a letter from the late Mr. Holland, of Sheffield, dated March 28, 1861, is the following mention of this wild hunt, with a sonnet by him, embodying local feelings on the subject: "I can never forget the impression made upon my own mind when once arrested by the cry of these Gabriel hounds as I passed the parish church of Sheffield, one densely dark and very still night. The sound was exactly like the questing of a dozen beagles on the foot of a race, but not so loud, and highly suggestive of ideas of the supernatural.

"Oft have I heard my honoured mother say,
How she has listened to the Gabriel hounds—
Those strange unearthly and mysterious sounds,
Which on the ear through murkiest darkness fell;
And how, entranced by superstitious spell,
The trembling villager not seldom heard,
In the quaint notes of the nocturnal bird,
Of death premonished, some sick neighbour's knell.
I, too, remember once at midnight dark,
How these sky-yelpers startled me, and stirred
My fancy so, I could have then averred
A mimic pack of beagles low did bark.
Nor wondered I that rustic fear should trace
A spectral huntsman doomed to that long moonless chase."

We have the authority of the distinguished ornithologist, Mr. Yarrell,[1] for stating the birds in question to be bean-geese, coming southwards in large flocks on the approach of winter, partly from Scotland and its islands, but chiefly from Scandinavia. They choose dark nights for their migration, and utter a loud and very peculiar cry. It has been observed in every part of England—in Norfolk, in Gloucestershire, and as far west as Cornwall. A gentleman was riding alone near the Land's End on a still dark night, when the yelping cry broke out above his head so suddenly, and to all appearance so near, that he instinctively pulled up his horse as if to allow the pack to pass, the animal trembling violently at the unexpected sounds.

Mr. Buckland[2] has reported portents of a somewhat similar

[1] *Notes and Queries*, vol. v. p. 596.

[2] *Curiosities of Natural History*, second series, p. 285.

character on the English Channel. A rustling rushing sound is heard there on the dark still nights of winter, and is called the Herring Spear or Herring Piece by the fishermen of Dover and Folkestone. This is caused by the flight of those pretty little birds the redwings, as they cross the Channel on their way to warmer regions. The fishermen listen to the sound with awe, yet regard it on the whole as an omen of good success with their nets. But they deprecate the cry of the "Seven Whistlers" (named in the sonnet above quoted from Wordsworth), and consider it a death-warning. "I heard 'em one dark night last winter," said an old Folkestone fisherman. "They come over our heads all of a sudden, singing 'ewe, ewe,' and the men in the boat wanted to go back It came on to rain and blow soon afterwards, and was an awful night, Sir; and sure enough before morning a boat was upset, and seven poor fellows drowned. I know what makes the noise, Sir; its them long-billed curlews, but I never likes to hear them."

But to return to the Gabriel hounds. In the neighbourhood of Leeds the phenomenon assumes another name and another character. It is there called "Gabble retchet," and held to be the souls of unbaptized children doomed to flit restlessly around their parents' abode. Now it is a widespread belief that such children have no rest after death. In North Germany they are said to be turned into the meteors called Will-o'-the-wisp, and so to flit about and hover between heaven and earth. In Scotland, unbaptized infants are supposed to wander in woods and solitudes lamenting their hard fate, and I know that a few years back, at Chudleigh, in Devonshire, a servant in the clergyman's family asked her mistress whether what the people of the place said was really true, about the souls of unchristened babies wandering in the air till the Judgment Day. And it is very remarkable that German Folk-Lore connects unbaptized infants with the Furious Host or wild hunt, which is evidently the same as the Gabriel hounds of the North and the Wisht hounds of the West of England. The mysterious lady Frau Bertha is ever attended by troops of unbaptized children, and she takes them with her when she joins the wild huntsman, and sweeps with him and his wild pack across the wintry sky. In North Devon the local name is "Yeth hounds," heath and heathen being both "Yeth" in the North Devon dialect. Unbaptized infants are there buried in a part of the churchyard set apart for the purpose called "Chrycimers," *i. e.* Christianless hill, and the belief seems to be that their spirits, having no admittance into Paradise, unite in a pack of "Heathen" or "Yeth" hounds, and hunt the Evil one, to whom they ascribe their unhappy condition.

Mr. Baring-Gould heard of this hunt in Iceland from his guide, Jón, under the name of the Yule host; and in his *Iceland, its Scenes and Sagas*, pp. 199-203, he gives so lucid an account of the myth that I am thankful, by his kind permission and that of his publishers, Messrs. Smith, Elder, and Co., to insert it in these pages. My readers will observe that he lays all the rout to the charge of the wind, not of the bean-geese; and certainly a winter wind would account for any amount of confusion and turmoil, especially on the wild moors and hills of the North. Still I do think that some of the wild stories and superstitions point to the birds in question as their originators, at least in part:—

"Odin, or Wodin, is the wild huntsman who nightly tears on his white horse over the German and Norwegian forests and moor-sweeps, with his legion of hellhounds. Some luckless woodcutter, on a still night, is returning through the pinewoods; the air is sweet-scented with matchless pine fragrance. Overhead the sky is covered with grey vapour, but a mist is on all the land; not a sound among the fir-tops; and the man starts at the click of a falling cone. Suddenly his ear catches a distant wail: a moan rolls through the interlacing branches: nearer and nearer comes the sound. There is the winding of a long horn waxing louder and louder, the baying of hounds, the rattle of hoofs and paws on the pine-tree tops. A blast of wind rolls along, the firs bend as withes, and the woodcutter sees the wild huntsman and his rout reeling by in frantic haste.

"The wild huntsman chases the wood spirits, and he is to be seen at cockcrow, returning with the little Dryads hanging to his saddlebow by their yellow locks. This chase goes by different names. The huntsman in parts of Germany is still called Wôde, and the chase after him Wüthendes Heer.[1] In Danzig the huntsman is Dyterbjernat, *i. e.* Diedrick of Bern, the same as Theodoric the Great. In Schleswig he is Duke Abel, who slew his brother in 1250. In Normandy, in the Pyrenees, and in Scotland, King Arthur rides nightly through the land. In the Franche-Comté he is Herod in pursuit of the Holy Innocents. In Norway the hunt is called the Aaskarreya, the chase of the inhabitants of Asgarth. (Hence perhaps our word skurry.) In Sweden it is Odin's hunt. This is the Netherlands account of it: In the neighbourhood of the Castle of Wynedal there dwelt, a long time ago, an aged peasant, who had a son that was entirely devoted to the chase. When the old peasant lay on his deathbed, he had his son called to him, for the purpose of giving him a last Christian exhortation. He came not, but whistling to his dogs went out into the thicket. At this the old man was struck with despair, and he cursed his son with the appalling words: 'Hunt, then, for ever!—ay, for ever!' He then turned his head and fell asleep in Christ. From that time the unhappy son has wandered restless about the woods, and the whole neighbourhood re-echoes with the voice of the huntsman and the baying of dogs.

"In Thuringia and elsewhere it is Hakelnberg, or Hackelnbärend, who thus rides, and this is the reason:

"Hakelnberg was a knight, passionately fond of the chase. On his deathbed he would not listen to the priest, nor hearken to his mention of heaven. 'I care not for heaven,' growled he, 'I care only for the hunt!' 'Then hunt until the last day!' exclaimed the priest. And now, through storm and rain, the wild huntsman fleets. A faint barking or yelping in the air announces his approach, a screechowl flies before him, called by the people *Tutösel*. Wanderers who fall in his way throw themselves on their faces, and let him ride over them.

"Near Fontainebleau, Hugh Capet is believed to ride; at Blois, the hunt is called the Chasse Macabée.

"Children who die unbaptized often join the rout. Once two

[1] The German word *wuth* is cognate with the name Odin. Our old English word "wood," equivalent to mad, is similarly related.

children in the Bern Oberland were on a moor together; one slept, the other was awake; suddenly the wild hunt swept by, a voice called, 'Shall we wake the child?' 'No!' answered a second voice, 'it will be with us soon.' The sleeping child died that night. Gervaise of Tilbury says, that in the thirteenth century, by full moon towards evening, the wild hunt was frequently seen in England traversing forest and down. In the twelfth century it was called in England the Herlething; it appeared in the reign of Henry II. and was witnessed by many. The banks of the Wye were the scene of the most frequent chases; at the head of the troop rode the ancient British Herla.

"King Herla had once been to the marriage-feast of a dwarf who lived in a mountain. As he left the bridal hall, the host presented him with horses, dogs, and hunting gear; also with a bloodhound, which was set on the saddlebow before the king, and the troop was bidden not to get off their horses till the dog leaped down.

"On returning to his palace, the king learned that he had been absent for two hundred years, which had passed as one night, whilst he was in the mountain with the dwarf. Some of the retainers jumped off their horses and fell to dust, but the king and the rest ride on till the bloodhound bounds from the saddle, which will be at the Last Day.

"In many parts of France the huntsman is called Harlequin, or Henequin; and I cannot but think that the Italian Harlequin on the stage, who has become a necessary personage in our Christmas pantomime, is the wild huntsman. It is worth observing that the Yule or Christmas, the season of pantomimes, is the time when the wild huntsman rides, and his host is often called the Yule troop.

"I have said that the wild huntsman rides in the woods of Fontainebleau. He is known to have blown his horn loudly, and rushed over the palace with all his hounds, before the assassination of Henry IV.

"On Dartmoor, in Devonshire, the same chase continues; it is called the Wisht hunt, and there are people now living who have witnessed it.

"Now for the names, Wôd, Herod, Hackelnbärend, &c. Perhaps Icelandic will help us to explain the myth. Wôd is evidently Woden; the name is derived from the preterite of a verb, signifying to rage:—

	Infinitive.	*Perfect.*	*Hence the Names.*
Icelandic	Vatha	Oth	Othr, Othinn
Old High German	Watan	Wuot	Wuotan, Wodin
Old Saxon	Wadan	Wôd	Wôd, Wôdan

"Hackelnbärend is the Icelandic Hekluberandi, the mantle-bearer; Herod is derived from Her-rauthi, the red lord. This name is known in the north (Hernath's Saga, *Kormak Saga* and *Fornmana Sögur*, ii. 259). But Dr. Mannhardt derives the name from Hrôths, rumour, fame. The name of Chasse Macabée is given from the allusion to it in the Bible (2 Maccabees, v. 2–4). 'Then it happened, that through all the city, for the space almost of forty days, there were seen horsemen running in the air, in cloth of gold, and armed with lances, like a band of soldiers. And troops of horsemen in array, encountering and running one against another, with shaking of shields, and multitudes of pikes, and drawing of swords, and casting of darts, and glittering of golden ornaments, and harness of all sorts, Wherefore every man prayed that that apparition might turn to good.'

"When men began to name the different operations of nature, they called the storm, from its vehemence, its *rage*, 'the raging' —Wuothan, Wôden; or from its coming at regular *times*, tempestus; or from its *outpourings* λαῖλαψ (cogn. λαπάζω, λαπασσω, λάπτω); or again from its *breathing*, storm (styrma, Icelandic, to puff; sturmen, Teut., to make a noise; thus, Gisah trumbaro inti meniga, sturmenta, *Schilt*, *Thesaur.*, *sub voce*—Christ saw the musicians and the multitude making a noise); our word gale comes from its whistling and *singing*—the root is also preserved in nightingale, the night-singer (gala, Icel. cogn. yell), and from this Odin (the storm) got his name of Galdnir, or Göldnir, and Christmastide was hight Yule; or from its *gushing* forth like a flood we get the word gust (Icel. geysa and gjósa); or, once more, from the storm *cloaking* the sky, covering the fair blue with a mantle of cloud, it got its name of Procella (cogn.

celo, προκαλύπτω, I screen with a cloak); and so we find the wild huntsman, who, you see, is the storm, called Hackelnbärend, from Hekluberandi, the cloak-bearer.

"Now, in the first ages, there was no intention whatever of making the raging storm into a god, nor expressing a divine act in saying that the storm chased the sere leaves; yet, by degrees, the epithet Wôden was given form and figure, and became personified as a deity; then, too, the idea of the storm chasing the leaves became perverted into a myth representing Wôden as pursuing the yellow-haired wood-nymphs."

But to return to auguries and portents. The mention of sneezings in the passage quoted in page 128 from Alcuin is remarkable, for here again a very early superstition holds its ground in the nineteenth century. Nurses in Durham, not to say mothers, still invoke a blessing on children when they sneeze; indeed, some extend the practice to adults. In Germany such is certainly the case. A young cousin of mine, lately at school in the Duchy of Wurtemburg, was greatly astonished to find that a fit of sneezing in which one of the professors indulged was responded to by a cry from all the pupils of "Gesundheit," or "good health;" an attention which he seemed to expect as much as the Emperor Tiberius, who was extremely particular in requiring it from his courtiers. The practice comes from early pagan days. The ancient Greeks, in observing it, claimed to follow the example of Prometheus, who stole celestial fire to animate the beautiful figure he had made of clay; as the fire permeated its frame, the newly-formed creature sneezed,[1] and the delighted Prometheus invoked blessings on it. At any rate the custom was of long standing in Aristotle's days. St. Chrysostom names sneezing among other things of which people made a sign, and St. Eligius warns his flock to take no notice of it. It has, however, been noticed, and good wishes have been uttered on the occasion far and near, in Christendom and heathendom alike —in the remotest parts of Africa, and as far east as Siam. Clarke,

[1] It is remarkable that in the account of the raising of the Shunammite's son by Elijah the lad is said to have given his first signs of renewed vitality by sneezing seven times.—S. B. G

in his *Travels*, refers to the usage as common in Scandinavia; and in the year 1542, when Hernando de Soto, the famous conquistador of Florida, had an interview with the Cacique Guachoya, the following curious incident occurred. In the midst of their conversation the Cacique happened to sneeze; upon this, all his attendants bowed their heads, opened and closed their arms, and making their signs of veneration, saluted their prince with various phrases of the same purport: "May the sun guard you!" "May the sun be with you!" "May the sun shine upon you, defend you, prosper you!" and the like.[1]

I will close this chapter with a verse on sneezing, which is current in Buckinghamshire to this day:—

> Sneeze on Monday, sneeze for danger,
> Sneeze on Tuesday, kiss a stranger,
> Sneeze on Wednesday, get a letter,
> Sneeze on Thursday, something better,
> Sneeze on Friday, sneeze for sorrow,
> Saturday, see your true-love to-morrow.

[1] Theodore Irving's *Conquest of Florida*, quoted in *Notes and Queries*, vol. v. p. 394.

CHAPTER V.

CHARMS AND SPELLS.

For Warts—Ringworm—Whooping-cough—Toothache—Use of South-running water—Weak Eyes—Epilepsy—Silver Rings—Sacrifice of Animals—Erysipelas—Ague—St. Vitus's Dance—Bleeding at the Nose—Goitre—Worms—Cramp—Healing of Wounds—Sympathy—Rheumatism—Foul (in Cattle)—Dean and Chapter—The Minister and the Cow—The Lockerby Penny—The Black Penny of Hume Byers—The Lee Penny—Loch Monar—Burheck's Bone—The Adder's Stone—Irish Stones—Calf hung up in the Chimney—Need-fire—Dartmoor Charms—Knife and Bone—Salt Spell—Passon Harris—Cumbrian Charm—Yorkshire Spell.

N the Borderland, as elsewhere, superstition is apt boldly to intrude into the physician's province, and proffer relief in every ill that flesh is heir to, by means which he does not condescend to recognise—that is, by charms and spells. Curiously enough, the Wilkie MS. is perfectly silent on this head, but, through the kindness of my friends, I have been enabled to collect a good deal of information respecting these byways to health and strength as practised in the northern counties of England. There is scarcely an ailment for which there is not some remedy at hand; for some a large variety are offered. Thus for warts, a schoolboy's first trouble, a Northumbrian lad has the choice of several modes of relief. He may take a large black snail, rub the wart well with it, and throw the poor creature against a thorn hedge, confident that as it perishes on one of the twigs the warts will disappear. This remedy has been practised very widely, and still lingers in Hampshire and in Devonshire, where

the victim slug or snail may yet be seen impaled on its thorn-bush. Again, he may count the number of warts which torment him, put into a small bag an equal number of pebbles, and drop the bag where four roads meet. Whoever picks up the bag will get the warts. This charm is practised, too, in the West of England. It is sometimes varied by the substitution of a cinder applied to the warts and then tied up in paper. A third plan is to steal a piece of raw meat, rub the warts with it, and throw it away. Southey mentions this little charm in "The Doctor." Did he learn it among the hills of Westmoreland? A fourth is to make as many knots in a hair as there are warts on the hands, and throw it away. A fifth is to apply eel's blood. A sixth, to whisper to the wart: "If you do not go away in a week, I'll burn you off with caustic." Again, boys take a new pin, cross the warts with it nine times, and fling it over the left shoulder; or they prick the warts with a number of pins and stick the pins into an ash tree, believing that as the pins become embedded in the growing bark the warts will disappear. Or, again, they rub the warts with the skin from lard, and nail up the skin in the sun. This remedy is a very ancient one. Lord Bacon writes: "The taking away of warts by rubbing them with somewhat that afterwards is put to waste and consume, is a common experiment: and I do apprehend it the rather because of mine own experience. I had from my childhood a wart upon one of my fingers; afterwards when I was about sixteen years old, being then at Paris, there grew upon both my hands a number of warts, at the least a hundred, in a month's space. The English ambassador's lady, who was a woman far from superstitition, told me one day she would help me away with my warts: whereupon she got a piece of lard with the skin on, and rubbed the warts all over with the fat side; and amongst the rest that wart which I had had from childhood; then she nailed the piece of lard, with the fat towards the sun, upon a post of her chamber window, which was to the south. The success was that within five weeks' space all the warts went quite away, and that wart which I had so long endured for company. But at the rest I did little marvel, because they came in a short time and might go away in a short time again; but the going away of that which had stayed so long, doth yet stick with me."[1] But to return to our North-country school-boys. Others cut an apple in two, rub the wart with each part, tie the apple together, and bury it, confident that as the apple decays the warts will disappear. This, too, is done in Devonshire, where they also take a wheat-stalk with as many knots as there are warts on the hand to be dealt with, name over the stalk the person afflicted, and then bury it. As it decays the warts will disappear.

My informant, a clergyman from Devonshire, pleads guilty to having used this charm himself, and by means of it cured his brother of some stubborn warts. He adds: "Gypsies charm away warts. I have known an instance of their curing them in this way. I know, too, a curious case of the kind, substantiated by the master and boys of Marlborough Grammar School. A boy had his hands covered with warts, which disfigured them most unpleasantly. As the lad passed the window of an old woman in the town who dabbled a little in charms and spells, she looked out and called to him to count his warts. He did so, and told her the exact number. 'By such a day,' she said, naming a day within the fortnight, 'they shall all be gone.' She shut the window and the boy passed on, but by the day indicated every one of the warts, which had troubled him for years, was gone." Modern Greeks and Armenians, however, deem it unlucky to count warts, and say that if counted they increase in number.

The vicar of Stamfordham, in Northumberland, tells me of an old man in that village who charmed away that obstinate complaint the ringworm. His patients were obliged to come to him before sunrise, when he used to take some earth from his garden and rub the part affected while repeating certain words not recorded. The secret of this charm might be communicated by a man to a woman or *vice versâ*, but if man told it to man or woman to woman the spell would be broken.

Several cures for whooping-cough are practised in this village, and doubtless in the whole neighbourhood: such as putting a

[1] *Natural History*, cent. x. 997.

trout's head into the mouth of the sufferer, and, as they say, letting the trout breathe into the child's mouth; or making porridge over a stream running from north to south. This last rite was performed not very long ago at a streamlet, near a spring-head, which runs for above fifty yards due south, through a field called Fool or Foul Hoggers, near West Belsay. A girdle was placed over this stream, a fire made upon the girdle, and porridge cooked upon it, and the number of candidates was so great that each patient got but one spoonful as a dose. This story was related to the Rev. J. F. Bigge by one of the recipients; it took place when she was a girl.

The belief in the efficacy of south-running water is apparently of very old date. Mention is made of it in a case of witchcraft recorded in a Book of Depositions from the year 1565 to 1573, extracted in *Depositions and other Ecclesiastical Proceedings from the Courts of Durham*, which forms vol. xxi. of the publications of the Surtees Society. The alleged witch was one Jennet Pereson, who was supposed to use witchcraft in measuring belts to preserve folks from the fairy, and who took at one time 6*d.* at another 3*d.* to heal persons taken with the fairy. Of her a girl named Catherine Fenwicke deposed thus: "She saithe that about two yeres ago, hir cosyn Edward Wyddrington had a child seke, and Jenkyn Pereson wyfe axed of Thomas Blackberd, then this deponent's mother's servaunte, how Byngemen (Benjamin) the child did, and bade the said Blackberd comme and speke with hir. And upon the same this deponent went unto him; and the said Pereson wyfe said the child was taken with the farye, and bade her send 2 for south-rowninge (south-running) water, and theis 2 shull not speak by the waye, and that the child shuld be washed in that water, and dip the shirt in the water, and so hang it upon a hedge all that night, and that on the morrow the shirt should be gone and the child shud recover health: but the shirt was not gone, as she said. And this deponent paid to Pereson's wyfe 3*d.* for her paynes; otherwais she knoweth not whether she is a wytche or not."

Another plan consists in tying round the child's neck a hairy caterpillar in a small bag. As the insect dies the cough vanishes.

And another in carrying the patient through the smoke of a limekiln. Children have lately been brought from some distance to the limekilns at Hawkwell near Stamfordham, and passed backwards and forwards. A variation of this treatment prevails in my native city. Last winter a little girl suffering from whooping-cough was taken for several days successively to the gas-works, to breathe what her mother called "the harmonious air" (I imagine she had some notion of ammonia in her head!) and I learnt from her that several other children were in attendance at the time for the same purpose.

Again, the little sufferer may be passed under the belly of an ass or a piebald pony with good hopes of a cure in consequence. This is carried out more fully at Middlesborough, where a friend of mine lately saw a child passed nine times over the back and under the belly of a donkey, and was informed by the parents that they hoped thus to cure it of whooping-cough.

This piece of superstition does not seem on the decline. In September, 1870, a woman was seen passing a child under a donkey in order to cure it of this complaint on the Sandhill, Newcastle-on-Tyne. She did it three times consecutively. In Worcestershire it is requisite to place the child upon the cross on the donkey's back, and lead the animal nine times round a sign-post. Something like this is done in Sussex, where in addition a silk bag containing hair cut from the cross on the donkey's back is hung round the child's neck. In the instance related to me the hair was sewn up in bags by the clergyman's wife, who also lent the donkey for two sick children to ride on.[1] The mention of a piebald pony is curious, for Abp. Whately observes in his *Miscellaneous Remains* (p. 273), that a man riding on such a horse is supposed, in virtue of his steed, to have the power of prescribing with success for the whooping-cough, and is promptly obeyed; so that when such a person once said to the inquiring

[1] In 1876 my children were suffering from whooping-cough, at Lew Trenchard, Devon. Our coachman's wife cut hair off the cross on an ass's back, and put it in little red silk bags, and begged me to hang these round the necks of the children. I complied with her request, of course, and for six weeks they wore the little bags, to the good woman's great satisfaction.—S. B. G.

parents, "Tie a rope round the child's neck," the rope was tied without the least hesitation.

Of this belief a contributor from Sussex writes, "A man who owned a piebald horse lived a few years ago at Petworth, and he never rode out on it without being accosted by some mother of a family and asked what was the best cure for whooping-cough. Sometimes he would reply, "Ale and butter," sometimes "honey and vinegar;" anything, in short, that occurred to him. But, however strange the advice might be, it was implicitly followed; "and," said Mrs. Cooper, my informant, "the result has always been that the sick children were cured." The same thing is believed in Gloucestershire. And in Suffolk rum and milk were freely administered to a little sufferer by his mother on the same authority.

In the Midland Counties the patient must go about till he finds a married couple whose names are Joseph and Mary, and must then ask them what will cure the cough. Whatever they prescribe will be efficacious. A Staffordshire remedy is to hang an empty glass bottle up the chimney.

From the late Dr. Johnson I learnt of another remedy current in Sunderland: the crown of the head is shaved and the hair hung upon a bush or tree, in firm belief that the birds carrying it away to their nests will carry away the cough along with it. A similar notion lies at the root of a mode of cure practised in Northamptonshire and Devonshire alike. Put a hair of the patient's head between two slices of buttered bread and give it to a dog. The dog will get the cough and the patient lose it, as surely as scarlet fever is transferred from a human being to an ass by mixing some of the hair of the former with the ass's fodder. Another Devonian remedy is to place a smooth mullein leaf under the heel of the left foot.

A Yorkshire lady kindly communicates to me another mode of cure which was practised upon herself and her brother in their childhood, their residence being in the neighbourhood of York. It consisted in eating while fasting, and early in the morning, unleavened bread made by a fasting virgin. They had to eat it in silence. A Dorsetshire remedy for the same complaint is, she informs me, to seat the patient on a donkey with its face towards its tail, and give him a roast mouse to eat. It is hardly necessary to say that he must not know what he is eating. The same practice has prevailed in Leicestershire and Northamptonshire. A Sussex remedy, said to be very efficacious, is to hang round the patient's neck the excrescence often found upon the briar-rose, and locally called Robin redbreast's cushion.

Another mode of cure for this scourge of childhood prevails in the North of Ireland. A lady residing in the county of Derry, my own near relation, tells me that a short time ago her servants summoned her out of doors to see a stranger who was peering about in the yard but would not speak to any of them. She went and found a respectable middle-aged woman, apparently a farmer's wife, who, seeing her to be the mistress of the house, eagerly went up and prayed her to save her child. In answer to the lady's inquiries the woman said, "My child is dying of whooping-cough; the doctors can do nothing more, so I went to a skilled man, and he told me to fill a small bottle with milk and take it to a house I had never visited before. I must cross the water three times to get to it, and must speak no word by the way till I see the master or the master's wife of this strange house. Then I must tell my tale and ask whether they keep a ferret. If they do I must pour the milk in a saucer, see the ferret drink half of it, return the other half into the bottle, take it home and give it to the child. He will drink it and be cured at once. Now I see you have ferrets, let me have one at once. I have been out so many days and have not been able to find a strange house where they kept them." My friend, as kindly as she could, endeavoured to disabuse the poor woman's mind of this strange superstition, but a belief in it was deeply rooted in her mind.

Since I received this narration I find that something similar holds its ground in my own county. The following instance was communicated to me by the late Rev. J. W. Hick, of Byer's Green: "A boy came into my kitchen the other day with a basin containing a gill of new milk, saying his mother hoped I would let my son's white ferret drink half of it, and then he would take the other half home to the bairn to cure its cough. I found the boy had been getting milk in the village for some days, and thus giving our ferret half of it."

For toothache there is remedy also. The inhabitants of Stamfordham, the Northumbrian village named already, have been accustomed to walk to Winter's Gibbet, on Elsdon Moor, some ten or twelve miles off, for a splinter of the wood to cure toothache, as those of Durham and its neighbourhood to "Andrew Miles's Stob," *i. e.* the gibbet near Ferry Hill, on which the wretched boy of that name was executed for the murder of his master's three little children A.D. 1683. Our county historian, Mr. Surtees, relates that a portion of the gibbet still remains, but is in a fair way to be carried off piecemeal for use as a charm against ague and toothache. How in either case the wood was to be applied we are not told, but the remedy sounds almost as ghastly as that resorted to for the same purpose at Tavistock in Devonshire—biting a tooth out of a skull in the churchyard, and keeping it always in the pocket. There is a ferocious character, too, about the Staffordshire mode of cure. It consists in carrying about a paw cut off from a live mole. A mole catcher stated to Mr. B— S— that he had been often asked for moles' paws for this purpose.

Nor is weakness of the eyes uncared for. Where the teasle is grown for use in the manufacture of broad-cloth, a remedy for weak eyes is found in the water which collects in the hollow cups of that plant. Again, I have myself seen and handled a talisman from the Tweedside, which, in the hands of an old witch-woman, was deemed powerful to heal them. It was called a lammer-bead, lammer being the Scotch for amber, from the French "l'ambre;" and wondrous were the cures it wrought, in the witch-woman's hands, when drawn over inflamed eyes or sprained limbs. It is apparently of amber, and probably was dug out of an ancient British grave or barrow. The old woman has recently died, but the bead is cherished in her family as an heirloom.[1]

[1] Compare this with a Devonshire talisman. In the parish of Thrustleton, North Devon, lives an old lady (Miss Soaper), possessed of a bluish-green stone called the "kenning stone," which is much resorted to by people troubled with sore eyes. If the eye be rubbed with the stone, the sufferer is cured.—S. B. G.

Of epilepsy the Rev. George Ornsby writes: "I remember, when a boy, application being made to my father for a halfcrown, to be offered by him the next time he went to Holy Communion at Lanchester church, and asked for again on behalf of the applicant, in order that it might be made into a ring to be worn by an epileptic patient." In Yorkshire the charm is rather different. The ring must be made of a halfcrown from the Offertory collection, but thirty pence are tendered for it, collected from as many different persons. Not ten years ago, the Vicar of Danby, near Whitby, was asked for a halfcrown after Holy Communion, by a farmer, one of his most respectable parishioners, the thirty pence being prepared in exchange. I may, perhaps, fitly add here, that a belief in the efficacy of the sacred elements in the Eucharist, for the cure of bodily disease, is widely spread throughout the North. A clergyman has informed me that he knows of one element having been secreted for this purpose, and that he has found it necessary to watch persons who appeared to have such an intention.

Certain superstitious beliefs are undoubtedly very widely spread. Silver rings made from Offertory money are still worn by epileptic patients in the Forest of Dean, and, with some variation, the charm is in use in Devonshire. A relation of mine in that county writes of it thus: "Twenty years ago, soon after we settled in this place, we were surprised by a visit from a farmer, a respectable-looking man, from Ilsington, a village about six miles off. With a little hesitation he introduced himself, and told us that his son had long been a sufferer from the falling sickness, that medical care had utterly failed, and, as a last resource, he had been advised to collect seven sixpences from seven maidens in seven different parishes, and have them melted down into a ring for the lad to wear. "I can't tell you," he went on, "how many miles I have travelled on this business, for the villages hereabouts are far apart. So hearing a family of ladies had settled here, I thought I would come up the hill to see if one among them had a heart kind enough to help my poor Bill." The appeal was irresistible; the sixpence was given, and the simple-hearted countryman went away full of gratitude, but not daring to utter it for fear of breaking the spell. Some such superstition has doubtless prevailed, more or less, at some period through the length and breadth of England. My kind contributor, Mrs. Lambert, has forwarded to me the following extract from a curious old journal and account-book, kept by a Lincolnshire gentleman, the uncle of her grandfather, in the year 1754:—

	£ s. d.
A poor woman at Barton, who had fits, towards buying a silver ring, 1*d*.	00 00 01

Very different is the treatment of epilepsy in the North of Scotland, as made known to us by Dr. Mitchell, in his deeply interesting paper on the Superstitions of the North-west Highlands and Islands of Scotland.[1] For a cure of this disease, he informs us that a literal downright sacrifice to a nameless but secretly acknowledged power is practised there: "On the spot where the epileptic first falls, a black cock[2] is buried alive, along with a lock of the patient's hair and some parings of his nails. I have seen at least three epileptic idiots for whom this is said to have

[1] Edinburgh: Mill and Co. 1862.

[2] Black cocks have been extensively used in magical incantations and in sacrifices to the devil. A French receipt for raising the devil runs as follows: Take a black cock under your left arm, and go at midnight to where four cross-roads meet. Then cry three times, "Poule noir!" or "Poule noir à vendre!" or else utter "Robert" nine times; and the devil will appear, take the cock, and leave you a handful of money. The famous Jewish banker, Samuel Bernard, who died in 1789, leaving an enormous property, had a favourite black cock, which was regarded by many as uncanny, and as unpleasantly connected with the amassing of his fortune. The bird died a day or two before his master.

Further, a black cock sings in the Scandinavian Niflheim, or "land of gloom," and the signal of the dawn of Ragnarok, "the great day of arousing," is to be the crowing of a gold-coloured cock. Guibert de Nogent writes (*De vita sua*, l. i. c. 26): "A certain clerk lived in the country of Beauvais; he was a scribe, and I knew him. Once he had a conversation with another clerk, a sorcerer, in the castle of Breteuil, who said to him, 'If it were worth my while, I would show you how you might daily make money without having to work for it.' The other having asked him how this could be accomplished, the sorcerer replied, 'You must make a sacrifice to the citizen of hell, that is, the devil.' 'What victim should I have to offer?' asked the other. 'A cock,' replied the sorcerer, 'but it must be a cock born of an egg laid of a Monday in the month of March. After having roasted the cock at the beginning of night, take it with you, still on the spit, and come with me to the nearest fishpond,'" &c.—S. B. G.

been done. A woman who assisted at such a sacrifice minutely described to me the order of procedure." According to Dr. Mitchell this sacrifice dates from remote antiquity, and is very widely spread. The cock, a creature consecrated to Apollo, who in classic mythology was in some measure connected with the healing art, was in Egypt sacrificed to Osiris, whom we may regard as the same divinity under another title. This bird has, throughout the East, been sacrificed during the prevalence of infectious disease, and in Algeria it is still drowned in a sacred well to cure epilepsy and madness. As to the mention of the patient's hair and nails, it is remarkable that the savages of the South Sea Islands at the present day perform most of their cures and incantations with the use of the hair, nails, and fragments left from the meals of the persons to be operated upon.

The purely Celtic superstitions have, indeed, an unmistakably heathen character about them which is almost appalling. Our author transcribes, from the old records of the Presbytery of Dingwall, extracts which show that down to A.D. 1678 bulls were sacrificed on August 25 at the little island of Innis Maree, in Loch Maree, and milk poured forth upon the hills as a libation. Several members of the Mackenzie family were cited that year before the Presbytery, "for sacrificing a bull in an heathenish manner, in the island of Saint Rufus, commonly called Ellan Moury, in Lochew, for the recovery of the health of Cirstane Mackenzie, who was formerly sick and valetudinarie," and it appears that the rite was one frequently performed. The 25th of August is the feast day of St. Malruba, now called Mourie or Maree, the patron saint of the district; but the people of the place often call him the god Mourie, which plainly shows that the worship formerly paid to some local Celtic divinity has been transferred to the saint. When it finally disappeared we are not informed, but a similar observance has been handed on to our own day in the county of Moray. Not fifteen years ago, a herd of cattle in that county being attacked with murrain, one of them was sacrificed by burying alive, as a propitiatory offering for the rest; and I am informed by Professor Marecco that a live ox was burned near Haltwhistle, in Northumberland, only twenty years ago, with the same intent. A similar observance has also lingered on among the Celtic population of Cornwall almost, if not quite, to the present day. In Hunt's *Romances and Drolls of the West of England*, 1st series (page 237), we read: "There can be no doubt but that a belief prevailed until a very recent period, amongst the small farmers in the districts remote from towns in Cornwall, that a living sacrifice appeased the wrath of God. This sacrifice must be by fire; and I have heard it argued that the Bible gave them warranty for this belief." He cites a well-authenticated instance of such a sacrifice in 1800, and adds: "While correcting these sheets I am informed of two recent instances of this superstition. One of them was the sacrifice of a calf by a farmer near Portreath, for the purpose of removing a disease which had long followed his horses and his cows. The other was the burning of a living lamb, to save, as the farmer said, 'his flocks from spells which had been cast on 'em.'"

The same ferocious character may be traced in the remedy for erysipelas, lately practised in the parish of Lochcarron, in the North-west Highlands: it consists in cutting off one-half of the ear of a cat, and letting the blood drop on the part affected.

Of a different character is the following mode of healing practised in the year 1870 in a rural district in ———. I give it in the words of the Vicar of K——: "A respectable farmer's wife told me to-day that she was effectually charming away erysipelas from the foot of her father, a paralysed old man. On my asking the nature of the charm, she allowed herself, after some hesitation, to confide to me the following mystic words: adding (1) 'that they would be powerless, unless communicated by a man to a woman, or *vice versâ*; and (2) that the spell must be administered before bedtime, or immediately on rising.' The words are verbatim as I copied them:

A RECET FOR THE CERONSEPELS.

As our blessed Lady sat at her bowery Dower,
With hir dear Daughter on her nee,
Wating on the snock[1] snouls and the wilfier[2]

[1] Blotches.

[2] Heat-spots, like crown pieces.

> And the Ceronsepel coming in at the town end,
> By the name of the Lord I medisen thee."

After this, who shall congratulate himself on the decay of superstition as a thing of the past?

Ague is a disease which has always been deemed peculiarly open to the influence of charms. It is said in Devonshire that you may give it to your neighbour, by burying under his threshold a bag containing the parings of a dead man's nails, and some of the hairs of his head; your neighbour will be afflicted with ague till the bag is removed. In Somersetshire and the adjoining counties, the patient shuts a large black spider into a box, and leaves it to perish; in Flanders he imprisons it between the two halves of a walnut-shell, and wears it round his neck; in Ireland he swallows it alive. The Sussex peasant imprisons a caterpillar, and carries it about in his pocket, confident that as the poor insect wastes away the ague-fits will diminish in violence. He has the alternative of wearing tansy leaves in his shoes, or eating sage leaves, fasting for nine mornings consecutively. Flemish Folk-Lore enjoins any one who has the ague to go early in the morning to an old willow, make three knots in one of its branches, and say "Good morrow, Old One; I give thee the cold; good morrow, Old One." Compare with this a mode of cure practised in Lincolnshire. It was thus described by one who had suffered from the disease, and tried the remedy in her young days. She was an old woman when her clergyman, the Rev. George Ornsby, wrote it down in her own words. I may add that she has but recently died:

"When I wur a young lass, about eighteen years auld, or thereabouts, I were living sarvant wi' a farmer down i' Marshland (borders of Lincolnshire). While I were there I were sorely 'tacked wi' t'ague, and sorely I shakked wi' it. Howsomever, I got mysen cured, and I'll tell ye how it were. They were on mawing, and I hed to tak t'dinner t'it men 'at were mawing i' t' field. Sae I went wi' t' dinner, and ane o' t' men were an auld man, and while he were sitting o' t' grass eating him dinner, I were stood looking at him, and talking t'him, and shakking all t' time. 'Young woman,' says he, 'ye've gotten t' shakking (a name they commonly give to the ague) very bad.' 'Ay,' says I, 'I have that.' 'Wad ye like to be shot on't?' says he. 'Ay, that wud I,' says I. 'Why then,' says he, 'thou mun do as I tell thee. Dost thou see yon espin-tree t'other side o' the field, ther?" 'Ay, dif I,' says I. 'Why then, ma lass, thou mun gang along to where thou sees ma coat lying yonder, and thou'lt fin' a knife in ma pocket, and thou mun tak t' knife and cut off a long lock o' thy heer (and lang and black ma heer were then, ye may believe me); and then thou mun gan to t' espin-tree, and thou mun tak a greet pin and wrap thy heer around it, and thou mun pin it t'it bark o' t' espin-tree; and while thou'st daeing it thou mun say, 'Espin-tree, espin-tree, I prithee to shak an shiver insted o' me.' An it'll come to pass 'at thou'lt niver hae t' shakking more, if thou nobbut gans straight home, and niver speaks to naebody till thou gets theer.' Sae I did as he tell't me, but if ye believe me I were sorely flayed; but howsomever t'auld man cured me that way, and I've niver had t' shakking fra that day to this."

I suppose that the ceaseless trembling of the aspen-leaves, even when all around is still, is suggestive of mystery; for certain it is that this tree comes forward a good deal in the Folk-Lore of different nations. The Bretons explain the phenomenon by averring that the cross was made from its wood,[1] and that the trembling marks the shuddering of sympathetic horror.[2] The

[1] The *Legenda Aurea* asserts that the cross was made of four kinds of wood: the palm, the cypress, the olive, and the cedar.—S. B. G.

[2] Mrs. Hemans came across this belief in Denbighshire, and therefore called it a Welsh legend, on which De Quincey (in his essay on Modern Superstition) remarks that it is not simply Welsh but European, or, rather, co-extensive with Christendom. I have met with some verses which, after telling how other trees were passed by in the choice of wood for the cross, describes the hewing down of the aspen and the dragging it from the forest to Calvary:—

On the morrow stood she trembling
At the awful weight she bore,
When the sun in midnight blackness
Darkened on Judea's shore.

Still when not a breeze is stirring,
When the mist sleeps on the hill,
And all other trees are moveless,
Stands the aspen trembling still.

Germans have a theory of their own, embodied in a little poem, which may be thus translated:—

Once, as our Saviour walked with men below,
His path of mercy through a forest lay;
And mark how all the drooping branches show,
What homage best a silent tree may pay!

Only the aspen stands erect and free,
Scorning to join that voiceless worship pure;
But see! He casts one look upon the tree,
Struck to the heart she trembles evermore!

If the Cross was thought to be made of aspen-wood, the Crown of Thorns was in the Middle Ages said to have been formed of white-thorn branches, and the white-thorn was reverenced accordingly. Mr. Kelly, however, affirms that this tree possessed a sacred character in ancient heathen days, as having sprung from the lightning, and being, in consequence, scatheless in storms. It was used for marriage torches among the Romans, and wishing-rods were made from it in Germany.[1]

But to return. The Rev. J. Barnby informs me of the following cure for St. Vitus's Dance, the patient having been daughter to his parish clerk, in a Yorkshire village. Medical aid having failed, the parents deemed the girl bewitched, and would not be dissuaded from consulting a wise man, who lived at or near Ripon, thirty miles off. The wise man told them that if the disease came from an evil eye, an evil wish, or an evil prayer, he could remove it, but if by the direct visitation of God he could not. Accordingly he tried the remedies for the first and second causes, but in vain. He then resorted to the proper measures for the third cause, which consisted chiefly in prayers; and the parents aver that at the very time of his praying the girl began to amend, she being ignorant meanwhile of what was going on. The wise man gave her a charm, to wear as a preservative against the person who had bewitched her, and the recovery was perfect.

[1] *Indo-European Folk-Lore*, p. 181.

The following curious history was communicated to me by the Rev. J. F. Bigge. A farmer's wife who lived at Belsay-dean-home, towards the south-west of Northumberland, was suddenly seized with a violent bleeding at the nose; and the usual modes of stopping it having been tried in vain, one of the neighbours, who had clustered round her, said, "Gan away to Michael W——, at Black Heddon, and fetch him quick. He'll ken o' summat to do her good." Now, this Michael W—— was and is esteemed a wizard. The husband went off at once for the wizard, who came with him homewards across the Belsay burn, but stopped at that point, muttered some words, and saying, "She'll be well now," turned and went straight home. However, when the farmer got back, he found his wife as bad as ever; so turning round he retraced his steps to Michael's door, and told him the state of affairs. "It's strange she's no better," said Michael; "but, eh! I've forgotten; there's another burn which runs under the road near the lodge." Back he went, crossed over that burn, repeated his charm, and confidently stated that the patient was better. The farmer went home and found that the bleeding had stopped.

Goitre, the scourge of the Swiss valleys, is sometimes found in our country, and superstition offers a remedy for it, though a revolting one. The late Rev. J. W. Hick, Incumbent of Byer's Green, informed me that on asking a parishioner thus afflicted whether she had tried any measures for curing it, she answered: "No, I have not, though I have been a sufferer eleven years. But a very respectable man told me to-day that it would pass away if I rubbed a dead child's hand nine times across the lump. I've not much faith in it myself, but I've just tried it." Somewhat similar measures were resorted to by another sufferer not many years ago. The body of a suicide who had hanged himself in Hesilden-dene, not far from Hartlepool, was laid in an outhouse, awaiting the coroner's inquest. The wife of a pitman at Castle Eden Colliery, suffering from a wen in the neck, according to advice given her by a "wise woman," went alone and lay all night in the outhouse, with the hand of the corpse on her wen. She had been assured that the hand of a suicide was an infallible cure. The shock to the nervous system from that terrible night was so great that she did not rally for some months, and eventually she died from the wen. This happened about the year 1853, under the cognisance of my informant, the Rev. Canon Tristram. This belief extended, not many years back, as far south as Sussex. "Some five-and-twenty years ago," writes the Sussex lady, to whom I am so much indebted, "there stood a gibbet within sight of the high road that wound up Beeding Hill, our nearest way to Brighton. . . . . Among my nurse's fearful stories about it was one relating to the curing of a wen by the touch of the dead murderer's hand, and she described most graphically the whole frightful scene: how the patient was taken under the gallows in a cart, and was held up in order that she might reach the dead hand, and how she passed it three times over the wen and returned home cured. This practice has happily become extinct with the destruction of the gibbet; but the remedy of a dead hand is still sometimes resorted to. Not very long ago, in the neighbouring village of Storrington, a young woman afflicted with goitre was taken by her friends to the side of an open coffin in order that the hand of the corpse might touch it thrice." It may be observed that they say in North Germany that tetters and warts disappear if touched by the hand of a corpse.

Another friend, the Rev. J. Cundill, tells me how, while he was fishing a short time ago in Stainsby Beck, in Cleveland, a peasant came along the stream in search of a "wick" (*anglicè*, quick or live) trout, to lay on the stomach of one of his children who was much troubled with worms, a trout so applied being a certain cure for that complaint. A different mode of treatment was made known to me, in the autumn of 1863, by the fireside of my landlady's kitchen at Sprouston, by the Tweedside, after a long day's fishing. I was informed that water in which earthworms had been boiled was an infallible remedy in such a case. I ventured to demur to its efficacy, on which the old woman broke out, "Bless me, Mr. Henderson! will ye no believe that? Why, wasn't Jeanie Wright fair brought back frae the grave when she was as gude as dead? A' the doctors had gi'en her up, but there were them about her that wudna knuckle down without ane mair attempt. So they houkit a pint o' worms, and biled them in fresh water, and gaed her the broo to drink. Frae that hour she began to mend, an' now she's as stout a woman as ony, an' ye may see her for yersell an ye gan to the west end o' the town, for there she's livin' yet."

For cramp our Durham remedy is to garter the left leg below the knee. An eel's skin worn about the naked leg is deemed a preventive too, especially by schoolboys. The eel's skin comes to light again in Northumberland. A sprained limb is bound up with it after the "stamp-strainer" has stamped upon it with his foot. This stamp-straining is practised in that county, and is said to have great efficacy. When the first pang is over, they declare that the operation is painless. The Rev. J. F. Bigge has noted down how one W. R., of Belsay Lake House, who was skilled in the art, stamped for a sprain the arm of J. R., and cured her.

But to return to the subject of cramp. Some people lay their shoes across to avert it; others wear a tortoiseshell ring; others place a piece of brimstone in their beds. Coleridge, in his *Table-Talk*,[1] records the approved mode of procedure in Christ's Hospital, which he believed had been in use in the school since its foundation in the reign of Edward VI. A boy when attacked by a fit of cramp would get out of bed, stand firmly on the leg affected, and make the sign of the cross over it, thrice repeating this formula:

> The devil is tying a knot in my leg,
> Matthew, Mark, Luke, and John unloose it, I beg;
> Crosses three we make to ease us,
> Two for the thieves, and one for Christ Jesus.

Archbishop Whately deems it unworthy of observation that the "cramp-bone" of a leg of mutton, *i. e.* the patella or knee-cap, has been in repute as a preservative against this complaint.[2] I learn from the Rev. George Ornsby that rings or handles from

[1] Vol. ii. p. 59.

[2] *Miscellaneous Remains*, p. 274.

coffins, made up and worn as finger-rings, are deemed efficacious in the West Riding. So they are in Cleveland. An old watchmaker at Stokesley, Robert Stevenson by name, used to cure "scores of people" that way. But he confided to his choice friends that he never really made up the coffin-tyre they brought him: he took it from them, but it was less trouble to give them rings which he had by him.

This may, perhaps, be a not unsuitable place for introducing an instance of Devonshire superstition, so peculiar that it seems worthy of record. It was related to my fellow-worker by her friend the late Dr. Walker, of Teignmouth, a physician of some local celebrity. Within the last twenty years he had under his care a poor woman of that place, who was suffering from an extensive sore on the breast. When he visited her one day he was surprised to find the entire surface of the wound strewn over with a gritty substance, and a good deal of inflammation set up in consequence. In some displeasure he asked what they had been putting on, but for a long time he could get no answer beyond "Nothing at all, Sir." The people about were sullen, but the doctor was peremptory; and at last the woman's husband, rolling a mass of stone from under the bed, muttered, in genuine Devonshire phrase, "Nothing but Peter's stone, and here *he* is!" On further inquiry it appeared that, incited by the neighbours, who had declared his wife was not getting well as she should, the poor fellow had walked by night from Teignmouth to Exeter, had flung stones against the figures on the west front of the cathedral (which is called St. Peter's by the common people), had succeeded at last in bringing down the arm of one of them, and had carried it home in triumph. Part of this relic had been pulverised, mixed with lard, and applied to the sore. I have never met with another instance of the kind, but doubtless it is not a solitary one. If the practice was ever general, we need not lay to the charge of Oliver Cromwell's army all the dilapidation of the glorious west front of Exeter Cathedral.

The treatment of surgical cases in the North by no means corresponds to that pursued by the faculty. When a Northumbrian reaper is cut by his sickle, it is not uncommon to clean and polish the sickle. Lately, in the village of Stamfordham, a boy hurt his hand with a rusty nail. The nail was immediately taken to a blacksmith to file off the rust, and was afterwards carefully rubbed every day, before sunrise and after sunset, for a certain time; and thus the injured hand was perfectly healed.

How well this mode of treatment corresponds with that pursued by the Ladye of Buccleugh towards the wounded moss-trooper, William of Deloraine, as recounted by the *Last Minstrel:*

> She drew the splinter from the wound,
> * * * *
> No longer by his couch she stood,
> But she hath ta'en the broken lance,
> And washed it from the clotted gore,
> And salved the splinter o'er and o'er.
> William of Deloraine, in trance,
> Whene'er she turned it round and round,
> Twisted as if she galled his wound.
> * * * *
> Full long she toiled, for she did rue
> Mishap to friend so stout and true!

Probably Sir Walter Scott borrowed it as much from Border practice as from Border records. It seems in early days to have been very prevalent. Lord Bacon avers, "It is constantly received and avouched that the anointing of the weapon that maketh the wound will heal the wound itself," *Nat. Hist.* cent. x. 998. And the "sympathetic powder," which Sir Kenelm Digby prepared "after the Eastern method," was applied by him to the bandages taken from the patient's wound, not to the patient himself. This curious mode of treatment still lingers here and there. Not long ago it was practised on a hayfork in the neighbourhood of Winchester, and I lately heard a reference to it in Devonshire. A young relation of mine, while riding in the green lanes of that county, lamed his pony by its treading on a nail. He took the poor creature to the village blacksmith, who immediately asked for the nail, and, finding it had been left in the road, said, as he shook his head, "Ah, Sir, if you had picked it up and wiped it, and kept it warm and dry in your pocket, there'd have been a better chance for the pony, poor thing!"

The Rev. Hugh Taylor has kindly communicated to me the following story in illustration of this belief: "A cousin of mine, when a boy, ran a pitchfork into his foot. As he was in much pain, in the absence of a surgeon, an old bone-setter named Harry Stephenson was sent for. Old Harry applied some lotion, consisting, as he said, of 'three consarns,' and sent for the pitchfork. He cut a little hair exactly from the back of his patient's head, and very carefully wiped the pitchfork with it; then, instructing him to place the hair under his pillow, he took the fork home and hung it up behind the door. Whether the treatment of the wound or the pitchfork deserve the credit, the patient was certainly quite well in the morning." Again, my Sussex informant writes: "Several instances of this old superstitious remedy have come under my observation, but the most remarkable one occurred in the house of an acquaintance, one of whose men had fallen down upon a sword-stick, and inflicted an injury on his back which confined him to his bed for several days. During the whole of this time the sword-stick was hung up at his bed's head, and polished night and day at stated intervals by a female hand. It was also anxiously examined lest a single spot of rust should be found on it, since that would have foretold the death of the wounded man."

The following communication from Mr. G. M. Tweddell tells of the same belief in Yorkshire: "Some years ago, a relation of mine was crossing the moors from Whitby to his home at Stokesley, when he heard a woman's voice calling out loudly, 'Canny man, canny man, d'ye come frae Stousley?' On his replying that he did, she begged him to take a harrow-tooth to the wise man of that place, as her husband had been injured by it, and she wished the wise man to polish and charm it. He took the harrow-tooth and placed it in his pocket, but, truth to tell, as soon as she was out of sight, he flung it away among the heather. However, when, some time after, he passed that way again, the poor woman recognised him and thanked him heartily for doing her errand, saying that her husband had mended from the day the wise man got the bit of iron."

It is curious to compare with these narrations the mode of

procedure prescribed in North Germany. If a person has wounded himself, let him cut, in an upward direction, a piece from a branch of a fruit-tree, and apply it to the recent wound so that the blood may adhere to it, and then lay it in some part of the house where it is quite dark, when the bleeding will cease. Or, when a limb has been amputated, the charmer takes a twig from a broom, and presses the wound together with it, wraps it in the bloody linen, and lays it in a dry place, saying,—

> The wounds of our Lord Christ
> They are not bound;
> But these wounds they are bound,
> In the name, &c.[1]

My friend the late Canon Humble told me of a strange Irish belief which he learnt from a poor woman whom he visited in sickness, that a fox's tongue was a specific for extracting obstinate thorns. "A neighbour of hers, she said, broke a very long thorn into the ancle joint. The doctor tried poultices and everything he could think of without result. She sent her fox's tongue. It was applied at night, and in the morning the thorn was found lying beside it, having come out in the night. The woman added that it was so valuable that in the long run she lost it through the cupidity of her neighbours."

The sympathy assumed between the cause of an injury and the victim is in Durham held strongly to exist between anyone bitten by a dog and the animal that inflicted the bite. An inhabitant of that city recently informed me, that, having been bitten in the leg by a savage dog about a month before, he took the usual precautions to prevent ultimate injury, but without satisfying his friends, more than twenty of whom had seriously remonstrated with him for not having the dog killed. This alone, they said, would insure his safety; otherwise, should the dog hereafter go mad, even years hence, he would immediately be attacked with hydrophobia. These persons were of the

[1] Thorpe's *Mythology*, vol. iii. p. 162.

middle class, and many of them had received a good education. The same belief, I find, prevails throughout Yorkshire.[1]

It is with reluctance that I approach the next anecdote, for, in truth, I can never recall it without pain; it tells the sad effects of local treatment of rheumatism. About twenty years have passed, since, after a long day's angling in the College (a small river which winds round the northern side of the Cheviot), I entered the thatched cottage of a shepherd, which stood near the confluence of that stream with the Bowmont. The man and his wife bade me welcome, after the kindly hospitable fashion of that district. I grew interested in their conversation, and promised to visit them again when I came next into their neighbourhood. I did so during the following spring, but what was my grief at finding the man, who had seemed to me a model of strength, now a complete wreck; he was lying on a long settle by the fire side, wrapped in blankets. The poor woman, on seeing me, burst into tears, and it was some time before her suffering husband could tell me his tale of too-confiding simplicity.

In the latter part of the preceding autumn, he had caught cold while tending his flock on the mountain side; acute rheumatism had followed; he suffered a good deal, and, being of a sanguine temperament, chafed at the slow but safe steps adopted by the surgeon of the district. As week after week passed by with little amendment, constant pain and impending poverty induced him at last, in an evil hour, to give heed to his neighbours' advice, and resort to "the wise man who lived far over the hills." The wise man declared that the case was desperate, and demanded desperate remedies. As the first step, he directed

[1] Compare this with the Devonshire belief that if anyone is bitten by a viper the viper is to be killed, and the fat applied to the wound as an infallible remedy. I remember a cow being bitten by a viper and cured in this manner. And, again, with the Sussex remedy for hydrophobia: "A slice of the liver of the dog that bit you, boiled and eaten." Again, a relation of the late vicar of Heversham, Westmoreland, informs me that on one occasion, when a beggar had been bitten by a dog at the vicarage, the man came back to the house to ask for some of the animal's hair to put to the wound.—S. B. G.

that the sufferer should be wrapped in a blanket and laid in the sharp running stream which flowed a few yards from the cottage. This was done with full faith, though it was the depth of winter. Never shall I forget the poor victim as he turned his dying eyes on me and said, "Oh, Sir, I laid there twenty minutes, but could endure it no longer; and I just said, 'Lift me out—I'm dead.' They took me out, and I've laid on this settle ever since." A few days more, and the poor fellow had passed (as we humbly trust) to a better life, a sacrifice to one of the most cruel and heartless impostures I ever heard of. Had not death intervened, who can tell what further tortures might not have been in store for him at the hands of this ignorant and presuming monster?

The late Canon Humble communicated to me a story respecting the treatment of rheumatism in Dundee, widely different in its nature and results. A clergyman went to see an old woman of that place, who had not moved off her chair for years in consequence of severe rheumatism, which had settled in the knee. As is common among the poor, she would make the minister feel the painful swelling. I should add that he is a man of great muscular power, and not always aware of the force with which he uses it. He laid his hand on the part affected, and soon left the room to visit at some other tenements in the same row. Before he had gone his rounds in that quarter, he heard some one call him, and turning round, beheld his old friend up and about, loudly proclaiming that the priest's touch had cured her. Certain it is, she has walked ever since.[1]

Different again is the Sussex remedy of placing the bellows in the sufferer's chair that he may lean against them and the rheumatics be charmed away.

Through the kindness of the Rev. T. H. Wilkinson, vicar of Moulsham, Chelmsford, I have been permitted to enrich this volume by extracts from a MS. book of old sayings and customs, jotted down by his father, once an inhabitant of Durham. In it

[1] The present incumbent of B——, Devonshire, has the reputation of performing remarkable cures with his hand. He cured a child at Okehampton of a wen in the throat by touch when the doctor had been of no service.—S. B. G.

is mentioned a very singular specific, which it seems was formerly held in high repute in that city. The remnants of every medicine bottle in the house, the more the better, were poured together, well shaken, and a spoonful of the mixture administered to a patient, of whatever nature his complaint might be. This strange remedy, it appears, was called "Dean and Chapter."

Passing by, for the present, different modes of cure for persons who have been bewitched, we will turn to the diseases of animals, for local superstition does not deem these beneath their notice. A gentleman farmer in the West Riding of Yorkshire, having some cattle affected by the foul or fellen (my informant, the Rev. George Ornsby, forgets which), and having heard that an old man in the neighbourhood, who had long practised farriery, was famous for curing the disease, went to consult him. The case was duly laid before the old man, who replied, with the utmost gravity, that he had cured "a many," and that, as he had given up practice, he did not mind if he told him his secret. His directions were few and simple; the owner of the horse was to go at midnight into his orchard and *grave* a turf at the foot of the largest apple-tree therein, and then hang it carefully on the topmost bough of the tree, all in silence and alone. If this was duly performed, as the turf *muddered* away so would the disease gradually leave the animal. The old farrier added that he had never known this mode of cure to fail.

This remedy is also mentioned in the late Mr. Denham's *Folk-Lore of the North of England*, with one addition—the turf cut must be one on which the beast has trodden with its diseased foot. Many people, he says, use no other remedy for the foul, looking upon this as an infallible cure.

Another tale from Northumberland must be given in the very words in which I received it from the Rev. J. F. Bigge, only premising that a poor woman had a cow, and that the cow was taken ill. The woman described its recovery as follows: "I was advised, ye ken, to gan to the minister, ye ken, and I thought he might do something for her, ye ken; so a gaes to the minister, ye ken, and a sees him about her. 'Well, Sir,' says I, 'the coo's bad; cuddn't ye come and make a prayer o'er her like?'

'Well, Janet,' says he, 'I'll come.' And come he did, ye ken, and laid his hand on her shoulder, ye ken, and said, 'If ye live ye live, and if ye dee ye dee.' Weel, ye ken, she mended fra that hour. Next year who but the minister should be ta'en ill, and I thought I wud just gan and see the auld minister—it was but friendly, ye ken. I fund him in bed, and I gans up till him, and lays my hand on his shoulder, and I says, 'If ye live ye live, and if ye dee ye dee.' So he burst out a-laughing, ye ken, and his throat got better fra that moment, ye ken." It would appear that the poor man was suffering from quinsy, which broke from the effects of laughing.

At Lockerby, in Dumfriesshire, is still preserved a piece of silver called the Lockerby Penny, which is thus used against madness in cattle. It is put in a cleft stick, and a well is stirred round with it, after which the water is bottled off and given to any animal so affected. A few years ago, in a Northumbrian farm, a dog bit an ass, and the ass bit a cow; the penny was sent for, and a deposit of *50l.* actually left till it was restored. The dog was shot, the cuddy died, but the cow was saved through the miraculous virtue of the charm. On the death of the man who thus borrowed the penny, several bottles of water were found among his effects, stored in a cupboard, and labelled "Lockerby Water."

The Lockerby Penny is not, however, without a rival on the Borders. From time out of mind, the family of T. of Hume-byers have possessed a charm called the "Black Penny;" it is said to be somewhat larger than a penny, and is probably a Roman coin or medal. When any cattle are afflicted with madness, the Black Penny is dipped in a well the water of which runs towards the south (this is indispensable); sufficient water is then drawn and given to the animals affected. Popular belief still formally upholds the value of this remedy; but alas! it is lost to the world. A friend of mine informs me that half a generation back the Hume-byers Penny was borrowed by some persons residing in the neighbourhood of Morpeth, and never returned.

Again, there is the Lee Penny, of Saracen origin, which Sir

Walter Scott was pleased to identify with his Talisman. As he informs us in a note to the romance of that name, a complaint was brought early in the seventeenth century before a kirk synod, against Sir James Lockhart, of Lee, for curing "deseasit cattle" by the use of this stone. But the Assembly considered "that in nature thair are many things seen to work strange effects," so they only admonished the Laird of Lee, in the using of the said stone, "to take heid that it be usit hereafter with the least scandle that possibly may be." One of my friends, a descendant of the very Sir Simon Lockhart, of Lee, who accompanied James, the good Lord Douglas, to the Holy Land with the heart of Robert Bruce, and who brought home the Lee Penny, informs me that it is still in existence. She adds that it is to this day in high repute for curing diseases in cattle. Not very long ago it was asked for as far off as Yorkshire for this purpose, and sent there, a deposit of a large sum of money being required for it. Strange to say, the parties having paid this, begged to retain the stone and forfeit the penalty. This was declined, and the stone was returned.

The waters of Loch Monar, a secluded lake near the Strath in the Highlands, claim to have a healing power of a somewhat similar character. Tradition avers that a woman who came from Ross-shire to live at Strathnaver possessed certain holy or charmed pebbles, which, when put into water, imparted to it the power of curing disease. One day, when she was walking out, a man assaulted her, and tried to rob her of the stones; but she escaped from his hands, ran towards the lake, and exclaiming, in Gaelic, "Mo nar shaine," flung the pebbles into the water; the lake was forthwith endowed with marvellous powers of healing, put forth especially on the first Mondays in February, May, August, and November. During February and November, however, it remains unvisited, probably on account of the severity of the season; but the Rev. D. Mackenzie, minister of Farr, attests that in May and August multitudes of people make pilgrimages to the Loch from Sutherland, Caithness, Ross-shire, and even from Inverness and the Orkneys. The votaries must be on the banks of the Loch at midnight, plunge thrice into the waters, drink a small quantity, and throw a coin into the lake as a tribute to its presiding genius. They sedulously get out of sight of the Loch before sunrise, else they consider that their labour will all have been in vain.[1]

Dr. Mitchell states, in the pamphlet already quoted, that in Lewis the diseases of cattle are attributed to the bite of serpents, and that the suffering animals are made to drink water into which charm-stones are put. He does not describe these stones, but says that he has presented two, recently in use, to the Museum of Antiquities; they have been more resorted to for the diseases of cattle than of men. "Burbeck's Bone," however—a tablet of ivory, long preserved in the family of Campbell of Burbeck—was esteemed a sovereign cure for lunacy; when borrowed, a deposit of 100*l.* was exacted, in order to secure its safe return.

Dr. Mitchell's allusion to serpents is curious in connexion with the following anecdote, transmitted to me by the late Canon Humble: "An intelligent sensible labourer, a Scotchman, was attacked by an adder while employed in levelling some ground near Pitlochry, in the county of Perth. Severe pain came on, and a terrible swelling, which grew worse and worse, till a wise woman was summoned with her adder's stone. On her rubbing the place with the stone, the swelling began to subside." The sufferer himself related the story to Canon Humble, saying also that the stone was produced by a number of adders who are accustomed to meet together and manufacture this antidote to their own venom.

Here we come upon a belief which extends, in part at least, even to Syria. In Kelly's *Syria and the Holy Land*, 1844, page 127, we read: "They have a sovereign remedy, which absorbs, as they assert, every particle of venom from the wound. This is a yellowish porous stone, *of a sort rarely met with* (the very words used by the Scottish labourer of his adder-stone). A fragment of such a stone always commands a high price, but, when the piece has acquired a certain reputation by the number of marvellous cures wrought with it, it becomes worth its weight in gold. Madame Catafugo, the wife of a wealthy merchant, is

[1] From *Two Months in the Highlands*, by C. R. Weld.

mistress of one of these stones. It is a small piece of great renown, and cost her 680 piastres, *i. e.* nearly 7*l.* sterling."

In the neighbourhood of Stamfordham, Irish stones are the favourite charms. The Rev. J. F. Bigge informs me that he knows of three, all in high estimation. A servant of Mrs. ——, of Kyloe House, related to him how he was once sent to the house of a neighbouring lady to borrow such a stone. It had been brought from Ireland, and was never permitted to touch English soil. The stone was placed in a basket, carried to a patient with a sore leg, the leg rubbed with it, and the wound healed. People came many miles to be touched with these stones, but they were considered more efficacious in the hands of an Irish person. We learn from Mr. Denham's Notes that Irish stones were at one time common in the Northumbrian dales, and in high repute as a charm to keep frogs, snakes, and other vermin from entering the possessor's house. Evidently the blessing bestowed by St. Patrick upon the Emerald Isle was supposed to dwell in its very stones. Mr. Denham describes one of these stones, which belonged to Mr. Thomas Hedley, son to a gentleman of the same name, at Woolaw, in Redesdale. It was of a pale-blue colour, three-and-a-quarter inches in diameter, and three-quarters of an inch thick. It is not perforated, and therein differs from the holy or self-bored stones of the North.[1]

Nor does it seem that the blessing stopped here. It is believed at Chatton, in Northumberland, that, if a native of Ireland draw a ring round a toad or adder, the creature cannot get out and will die there. My informant, the Rev. Hugh Taylor, adds, "My groom mentions, that, when a dog is bitten by an adder, the only remedy is to wash the place with the milk of an Irish cow."

The late Canon Humble mentioned to me the following mode of

[1] As to this later description of stone, however, we often come across it in the Folk-Lore of the whole of England. Self-bored stones are considered charms against witchcraft, and they keep away nightmare both from man and beast. They are therefore suspended at the head of the bed as well as in stables. I have heard of this belief in the North of England, and also in Suffolk and in Cornwall.

cure resorted to by a woman of that place whose young daughter was afflicted by an eruption which broke out all over the body. It is warranted to have been a *sovereign* remedy. She borrowed a half-sovereign of her neighbour, and after pronouncing the words, "In the name of the Father," &c. she proceeded to rub the child on the chest with the gold. The eruption went in and the child has never since been afflicted.

A curious aid to the rearing of cattle came lately to the knowledge of Mr. George Walker, a gentleman of the city of Durham. During an excursion of a few miles into the country, he observed a sort of rigging attached to the chimney of a farmhouse well known to him, and asked what it meant. The good wife told him that they had experienced great difficulty that year in rearing their calves; the poor little creatures all died off, so they had taken the leg and thigh of one of the dead calves, and hung it in a chimney by a rope, since which they had not lost another calf.[1]

It is strange to find the custom of lighting "need-fires" on the occasion of epidemics among cattle still lingering among us, but so it is. The Vicar of Stamfordham writes thus respecting it: "When the murrain broke out among the cattle about eighteen years ago, this fire was produced by rubbing two pieces of dry wood together, and was carried from place to place all through this district, as a charm against cattle taking the disease. Bonfires were kindled with it, and the cattle driven into the smoke, where they were kept for some time. Many farmers

[1] I have often observed in the Weald of Sussex dead horses or calves hung up by the four legs to the horizontal branch of a tree. It is a sufficiently ghastly sight. A magnificent elm in Westmeston, just under the Ditchling Beacon, was constantly loaded with dead animals: one spring I saw two horses and three calves. I never could ascertain the reason of this strange custom, further than that it was thought lucky for the cattle. I have no doubt myself that they were originally intended as a sacrifice to Odin, hanging being the manner in which offerings were made to him. Odin himself on one occasion is said to have hung between heaven and earth. It was customary for the ancient Germanic tribes to hang upon trees the heads of the horses which had been killed in battle, as offerings to the god. When Cæcina visited the scene of Varus' overthrow (A.D. 15), he saw horses' heads hanging to the trees in the neighbourhood of the altars, where the Roman tribunes and centurions had been slaughtered.—S. B. G.

hereabouts, I am informed, had the need-fire." And Mr. Denham relates that his father, who died A.D. 1843, in his 79th year, perfectly remembered a great number of persons belonging to the upper and middle classes, from his native parish of Bowes, assembling on the banks of the river Greta to work for need-fire, a murrain among cattle being then prevalent in that part of Yorkshire. The fire was produced by the violent and continuous friction of two pieces of wood; and if cattle passed through the smoke thus raised their cure was looked upon as certain.

The North-country proverb, "to work as if working for need-fire," shows how prevalent this custom has been in the border counties as in Scotland. That it is of very ancient origin, and widely spread, Mr. Kelly proves.[1] Originally, the mystic fire was originated by the friction of a wooden axle in the nave of a waggon-wheel, all the fires in the adjacent houses having been previously extinguished. Every household furnished its quota of straw, heath, and brushwood for fuel, laying them down altogether in some part of a narrow lane. When the fire thus made was burned down sufficiently, the cattle were all forcibly driven through it, two or three times, in order, beginning with the swine, and ending with the horses, or *vice versâ*. Then each householder took home an extinguished brand, which, in some districts, was placed in the manger; and, finally, the ashes were scattered to the winds, that their health-giving influence might be spread far and near. It is on record also that a heifer has been sacrificed on this occasion.

In the fire-giving wheel Mr. Kelly sees an emblem of the sun, and in the whole ceremonies of the need-fire the remains of an ancient and solemn religious rite, handed down from early pagan times.

Some of the above narrations make mention of charms uttered over a wounded or diseased part of the body, but I have not been able to learn the words spoken. Two charms have, however, been sent me from the neighbourhood of Dartmoor, in

[1] *Indo-European Tradition* p. 48.

Devonshire, where they are held in high esteem. The first was repeated over the upper nurse in the family of the Rev. George Arden, late Vicar of North Bovey, after a hurt by a fish-bone, in September 1860, and has the credit of curing her:

"When our Lord Jesus Christ was upon earth, He pricked himself with a [*here name the cause of the injury*], and the blood sprang up to heaven. Yet His flesh did neither canker, mould, rot, nor corrupt; no more shall thine. I put my trust in God. In the name," &c.—Say these words thrice, and the Lord's Prayer once.

The second runs thus:—

TO STOP BLEEDING.

Our Saviour Christ was born in Bethlehem,
And was baptized in the river of Jordan;
The waters were mild of mood,
The Child was meek, gentle, and good,
He struck it with a rod and still it stood,
And so shall thy blood stand,
In the name, &c.

Say these words thrice, and the Lord's Prayer once.[1]

[1] I obtained the following charm from the neck of a dead man at Hurstpierpoint, and give it in the original spelling:

"When Jesus Christ came upon the Cross for the redemption of mankind, He shook, and His Rood trembled. The Cheaf Preast said nnto him, Art thou afraid, or as thou an ague? He said unto them, I am not afraid, neither have I an ague, and whosoever Believeth in these words shall not be troubled with anney Feaver or ague. So be it unto yon.

"HENRY WICKHAM."

I have fonnd a very similar charm written out, and dated 1708, in an old copy of Gould's *Poems*, but I do not know to what county it belongs:

"When Jesns went np to the Cross to be crucified, the Jews asked him, saying, Art Thou afraid, or hast Thou the ague? Jesus answered and said, I am not afraid, neither have I the ague. All those which bear the name of Jesus about them shall not be afraid, nor yet have the agne. Amen, sweet Jesus! Amen, sweet Jehovah! Amen, amen!"

Compare with these the following German charms:

A CHARM FOR EASY DELIVERANCE.

Thus said Christ: I received 102 blows on the mouth from the Jews in the Court, and 30 times was I struck in the garden. I was beaten on head, arm, and

It would be interesting to compare these lines with those used under similar circumstances in the North of England. But there is always a difficulty in drawing from a Northern his little superstitions; he is too reticent. One still in use in the Isle of Man was communicated by Mr. Crombie, of Woodville House. It was given him by a farmer named James Kelly, formerly troubled with bleeding at the nose, which he declared he could now always stop at once by its use. He adds that a belief in such charms, and in the power of the Evil eye, is almost universal in that island.

TO STOP BLEEDING.

Three wise men came from the East,
Christ, Peter, and Paul—
Christ bleeding crucified,
Mary on her knees at the foot of the cross.

And Christ drew a cross over the three women that were crossing the waters.

One said, Stop,
One said, Stand,
One said, "I will stop the blood of [here name the person.]
In the name, &c.

---

breast 40 times, on shoulders and legs 30 times; 30 times was my hair plucked, and I sighed 127 times. My beard was pulled 72 times, and I was scourged with 6666 strokes. A thousand blows were rained on my head with the reed, smiting the thorny crown. Seventy-three times was I spat in the face, and I had in my body 5475 wounds. From my body flowed 30,430 blood drops. All who daily say seven Our Fathers and seven Hail Maries, till they have made up the number of my blood drops, shall be relieved of pain in childbirth.

A CHARM AGAINST STORMS.

Jesus, King of Glory, is come in peace + God is made man + Christ is born of a Virgin + Christ has suffered + Christ has been crucified + Christ has died + Christ arose + Christ ascended + Christ conquers and rules + Christ stands between me and thunder and lightning + He passed through them unhurt + Holy God + Holy strong God + Holy undying God + Have mercy!

A CHARM FOR CATTLE.

Our Lord Jesus Christ went over the land
With His staff in His hand,
The Holy Ghost in His mouth,
In the name, &c.

And the sign of the cross is made nine times over the cattle.—S. B. G.

In Shetland the following words are used to heal a burn:—

Here come I to cure a burnt sore,
If the dead knew what the living endure
The burnt sore would burn no more.

The Sussex charm for the same purpose is different and can only be used with good effect on Sunday evening. Mrs. Latham informs me that a poor person of that county who was severely scalded peremptorily refused to see a doctor or try any remedy till Sunday evening came round. She then sent for an old woman who "bowed her head over the wound, crossed two of her fingers over it, and after repeating some words to herself huffed or breathed quickly on it." The words were as follows:

There came two angels from the north,
One was Fire and one was Frost.
Out Fire, in Frost,
In the name of Father, Son, and Holy Ghost.

In the same village dwelt an ancient dame who kept a small day-school, and was also a celebrated compounder of ointments, a collector of simples, and charmer of wounds caused by thorns. She boasted of the numbers who came to her with bad wounds begging her "to say her blessing over them, and a power of people had she cured with it in the course of her life." She had received the charm when a young girl from an old shepherd who lodged with her mother. It ran thus:

Our Saviour Christ was of a virgin born,
And He was crowned with a thorn.
I hope it may not rage or swell,
I trust in God it may do well.

She had inherited from her mother a charm for the bite of a viper, and one for the cure of giddiness in cattle, but had lost them in charming horses. The former she much regretted, it had done "such a power of good." She had tried it once on a lad who had been stung by a viper coiled up in a bird's nest into which he had put his hand. His arm went on to rage and swell till it was as big round as his body, and a power of doctors came to see him but could do him no good. So she watched her opportunity and went upstairs one day when she knew he was quite alone, and said her blessing over his arm, and he was soon quite hearty again. "And since he has been a man grown," she exclaimed in a tone of exultation, "hasn't he been to see me, and didn't he say you're the best friend I ever had, for I shouldn't be here now but for your viper-blessing."

The following charm for toothache is copied verbatim et literatim from the fly-leaf of a common prayer-book lately belonging to a Sussex labourer, and now in the possession of my informant:

As Peter sat weeping on a marvel stone Christ came by and said unto him, Peter, what ailest thou ? Peter answered and said unto him, My Lord and my God, my tooth eaketh. Jesus said unto him, Arise, Peter, and he thou hole, and not the only but all them that carry these lines for my sake shall never have the tooth ake.—Joseph Hylands, his book.

A Bible or prayer-book with this legend written in it is a charm against the toothache in great repute through the south-eastern counties of England and I believe in Ireland.

We may mention here that this sort of charm is much used in Prussia by persons of a higher station in life than those who resort to them in any part of England. A friend informs me that in a family at Berlin, of more than average education and cultivation of mind, she has heard a lady blamed for persisting in consulting the doctor for chronic rheumatism in the arm, instead of having the limb "*besprochen.*"

In the North of England, at any rate, charms and spells are not all spent upon the sick and wounded. Witness the following dialogue between two servant-girls in the city of Durham, communicated to me by the Rev. Canon Raine. One of them, it seems, peeped out of curiosity into the box of her fellow-servant, and was astonished to find there the end of a tallow-candle stuck through and through with pins. "What's that, Molly," said Bessie, "that I see'd i' thy box?" "Oh," said Molly, "it's to bring my sweetheart. Thou see'st, sometimes he's slow a-coming, and if I stick a candle-end full o' pins it always fetches him." A member of the family certifies that John was thus duly fetched from Ferryhill, a distance of six miles, and pretty often too.

It is remarkable that a somewhat similar use of candles and pins prevailed in the remote county of Buckingham at no very distant date. My friend Miss Young has given me the following particulars on the subject, which she learned from her nurse, an old servant still in the family. Buckinghamshire damsels desirous to see their lovers would stick two pins across through the candle they were burning, taking care that the pins passed through the wick. While doing this they recited the following verse:—

It's not this candle alone I stick,
But A. B. heart I mean to prick;
Whether he be asleep or awake,
I'd have him come to me and speak.

By the time the candle burned down to the pins and went out, the lover would be certain to present himself.

The nurse declared that she knew three instances in which this spell had been practised, and that successfully, so far as the appearance of the lover was concerned; but only one of the girls was married to the man in question, and her after-life was most unhappy. Of the other two, one lost her sweetheart immediately. He came to her that evening because he could not help himself, but he came in a very ill-humour, declaring that he knew the girl "had been about some devilment or other." "No tongue," he said, "could tell what she had made him suffer," and he never would have another word to say to her from that hour.[1]

[1] On reading this narration my friend the late Canon Humble wrote: "A servant in our family at Durham used to stick pins in the candle in the same manner, only I believe two persons were to stick each a pin, and if both remained in the wick after the candle had burnt below the place in which they were inserted the lovers of both would appear. If a pin dropped out the lover was faithless. If on sticking in the pin "swealing" began in the candle the lover was sure not to come that night. One person might practise this charm alone, but two were preferred. I do not believe the pins were always crossed. They were sometimes placed on opposite sides but not quite in a line.

It is interesting to compare this history with the following, from the neighbourhood of the Hartz Mountains. In that district girls obtain a glimpse of their future husbands in the following manner. At nightfall a maiden must shut herself up in her sleeping-room, take off all her clothes, and place upon a table, covered with a white cloth, two beakers, the one filled with wine, the other with pure water. She must then repeat the following words:—

My dear St. Andrew,
Let now appear before me
My heart's beloved;
If he shall be rich,
He will pour a cup of wine;
If he shall be poor,
Let him pour a cup of water.

This done, the form of the future husband will appear, and drink from one of the cups. If poor he will sip the water, if rich the wine.

An over-curious maiden once summoned her future husband in this manner. Precisely as the clock struck twelve he appeared, drank from the wine-cup, laid a three-edged dagger on the table and vanished. The girl put the dagger in her trunk. Some years afterwards a man arrived in that place from a distant part of the country, bought property there, saw the girl, and married her. It was the same whose form had appeared to her that night. After a time he chanced to open his wife's trunk, and there beheld the dagger. At the sight of it he became furious. "Thou, then, art the woman," he exclaimed, "who, years ago, forced me to come hither from afar in the night, and it was no dream! Die, therefore!" and with these words he thrust the dagger in her heart.[1]

Something like this is named in the *Universal Fortune Teller*. "Any unmarried woman fasting on Midsummer Eve, and at midnight, spreading a clean cloth with bread, cheese, and ale, and sitting down to the table as if to eat, the street door being

[1] Thorpe's *Mythology*, vol. iii. p. 144.

open, the man whom she is to marry will enter the room, and bowing drink to her; then filling the glass will place it on the table, bow to her again and go out."

A variation of this spell extends into Yorkshire, and was thus practised by a young woman at Wakefield, not long ago. She obtained the blade-bone of a shoulder of mutton, and into its thinnest part drove a new penknife; then she went secretly into the garden, and buried knife and bone together, firmly believing that so long as they were in the ground her betrothed would be in a state of uneasiness, which would gradually increase till he would be compelled to visit her.

In this case his powers of endurance were not very great, for he arrived the next day, saying how wretched and miserable he had been ever since yesterday. The girl was thus firmly convinced of the potency of the spell, but at the same time she had been so uncomfortable while practising it, and her conscience pricked her so sharply for the sufferings she had inflicted on her lover, that she determined never to have recourse to it again.

In *The Universal Fortune Teller* the spell runs thus: "Let any unmarried woman take the blade-bone of a shoulder of lamb, and borrowing a penknife (without saying for what purpose) she must, on going to bed, stick the knife once through the bone every night for nine nights in succession in different places, repeating every night while so doing these words,—

'Tis not this bone I mean to stick,
But my lover's heart I mean to prick;
Wishing him neither rest nor sleep
Till he comes to me to speak.

Accordingly at the end of the nine days, or shortly after, he will come and ask for something to put to a wound inflicted during the time you were charming him." It would answer as well to wrap in paper some of the drug called dragon's blood, and throw it in the fire with these words,—

May he no pleasure or profit see
Till he come back to me.

The "salt spell" of the southern counties is somewhat akin to the foregoing. A pinch of salt must be thrown into the fire on three successive Friday nights while these lines are repeated:

> It is not this salt I wish to burn;
> It is my lover's heart to turn;
> That he may neither rest nor happy be
> Until he comes and speaks to me.

On the last night he will surely appear.

The following account of a spell cast for a similar purpose by a former vicar of Hennock, South Devon, was taken down from the lips of Robert Coombes, an old inhabitant of that place: "Passon Harris was a wonderful man; he knew a thing or two more than other people, and could cast a spell or recover stolen property. Passon Harris had a pretty housemaid, and she had a young man; but he deserted her and went off to North Devon. She cried all the week, and on Saturday evening her master found out what was the matter. 'Never mind, my girl,' said he, 'depend upon it he will be glad to come back to you before to-morrow night.' So Passon Harris laid a spell the next morning. But the young man never came back all day, and good reason too, for when he dressed himself in the morning he put his Common Prayer-book in his pocket ready for church, so the spell could not take effect any way. However at night, when he took off his coat and waistcoat to go to bed, the spell began to work. Off he started just as he was in his shirt-sleeves and ran all night as fast as he could, and when the girl came down in the morning who should she see at the back-door but her young man, panting and breathless." It may be added that the tomb of "Passon Harris" is still to be seen in Hennock churchyard, and that he died about A.D. 1778.

But this is not all. Local superstition interferes in a yet more delicate matter—the quarrels of husband and wife, as the following narration shows, which was communicated to me by the late Mrs. Wilson, of Durham:—

About the year 1825 there lived at Bothal, in Cumberland, a farmer named Billy Briscoe, who had married a widow, and a wealthy one for that part of the country, since her fortune was 60*l*. a year. But, unfortunately, she had also a strong will and high temper; and, as his were of the same character, the match did not prove a happy one. The ill-assorted couple were always quarreling. If anything went amiss in the house or the farm, the husband at once threw the blame on his wife, who for her part was never at a loss for an angry retort.

Things had gone on for some time in this wretched way, when in despair the husband applied to a wise woman for a charm to protect him from his wife's evil eye; and on receipt of a guinea she gave him two pieces of paper, each about three inches square, closely covered with writing, directing that one piece should be sewn inside his waistcoat, and the other fastened within the cupboard door. This was done, and the change that ensued was wonderful. All was peace and goodwill. The cat and dog were transformed into a pair of turtledoves.

But the harmony was, unhappily, of no long duration. After a few months the waistcoat was thoughtlessly popped into the washtub, and the charm disappeared among the suds, while about the same time its counterpart was swept off the cupboard door during a grand house-cleaning. The spell was broken; peace was over, and the home more miserable than ever. The unhappy wife told all this to my informant, who, as a last resource, asked her why she did not go back to her own friends, since she could not make her husband happy. "I've thought of that," she replied, "but my money's here, and how could I go away and leave other people to eat my meat?"

There is some resemblance between this charm and that which figures in a Yorkshire story communicated to me by Mr. Stott, formerly a resident in the county from which he gleaned so much valuable information. It runs thus: Mr. Y—— and his family lived at B——y. He kept a public-house, had a small farm, and went out sometimes as a "Higgler," *i. e.* a vendor of woollen cloth from house to house. On one occasion during the Peninsular war he went out thus with a large quantity of goods but did not return. No tidings respecting him reached his wife, so after a time she sold off everything and went back to her father's house. Her husband's mother, however, persuaded her to visit the Wise-man, see whether he was alive or dead, and if alive procure a charm to bring him back. She went, and learnt that her husband was on *terra firma* and quite well. She then asked for a charm to bring him back. The Wise-man hesitated; he *could* do it, but did not like to meddle with such things. She pressed him, and at last he consented on payment of 10*s*. He gave her three very small notes folded in a peculiar manner and sealed. One was to be buried beside a spring on which the sun shone when it rose, another was to be worn near her person, and the third was to be placed behind the lock of the house-door, between the lock and the door. She disposed of the first and the third as directed, the second she sewed in her stays; but from that day she was most wretched. The thought of having dealings with the devil embittered her waking hours, and at night she was tormented by frightful dreams. At length she could bear it no longer, and rising early one morning before the rest of the family she ripped open her stays, tore out the paper, and threw it into the fire. After this she was more at ease in her mind. A few months later she received a letter sent by her husband to his brother; she answered it, and after another interval he returned back to the great joy of all.

When the good man was settled at home again he asked his wife if she had not been charming him. She was frightened and said "No." He then told her that soon after leaving home with his cloth he had been seized by a press-gang, carried on board ship, and taken to Brazil. There he had fallen sick and been left behind. On his recovery he had obtained a situation as under-master in a school, and been very comfortable until a violent wish to return home took possession of him. He had no rest till, having saved up money enough for his passage, he took ship and landed at Liverpool. There, however, a change came over him without any assignable cause, and within an hour of his arrival he went on board another ship outward bound. The wife found on inquiry that her husband had landed at Liverpool and sailed from it again at the identical time she threw the spell into the fire, but she took good care never to let him know it.

Through the kindness of J. S. Crompton, Esq. I have received the account of a very curious old Yorkshire spell discovered at his patrimonial estate of Eschott, between Leeds and Bradford, on the left or north bank of the river Aire. Mr. Crompton writes, "My father had a tenant at Eschott, by name John Gill, who died an old man. Upon his death an old cow-house was taken down to be replaced by a new one. Over every cow's head in a hole was a paper on which was written:

Omni Spiritones laudent Dominum
habentu Mosa et Prophetores
Excugat Deus et dissipentur
Manu segas amori.
Fiat. Fiat. Fiat.

My brother has the paper now, for only one was perfect. The others had been eaten by mice.

When they were found all the folks said, "Aye, old Gill was always lucky wi' his kye. *He* never lost a beast. It mun be a powerfu' writing."

I add a charm for the bite of a mad dog, communicated to me by the kindness of Professor Marecco :

To be written on an apple or a piece of fine white bread :

O King of Glory, come in peace,
Pax, Max, and Max,
Hax, Max, Adinax, opera chudor.

To be swallowed three mornings fasting.

CHAPTER VI.

WITCHCRAFT.

In the Borders—Drawing Blood above the Mouth—Witchcraft in Durham—In Devonshire—Witches in dairies—Elf-shooting—The Evil Eye—Witchcraft in Sunderland—In the West Riding—Changelings—The Blacksmith's Wife of Yarrowfoot—The Farmer's Wife at Bollebeck—The Miller of Holdean—The Giant of Dalton Mill—Ronaldson of Bowden—The Farmer's Wife of Deloraine—Hair tethers—Maydew—Laird Harry Gilles and the Hare—Tavistock Legend—Yorkshire Tales—Witches disguised as Hares—Toads—Cats—Ducks—Auld Nan Hardwick—Nannie Scott—Auld Betty—The Wise Man o' Stokesley—Willie Dawson—Black Jock—Black Willie—Incantation of a Heart and Pins—Rowan Wood—Pins—Corp-cré—Bible and Key—Riddle and Shears—Billy Pullen—The Hand of Glory—The Lost Watch—Kate Neirns.

ITCHCRAFT undoubtedly lies at the root of many of the practices recorded in the last chapter, but we must now deal with it more directly. The belief in this evil power, once universal throughout Christendom, took deep hold of the Borderland, especially of the Scottish portion of it. It is curious to observe how Mr. Wilkie speaks of witches as though they were recognised members of society, to be met and spoken with every day. Thus, he begins abruptly: "There is some difficulty in knowing how to act when a witch offers to shake hands with us. No doubt there is some risk in accepting the courtesy, since the action entails on us all the ill she may wish us. Still it insures us equally all the good she may wish us, and therefore it seems a pity to refuse one's hand. It is, however, unlucky to be praised by a witch, or indeed to hold any conversation with her, and our only safety against sudden death soon after consists in having the last word. Hence the old phrase, 'Some witch or other has shaken hands wi' him, *and gotten the last word.*' Should you receive money from a witch, put it at once into your mouth, for fear the donor should spirit it away and supply its place with a round stone or slate, which otherwise she might do at pleasure. Accordingly, it may be observed that old people constantly put into their mouths the money which is paid them. If you want to stop a witch lay a straw across her path. She cannot step over it."

To draw blood above the mouth from the person who has caused any witchery is the accredited mode of breaking the spell. The Rev. J. F. Bigge has recorded the following instance: A tenant of Sir Charles Monck, living at Belsay-bankfoot, had so many mischances that he felt no doubt his stock was bewitched. A cow broke her leg, a calf died, a horse got stuck, and so on. Who was his enemy? He settled that it must be a new servant of his own, quite a young lad, and by the advice of a skilled person he determined to break the spell, by drawing blood above the wizard's mouth. So at foddering time the farmer purposely quarrelled with the poor boy about some trifle, and flying upon him, scratched his face and made his nose bleed. The plan was considered quite a success, for no further misfortune happened to the stock. And as recently as December 1868, a family at Framwellgate Moor, near Durham, applied to a police officer for his sanction to assault an old woman of the adjoining hamlet of Pity-me, alleging that she had bewitched their daughter, and that they "only wanted to draw blood from her to break the spell." On this refusal they went to one Jonah Stoker, "a wise man," and induced him to go with them to the old woman's cottage. They seized her arm, wounded it till it bled, and then retired, quite satisfied that the spell was broken. Again, in the year 1870, a man eighty years of age was fined at Barnstaple, in Devonshire, for scratching with a needle the arm of a young girl. He pleaded that he had "suffered affliction" through her for five years, had had four complaints on him at once, had lost 14 canaries, and about 50 goldfinches, and that his neighbours told him this was the only way to break the spell and get out of her power. Another case in point has been communicated to me from Cheriton Bishop, a village near Exeter. Not many years ago a young girl in delicate health was thought to have been bewitched by an old woman of that place, and everybody declared that the only cure for her would be an application of the witch's blood. The girl's friends, therefore, laid wait for the poor old woman, seized her when she was alone and unprotected, scratched her with a nail till the blood flowed, and collected the blood. They carried it home, and smeared the sick girl with it, and the recovery, which took place in course of time, was attributed to this application.[1]

It is sometimes held, however, that no blood flows when a witch is wounded. In a case of assault brought before a bench of magistrates in West Sussex, the defendant declared that she should never have molested the plaintiff had she not found out she was a witch. She had long had her suspicions how it was, and she watched for an opportunity to set her mind at rest. At last she managed to scratch her arm with a crooked pin, and when no blood came then she "up with her fist and gave it her well."

There are still plenty of white witches in Devonshire, but one died a few years ago in the village of Bovey Tracey, who, unless she were greatly maligned, by no means deserved so favourable a designation. She was accused of "overlooking" her neighbours' pigs, so that her son, if ever betrayed into a quarrel with her, used always to say before they parted, "Mother, mother, spare my pigs." This son, a farm-labourer living in the adjoining parish of Hennock, came to a very remarkable end. While leading a cart through the river Teign, he stopped to rest his horse, and while arranging something about the cart it turned over upon him, so that he was imprisoned in the water and drowned. Neighbours remembered that he had "had words" with his mother when last they met, and were not slow in laying his death to her charge. But the most awful story about her is as follows: A man went to her asking for help to get rid of an enemy. The witch gave him a candle, and told him to take it into a secret

[1] Note that this is the case with werewolves also. In Brittany, if the lycanthropist be scratched above the nose, so that three blood-drops are extracted, the charm is broken. In Germany, the werewolf has to be stabbed with knife or pitchfork thrice on the brows before it can be disenchanted.—S. B. G.

place, light it, and watch it while it was burning. So long as it burned, his enemy would be in flames; when it expired he would die, which, said my informant, came to pass.[1]

One of the most common misdeeds of witches is to hinder the dairymaid in butter-making. When the butter fails to come in the churn as usual, it is at once set down as bewitched, and, curiously enough, this belief extends to Devonshire, though butter is there made without churning. A gentleman of that county informs me that he perfectly remembers how, when he was a child, the dairymaid would run to his mother and say, "Please, ma'am, to send somebody else to make the butter; I've been stirring the cream ever so long, and the butter won't come, and I know it's bewitched." In Lancashire the witch is driven away by putting a hot iron into the churn, in Northumberland by popping in a crooked sixpence. In Cleveland they keep her off thus: Before churning take a pinch of salt, and throw it into the churn; then a second pinch, and throw it into the fire, and so on nine times each way. Your butter will then come without fail.

The following story was told to the Rev. George Ornsby by an old man who used to work in the vicarage garden at Fishlake. A few years ago the old man was applied to by the tailor of the neighbouring village for two small branches from a mountain-ash which grew in his garden. Inquiry being made why they were wanted, the applicant stated that his wife had been churning for hours, and yet no butter would come; that they believed the

[1] At Hurstpierpoint there is a cottage in which lived a witch, of whom it was said she could not die till she had sold her secret. Her end was dreadful. She was dying for weeks. At last an old man from Cuckfield workhouse paid a half-penny for the secret, and she died with the money in her hand. A blue flame appeared on the roof as she breathed her last.

The mother of a man whom I know was struck dumb by this witch. The hag was wont to mumble as she walked along, and this woman asked her one day what curses she was muttering, whereupon she was struck dumb. At the end of three months the relations interfered, and persuaded the old woman to take off the charm. So she told her victim to walk to Sevenoaks, in Kent, where at the park-gate she would meet a man in black, and then and there recover her speech, which accordingly came to pass. I have heard this story corroborated by several persons.—S. B. G.

cream was bewitched; and that they had heard say that if the cream was stirred with one twig of mountain-ash, and the cow beaten with the other, the charm would be broken, and the butter come without delay.

On the Borders, if you suspect a woman of bewitching your cow and hindering the butter from coming, order the dairymaid to press down the churn staff to the bottom of the churn, and keep it there. The witch will be drawn to your house, enter it, and sit down without power to rise. Now you are mistress of the occasion. Tax her with her guilt, and make her promise to let your butter come. This done, you may permit her to rise and go away, which she will do at once, making many protestations of innocence. The Irish mode of procedure is somewhat different. In Leinster, when witchcraft is suspected in the dairy the doors are shut, and the plough-irons thrust into the fire and connected with the churns by twigs of the mountain-ash or quickenberry. The witch, wherever she may be, finds her inside tortured by the red-hot coulter, and *must* come and present through the window a bit of bewitched butter, which being thrown into the churn undoes the mischief. In North Germany, again, they believe that if the butter does not come the dairy is bewitched, but the remedy there is to smoke the cows, churns, and pails, in secret and at nightfall. This will bring the witch to the door, asking admittance, but she must on no account be let in.[1]

[1] See Thorpe's *Mythology*, vol. iii. p. 64.—At Bratton-Clovelly, in Devonshire, a farmer's cows were charmed, so that his milk yielded neither cream nor butter. He declared on oath that he had put whole faggots on the fire, but the milk would not boil, a proof that it was bewitched. He therefore resorted to the white witch at Exeter, who advised him to make a fire with sticks gathered out of four parishes, and set the milk upon them. The witch would thereupon look in at the door or window, and the charm would be broken. The man did as ordered, collecting wood from the parishes of Lewtrenchard, Germansweek, Broadwood Wigger, and Thrustleton. As soon as the milk was placed on the fire thus made, it boiled over; the witch peeped in at the window and muttered something, then went away, and the charm was broken.—S. B. G.

It is curious to trace something analogous in Swedish Folk-Lore. If on Midsummer Eve nine kinds of wood are collected, and formed into a pile and kindled, and some witch's butter cast upon it, or if the fire be only beaten with nine kinds of wood, witches are forced to come forward and discover themselves.—Thorpe's *Mythology*, vol. ii. p. 106.

The difficulty in churning milk, however, proceeds most commonly from the cow having been struck by an elf-stone while grazing in the field. However much the poor creature may suffer from the wound, no human eye will see it till she has been rubbed all over with the blue bonnet belonging to the chief of the family, or to some very aged man. The wound, or its scar, if the mischief be of old date, will then be plainly seen.

The elf-stone is described as sharp, and with many corners and points, so that whichever way it falls it inflicts a wound on the animal it touches. Popular belief maintains that the elves received these stones from old fairies, who wore them as breast-pins at the fairy court, and that the old fairies received them in turn from mermaidens. Such is Mr. Wilkie's account of the matter. Doubtless they are really the flint arrow-heads of our ancestors. Mr. Denham maintains this, and describes them as formed of flint about an inch long and half-an-inch broad. Irish peasants wear them about their necks, set in silver, as an amulet against elf-shooting. He adds that the disease, said to be produced by an elf-shot, consists really in an over-distension of the cow's first stomach, from eating to excess clover and grass with the morning dew upon it. Mention is made of elf-stones in the confession of Isabel Gowdie, who was tried for witchcraft in April 1662, and afterwards executed. She declared that the elves formed them from the rough flint, the archfiend himself perfecting or "dighting" them; and she gave the names of many persons whom she and her comrades had slain with them, stating that whoever failed to bless himself when the little whirlwind passed which accompanied their locomotion fell under their power, and they had the right of shooting at him.[1]

Mr. Wilkie records that a few years ago a ploughman in Ettrick Forest was said to have obtained an elf-stone thus. While ploughing a field he heard a whizzing sound in the air, and looking up perceived a stone aimed at one of his horses. He drove on, and it fell by the animal's side. He stopped and picked up the stone, but found its angles so sharp that they cut

[1] Scott's *Demonology*, letter v.

his hand as it lay there, though the weight of the stone was only one ounce troy.

The belief in elf-shooting extends, or has extended, from the Shetland Islands to Cornwall.[1] In the Shetland Islands a charm is repeated over the wounded creature, while a sewing-needle, wrapped in a leaf of the Psalter, is fastened into some part of her hair. Elsewhere the cow was made to drink water in which an elf-stone had been washed. Another mode of relief, called the "ordeal of blood," is prescribed in Scotland. Take some of the injured animal's blood, mix with it a quantity of pins, and boil it, taking care to stir it as soon as it begins to boil. The door must be carefully locked, and everyone kept out of the secret, except the members of the family. Presently the witch who has done the evil will come to the house-door, and ask to be let in; but you must take care not to admit her, for if she enters she will murder everyone concerned in the ordeal. Instead of opening the door, you must insist on her promising to take off the spell, after which you may admit her freely.

The following account of elf-shooting in County Derry is furnished by my Irish correspondent. The elves, she says, are considered bad jealous sprites, who envy the peasants all their little comforts, and especially their rough mountain cows, with the milk and butter they yield. Therefore the elves delight to injure the milch-cows. At dead of night, it is firmly believed, an elf will often enter the byre, and shoot a small sharp stone,

[1] Elf-shooting is, in fact, an ancient Scandinavian superstition. In the *Bandamanna Saga*, an Icelandic account of a law-feud in the eleventh century, occurs the following passage: "That same autumn Hermund gathered a party and went on his way to Borg, intending to burn down the house with Egil in it. Now, as they came out under Valfell, they heard the chime of a bowstring up in the fell; and at the moment Hermund felt ill, and a sharp pain under his arms, so that they had to turn about, and the sickness gained on him. When they reached Thorgautsstede they had to lift him down from his horse, and they sent after the priest at Sidumuli. When he arrived Hermund could not speak, and the priest remained with him. After awhile his lips moved, and the priest bending over him heard him say, 'Two hundred in the gill! Two hundred in the gill!' and so muttering he died."—(*Bandamanna Saga*, p. 41.) This is one of the earliest accounts of an elf-shot I know. In the old Norse ballad of "Sir Olaf," the Ellmaid strikes the hunter on the heart, and he dies.—S. B. G.

rather bigger than a pea, under and behind the left shoulder of the cow. Next morning the owner finds his cow lying down, breathing heavily, with the sweat running down its eyes and nose from pain, and he knows she has been elf-shot. So off he goes to the old man of the county who is skilled in healing cows. The old man comes "travelling" (*i.e.* on foot), it may be, many miles, and all are awed in his presence. He clears the room and makes his preparations. In a new clean pot he boils a pound of gunpowder and a crooked sixpence in a pint of water, and then carries the mixture to the byre and places it before the cow. She drinks it at once, well knowing it is her only hope of cure. The gunpowder immediately blows the elf-stone out again through the hole under the shoulder, and the sixpence, fitting on the heart, covers the wound made there by the stone. The doctor returns into the house with the stone in his hand, to be well praised and well paid. Should any one present indulge in impertinent doubts, he will take care to keep them to himself, for fear his cows should be "blinked" by the skilled man, and everybody believes in blinking. This is casting an evil eye on a cow, a less evil certainly than elf-shooting, because it is a human, not a spirit curse, but still troublesome, since the old man must be summoned and paid. When a cow has been blinked, the old man cures her by muttering a charm over her, making the sign of the cross over her back and down each leg, and pouring down her throat a compound of Epsom-salts, castor-oil, saltpetre, and sulphur. It is useless to argue against these superstitions. If after the skilled man's treatment for elf-shooting the cow *will* not recover, she dies because God chooses it, and not from the elf-shot.

When a child pines or wastes away, the cause is commonly looked for in witchcraft or the "evil eye." At Stamfordham a sickly puny child is set down as "heart-grown" or bewitched, and is treated as follows: Before sunrise it is brought to a blacksmith of the seventh generation, and laid naked on the anvil. The smith raises his hammer as if he were about to strike hot iron, but brings it down gently on the child's body. This is done three times, and the child is sure to thrive from that day.

In the north-west of Scotland, according to Dr. Mitchell, the "gold and silver water" is the accredited cure for a child suffering from an evil eye. A shilling and a sovereign are put into water, which is then sprinkled over the patient in the name of the Trinity.

An eminent physician of Sunderland, the late Dr. Johnson, wrote to me thus respecting a little sufferer of that town, only four days before his own death:—"A case of necromancy occurred in this town some months ago. A child about eighteen months old, belonging to a working man at Southwick, was suffering from the wasting which accompanies scrofulous disease of the bowels, and presented the withered, haggard, weird appearance attributed to those smitten by the witch's evil eye, or to the fairies' changelings. The parents firmly believed the former to be the case, and sought counsel of a reputed charmer (Irish, I think) yet living in this town. He told them to come at midnight with the child to a room occupied by himself; and there a magic circle was drawn, lighted by candles placed round the circumference, and ornamented by chalk drawings, supposed by the people to be representations of planets. He took the naked child in his arms, stepped within the circle, repeated something (alleged to be the Lord's Prayer backwards) three times over, anointed the breast and forehead of the child with some mysterious unguent, waved a magic wand over its head, addressed a sort of patron angel or imp in its behalf, and then pronounced the child whole and taken from under the evil spell. I find that a part of this superstition refers to a belief that the parents of sick children employ the 'evil eye' to transfer the disease from their own to other children, as well as to gratify malice or revenge. Within the last month a charge was seriously preferred against an elderly female for bewitching a child, about whom I was consulted; and there seemed to be a floating belief in the minds of the parents that the 'evil eye' had been cast upon it, not only because the witch had quarrelled with the father, but, because her own pigs being unhealthy, she had sought to transfer the sickness from her own stye to her neighbour's nursery."

In the West Riding of Yorkshire, also, a belief in witchcraft is still current. Mr. Stott who used to reside in that district wrote to me respecting two old men, whom he calls A and B. A maintains B to be a witch, keeps a hedging-bill at the end of his table to kill him should he dare to enter his house, and if he meets him, crosses himself, places the first finger of his right hand under his lower lip, and spits over it as a protection against witchery. One day a small farmer in the neighbourhood was showing off a fine calf to his friends and all were praising it as a great beauty. A was among them, and soon B came up, paused a few minutes, and then passed on. A grew excited and soon said to the others, "Did yo' see him setting his tricks at it? It'll dee." They laughed at him as they dispersed, but the next morning the calf was dead.

Even in our own country it appears that the fairies share with the witches the odium of molesting our nurseries. In the Western Islands idiots are believed to be without doubt changelings of the fairies. Dr. Mitchell knew of three such cases, and he records the only means of redress there open to the parents. If they place the changeling on the beach, below high water-mark, when the tide is out, and pay no heed to its screams, the fairies, rather than suffer their offspring to be drowned by the rising waters, will convey it away and restore the child they had stolen. The sign that this has been effected is the cessation of the child's crying.

Danish Folk Lore speaks much of these changelings, which the underground folk substitute for human children before their baptism if the lights are extinguished in the lying-in chamber. Once, the room being darkened to give the mother sleep, and the baby considered safe in its father's arms, he dozed off for a few minutes, and awoke with a child in each arm and a tall woman standing before him. The woman vanished, and he was left in terrible perplexity as to which was his own child. By the advice of the priest, the two infants were laid upon the ground, and a wild stallion colt led up to them. The creature licked the one but snorted at the other, and strove to kick it, on which a tall woman appeared, caught up the false child, and ran away with it.

Two methods of getting rid of such changelings are recorded. One mother, who was greatly distressed at the loss of her own child and the substitution of a puny wretched creature, at length heated her oven very hot, and having instructed her servant-maid to ask, in a very loud voice, "Why do you heat the oven so hot, mistress?" replied, "I am going to burn my child." The question was asked and answered three times; then she took the changeling and put it on the peel, as if to thrust it in the oven. At this moment the underground woman rushed in, took her child from the peel, and returned the other saying, "There is your child! I have done by it better than you have by mine." And, in fact, the baby was thriving and strong. In the other case a pudding was made of pork, with skin, hair, and all mixed up in it. When this was placed before the changeling he exclaimed, as he eyed it for some time, "Pudding with hide and pudding with hair, pudding with eyes and pudding with bones in it. Thrice have I seen a young wood spring up on Tiis lake, but never before did I see such a pudding! The fiend will stay here no longer." So saying, he turned and went away. In each instance it is specified that the change of children was effected because the parents had been negligent in bringing the infants to be christened.[1]

But to return to witchcraft proper. The Wilkie MS. is rich in stories on this subject. Witches and warlocks, it seems, are wont to kindle their fires in deep glens, on the wildest moors, or on the tops of high hills, there to dance or sit in ring, and hold converse while they devour the plunder of rifled graves with the choicest wines from their neighbours' cellars. Now, some years back, the blacksmith of Yarrowfoot had for apprentices two brothers, both steady lads, and, when bound to him, fine healthy fellows. After a few months, however, the younger of the two began to grow pale and lean, lose his appetite, and show other marks of declining health. His brother, much concerned, often questioned him as to what ailed him, but to no purpose. At last, however, the poor lad burst into an agony of tears, and con-

[1] Thorpe's *Mythology*, vol. ii. pp. 174-176.

fessed that he was quite worn-out, and should soon be brought to the grave by the ill-usage of his mistress, who was in truth a witch, though none suspected it. "Every night," he sobbed out, "she comes to my bedside, puts a magic bridle on me, and changes me into a horse. Then seated on my back, she urges me on for many a mile to the wild moors, where she and I know not what other vile creatures hold their hideous feasts. There she keeps me all night, and at early morning I carry her home. She takes off my bridle, and there I am, but so weary I can ill stand. And thus I pass my nights while you are soundly sleeping."

The elder brother at once declared he would take his chance of a night among the witches, so he put the younger one in his own place next the wall, and lay awake himself till the usual time of the witch-woman's arrival. She came, bridle in hand, and flinging it over the elder brother's head, up sprang a fine hunting horse. The lady leaped on his back, and started for the trysting-place, which on this occasion, as it chanced, was the cellar of a neighbouring laird.

While she and the rest of the vile crew were regaling themselves with claret and sack, the hunter, who was left in a spare stall of the stable, rubbed and rubbed his head against the wall till he loosened the bridle, and finally got it off, on which he recovered his human form. Holding the bridle firmly in his hand he concealed himself at the back of the stall till his mistress came within reach, when in an instant he flung the magic bridle over her head, and behold, a fine grey mare! He mounted her and dashed off, riding through hedge and ditch, till, looking down, he perceived she had lost a shoe from one of her forefeet. He took her to the first smithy that was open, had the shoe replaced, and a new one put on the other forefoot, and then rode her up and down a ploughed field till she was nearly worn out. At last he took her home, and pulled the bridle off just in time for her to creep into bed before her husband awoke, and got up for his day's work.

The honest blacksmith arose, little thinking what had been going on all night; but his wife complained of being very ill, almost dying, and begged him to send for a doctor. He accordingly aroused his apprentices; the elder one went out, and soon returned with one whom he had chanced to meet already abroad. The doctor wished to feel his patient's pulse, but she resolutely hid her hands, and refused to show them. The village Esculapius was perplexed; but the husband, impatient at her obstinacy, pulled off the bed-clothes, and found, to his horror, that horse-shoes were tightly nailed to both hands! On further examination, her sides appeared galled with kicks, the same that the apprentice had given her during his ride up and down the ploughed field.

The brothers now came forward, and related all that had passed. On the following day the witch was tried by the magistrates of Selkirk, and condemned to be burned to death on a stone at the Bullsheugh, a sentence which was promptly carried into effect. It is added that the younger apprentice was at last restored to health by eating butter made from the milk of cows fed in kirkyards, a sovereign remedy for consumption brought on through being witch-ridden.

A similar story is told in Iceland, and is translated in Powell's *Legends of Iceland*, p. 85. It appears again in Belgium in the following form:—

At a large farm at Bollebeck dwelt a serving-man, who, though well-fed by the farmer's wife, grew thinner every day. His fellow-servants questioned him as to the cause of this, but to no purpose, till at length the shepherd, who was his best friend, drew the following history from him. His mistress was a witch, and used to come at night to his bedside, throw a bridle over his head, turn him into a horse, and ride him about all night. "This seems to me incredible," said the shepherd, "but let me lie in thy bed to-night. I should like to try the thing for once." The man agreed, and the shepherd took his place in bed.

About ten o'clock the farmer's wife came in, and would have thrown the bridle over him, but the shepherd was too quick for her. He snatched it out of her hand, and threw it over her, on which she was instantly changed into a mare. He rode her about the fields all night, then brought her home and led her to the farmer, saying, "Master, there is a horsedealer in the village who wishes to dispose of this mare, and asks five hundred francs for her." "She is sold," said the farmer; "come in, and I will give thee the money." "But it's without the bridle," said the shepherd; "he requires to have that back." "Be it so," said the farmer, laughing; "the bargain stands." He counted out the money, the shepherd pocketed it, then took off the bridle, and, behold! the woman stood before them. Shedding bitter tears, she fell at her husband's feet, promising never again to do the like, on which he forgave her, and the shepherd was bound over to secrecy.[1]

The Danish version of the story is slightly different. In it the victim is unconscious of the cause of his declining health and strength till he learns it from a Wise-man. The Wise-man gave him an ointment to apply to his head at night. The tingling it produced awoke him, and, lo! he was standing outside Tron Church in Norway with a bridle in his hand. He had torn it off in scratching his head. He flung the bridle over his mistress, transformed her into a handsome mare, rode her home, had four new shoes fastened on her, sold her to her husband; and taking off the bridle, there she stood, with horseshoes nailed to her hands and feet. The indignant husband turned her out-of-doors, and she never was able to free herself from the iron shoes.[2]

On these histories my friend, the late Canon Humble, wrote: "The stories of witches turning men and women into horses must have originated in places where the real animal was not to be had without the transformation. Witches were dreadful harriers of horseflesh, but were effectually excluded from stables which were guarded by a horseshoe nailed upon or over the door. This is still very commonly done in the county of Durham as elsewhere. I remember a farmer there telling me how one of his horses had been more than once ridden by the witches, and he had found it in the morning bathed in sweat, but he had nailed a horseshoe over the stable door, and hung some broom over the rack, and the horse had not been used by the witches

[1] Thorpe's *Mythology*, vol. iii. p. 235. [2] Ibid. vol. ii. p. 190.

since." In the North, a self-bored stone is also considered efficacious against witchcraft and the evil eye; in the South, a copy of the apocryphal letter of our Lord to Abgarus, King of Edessa, is often pasted on cottage walls for the same purpose. I have in my possession one of these letters, curiously interpolated with Methodist hymns, which was bought from a pedlar by the Rector of Kenn, near Exeter.

The next story relates how the miller of Holdean Mill, Berwickshire, received some uncannie visitants, of what precise nature it does not specify. It is to this effect. While the miller was drying a melder of oats belonging to a neighbouring farmer, tired with the fatigues of the day, he threw himself down upon some straw in the kiln-barn, and soon fell fast asleep. After a time he was awakened by a confused noise, as if the killogee were full of people, all speaking together; on which he pulled aside the straw from the banks of the kiln, and, looking down, observed a number of feet and legs paddling among the ashes, as if enjoying the warmth from the scarcely-extinguished fires. As he listened, he distinctly heard the words, "What think ye o' my feeties?"—a second voice answering, "An' what think ye o' mine?" Nothing daunted, though much astonished, the stout-hearted miller took up his "beer-mell," a large wooden hammer, and threw it down among them, so that the ashes flew about; while he cried out with a loud voice, "What think ye o' my meikle mell amang a' thae legs o' yourn?" A hideous rout at once emerged from the kiln amid yells and cries, which passed into wild laughter; and finally these words reached the miller's ears, sung in a mocking tone:

> Mount and fly for Rhymer's tower,
> Ha, ha, ha, ha!
> The pawky miller hath beguiled us,
> Or we wud hae stown his luck
> For this seven years to come,
> And mickle water wud hae run
> While the miller slept.

I may perhaps be permitted here to introduce a very remarkable story communicated to me by Mr. Baring Gould. He remarks that it is the only trace of the Polyphemus myth he has met with in England, but that it has its correlatives in Scandinavian sagas: "At Dalton, near Thirsk, in Yorkshire, is a mill. It has quite recently been rebuilt, but when I was at Dalton, six years ago, the old building stood. In front of the house was a long mound, which went by the name of 'the giant's grave,' and in the mill was shown a long blade of iron something like a scythe-blade, but not curved, which was said to have been the giant's knife. A curious story was told of this knife. There lived a giant at this mill, and he ground men's bones to make his bread. One day he captured a lad on Pilmoor, and instead of grinding him in the mill he kept him as his servant and never let him get away. Jack served the giant many years and never was allowed a holiday. At last he could bear it no longer. Topcliffe fair was coming on, and the lad entreated that he might be allowed to go there to see the lasses and buy some spice. The giant surlily refused leave; Jack resolved to take it.

"The day was hot, and after dinner the giant lay down in the mill with his head on a sack and dozed. He had been eating in the mill and had laid down a great loaf of bone bread by his side, and the knife was in his hand, but his fingers relaxed their hold of it in sleep. Jack seized the moment, drew the knife away, and holding it with both his hands drove the blade into the single eye of the giant, who woke with a howl of agony, and starting up barred the door. Jack was again in difficulties, but he soon found a way out of them. The giant had a favourite dog which had also been sleeping when his master was blinded. Jack killed the dog, skinned it, and throwing the hide over his back ran on all fours barking between the legs of the giant, and so escaped."[1]

A man named Ronaldson, who lived in the village of Bowden, is reported to have had frequent encounters with the witches of

[1] Mr. Baring Gould writes further on this subject:

"I do not think the miller's story at Dalton is taken bodily from the Polyphemus tale, for there are extraordinary similarities to it to be found all over the

that place. Among these we find the following. One morning at sunrise, while he was tying his garter with one foot against a low dyke, he was startled by feeling something like a rope of straw passed between his legs, and himself borne swiftly away upon it to a small brook at the foot of the southernmost hill of Eildon. Hearing a hoarse smothered laugh, he perceived he was in the power of witches or sprites; and when he came to a ford called the Brig-o'-stanes, feeling his foot touch a large stone, he exclaimed, "I' the name o' the Lord, ye'se get me no farther!" At that moment the rope broke, the air rang as with the laughter of a thousand voices; and as he kept his footing on the stone he heard a muttered cry, "Ah, we've lost the coof!"

This adventure reminds us how the ancestor of the Duffus family was spirited away from his paternal fields, and found the next day at Paris, in the royal cellars, with a silver cup in his hand. In that case, however, the victim provoked his destiny by echoing the cry of "Horse and hattock," the elfin signal for mounting and riding off.

world. See on this *Die Saga von Polyphem*, by W. Grimm, Berlin, 1857. He quotes:

"1. Homer's story of Polyphemus.

"2. A story of French origin in Dolopathes, written between 1184-1212.

"3. A story told by the Oghuzi, a Tatar-Turkish race, in Diez's *Des Neuentdeckte oghuzische Cyklop veglichen mit dem kanerischen*, 1815.

"4. The third adventure of Sinbad.

"5. A Serb tale.

"6. A Roumanian tale, collected in Transylvania by Obert.

"7. An Esthonian tale.

"8. A Finn tale.

"9. A tale picked up by Castrin, the ethnologist of the northern tribes of Russia, in Karelia.

"10. A Folk-tale in the Harz Mountains.

"11. A Norse tale in Asbjörnsen.

"The preservation of the knife and the mound called the Giant's Grave show that the myth I heard is not of recent origin at Dalton. I am told by one of our servants from Dalton that at the rebuilding of the farm the mound was opened, and a stone coffin found in it; but whether this be a kistvaen or a mediæval sarcophagus I cannot tell. I wrote some time ago to my successor at Dalton for another version of the Giant story to compare it with mine, and about the stone coffin, but have had no answer."

Witchcraft is not named in the next story, but we can scarcely be wrong in assuming it to be the agent at work in it. We must premise that it was, perhaps still is, customary in the Lowlands of Scotland, as in other secluded districts, for tailors to leave their workshops and go into the farmhouses of the neighbourhood to work by the day. The farmer's wife of Deloraine thus engaged a tailor with his workmen and apprentices for the day, begging them to come in good time in the morning. They did so, and partook of the family breakfast of porridge and milk. During the meal, one of the apprentices observed that the milk-jug was almost empty, on which the mistress slipt out of the back-door with a basin in her hand to get a fresh supply. The lad's curiosity was roused, for he had heard there was no more milk in the house; so he crept after her, hid himself behind the door, and saw her turn a pin in the wall, on which a stream of pure milk flowed into the basin. She twirled the pin, and the milk stopped. Coming back she presented the tailors with the bowl of milk, and they gladly washed down the rest of their porridge with it.

About noon, while our tailors were busily engaged with the gudeman's wardrobe, one of them complained of thirst, and wished for a bowl of milk like the morning's. "Is that a'?" said the apprentice; "ye'se get that." The mistress was out of the way, so he left his work, found his way to the spot he had marked in the morning, twirled the pin, and quickly filled a basin. But, alas! he could not then stay the stream. Twist the pin as he would, the milk still continued to flow. He called the other lads, and implored them to come and help him; but they could only bring such tubs and buckets as they found in the kitchen, and these were soon filled. When the confusion was at its height, the mistress appeared among them, looking as black as thunder; while she called out, in a mocking voice, "A' ye loons! ye hae drawn a' the milk fra every coo between the head o' Yarrow an' the foot o't. This day ne'er a coo will gie her maister a drop o' milk, though he war gawing to starve." The tailors slunk away abashed, and from that day forward the wives of Deloraine have fed their tailors on nothing but chappit 'taties and kale.[1]

Now it is clear from Kelly's *Indo-European Traditions* (p. 229) that witchcraft has always been potent in the dairy, and he accounts for it thus. The Aryan idea that the rain-clouds were the cows of heaven has been well preserved among the northern nations. As Indra used to milk the cloud cows, and churn the milk lakes and fountains with his thunderbolt, so did Thor with his axe. Our ancestors' mythology has passed into our own superstitions, and so witches of modern days draw milk from the handle of an axe stuck in a doorpost. We find a close parallel to the history of the wife of Deloraine at Caseburg, in North Germany, where a farmer who got no milk from his dairy put the affair in the hands of a Wise-man, and the Wise-man detected the culprit in the person of a neighbour's wife. This woman had stuck a broom-handle into the wall of her own cow-house which was nearest to the farmer's dairy. To the handle she had hung a bucket, and was milking the broom-stick, which under her hands yielded a plentiful flow of milk.[2]

The rich dairies of Holland and Belgium are not proof against such evil practices, but the means of redress are well known. They are as follows: "When a sorceress has by her arts milked all the milk from a cow, the cow must soon afterwards be milked again. Let the milk thus obtained be set on the fire and made warm, and then beat with a stick till not a drop remains in the vessel. Any milk that flows over on the ground may also be beaten, for the more beating there is the better, since every stroke given to the milk is received by the sorceress on her back

[1] In the curious old volume of sermons in German, by Dr. Johann Geyler von Keysersperg, entitled *Die Emeis*, preached in Strasbourg A.D. 1508, and published in 1517, is a quaint woodcut of witches milking pump-handles, and a sermon on the iniquity of those old hags who thus drain their neighbours' cows of milk. That portion of the wife of Deloraine's story concerning the inability of the apprentice to stop the milk closely resembles the German tale of the magician and his pupil, which Göthe has versified in his *Zauberlehrling*.—S. B. G.

[2] Thorpe's *Mythology*, vol. iii. p. 78.

from the devil. It has often happened here (at Laeken) that sorceresses have been confined to their beds for a week or more from having been thus beaten." One Dutch farmer, however, preferred actually administering the blows himself: so, observing one day an old witch go with a knife outside his dairy, turn to the moon, and repeat these words—

Here cut I a chip
In the dairy's wall,
And another thereto,
So take I the milk from this cow,

he took a thick rope, ran up to the sorceress and beat her well, exclaiming:

Here strike I a stroke,
And another as I may,
And a third thereto,
So keep I the milk with the cow,

And this, it is quaintly said, was the best method he could adopt.[1]

In Motherwell's preface to Henderson's *Proverbs* is a narration which bears on this part of our subject. The author says, that the ancestor of one of his neighbours in a Scottish village, going out early with his gun one May-day or Beltane morning, found two carlines long suspected of witchcraft, but never yet caught in the fact, brushing the May-dew off the pasture-fields with a long hair tether. They fled at his approach, leaving behind them the instrument of their incantations, which he gathered up, carried home, and placed above the cow-house door. The consequence was that the next milking-time the dairy-maids could not find pails to hold the supply of milk which the cows yielded till the old gentleman took down and burnt the tether, after which things went on in the usual way. There were a number of knots in the rope, every one of which went off like a pistol-shot when it was burnt. Mr. Kelly tells of a hair rope too, which in the hands of a witch would yield milk, adding that it must be made from the

[1] Thorpe's *Mythology*, vol. iii. p. 277.

hair of different cows with a knot for each cow. The following verse was sung by way of incantation on such occasions:

Meare's milk, and deer's milk,
And every beast that bears milk,
Between St. Johnston and Dundee,
Come a' to me, come a' to me!

As to May-dew, the belief in its virtue extends to Germany, or rather seems to have originated there, since the Germans have an appellation for a witch derived from her connection with it. They call her Daustriker (*Thaustreicher*), dew-striker or scraper. When the dew falls on May-morning, they say, it will be a good butter year. On such a morning a witch went out before sunrise into her neighbours' fields, took up the dew with large linen cloths, then wrung them out, and so collected the dew in a vessel. Afterwards, every time she wished to make butter, she took a spoonful of it and poured it into the churn, saying at the same time "From every house a spoonful." By this process she took on each occasion so much butter from every one of the owners of the fields she had swept of dew. Once, however, she left her man to churn, but not rightly understanding the matter he blundered out, "From every house a bushelful;" so when he churned there came so much butter that it spread out over the whole house, and people were at a loss what to do with it.[1]

The German witches seem, indeed, to have been unremitting in their attacks on the dairy. "There was a time when they were particularly mischievous. It was then indispensable for every housewife to have a handle made of the wood of the service (quicken) tree to her churn, else she could never be sure of getting butter. A man one morning early, on his way from Jägerup to Hadersleben, heard, as he passed by Woiensgaard, that they were churning in the yard; but at the same time he observed that a woman whom he knew was standing by the side of a running brook, and churning with a stick in the water. On that same day he saw her again selling a large lump of butter in

[1] Thorpe's *Mythology*, vol. iii. p. 681.

Hadersleben. In the evening, as he again passed by Woiens, they were still churning; whereupon he went to the house, and assured them that their labour was all in vain, for the butter was already sold at Hadersleben."[1]

According to Mr. Kelly, the proper antidote for witchcraft in the dairy is a twig of rowan-tree, bound with scarlet thread, or a stalk of clover with four leaves, laid in the byre. To discover the witch the gudeman's breeks must be put upon the horns of the cow, one leg upon each horn, when she, being let loose, will for certain run straight to the door of the guilty person.

He also mentions a Scottish witch having been seen milking the cows in the shape of a hare, a creature closely connected with witchcraft since the memorable day when the prince of necromancers, Sir Michael Scott, was turned into a hare by the witch of Falsehope, and hunted by his own hounds, till, jaded and discomfited, he was fain to take refuge in his own jawhole (*anglicè*, common sewer); while to this day in Sussex the right forefoot of a hare is worn in the pocket as a spell against rheumatism, and in Warwickshire round the neck for cramp. In fact, the cat and the hare are the two creatures into which the witch ever transforms herself when in extremity. Stories of cunning hares, defying all hounds and hunters, are to be found in every part of the country. That recorded by Mr. Wilkie is as follows:—

"The Laird (Harry Gilles) of Littledean was extremely fond of hunting. One day, as his dogs were chasing a hare, they suddenly stopped, and gave up the pursuit, which enraged him so much that he swore the animal they had been hunting must be one of the witches of Maxton. No sooner had he uttered the word than hares appeared all round him, so close that they even sprang over the saddle before his eyes, but still none of his hounds would give them chase. In a fit of anger, he jumped off his horse and killed the dogs on the spot, all but one large black hound, who at that moment turned to pursue the largest hare. Remounting his horse, he followed the chase, and saw the black

[1] Thorpe's *Mythology*, vol. iii. p. 25.

hound turn the hare and drive it directly towards him. The hare made a spring as if to clear his horse's neck, but the laird dexterously caught hold of one of her forepaws, drew out his hunting-knife, and cut it off; after which the hares, which had been so numerous, all disappeared. Next morning Laird Harry heard that a woman of Maxton had lost her arm in some unaccountable manner; so he went straight to her house, pulled out the hare's foot (which had changed in his pocket to a woman's hand and arm), and applied it to the stump. It fitted exactly. She confessed her crime, and was drowned for witchcraft the same day in the well by the young men of Maxton."[1]

Mrs. Bray, Southey's correspondent, tells of a similar legend in Devonshire. The grandson of a witch at Tavistock was accustomed to get sixpences from a neighbouring huntsman by pointing out where he would find a hare, which hare was never caught. At last, measures were taken for a very vigorous chase; the hare was hard pressed, and the boy was heard crying out, "Run, granny—run for your life!" She did so, and just gained her cottage, where her pursuers found her panting and bleeding. The culprits were let off that time with a whipping, but the old woman is said to have ended her days at the stake, a convicted witch.[2]

Through the Dales of Yorkshire we find hares still in the same mysterious relationship with witches. The Rev. J. C. Atkinson informs me, that, a new plantation having been made near Eskdale, great havoc was committed among the freshly-planted trees by hares. Many of these depredators were shot, but one hare seemed to bid defiance to shot and snare alike, and returned to the charge night after night. By the advice of a Wise-man (I believe of the Wise-man of Stokesley, of whom more

[1] Nyauld (*De la Lycanthropie*, Paris, 1615) relates (p. 52) that in a village of Switzerland, near Lucerne, a peasant was once attacked by a wolf while he was hewing timber. He defended himself, and smote off the foreleg of the beast. The moment that the blood began to flow the creature's foot changed, and he recognised in his enemy a woman of his acquaintance without her arm. She was burnt alive.—S. B. G.

[2] *Traditions of Devon*, vol. ii. p. 277.

will be said bye-and-bye), recourse was had to silver shot, which was obtained by cutting up some small silver coin. The hare came again as usual, and was shot with the silver charge. At that moment an old lady who lived at some distance, but had always been considered somewhat uncannie, was busy tamming, *i. e.* roughly carding wool for her spinning. She suddenly flung up both hands, gave a wild shriek, and crying out, "They have shot my familiar spirit," fell down and died.

In another dale, he adds, higher up the course of the Esk, was a hare which baffled all the greyhounds that were slipped at her. They seemed to have no more chance with her than if they were coursing the wind. There was at the time a noted witch residing near, and her advice was asked about this wonderful hare. She seemed to have little to say about it, however, only she thought they had better let it be, and above all they must take care how they slipped a black dog at it. Nevertheless, either from recklessness or from distrust of their adviser, the party did go out coursing soon after with a black dog. The dog was slipped, and they perceived at once that the hare was at a disadvantage. She made as soon as possible for a stone wall, and attempted to escape through a "smout" or sheephole at the bottom. Just as she reached it, the hound threw himself upon her and caught her in the haunch, but was unable to hold her. She got through, and was seen no more. The sportsmen, either in bravado or from terror of the consequences, went straight to the house of the witch to say what had happened. They found her in bed, hurt, she said, by a fall; but the wound looked very much as if it had been produced by the teeth of a dog, and it was on a part of the person corresponding to that by which the hare had been seized before their eyes by the black hound. Whether this Wise-woman recovered from the effects of the accident, I do not know; but the Guisborough witch, who died within the memory of man, was lame for several years, in consequence, it was said, of a bite she received from a dog while slipping through the keyhole of her own door in the shape of a hare.

The witch of Hawkwell, in Northumberland, transformed herself into a hare, and the trap-hole in a door through which she used to bolt in when hard-pressed is still pointed out. A whinstone on the roadside is also shown, melted down from her sitting on it. This witch used to show her spite by disabling the young horses that fed behind her cottage.

In Sir Walter Scott's *Demonology and Witchcraft* (letter ix.) we find the disenchanting rhyme, by virtue of which disguised witches could recover their own shape, if only they gained time to repeat it:

> Hare, hare, God send thee care!
> I am in a hare's likeness now,
> But I shall be a woman even now.
> Hare, hare, God send thee care!

It appears that in Orissa the witch transforms herself at will into a tiger; in Cumberland one is said to have been hunted in the form of a red-deer stag; but the hare is her most common disguise in the northern counties of Europe, and hence no doubt the wide-spread belief that it is unlucky for a hare to cross one's path—a belief which dates at least from the Roman occupancy of our country, and which prevails, or has prevailed, in every part of Great Britain, as well as in many other countries. The Thugs in India are guided in their murderous expeditions by this omen. Lord Lindsay's Arab attendants looked out for disasters after a hare had crossed their road in the desert. The Laplanders regard the creatures with terror, as do the Namaquas, a South African tribe. Thorpe's *Mythology*[1] contains many instances of witches disguised as hares; but there is one in which, by a strange caprice, the sorceress assumed the form of a toad. About the end of the sixteenth century, in West Flanders, a peasant had a quarrel with the landlady of the alehouse in which he had been drinking, and at last she uttered this threat: "For this thou shalt not reach home to-night, or I'll never come back." Accordingly, when he went down to the canal and got into his boat, he could not, with all his exertions, move it from the shore. In his distress, seeing some soldiers pass by, he asked them to come and help him. They did so, but all in vain, till one of

[1] Vol. iii. p. 278.

them proposed to throw out some things which were lying at the bottom of the boat. When these things were moved the men discovered beneath them an enormous toad, with eyes like glowing coals. One of the soldiers stabbed the reptile through the body and flung it into the water, and the others gave it several wounds in the belly as it floated by the boat upon its back. They tried again to move the boat, and now it glided off without any further trouble, which so pleased the peasant that he took the soldiers back to the alehouse for some refreshment. Asking for the landlady, they were told she was at the point of death, from wounds which could not be accounted for, since she had not left the house. On inquiry the wounds exactly corresponded with those inflicted on the reptile.

I do not know any other instance in which the witch assumes this loathsome shape, but the toad has ever figured largely in the records of superstition. It stands first in the horrible list of ingredients which the witches in Macbeth throw into their cauldron:

> Toad, that under coldest stone,
> Days and nights hast thirty-one
> Sweltered venom sleeping got,
> Boil thou first i' the charmed pot!

Thus, again, in Middleton's play, "The Witch," in the charm song, beginning

> Black spirits and white, red spirits and grey,
> Mingle, mingle, mingle, you that mingle may;

after the blood of a bat and libbard's bane, comes—

> The juice of toad, the oil of adder,
> Those will make the younker madder.

And, to descend to modern times, the hind-leg of a toad dried, placed in a silk bag, and worn round the neck, is in Devonshire the common charm for the king's evil. White witches and Wisemen supply these charms for a fee of five shillings. Sometimes they cut from the living reptile the part analogous to that in which the patient is suffering, bury the rest of the creature, wrap that part in parchment, and tie it round the patient's neck. A cure for rheumatism in the same county runs thus: burn a toad to powder, tie the dust in silk, and wear it round the throat.

In my next story the cat is the creature simulated by the witch. Like the hare, the cat mixes largely in the mythology of all the Indo-European nations. If the goddess Freya was attended by hares as her train-bearers and light-bearers, her chariot was drawn by cats. Perhaps these cats were originally tigers; perhaps Pussy's gleaming eyes and weatherwise propensities procured her the distinction, by inspiring belief in her supernatural powers. To this day she supplies portents as to the weather,—

If the cat washes her face o'er the ear
'Tis a sign that the weather 'll be fine and clear;

and also as to the health of the family she lives with. In Sussex the most petted cat is turned at once out of doors if she sneezes, for should she stay and sneeze three times in the house everybody within its walls will have colds and coughs. In the present instance, an honest Yorkshireman, who bred pigs, often lost the young ones. He therefore applied to the wise man of Stokesley, who told him they were bewitched by an old woman who lived near, and to whom my informant had long paid parochial relief. The owner of the pigs called to mind that he had often seen a cat, a suspicious-looking creature, prowling about his yard, and he jumped to the conclusion that this was the old woman in disguise. He watched for her, armed with a poker, and when she made her appearance flung it at her with all his force. The cat disappeared, and curiously enough, the poor old woman in question, while getting up that same night, fell and broke her leg. This of course was conclusive; the man was fully assured that the poker he had hurled at the cat had broken the witch's leg, and that the witch was no other than the old woman lying lamed in her bed.[1]

[1] Sprenger relates that a labourer was attacked by three young ladies in the form of cats, and that they were wounded by him. They were found bleeding in their beds next morning. Bodin says that in Vernon, about the year 1566, the

The connection between cats and witches is notorious enough, dating at least from the classic story of Galanthis being turned into a cat, and becoming, through the compassion of Hecate, her priestess. The picture of a witch is incomplete without her cat, by rights a black one. It is curious that at Scarborough, a few years back, sailors' wives liked to keep black cats in their homes, to insure the safety of their husbands at sea. This gave black cats such a value that no one else could keep them; they were always stolen. Mr. Denham has recorded some curious old north-country rhymes on the subject:

> Whenever the cat o' the house is black,
> The lasses o' lovers will have no lack.
>
> Kiss the black cat,
> An' 'twill make ye fat;
> Kiss the white ane,
> 'T will make ye lean.

In accordance with the former, an old north-country woman said lately to a lady, "It's na wonder Jock ——'s lasses marry off so fast, ye ken what a braw black cat they've got." Naturally enough it is considered extremely lucky for a cat of this kind to come of her own accord and take up her residence in any house. During the November of 1867, in Pennsylvania, a woman was publicly accused of witchcraft for administering three drops of a black cat's blood to a child as a remedy for croup. She admitted the fact, but denied that witchcraft had anything to do with it, and twenty witnesses were called to prove its success. Professor Marreco, of Newcastle, has communicated to me the following curious

witches and warlocks gathered in great multitudes under the shape of cats. Four or five men were attacked in a lone place by a number of these beasts. The men stood their ground with the utmost bravery, succeeded in slaying one puss, and wounded many others. Next day a number of wounded women were found in the town, and they gave the judge an accurate account of all the circumstances connected with their wounding.—*The Book of Werewolves*, by the Rev. S. Baring Gould, pp. 64, 65.

Note that in England the extirpation of wolves under the Anglo-Saxon kings has altered the ancient legends of lycanthropy into stories of transformation into hares and cats.—S. B. G.

belief: "He who ties up a black cat with ninety-nine knots, and sells it for a hare at the church door to the Evil One, will receive a large sum of money for it. But he had better get well away before the cat is let out of the bag. Also that throwing a cat overboard at sea is held by sailors to provoke a storm."

We find witches and cats constantly together in the Folk-Lore of the northern countries of Europe. Thus in Eiderstedt, in North Germany, there was a miller who was unfortunate enough to have his mill burned down every Christmas Eve. At last a courageous servant undertook to keep watch in the mill on the fatal night. The fellow kindled a fire and made himself a good kettleful of porridge, which he stirred with a large ladle, while an old sabre lay beside him. Ere long a troop of cats entered the mill, and he heard one say in a low tone to another, "Mousekin! go and sit by Hanskin!"—on which a beautiful milk-white cat came creeping softly to him, and placed herself by his side. In a moment, taking a ladleful of the scalding porridge, he dashed it in her face, then seizing the sabre cut off one of her paws. On this the cats all disappeared, and instead of the paw appeared a delicate woman's hand, with a gold ring on one of the fingers bearing his master's cypher. Next morning the miller's wife lay in bed and would not rise. "Give me thy hand, wife," quoth the miller. She refused, but she could not long conceal the mutilated arm, and at last was burnt for a witch.[1]

There is a Norwegian tradition to the same effect, in which a courageous tailor discovers the witchery. Again, in the Netherlands, one bold Jan undertakes to lodge for a night in the haunted castle of Erendegen, provided only he is supplied with every requisite for frying pancakes. He makes a fire and begins his work, when a black cat walks in, sits down before the fire, and asks Jan what he is about. "I am making pancakes, my little friend," answered the hero. Seven more cats entered, put the same question, and are answered as before. Then, taking each other's paw, they danced round and round, on which Jan

[1] Thorpe's *Mythology*, vol. iii. p. 26.

flings over them the scalding batter from his frying-pan, and they all vanish. The next day it was reported in the village that the shoemaker's wife was burnt all over the body. Bold Jan showed no surprise at the news; he simply said that the castle would not be haunted any longer, which proved to be the case.

"Auld Betty," the Halifax witch, of whom more will be said by-and-bye, once figured in the form of a cat. Mr. J. Stott writes of her: "An old man, whom I knew well in my boyhood, was said to have undertaken the dangerous task of catching this witch, and drawing blood from her. Armed with a three-pronged table-fork he stationed himself beside the fire in the house where she was suspected of doing mischief, by night, in the form of a black cat. According to the directions for the capture of witches, he had a cake baking before the fire. All at once he perceived a large black cat sitting by the hearth washing its face, though he had not seen or heard it come in. 'Cake burns,' cried the cat. 'Turn it, then,' replied the witch-catcher. 'Cake burns,' it said once more, and he made the same answer again and again. The man had been especially charged on no account to mention any holy name while watching the doings of the cat, and for a long time he remembered this, but, worn out with watching, and worried by the continued cry of 'Cake burns,' he lost his temper, and answered with an imprecation. Instantly the cat sprang up the chimney, and after it scrambled the witch-catcher, trying to pierce it with the three-pronged fork. This he accomplished at last, but not till he had been dreadfully scratched by his antagonist. The next morning the old witch-woman was ill in bed, and continued there for some days, but the person who had been witched was relieved."

Cats and witches appear together in the following Flemish story, from Thorpe's *Mythology* (vol. iii. p. 237): "An inhabitant of Stockham, on the birth of a child, goes to acquaint his mother, and is astonished to find her already informed of the event, though she lived half-an-hour's walk from the village, and no communication had taken place to his knowledge. On his way home the good man was molested by a perpetually increasing swarm of cats, who crowded about him and obstructed his way.

He struck at them with his stick, but to no purpose; they tore away his silver shoe-buckles, and pushed him into the brook which ran by the wayside. On returning home, wet and tired, the man sent for the priest and related his adventure. 'Ah,' said the priest, 'I see what it all is! Now, if you desire your wife and child to do well, take care you give nothing out of your house to any one who may beg at the door.' The man promised to follow the advice, and for three weeks he did so, though the door was besieged by beggars of every age and condition. At last an old woman came and begged for a crust of bread so piteously that the wife, who was sitting up with the child in her lap, entreated her husband to give it. Against his better judgment he did so. Instantly the infant was torn from its mother's arms by invisible hands, and dashed against the ceiling, while the mother received a shock which threw her into a corner. The priest was summoned, but could do nothing: he pronounced mother and child past human help, and, in fact, both died within a week."

Danish witches transform themselves also into ducks. A huntsman, who used to pass the farm of Baller, near Ostrel, observed, constantly in its neighbourhood, a hare or a wild duck, neither of which could he ever hit. At last he shot at the duck with a silver button from his jacket, and wounded it, but it fluttered away into the poultry-house. Going into the farm-kitchen to ask for the duck, he saw by the chimney an ugly old woman, with one shoe off, and blood streaming from her leg. She said she had fallen down and hurt herself, but the huntsman felt convinced he saw before him the witch he had shot, and hurried away with the utmost speed.[1]

But to return to our own country. The Rev. J. C. Atkinson has communicated to me some particulars respecting a noted Yorkshire witch, Nan Hardwick by name, which were communicated to him by an inhabitant of Danby. This old woman lived in one of the two lonely old-fashioned huts known as the Spital Houses, and her habit was to go every evening, a little before

[1] Thorpe's *Mythology*, vol. ii. p. 191.

dark, and squat among the whins on a bank at Oenthorpe, about a mile from her dwelling, for what purpose or in what form the narrator sayeth not. This being her custom, the young men of the neighbourhood took up the practice of collecting the five or six hounds kept in that part of the parish, with any other dogs they could get hold of, to hunt, as they said, "Auld Nan Hardwick." When they found her, as they usually did, a loud clatter was heard along the "causey," or ancient horse-road leading to Oenthorpe in the direction of the witch's residence, all the dogs following in full cry.[1]

One evening, a little before the usual hour of the hunt, a young man, who was generally foremost in the sport, happened to be on the "causey" in question, and to see Nan Hardwick on the way to her place of evening resort. "She was all black that night," said the narrator (one William Agur, a parishioner of Danby), "for ye ken she wur not alla's the same to look at;" and the young man (T. P. by name) determined that she should not pass him on the "causey." So he drew himself up, set

[1] It is curious to compare this account with that Ben Jonson gives in his "Sad Shepherd" of "the sport of witch-hunting, or starting of a hag":

Within a gloomy dingle she doth dwell,
Down in a pit o'ergrown with brakes and briars,
Close by the ruins of a shaken abbey,
Torn with an earthquake down unto the ground,
'Mongst graves and grots, near an old charnelhouse.
* * * * *
All this I know, and I will find her for you,
And show you her sitting in her form. I'll lay
My hand upon her; make her throw her scut
Along her back, when she doth start before us.
But you must give her law, and you shall see her
Make twenty leaps and doubles, cross the paths,
And then squat down before us.

John. Crafty Croan,
I long to be at the sport and to report it.

Scarlet. We'll make this hunting of the witch as famous
As any other blast of venery.

his legs close together, and squared himself so as to engross the entire width of the narrow gangway. The witch neither paused nor turned aside; she came straight on, and in a minute was in the rear of him who would have arrested her. How she went by him T. P. could never tell; he was still occupying the whole space, his legs were still close to each other, but, as far as he could pronounce upon any part of the transaction, he felt convinced she had passed between them.

The young man's father, himself a T. P. too, was about this time overseer of the poor, and, witch though she was, "Au'd Nan Hardwick" applied for parish relief. T. P. stoutly refused her, though he knew well that he thus exposed himself to her illwill. One day, as he was leaving Castleton, he met her coming in the other direction. Between them ran the small stream which drains Danby Dale, now crossed by a "draught bridge," then merely by a single stone, just wide enough to let one person pass at a time, with a "hemmel" or handrail on either side. T. P. reached the bridge first. No feeling of courtesy prompted him to stand back till Auld Nan had crossed, so he marched sturdily on to the middle of the bridge, but no further. There her power fell upon him, and he stood like a statue, unable to move hand or foot, till she was pleased to set him free—which was not at once.

This anecdote is curious as an instance of a spell undestroyed by the power of running water, and I believe a solitary one. The law is all but absolute, that every species of magic and witchcraft is annihilated by the force of a running stream. The Goblin Page might counterfeit the heir of Buccleugh:

> But as a shallow brook they crossed,
> The elf, amid the running stream,
> His figure changed, like form in dream,
> And fled, and shouted, "Lost! lost! lost!"

And young Keeldar, in the ballad, secure in the protection of his plume of holly and rowan, and his casque of sand formed by the mermaid, yet fell a prey to Lord Soulis and the Liddesdale Lancers when they forced him into the brook, for—

> No spell can stay the living tide,
> Or charm the rushing stream.

Auld Nan Hardwick possessed, it would seem, a power beyond that of the mighty masters of the black art in old days. By the kindness of the late Dr. Johnson, of Sunderland, we may compare this Cleveland witch with her Northumbrian sister Nannie Scott. He wrote thus to me respecting her: "We find in this locality many relics of the Scandinavian superstitions, varied and mixed up with modern customs and phraseology. The old keelmen (once numbering some hundreds) on the Weir were brimful of superstitious stories and legends, and their nightly rambles on shore and river, to seek their vessels and bring them in with the tide, are very amusing. I remember, when a boy, a witch who resided in a little hovel near us, in Sunderland, and with whom I was on most friendly terms, much to the disgust of my nurse. She told fortunes by the stars, practised the black art, and sold a compound of treacle, &c. called by us "claggum." Her hatred was considered certain death; and children once under her protection were sure to be lucky in life. She had a black cat and a black dog, both unmitigated savages and thieves (the poor animals, being deemed familiars, were pelted and persecuted into ferocity), and few women were more coaxed and toadied than was Nannie Scott. She prayed for fair winds for sailors' wives; she sold love-charms to bring together sulking sweethearts; and she did all with an air of solemn strong-mindedness that bore down any approach to discredit. She lived to a very great age, and died about twenty years ago."

From Mr. J. Stott, of Perth, formerly a schoolmaster in the West Riding of Yorkshire, I learn some particulars respecting "Auld Betty," who was held in great dread as a witch not many years ago by both old and young for miles round in a neighbourhood not twenty miles from Halifax. My informant knew her well in his youth, and tells me that she gained her livelihood by the sale of linsey-woolsey. The following story exhibits her in the darkest point of view:

The infant daughter of Mr. and Mrs. H. though born a healthy child, began to pine away, and no medical advice was of any avail. The mother thought she was bewitched, and proposed to her husband that they should consult a certain doctor in a neighbouring village, a Quaker, who was noted for his skill in such cases. Mr. H. only laughed at his wife's superstition, but the child wasting away more and more he yielded at last, and all set out one morning to consult the Quaker.

On arriving at his house Mrs. H. took the little girl in, while her husband went with the horse to the inn. She told the doctor's assistant that her child was unwell and that she wished to know what was the matter, but she made no mention of her own suspicions. After examining the child and putting several questions, he went into another room to his master, returned to ask some more questions, and went back again. Then the old gentleman came out and examined the child, and just as Mr. H. came in from the inn he said, "The child's hurt done," *i. e.* bewitched. "Do yo think soa," asked the father. "Nay," replied the doctor, "om sure soa." "Can ye do hur onny good?" pursued he. "If thah'll do as oi tell thee oi can," was the reply. "Oh, we'll do onny thing yo tell uz," exclaimed the mother. "Well, then," said the doctor, "tack some o'thyh hair, the wife's, and some o't child's; some o'th cuttings o'th finger-nails and toe-nails, and some o'th water o' all yo three, put all into this bottle, cork it up an' seal it, an' when thah rakes t' fire at neet put t'bottle under t' stuff thah rakes wi'; an' tack care thah dosen't let a woman come into t' house first in t' morning." With these directions Mr. and Mrs. H. returned home.

The child having for some time been very restless at night, the parents had brought their bed downstairs and placed it in a corner near the fire, which they kept in by "raking" for the sake of their little patient. So this night, after fulfilling so far the doctor's directions, they went to bed as usual, but to their surprise the little one was soon fast asleep and did not once disturb them in the night. About 4 o'clock in the morning the father rose, broke up the fire, and carried the ashes into the back yard to riddle them. He had scarcely got into the yard when Mrs. H. heard some one coming toward the house, which stood only a few yards from the high road. She jumped out of bed, and looking out of window was horrified to see Auld Betty the witch coming towards the house. Seizing the poker she rushed forwards just in time to stop her on the doorstep. "Does yor husband want t'as riddle mending?" cried the old woman. "Ha! burn yo," replied Mrs. H.; "if yo' come here oi'll kill yo." Upon this Auld Betty took to her heels, and from that hour the little girl began to improve, till she became as fine a child as any in the neighbourhood.

Auld Nan Hardwick, Nannie Scott, and Auld Betty, however, sink into insignificance before the Wise-man of Stokesley, long the oracle of South Durham, as well as of Cleveland. The name of this personage was Wrightson. He flourished at Stokesley above fifty years ago; and such ascendancy did he obtain in the neighbourhood that he was at once resorted to in cases of sickness, distress, or loss of property, and this not by the lower orders alone. His private character appears to have been very bad; still his influence in Stokesley was so great that he was constantly in request as godfather to the children of the place; and on these occasions he used to attend church in a scarlet coat, a long white waistcoat and full-starched shirt-frill, crimson knee-breeches, and white stockings. Several stories of his craft have come to me from an eye-witness, having been repeated to the Rev. J. C. Atkinson by an old man turned eighty-two, but in possession of his faculties, and of entire respectability of character. Wrightson used always to say that he had no power or knowledge beyond other men except when fasting, that he owed his power to his being a seventh son of a seventh daughter, and that he was quite unable to transmit them to his own son. The following stories, if true, go towards proving him to have been a natural clairvoyant:—

Years ago, when the old man at Danby was young, a relation of his had a cow, which fell ill of a disease which baffled the skill of every cow-leech in the neighbourhood. Our informant was therefore mounted on a horse belonging to his relative, and despatched to Stokesley to consult the Wise-man. On opening his door—before he had time to explain his errand—the wizard said, "I know what has brought you here; you have come about a cow, and, if I cannot tell you as much about the creature as you can tell me, it is not likely I can help you." Then he proceeded to describe the cow, her colour and appearance, her symptoms—constant restlessness, and uneasy movements, and a peculiar sound she uttered; also her position in the cow-house. "The door opened," he said, "right upon her rump." The Wise-man went on to specify her disease, and added that nothing could save her. She died accordingly, and a post-mortem examination verified all that "auld Wrightson" had said. But what seems to have struck our informant most was the wizard's remark on the careful way in which he had ridden the horse which brought him to Stokesley—the sender had no son who would have been so careful with the beast.

Another instance of the Wise-man's strange foreknowledge was as follows. Some pitmen were working together at the Try-up-Trough pits, and left their clothes above, as usual, on descending to their work. In the afternoon, when work was over, one of them missed his shirt, and could not find it anywhere. Borrowing one from a friend, the man started straight from the pits to Stokesley to consult "auld Wrightson," taking with him a comrade whose Christian name was Elijah. They passed a place called West House, and there Elijah deposited his overcoat, which was hot and heavy, observing to his friend that they should be able to trust the Wise-man in the matter of the shirt by seeing whether he knew where the coat was.

Here, too, the wizard forestalled all inquiries by announcing to the men what they had come about; and turning to the comrade, addressed him thus by his Christian name, "What hast'ee decan wi' thy coat, Elijah? I think thee's left it a' West House. Thinkst'ee t'wise man knaws aught about t'shart?" As these were the very words the man had used, he was struck dumb with astonishment. The wizard then described the shirt, saying it had been made by a left-handed person (which was true), and finally said its owner would find it at home on his return. He added a warning on giving salt out of the house, a most dangerous thing, and one which the pitman's mother had done that day.

Returning home, they found that the shirt had been left there by a fellow-workman, who had carried it away in mistake, and that the house-mother had been guilty of the "dangerous act" of giving salt away. This danger is thus explained: If the salt passes into the hands of any person who has the power of wishing, *i. e.* of bringing down harm on another by uttering an ill wish, the possession of the salt places the giver entirely within the power of the wish. The same belief holds in Northumberland with regard to leaven. Mrs. Evans of Scremerston Vicarage, near Berwick, kindly informs me that there is only one person in the place who will give her a "set-off" if she has lost her leaven. All excuse themselves on one plea or another rather than give it even to the parson's wife. Curiously enough this piece of superstition appears in Spain also.

The next Stokesley story is as follows. A miller, named W——, lost a set of new weights very mysteriously, and all his searchings and inquiries ended in disappointment; he could make out nothing about them. So he applied to the Wise-man. The miller seems to have been allowed the unusual privilege of stating his case, and the wizard, after consulting his books, announced that he knew about the weights; they should be restored; at present they were concealed in an "ass-midden." Accordingly, in the course of a night or two, the weights appeared as mysteriously as they had vanished, being placed at the miller's door, and "all clamed wi' ass," which, of course, was satisfactory.

Again, a young bull belonging to an inhabitant of the district was attacked by sickness, and in spite of all remedies was soon at what appeared the point of death—too weak to stand, and slung up by ropes to keep it from falling. The wise man was sent for, and in due time arrived at the house, but declined to speak of the animal; saying, in his usual way, that unless he could tell them all they could tell him, and a little more, it was not likely he could be of much use. At last he condescended to light his pipe, and stroll out to the "beast-house." After a little time, curiosity prompted one or two men who were standing about to follow him, and approaching the byre they were surprised to see the bull apparently as well as ever, standing without any aid from slings, and eating his provender with a very hearty appetite. The mode of cure remained a secret.

The concluding anecdote respecting "auld Wrightson," like that of Nan Hardwick fixing the relentless overseer on the bridge, suggests a notion that, consciously or unconsciously, these worthies practised something like electro-biology. Two men, one of them bearing the name of Bob Bennison, and brother to a person still living at Danby, were on their way to Stokesley Fair, when one of them proposed to turn aside in order to "see auld Wrightson, and have a bit o' sport wi' him." On reaching the Wise-man's house, he gave them an apparently cordial welcome, seated them in front of the fire, and proceeded to mend it by heaping on fuel. Fiercer and fiercer it blazed up, and Wrightson's guests, feeling somewhat too warm, tried to edge their chairs backwards, but their efforts were in vain; they found themselves immovably fixed in their seats, and the seats immovably fixed in front of the fire, which all the time was burning hotter and hotter. After giving the men such a roasting as he deemed sufficient, the wizard at length set them free, scornfully bidding them go on to the fair, and there tell their friends "the sport they had had wi' auld Wrightson."

Though the wizard doctor of Stokesley professed himself unable to transmit his mysterious powers to his son, one William Dawson pretended to have inherited his books and some of his gifts, and he too was consulted by persons of a respectable position in life. A substantial Yorkshire farmer, having sustained heavy and continuous losses among his stock, consulted this William Dawson, and was instructed by him how to find out whether witchcraft was really the cause of the mischief. The farmer was to take six knots of bottree (bore-tree or elder) wood, and, placing them in orderly arrangement beneath a new ashen bowl or platter, was so to leave them. If, on looking at them some little time afterwards, they were found in confusion, "all squandered about," as he phrased it, there could be no doubt the beasts were perishing from the effects of witchcraft. This was done, and on inspection the knots were found in utter confusion. So the farmer was directed to take the heart of one of the dead beasts, and stick in it nine new nails, nine new pins, and as many new needles. The heart thus prepared was to be burnt on a fire made and fed with witchwood (rowan-tree) a little before midnight, at which hour a certain verse of the Bible was to be read over the flames, and the spell would be broken. All was made ready, and the doors of the farmhouse secured with bolt and bar, to say nothing of tables and chairs heaped against them for additional security. The heart lay on the mystic fire; as midnight approached, the operator touched it with the poker, and it burst asunder into many pieces. Gathering them together upon the hot embers, that they might be thoroughly consumed, he read the appointed verse, and at the same moment a rushing and clattering was heard down the paved causey which led from the house-door to the turnpike (the high road) in front, as if a carriage-and-four were driven down it furiously. Next began a terrible knocking and hammering, first at the front door, then at the back; but as the embers of the heart wasted in the fire the sounds without grew weaker and fainter, till, as the last spark disappeared, the noise ceased; and from that night no further harm befell the stock.

The mention of the six knots of elderwood is curious, for that tree mixes largely in Folk-lore. In Sussex an elder stick, with three, five, or seven knots upon it, is carried in the pocket as a charm against rheumatism. Some say the cross was made from its wood; others, that on it Judas hanged himself. Mr. Wilkie observes that the tree is obnoxious to witches, because their enemies use the green juice of its inner bark for anointing the eyes. Any baptized person whose eyes are touched with it can see what the witches are about in any part of the world. Compare with this the Danish belief, that he who stands under an elder-bush at twelve o'clock on Midsummer Eve will see Tolv, the king of the elves, go by with all his train. A Danish remedy for toothache is to take an elder twig, put it into the mouth, then stick it in the wall, saying, "Depart thou evil spirit!" As appears by Hans Andersen's stories, it is thought in Denmark that there dwells in the elder-tree a being called Hyldemoer, or elder-mother, who avenges all injury done to the tree: hence it is not advisable to have moveables of elderwood. The elder-mother once pulled a baby by the legs, and molested it till it was taken out of an elderwood cradle. Danish peasants will not cut this tree without asking permission thus,—"Hyldemoer, Hyldemoer, permit me to cut thy branches."[1] In Lower Saxony, the formula is as follows, to be repeated three times, with bended knees and folded hands:—

Lady Elder,
Give me some of thy wood,
Then will I give thee some of mine,
When it grows in the forest.[2]

But to return to Willie Dawson. All his powers, such as they were, failed to help him in the battle of life, for, from being a farmer at Quaker's Grove, near Stokesley, he sank into poverty, and ended his days in very reduced circumstances in South Durham. I have received another account of his magical incantations from a correspondent, who himself witnessed them when a boy. The object of them was to restore to health a young man said to be bewitched. A fire was made by midnight, as before, and the doors and windows closed. Clippings from every finger and toe-nail of the patient, with hair from each temple and the crown of his head, were stuffed into the throat of a pigeon which had previously been placed between the patient's feet, and there had died at once, thus attesting the witchery from which he was suffering. The bird's bill was riveted with three pins, and then the wise man thrust a pin into its breast, to reach the heart, everybody else in the room in turn following his example. An opening was then made in the fire, and the pigeon dropped into it. The Wise-man began to read aloud Psalms from the

[1] Thorpe's *Mythology*, vol. ii. p. 168.

[2] Ibid. vol. iii. p. 182.

prayer-book, and a loud scratching and whining began outside. All in the house, save my informant, were satisfied that the young man's enemy had appeared outside, perhaps in the form of a dog; he alone attributed the sounds to the wizard's own dog, which had not been allowed to enter the house. His scepticism, however, annoyed the wizard and his dupes so much that the lad was fain to keep it to himself.

A parallel to William Dawson's wild incantations has been communicated to me by the Rev. J. F. Bigge. Not many years ago there lived at Newcastle a wizard named Black Jock, who was much consulted by the neighbouring people in all cases of doubt and difficulty. On one occasion, a farmer named William P——, who was tenant of Richmond Hill, lost a valuable horse by a sudden attack of disease so peculiar that it suggested the idea of unhallowed charm and evil eye, or at least of some strange injury inflicted by a spiteful neighbour. So to Black Jock went Farmer P——, and told his tale. The wizard listened, and then announced that the horse had been killed by poison administered to it in brewers' grains; and on payment of one pound he gave the following directions for discovering the poisoner. The farmer and one chosen friend were secretly to cut up the horse and take out its heart, which they were to stick full of pins and roast before the fire between eleven and twelve o'clock at night, having previously closed carefully every aperture communicating with the outer air, whether door, window, or other opening, and stuffed every interstice with tow or some such material. When the clock struck the midnight hour, they might open the door, and, looking out, they would assuredly see passing by the form of him who had done the injury.

The wizard's injunctions were obeyed with right good will by the farmer and his trusty servant, Forster Charlton; but when they looked out they saw with astonishment no faint and flitting shadow of a suspicious-looking form, but, as it chanced, one of the most respectable and kindly-disposed among their neighbours, passing by in the flesh, on his way to his own home. To accuse such a man of being privy to the poor horse's death was plainly impossible, yet what were they to think? So, after much consultation, the watchers went to bed in a very perturbed state of mind, determined only on one point, the calling the wizard into council again. Summoned, accordingly, to the spot the very next day, Black Jock carefully inspected the premises, and having discovered a certain round hole on the stairs which opened into the outer air, and which they had overlooked and omitted to stuff up, he proclaimed with an oracular and impressive demeanour, from which there was no appeal, that such carelessness and disregard of his injunctions could have ended in no other way; that of course the person who had passed by was not the delinquent, but that it was owing to the non-fulfilment of the conditions imposed that they had not seen him; and, what was more, see him now they never would.

These grisly incantations appear to have taken deep root in our "north countrie." A farmer near Durham, on the death of a horse, has lately pursued exactly the same plan prescribed by Black Jock, but with better success than attended the Northumbrian farmer; for, after the poor steed's heart had been pierced and roasted, the watchers distinctly heard the howling of spirits round the house, and thus satisfied themselves that evil spirits had done the horse to death! The owner of the animal narrated this himself to my informant, who exclaimed in astonishment, "Why, surely you don't believe that?" "But I do," rejoined the farmer stoutly, "for I heard them myself."

In a well-authenticated instance which took place not very long ago near Alnwick, a cow, supposed to be influenced by the evil eye, was actually slaughtered for the purpose of discovering by the burning of its heart the person who had caused the injury. The unusual light and smell attracted a neighbour to the spot, and she was at once condemned as the culprit. It should be added, however, that the villagers blamed the owner of the victim, declaring that the knowledge was ill-purchased by the loss of even a sick cow.

A somewhat similar case transpired at Durham not long ago. A poor woman, the wife of a pitman, was brought before the bench of magistrates on the charge of stealing a fowl. She made no attempt to deny the fact; indeed, she had previously admitted it to the policeman who apprehended her, saying that she had committed the theft for the purpose of working out a charm which was to restore her sick child to health. The child, it appeared, had long been ailing, and was now fast pining away, when its mother, full of uneasiness about it, consulted a witch who lived near. The witch solemnly charged her to steal a hen, take out the heart, stick it full of pins, and roast it at midnight over a slow fire, first closing up every communication with the outer air. If this were duly done, the hag promised that, as the heart was gradually consumed, health would return to the suffering child. The magistrates, considering the delusion under which the woman had acted, dismissed the case.

The following tale is from the West Riding of Yorkshire, communicated to me by Mr. J. Stott, of Perth, formerly a resident in that district; a variation will be observed in the treatment of the heart and the pins. There was a woman in the village of L—— who pined and wasted away till, as her neighbours said, she was nothing but skin and bones. She had no definite illness, but complained that she felt as if pins were being run into her body all over her. The village doctor was resorted to, but in vain. At last they applied to the Wise-man, who pronounced that some person was doing her harm, and advised them to search the garden for hidden spells. They did so, and found buried under the window a sheep's heart stuck full of pins like a pin-cushion. The thing was removed and destroyed and the woman recovered.

Again, in a village near Preston a girl, when slighted by her lover, got a hare's heart, stuck it full of pins, and buried it with many imprecations against the faithless man whom she hoped by these means to torment.

The Rev. Canon Tristram has communicated to me another case from the south of the county of Durham: "In November of the year 1861 I was sent for by a parishioner, the wife of a small farmer, who complained that she had been scandalized by her neighbours opposite, who accused her of witchcraft. These neighbours had lost two horses during the last year, and therefore consulted 'Black Willie' at Hartlepool, who assured them that they had been bewitched. Acting on his advice, they adopted the following means for discovering the witch. Having procured a pigeon, and tied its wings, every aperture to the house, even to the key-holes, was carefully stopped, and pins were run into the pigeon whilst alive by each member of the family, so as to pierce the poor bird's heart. The pigeon was then roasted, and a watch kept at the window during the operation, for the first person who passed the door would, of course, be the guilty party. The good woman who appealed to me had the misfortune to be the first passer-by, and the family were firmly convinced she had exercised the 'evil eye' upon the dead horses, though she was a comely matron, not yet fifty years of age. This happened in a village close to the river Tees."

The last instance I shall record took place at Whitby in the year 1827. A woman residing in that town was suffering from fever, attended with soreness and swelling of the throat. Among other remedies, camphorated spirits of wine were applied externally to the part affected; but the patient growing worse, her mother took up a notion that she was bewitched, and that the spell had been fixed by the spirits of wine. The old woman therefore determined to resort to what she called the ancient ordeal. She procured a sheep's heart, stuck it full of new pins, and placed it on the fire to be burnt, watching anxiously all the time for the appearance of the witch who had troubled her daughter. She looked in vain, however, for no one appeared.

This superstition is not altogether without a parallel in the South of England. A publican at Dittisham, a pretty little village on the banks of the river Dart, lost several pigs in an unaccountable manner. Persuaded that they had been bewitched, he took out the heart of one of the victims, stuck it over with pins and placed it in front of the fire till it was charred to a cinder, in order, he said, to counteract the evil designs of the witch.

There are two or three points worth notice in these grisly rites for the discovery and baffling of witchcraft. First, the employment of mountain-ashwood for the roasting of the heart. Now the rowan, or mountain-ash, is ever the dread of witches, as we see by the old rhyme—

Black luggie, lammer bead,
Rowan-tree and red thread,
Put the witches to their speed.

Mr. Wilkie alleges the following very good reason for their apprehension. The witch who is touched with a branch of this tree by a christened man will be the victim carried off by the devil when he comes next to claim his tribute. This tribute is alluded to in the ballad of young Tamlane—

O pleasant is the fairyland,
  And happy there to dwell,
But aye, at every seven years' end,
  We pay a tiend to hell.

Mr. Kelly considers the mountain-ash to be the European representative of the Indian palasa, which it resembles in its light luxuriant foliage and red berries, or of the mimosa, a tree of the very same genus as well as general character. These Indian trees are in as high repute in Hindostan as preservatives against magic as is the rowan in Scotland, in Cornwall, or in Yorkshire. In Cornwall it is called "care," and if there is a suspicion of a cow being "overlooked" the herdsman will suspend it over her stall, or wreath it round her horns. That it is still in repute in Yorkshire let this little anecdote witness. I give it in the words of the narrator, as he told it to the Rev. J. C. Atkinson:—

"A woman was lately in my shop, and in pulling out her purse brought out also a piece of stick a few inches long. I asked her why she carried that in her pocket. 'Oh,' she replied, 'I must not lose that, or I shall be done for.' 'Why so?' I inquired. 'Well,' she answered, 'I carry that to keep off the witches; while I have that about me, they cannot hurt me.' On my observing that I thought there were no witches nowadays, she observed quickly, 'Oh yes; there are thirteen at this very time in the town, but so long as I have my rowan-tree safe in my pocket they cannot hurt me.'"

This good dame evidently agreed with the old rhymer, who said:

> If your whipstick 's made of row'n,
> You may ride your nag through any town ;

but, on the contrary—

> Woe to the lad
> Without a rowan-tree gad !

A bunch of ash-keys is thought as efficacious as the rowan-stick. An incident mentioned to me by the Rev. George Ornsby may be introduced here: "The other day I cut down a mountain-ash (or wiggan-tree, as it is called here) in my carriage-road. The old man who gardens for me came a day or two after, and was strangely disconcerted on seeing what 'master' had done in his absence; 'for,' said he, 'wherever a wiggan-tree grows near a house, t' witches canna come.' He was comforted, however, by finding, on closer investigation, that a sucker from the tree had escaped destruction."

Mr. Wilkie assures us, that, like the mountain-ash, the yew is a very upas tree to the witches, possibly because of its constant proximity to churches. They hate the holly, too, and with good reason: its name is but another form of the word holy, and its thorny foliage and blood-red berries are suggestive of the most sacred Christian associations. The bracken also they detest, because it bears on its root the letter C, the initial of the holy name Christ, which (says Mr. Wilkie) may plainly be seen on cutting the root horizontally. A friend suggests, however, that the letter intended is not the English C, but the Greek χ, the initial letter of the word χριστος, which really resembles very closely the marks in the root of the bracken, or *Pteris aquilina.* These marks have, however, been interpreted in many ways. Some say they resemble the Austrian double-headed eagle, and derive from hence the Latin name for the plant: others see in them Adam and Eve standing on either side of the tree of knowledge, or King Charles in the oak; or, again, they try to discover the initials of their future husband or wife.

But witches have their favourite plants as well. They love the broom and the thorn, as well as the ragwort, which is called in Ireland the fairies' horse, and use them all as means for riding about at midnight. They are also fond of hemlock, nightshade, St. John's-wort, and vervain, and infuse their juices into the baleful draughts prepared for their enemies. This statement, however, contradicts that in St. Colne's charm, as sung by Meg Merrilies at the birth of Harry Bertram—

> Trefoil, vervain, John's-wort, dill,
> *Hinder* witches of their will.

It contradicts, also, the old rhyme given in the notes to the Demon Lover, in the *Minstrelsy of the Scottish Border* :—

> Gin ye wud be leman mine,
> Lay aside the St. John's-wort and the verveine ;

for here these plants appear as countercharms, protecting a maiden from the approach of a very uncannie sprite in the form of a lover.

Of the St. John's-wort the following little notice has reached me from the Isle of Man. Peasants there say (or did say, before the incursion of visitors drove away all the individuality of the place) that, if you tread on the St. John's-wort after sunset, a fairy horse will rise from the earth and carry you about all night, leaving you in the morning wherever you may chance to be at sunrise.

As to the vervain, we know that in all times the Druids regarded it as the cure for many ills, and a fit offering to the divinity. At the present day, in Sussex, its leaves, dried and worn in a black silk bag, are recommended for weakly children, possibly as averting witchcraft.

Mr. Wilkie maintains that the *Digitalis purpurea* was in high favour with the witches, who used to decorate their fingers with its largest bells, thence called " witches' thimbles." Hartley Coleridge has more pleasing associations with this gay wild flower. He writes of " the fays,—

> That sweetly nestle in the foxglove bells,"

and adds in a note: " Popular fancy has generally conceived a connection between the foxglove and the good people. In

Ireland, where it is called lusmore, or the great herb, and also fairy-cap, the bending of its tall stalks is believed to denote the unseen presence of supernatural beings. The Shefro, or gregarious fairy, is represented as wearing the corolla of the foxglove on his head, and no unbecoming headdress either. Is not the proper etymology 'folks' (*i.e.* fairies') glove? Surely Reynard does not wear gloves in popular tradition?"

But to return to the incantations of Black Jock and his brotherhood. The horse's heart, pigeon, fowl, or whatever else was consumed upon the rowan-tree fire, was pierced through with pins. Now, it is remarkable how often we come across pins in the records of superstition. Mary de Medicis and her favourite, Leonora Concini, were suspected of practising against the life of Louis XIII. of France, by making a waxen image of him, and impaling it with pins; and the Duchess of Gloucester, in the reign of our Henry VI. was imprisoned on the charge of similar practices. Such sorceries appear to have prevailed extensively in the northern countries of Europe. Thus, at Amreem, in North Germany, a man lay for a long time sick in bed, and nothing afforded him relief. Meanwhile a miller observed from his mill that a woman was in the daily habit of going to the Donkkàm. One day he followed her footsteps, and on digging in the sand found a little waxen image of a man, with a pin stuck through the heart. He drew the pin out, took the image home, and burned it; from that hour the patient recovered.[1]

[1] Thorpe's *Mythology*, vol. iii. p. 24.—In Devonshire witches and malevolent people still make clay images of those whom they intend to hurt, baptize the image with the name of the person whom it is meant to represent, and then stick it full of pins or burn it. In the former case that person is racked with rheumatism in all his limbs; in the second he is smitten with raging fever. Nider, in his *Hierarchy of Blessed Angels*, speaks of a witch named Æniponte, who, by making an effigy of wax, pricking it with needles in divers parts, and then burying it under the threshold of a neighbour's house whom she much hated, brought upon that neighbour insufferable torments and prickings in the flesh, till the image was found and destroyed, upon which those evils passed away. King James I. in his *Demonology*, speaks of the practice as very common, and attributes its efficacy to the devil. In Adam Davies's *Gest, or Romance of Alexander*, Neotabanus, a magician, discovers the machinations of his enemies by embattling them in wax figures. So, too, he bewitches a queen by making a wax puppet of her, and spreading over it herbs of power.—S. B. G.

And, as recently as 1869, in the county of Inverness, a "corp cré or criadt" was discovered in a stream. The body was of clay, into which were stuck human nails, birds' claws, &c. and pins. This image was the representatian of a person whose death was desired by some illwisher, and was placed in running water with the hope and expectation that as the waters washed away the clay so the life of the person represented by it would waste and be destroyed.

Again, if a person is robbed, he goes to a so-called "cunning man," who engages to strike out the eye of the thief. The following is the process: The troll-man puts a human figure on a young tree, mutters certain dire spells by the devil's aid, and then drives a sharp instrument into the eye of the figure, thus blinding its representative. Or he will shoot with an arrow or bullet at one of the members of the figure, thus entailing wounds and sores on the corresponding limbs of the living person.[1] The Flemish countercharm is as follows: Let a sorceress melt lead and pour it into water, where it will assume a human form. She must then ask the person bewitched whereabouts in the body of him who caused the evil it shall be sent. The part is named; the sorceress makes a cut or prick in the corresponding limb of the leaden image, saying where the person is who inflicted the evil, but not naming any name. The evil will leave the victim, and alight upon the perpetrator.[2]

It is strange to meet with the same kind of superstition in India also, yet such is the case; witness the following extract from a paper by the Rev. George Pettit, of the Tinnevelly Mission of the Church Missionary Society: "A man recently under instruction at Pakunari, now a catechist, brought me an ugly wooden image, about six inches long, with nails driven into it in several places, indicating the parts of his body to be attacked with disease. He had found it buried near his door, and brought it thirty miles to show me, trembling through every limb." And I am also informed that witches in that country are accustomed to sketch on the ground, or mould in clay, a figure resembling as much as possible the person they

[1] Thorpe's *Mythology*, vol. ii. p. 54. [2] Ibid. vol. iii. p. 279.

propose to injure. They then invoke the evil spirit every day at noon for a week, and finally cut the figure with a sword, or strike it with an arrow from a bow. Again, an Indian tale runs thus: A sorceress falls in love with a prince, who rejects her advances. In revenge she surprises him in coming out of the bath, draws a bag from her girdle, and blows on it; a shower of pins flies out, which stick all over the body of the prince, and he forthwith becomes insensible. Many years afterwards a princess, losing her way in the jungle, discovers a ruined city and palace. She enters the palace, sees the prince extended on a couch, pulls the pins out of his body, and thus destroys the spell.

Witch-finders too used to torment their victims by thrusting pins into them, with the view of discovering upon them the devil's stigma or mark, a spot which was supposed insensible to pain; and bewitched persons were said to vomit pins in large quantities. Throughout the North of England we have wishing-wells, where the passer-by may breathe his wish, and may rest assured of its fulfilment if only he drop a crooked pin into the water. The Worm Well at Lambton is one of these; there is another in Westmoreland, and another at Wooler, in Northumberland. Of this last a friend writes: "It is scarcely three months since I looked into the maiden or wishing-well at Wooler, and saw the crooked pins strewed over the bottom among the rough gravel." Certainly at St. Helen's Well, near Thorp Arch, in Yorkshire, the offering was a scrap of cloth fastened to an adjoining thorn, which presented a strange appearance under its burden of rags; and at the Cheese Well, on Minchmuir, in Peebleshire, it was a piece of cheese flung into the well; but the pin is used as a rule. The country girls imagine that the well is in charge of a fairy or spirit, who must be propitiated by some offering; the pin presents itself as the most ready and convenient, besides having a special suitableness as being made of metal.

Metallic substances are held throughout the North to counteract the influence of witchcraft and every kind of evil spirit. Thus, a knife or other utensil of steel is placed in the cradle of an unbaptized child in Sweden to protect it from all such dangers;

and, again, bathers there will throw a bit of steel into the water before they plunge into it, saying to the spirit of the stream, "Neck, neck, steel in strand; thy father was a steel thief, thy mother was a needle thief; so far shalt thou be hence as this cry is heard —Ho, hagler!" Those, too, who visit the holy wells of that country cast into them a piece of money, or a bit of iron, or some other metal.[1]

As to the crookedness of the pins dropped into our north-country wells, it would seem that, in Folk-Lore, crooked things are lucky things; witness the high repute of crooked sixpences. Wells reputed sacred under the tutelage, sometimes of saint sometimes of fairy, still exist in many parts of our island and in the Hebrides. As late as the year 1740, sickly children were dipped in St. Bede's Well, near Jarrow, and a crooked pin dropped into it; and the same was done when weak eyes were bathed in the well at Whitford, in Flintshire, and when water was drawn from Locksaint Well, in Skye, and drank as a specific for certain complaints. At Sefton, in Lancashire, is a well at which people try their fortunes. They throw in pins and draw conclusions as to the fidelity of lovers, the date of marriage, and so forth, by the turning of the pin to the north or any other point of the compass.

I will only add, in connection with this subject, a remarkable story noted down by my Sussex correspondent: "A lady of my acquaintance, Mrs. P. of Westdean, observed one day on a cottage hearth a quart bottle filled with pins, and on asking about it was requested not to touch the bottle for it was red hot, and besides, if she did so, she would spoil the charm. 'What charm?' she asked in some surprise, 'Why, Ma'am,' replied the woman, 'it has pleased God to afflict my daughter here with falling fits, and the doctors did her no good, so I was advised to go to a Wise-woman who lives on this side of Guildford. Well, she said if she were well paid for it she could tell me what ailed the girl and what would cure her. So I said I was agreeable, and she told me the girl was bewitched like other people with falling fits, and I must get a quart bottle and fill it

[1] Thorpe's *Mythology*, vol. ii. p. 82.

with pins, and let it stand upon the hearth close to the fire till the pins were red hot. When that came about they would prick the heart of the witch who brought this affliction on my poor girl, and she would be glad enough to take it off.' " A medical practitioner of the same neighbourhood (Mr. M. of Pulborough) told her, in illustration of this superstition, that during the repairing of a house in that village, on removing the hearth-stone of one of the rooms, a bottle containing upwards of 200 pins was discovered, every pin being bent, and some of them much curved. On a bystander expressing his astonishment at this discovery, the workmen told him that they often found such things, and that they were deposited under the hearthstone at the building of a house to insure its safety from witchcraft.

We pass now to some Tweedside stories of recovery of property by the aid of local superstition. The following anecdote is recorded by the Rev. R. O. Bromfield, of Sprouston, and I am glad to give it in his own words:—

" Some time since, when calling at the house of one of my oldest parishioners, who had been a handloom weaver, he fell to speak of other days; and, amongst other things, he told me of the disappearance, some years back, on a fine summer's evening, of a web of linen which had been laid to bleach by the riverside at the foot of the glebe. The fishermen, it seems, were burning the water in the Skerry, and the man who had charge of the web went off to see the salmon 'leistered,' and on his return the web was gone. Of course there was a sensation. The story was soon in everybody's mouth, with abundant suspicions of as many persons as there were yards in the web of linen.

" The web belonged to a very important personage, no less than the howdie, or old village midwife, who was not disposed to sit down quietly under her loss. So she called in the aid of a Wise-man from Leetholm, and next day told her friend the weaver, my informant, that she had found the thief, for the Wise-man had turned the key. The weaver being anxious to see something of diablerie, the howdie brought the Wise-man to his house; and, the door being locked on all within (four in number), the magician proceeded as follows. He took a small key and attached it to a string, which he tied into the family Bible in a particular place, leaving the key hanging out. Next he read two chapters from the Bible, one of which was the history of Saul and the witch of Endor; he then directed the howdie and another person to support the key between them, on the tips of their forefingers, and in that attitude the former was told to repeat the names of all the suspected parties.

"Many persons were named, but the key still hung between the fingers, when the Wise-man cried out, 'Why don't you say Jock Wilson?' This was accordingly done, and immediately the key dropped, *i. e.* turned off the finger-ends. So the news spread far and wide that the thief was discovered, for the key had been turned and Jock Wilson was the man! He proved, however, not to be the man to stand such imputations, and, being without doubt an honest fellow, he declared 'he wud'na be made a thief by the deevil.' So he went to consult a lawyer, but after many long discussions the matter died away; and my authority, the weaver, says it was believed that the lawyer was bribed, 'for he aye likit a dram.'"

Now here we have something very like an old superstition, which dates at least from the time of Theocritus (B.C. 282). Potter, in his *Grecian Antiquities*,[1] says that the Greeks called it coskiomancy, and practised it for the discovery of thieves and other suspected persons. They tied a thread to the sieve, by which it was upheld, or else placed under it a pair of shears, which they held up by two fingers; then they prayed to the gods for assistance, after which they repeated the names of the persons under suspicion; and he or she at whose name the sieve moved was thought to have committed the offence. Such was the rite resorted to in pagan Greece. Mr. Kelly finds the key to it in the marvellous powers with which the sieve was invested in days of yore through its connection with rainclouds. Throughout the Greek and Teutonic mythology the sieve may be seen in the hand of cloud-gods and cloud-goddesses, who employed it in watering the earth. Hence it became a sacred implement, and the Greeks, Romans, Germans, and Slavs used it alike in divi-

[1] Vol. i. p. 52.

nations and solemn ordeals. Cornelius Agrippa speaks of it as thus employed, and in *Hudibras* we find mention of—

> The oracle of sieve and shears,
> That turns as certain as the spheres.

There is a record of its use in the North of England in the 16th century. The private book of Dr. Swift, who was Vicar-General and official Principal of the diocese of Durham from 1561 to 1577, contains "A confession to be made by Allice Swan, wife of Robert Swan, in S. Nicole's church at Newcastle, for turning the ridle and shears, with certen others, after the minister upon Sonday after the sermon."

The practice has descended in Germany almost to our own day. It is thus carried on in Mecklenburg. They take a sieve that has been inherited from relations, lay it on the rim, open a pair of *inherited* scissors, and stick the points so deep into the rim of the sieve that it may be supported by them. Two persons then, of opposite sexes, go with the sieve into a perfectly dark place, hold the middle finger of the right hand under the ring of the scissors, and so raise up the sieve. One then inquires, "In the name, &c. I ask of thee; tell me truly, has Hans, Fritz, Peter, done it?" On naming the guilty one, the ring slides off, the sieve falls to the ground, and the thief is detected.[1]

In the passage above cited, from Potter's *Grecian Antiquities*, he says that the vulgar in many parts of England have an abominable practice of using a riddle and a pair of shears in divination. A book and key, however, appear commonly to have superseded the sieve and shears in this country. When Reginald Scott speaks of this species of divination (in his *Discovery of Witchcraft*, A.D. 1599), it is with a Psalter and a key; and in a case brought before the Thames Police, in 1832, the Bible was used. One Mr. White, it seems, had lost some property, and agreed with the neighbours to resort to the Bible and key in discovery of the thief. They placed the street-door key on the fiftieth Psalm, closed the volume, and fastened it tightly with a string. The Bible and key were then suspended to a nail, and the name of Mrs. Blucher (the person on whom suspicion had

[1] Thorpe's *Mythology*, vol. iii. p. 161.

fallen) was repeated three times by one of the women, while another recited these lines:—

> If it turn to thee,
> Thou art the thief, and we are all free.

The key then turned, or was thought to do so, and Mrs. Blucher was proclaimed to be the thief; on which she went into Mrs. White's house and beat her, and was finally brought before the police-court on a charge of assault.

A similar case occurred not long ago on board a collier off Southampton, in which the key was placed on the 1st chapter of Ruth. The Bible fell at the mention of a certain lad's name, and on this evidence alone he was brought before the bench of magistrates on a charge of theft. The bench of course discharged him.

Again, soon after the reconstruction of the Whitby and Pickering branch of the North Eastern Railway, a lady lost her boa, a large old-fashioned one, on Fenbog, near the line. Having ascertained that only one person had been seen near the spot that day she accused him of finding and keeping her boa, in spite of his respectable position as an inspector on the line and his unblemished character. He denied the charge, so she consulted the riddle and shears and he was found guilty. The oracle swayed public opinion so completely that he found himself obliged to give up his situation and leave the place. Some months later, however, he was unexpectedly cleared. A railway official spied a hairy monster floating in a little stream close to the line, called for help, and collected some men with forks and other implements, who soon brought to land the lost boa. While as recently as December 27, 1878, in a trial before the borough court of Ludlow, it transpired that "the Bible and key" had been appealed to for the discovery of a thief, and in the following way: The parties concerned touched the ends of their five fingers to form a cross over the open Bible, on which the key was laid, and the words, "Where thou goest I will go," &c. were uttered. Then certain names were repeated, and when the name was mentioned of the person who stole the articles the key began (it was said) to jerk about, and no power could keep it still.

A book and key are used, I believe, in a somewhat similar way by modern mesmerisers, to test the strength of will. If two persons thus hold them on the tips of their forefingers the key will turn, they say, to the one who possesses the strongest will.

The *Universal Fortune Teller,* a small pamphlet of which I have made mention already, prescribes the following method of discovering a theft by the sieve and shears: "Stick the points of the shears in the wood of the sieve, let two persons support it, balanced upright with their two fingers, then read a certain chapter in the Bible and ask S. Peter and S. Paul if A or B is the thief, naming all the persons you suspect. On naming the real thief the sieve will suddenly turn about."

The same authority prescribes the following plan for finding out the two first letters of the future wife or husband's name. "Take a small Bible and the key of the street-door, and having opened to Cant. viii. 6, 7, place the wards of the key on those two verses. Let the bow of the key be about an inch out of the top of the Bible. Then shut the book and tie it round with your garter so that the key will not move, and let the person who wishes to know his or her future partner's signature suspend the Bible by putting the middle finger of the right hand under the bow of the key, while another person stands in like manner on the other side of the bow of the key. The latter must repeat the above-named verses while the former person says the alphabet, one letter to each repetition of the verses. It must be observed that he who says the verses must be told before beginning which you intend to try first, the Christian or the surname; take care to hold the Bible steady, and when you arrive at the appointed letter the book will turn round under your finger; this shows it to be the first letter of your intended's name." These are the strange forms in which "coskiomancy" is now practised in the neighbourhood of the Seven Dials. In Sussex two young persons will hold the "Bible and key" to ascertain which will be married first. While they stand with the string suspended on their fingers they repeat Ruth i. 16, and he to whom the book turns is pronounced the fortunate one. I am assured that this rite has been a good deal practised there even by well-educated persons. It is remarkable that Eusebe de Salle, in his *Peregrinations en Orient,* states that he saw the book and key resorted to for the sake of ascertaining which of two parties spoke the truth. He was on a visit at the English consul's when a servant, a Syrian Christian, declared that he had given into the possession of his mistress a certain jewel which yet she could not find. The question of his truthfulness was submitted to the ordeal of the Bible and the key. The servant repeated a prayer, then pronounced alternately his mistress's name and his own. The Bible turned at her name, and he was considered clear of the offence. It is added that on a closer search the lady found her jewel.

But to return to the Tweedside. I am indebted to the Rev. R. O. Bromfield for the history of another web of linen stolen a few years back from the banks of the same river. In this instance the owner was one Tam Aldren, an elder in the Kirk, and he resorted to a Wise-woman at Berwick-upon-Tweed. She told him at once that the cloth was then hidden under a certain tree, which she described, and offered to evoke the forms of the thieves, and make them pass before him at that very moment. But honest Tam demurred: he said he didna want to ken wha had stolen the claith, but where the claith was put, that he might get it back; and no doubt he entertained, too, a lurking fear of being brought too near the de'il. So away he went in all haste to the tree indicated, to search for his cloth below it, but, alas! he found it not. Seeing, however, or fancying he saw, some traces there of the bleaching composition, he maintained ever after, that, without any doubt, the cloth had once been on that spot.[1]

[1] It is curious to remark the different forms which superstition assumes in different grades of society. While our peasants resort to the wizard or Wise-woman, our gentlemen, it seems, actually have recourse to the spirit-rapper. Witness the following anecdote:

In the early part of the year 1861 a robbery took place near S——, in the county of Durham; the sum taken was large, and the attendant circumstances mysterious. Great efforts were made by the police to discover the thieves, but to no purpose; so the gentleman whose property had been stolen actually sent to

It appears that Scarborough has its Wise-man, to whom resort is made on the loss of property. Thus the following notice was recently published by the bellman at Staithes: "Stolen yesterday afternoon a large fisherman's net belonging to Jock ——, and if it is not brought back before to-morrow at 1 o'clock he'll apply to the Wise-man at Scarbro'." At Shipley, near Leeds, resides another of these worthies, named Billy Pullein. A "land merchant," or dealer, who carried woollen goods to country markets, on returning from a tour in the north of Yorkshire, lost the proceeds of all his sales between Bingley and Shipley. Under these circumstances he consulted Billy Pullein, who after listening to the narration merely deigned to say, "I'll gie 'em a shak." A week later the dealer met near the Cloth Hall at Leeds an acquaintance who asked him whether he had heard anything about the lost money. On being answered in the negative, the man continued with much emotion, "But I can tell thee summat; there it is. I gie it thee just as I found it." And when the dealer thanked him he only said, "Thou canst have no more pleasure in getting it than I in giving it. I've been miserable indeed all this week." This was of course attributed to Billy Pullein's "shak."

In cases like these, it may be remarked that Devonshire superstition points more to the punishment of the thief than to the recovery of the stolen property. If a robbery has been committed, it enjoins you to pluck six blades of grass from the spot, and take them to a white witch; as many scratches as she makes

London for an eminent spirit-rapper to aid his search. The spirit having been evoked, it was announced that the lost treasure was deposited in a certain garden; and there at midnight the party set to work to recover it. While thus employed they perceived that they were watched, and, secrecy being requisite for such investigations, they hastily decamped. But what was the horror of the gentleman and his friends when a policeman called the next morning, and announced that he had got on the scent, for he had seen the thieves digging in the garden at midnight, and had heard them speak of the money they expected to find there! Little were they prepared for such a way of "turning the tables." What makes this incident the more singular is, that the gentleman who thus sought for the aid of spiritual agency was in the prime of life, and was a person of wealth and good position in the county.

with a pin in the grass blades, so many rents will there be in the face of the thief.

Wild and varied as I know the superstitions of my native county to be, I must plead guilty to some astonishment at discovering among them what Brand calls "the *foreign* superstition of the Hand of Glory, once firmly believed in many parts of France, Germany, and Spain." Sir Walter Scott brings it forward as a foreign charm. It is the German adventurer, Dousterswivel, who is conversant with it, and who (in *The Antiquary*) describes it thus racily to the assembled party among the ruins at St. Ruth's: "Why, my goot master Oldenbuck, you will only laugh at me. But de Hand of Glory is very well known in de countries where your worthy progenitors did live; and it is a hand cut off from a dead man as has been hanged for murder, and dried very nice in de shmoke of juniper-wood; and if you put a little of what you call yew wid your juniper it will not be any better—that is, it will not be no worse; then you do take something of de fatsh of de bear, and of de badger, and of de great eber (as you do call de grand boar), and of de little sucking child as has not been christened (for dat is very essentials); and you do make a candle, and put into de Hand of Glory at de proper hour and minute, with de proper ceremonish; and he who seeksh for treasuresh shall never find none at all."[1]

Dousterswivel asserts that the monks used the Hand of Glory as a spell to conceal treasures. Southey places it in the hands of

[1] The Hand of Glory is the hand of a man who has been hung, and is prepared in the following manner: Wrap the hand in a piece of winding-sheet, drawing it tight so as to squeeze out the little blood which may remain; then place it in an earthenware vessel with saltpetre, salt, and long pepper, all carefully and thoroughly powdered. Let it remain a fortnight in this pickle till it is well dried, then expose it to the sun in the dog-days till it is completely parched, or, if the sun be not powerful enough, dry it in an oven heated with vervain and fern. Next make a candle with the fat of a hung man, virgin wax, and Lapland sesame. The Hand of Glory is used to hold this candle when it is lighted. Wherever one goes with this contrivance those it approaches are rendered incapable of motion as though they were dead.—Colin de Planey's *Dictionnaire Infernal*, 1818. See also Grimm's *Deutsche Mythologie*, p. 1027. There is a Catalonian ballad to the same effect in Ferd. Wolf's *Proben Portug. u. Katalan. Volksromanzen*, Wien, 1853, p. 146.—S. B. G.

the enchanter-king Mohareb, when he would lull to sleep Zohak, the giant keeper of the caves of Babylon—

> Thus he said,
> And from his wallet drew a human hand,
> Shrivelled, and dry, and black.
> And fitting, as he spake,
> A taper in his hold,
> Pursued: "A murderer on the stake had died;
> I drove the vulture from his limbs and lopt
> The hand that did the murder, and drew up
> The tendon-strings to close its grasp.
> And in the sun and wind
> Parched it, nine weeks exposed.
> The taper . . . . but not here the place to impart,
> Nor hast thou undergone the rites
> That fit thee to partake the mystery.
> Look! it burns clear, but with the air around
> Its dead ingredients mingle deathiness.
> This when the keeper of the cave shall feel,
> Maugre the doom of heaven,
> The salutary spell
> Shall lull his penal agony to sleep,
> And leave the passage free;[1]

while Grose gives a full account of it, as used by French housebreakers, in a translation from the French of *Les Secrets du Petit Albert* (A.D. 1750), alleging that its use was to stupefy those to whom it was presented, and to render them motionless, so that they could not stir any more than if they were dead. There is one instance on record of its use in Ireland: "On the night of the 3rd instant (January 1831), some Irish thieves attempted to commit a robbery on the estate of Mr. Naper, of Loughcrew, county Meath. They entered the house, armed with a dead man's hand with a lighted candle in it, believing in the superstitious notion that a candle placed in a dead man's hand will not be seen by any but those by whom it is used; and also that if a candle in a dead hand be introduced into a house it will prevent those who may be asleep from awaking. The inmates, however, were alarmed, and the robbers fled, leaving the hand behind them."

[1] *Thalaba the Destroyer*, book v.

The Stainmore story, however, which has with difficulty been rescued from oblivion by the persevering kindness of friends, is much richer in detail. It is as follows:—One evening, between the years 1790 and 1800, a traveller, dressed in woman's clothes, arrived at the Old Spital Inn, the place where the mail coach changed horses, in High Spital, on Bowes Moor. The traveller begged to stay all night, but had to go away so early in the morning, that if a mouthful of food were set ready for breakfast there was no need the family should be disturbed by her departure. The people of the house, however, arranged that a servant maid should sit up till the stranger was out of the premises, and then went to bed themselves. The girl lay down for a nap on the long settle by the fire, but before she shut her eyes she took a good look at the traveller, who was sitting on the opposite side of the hearth, and espied a pair of man's trousers peeping out from under the gown. All inclination for sleep was now gone; however, with great self-command, she feigned it, closed her eyes, and even began to snore. On this the traveller got up, pulled out of his pocket a dead man's hand, fitted a candle to it, lighted the candle, and passed hand and candle several times before the servant-girl's face, saying as he did so, "Let those who are asleep be asleep, and let those who are awake be awake." This done, he placed the light on the table, opened the outer door, went down two or three of the steps which led from the house to the road, and began to whistle for his companions. The girl (who had hitherto had presence of mind enough to remain perfectly quiet) now jumped up, rushed behind the ruffian, and pushed him down the steps. She then shut the door, locked it, and ran upstairs to try and wake the family, but without success: calling, shouting, and shaking were alike in vain. The poor girl was in despair, for she heard the traveller and his comrades outside the house. So she ran down again, seized a bowl of blue (*i.e.* skimmed milk), and threw it over the hand and candle; after which she went upstairs again, and awoke the sleepers without any difficulty. The landlord's son went to the window, and asked the men outside what they wanted. They answered that if the dead man's hand were but given them, they would go away quietly, and do no harm to any one. This he refused, and fired among them, and the shot must have taken effect, for in the morning stains of blood were traced to a considerable distance.

These circumstances were related to my informant, Mr. Charles Wastell, in the spring of 1861, by an old woman named Bella Parkin, who resided close to High Spital, and was actually the daughter of the courageous servant-girl.

It is interesting to compare them with the following narrations, communicated to me by the Rev. S. Baring Gould:—"Two magicians having come to lodge in a public-house with a view to robbing it, asked permission to pass the night by the fire, and obtained it. When the house was quiet, the servant-girl, suspecting mischief, crept downstair and looked through the keyhole. She saw the men open a sack, and take out a dry withered hand. They anointed the fingers with some unguent, and lighted them. Each finger flamed, but the thumb they could not light; that was because one of the household was not asleep. The girl hastened to her master, but found it impossible to arouse him. She tried every other sleeper, but could not break the charmed sleep. At last, stealing down into the kitchen, while the thieves were busy over her master's strong box, she secured the hand, blew out the flames, and at once the whole household was aroused."[1]

But the next story bears a closer resemblance to the Stainmore narrative. One dark night, when all was shut up, there came a tap at the door of a lone inn in the middle of a barren moor. The door was opened, and there stood without, shivering and shaking, a poor beggar, his rags soaked with rain, and his hands white with cold. He asked piteously for a lodging, and it was cheerfully granted him; there was not a spare bed in the house but he could lie on the mat before the kitchen fire, and welcome.

So this was settled, and everyone in the house went to bed except the cook, who from the back kitchen could see into the large room through a pane of glass let into the door. She watched the beggar, and saw him, as soon as he was left alone, draw himself up from the floor, seat himself at the table, extract

[1] Delrio. See also Thorpe's *Mythology*, vol. iii. p. 274.

from his pocket a brown withered human hand, and set it upright in the candlestick. He then anointed the fingers, and applying a match to them, they began to flame. Filled with horror, the cook rushed up the back stairs, and endeavoured to arouse her master and the men of the house. But all was in vain—they slept a charmed sleep; so in despair she hastened down again, and placed herself at her post of observation.

She saw the fingers of the hand flaming, but the thumb remained unlighted, because one inmate of the house was awake. The beggar was busy collecting the valuables around him into a large sack, and having taken all he cared for in the large room, he entered another. On this the woman ran in, and, seizing the light, tried to extinguish the flames. But this was not so easy. She blew at them, but they burnt on as before. She poured the dregs of a beer-jug over them, but they blazed up the brighter. As a last resource, she caught up a jug of milk, and dashed it over the four lambent flames, and they died out at once. Uttering a loud cry, she rushed to the door of the apartment the beggar had entered, and locked it. The whole family was roused, and the thief easily secured and hanged. This tale is told in Northumberland.

A variation of the same belief prevailed in Belgium. Not far from Bailleul, in West Flanders, a thief was taken, on whom was found the foot of a man who had been hanged, which he used for the purpose of putting people to sleep. Again, in the village of Alveringen, there formerly lived a sorceress who had a thief's finger over which nine masses had been said; for, being acquainted with the sacristan, she had wrapped it in a cloth and laid it on the altar, telling him it was a relic. With this finger she performed wonderful things. When she had lighted it—for such fingers burn like a candle—everyone in the house where she might be was put to sleep. She would then steal money and everything else she fancied, till at last she was detected, and the stolen property found in her possession.[1]

In a note to the passage quoted above from Southey's *Thalaba*, it is mentioned that a somewhat similar practice is recorded by

[1] Thorpe's *Mythology*, vol. iii. pp. 274, 275.

Torquemada of Mexican thieves. They used to carry with them the left hand and arm of a woman who had died in her first childbed; with this they twice struck the ground before the house which they designed to rob, and the door twice, and the threshold twice: the inhabitants, if asleep, were hindered from waking by this charm, and, if awake, were stupefied and deprived of speech and motion while the fatal arm was in the house.

But I have wandered a little from the subject of witchcraft proper. Let me return to it and mention an incident more recent than the other illustrations I have adduced. I received it from a clerical friend, whose informant was a pupil in the house of the clergyman referred to.

In the autumn of the year 1851, a clergyman living in Rutlandshire gave a small party, to which a neighbour, also a country clergyman, brought his family and one young lady visitor. During the evening, this young lady went upstairs into the bedroom of one of her host's family, saw a gold watch hanging up on a nail, took it down, concealed it in her dress, joined the party again, and entered into the amusements of the evening. They dispersed in due time, and the young lady carried away the watch. When its owner retired to her room she at once missed it; inquiries were made, and even the police called in, but to no purpose. Suspicion fell, however, upon a poor woman and her daughter, who had come in as helpers from the village, and this in spite of the excellent character they had always borne. These persons were much hurt at the accusation, and annoyed at the visits and searchings of the police; so after a few days they called in a Wise-woman from Leicester, who was famous for aiding to recover lost property. This Wise-woman was thrown into a mesmeric state by her husband. At first she was violent, but she gradually calmed down, and when they questioned her spoke as follows:—

"I am going over hill and valley, and at length arrive at a village. I come to a gate, go through it into a yard, enter the house, and ascend the stairs." (She then described accurately the house and the room.) "I see a watch hanging on a nail. A short young lady in a pink dress, with dark hair, comes in, takes it, and puts it in her bosom. She goes away two miles. She is at this moment walking in a meadow with some children. The watch is in her bosom, and you will find it there; but you must be very quiet about it, for she is full of apprehension, and has been trying to get rid of the watch."

This history was brought to the family where the young lady was staying. The master of the house was not at all disposed to believe the circumstances, but, seeing the poor people persuaded of their truth, he felt himself obliged to order an investigation. The young lady's boxes were searched in vain, but on proceeding to a personal examination, the watch was found in the place specified. The Wise-woman had stated that this was not the first instance of appropriation on the young lady's part, and here too she proved correct.

Let me close this long rambling chapter with a few words about a Scottish witch, the last who was burned at Crieff. She suffered on the Knock. Her name was Kate Neirns, and many romantic tales are told of her. With her last breath she denounced her principal persecutor, Campbell, of Menzie, a neighbouring laird, and the effect of her curse is still believed to attach to his unfortunate house. No son, she said, should ever succeed his father in the property. On the contrary, she did what she could for the laird of Inchbrakie, Graeme, who had endeavoured to save her life. She told him that as long as he and his preserved a bead which she spit out of her mouth so long the property should continue in the family. The bead is still carefully kept, and the family, though not without many vicissitudes, still retain their lands. These particulars were communicated to me by the late Canon Humble.

CHAPTER VII.

LOCAL SPRITES.

The Bogle, Brownie, Dobie—Brown Man of the Muirs—Killmoulis—Redcap—Powries or Dunters—Wag-at-the Wa'—Habetrot—Cowlug E'en—Thrumpin—Dunnie—Hobhole Hob—Hob Headless—Hob Thrush—Peg Powler—Peg-o'-Nell—Cauld Lad of Hilton—The Radiant Boy—Silky—Picktree Brag—Hedley Kow—Kludde—Oschaert—Padfoot—Barguest—Capelthwaite—Northern Sprites compared with those of Devon—The Evil Spirit—Clontie's Croft—The Minister and Satan—The Devil trying all Trades—Praying aloud.

HE Land o' Cakes is well known to be haunted by many kinds of sprites and goblins, some of which have found their way across the Cheviots, while the North of England has unearthly denizens peculiarly its own. The Scotch peasant Barnaby, in the Ettrick Shepherd's tale of the "Woolgatherer," speaks thus of the sprites of his country, and the popular belief in them of his day:—

"Ye had need to tak care how ye dispute the existence of fairies, brownies, and apparitions: ye may as weel dispute the Gospel of Saint Matthew. We dunna believe in a' the gomral fantastic bogles an' spirits that flay light-headed folk up an' down the countree; but we believe in a' the apparitions that warn o' death, that save life, and that discover guilt. I'll tell ye what we believe ye see. The deil and his adjents, they fash none but the gude folk—the Cameronians and the prayin' ministers an' sic like. Then the Bogles, they are a better kind o' spirits; they meddle wi' nane but the guilty; the murderer, an' the mansworn, an' the cheaters o' the widow an' fatherless, they do for *them*. Then the Brownie, he's a kind of half-spirit, half-man; he'll drudge, and do a' the work about the town for his meat, but then he'll do no wark but when he likes for a' the king's dominions. That's what we a' believe here awa' auld and young."

I do not find that in Yorkshire the Bogle bears the peculiar character of a minister of retribution here assigned him. At least the following story, communicated by Mr. Robinson, does not represent him in exactly that light. In a village in Arkingarthdale a house had long been haunted by a Bogle, and various means had been resorted to in order to drive him out. At last the owner adopted the following plan. Opening his Bible he placed it on a table with a lighted candle and said aloud to the Bogle, "Noo, thoo can read or dance, or dea as ta likes." He then turned round and walked up stairs. The Bogle, in the form of a grey cat, flew past him and vanished into the air. Years passed without its being seen again. However one day as the man was going to work the thing met him on the stairs. He turned back, told his mother of the apparition, went out again, and was killed that day in the mines. A Bogle, or something akin to one, appears however in the following narration as the protector of a poor widow. At the village of Hurst, near Reeth, lived a widow who had been wronged out of some candles by a neighbour. This neighbour saw one night a figure in his garden, so he brought out his gun and fired it, on which the figure vanished. The next night while he was in an outhouse the figure appeared in the doorway and said, "I'm neither bone, nor flesh, nor blood, thou canst not harm me. Give back the candles, but I must take something from thee." So saying he pulled an eyelash from the thief's eyelid and vanished. The candles were promptly restored the next morning, but the thief "twinkled" ever after.

Of the good old Brownie, that faithful ally of the Scottish household, I have little new to tell. He seems a denizen of the Shetland Islands, the Highlands of Scotland, and the Western Isles, as well as of the Borderland. I must warn you, however, not to confound him with the Dobie, a creature of far less sense and activity. In fact, the Dobie was what I have heard a poor woman called her husband's ghost, "a mortal heavy sprite;" and hence the common border phrases, "Oh ye stupid Dobie!" or "She's but a senseless Dobie."[1] The Brownie was therefore

[1] Sir Walter Scott seems unaware of this peculiar character of the Dobie. He considers it merely another name for the Barguest, of whom more hereafter;

preferred as a guardian of hidden treasure, and to him did the Borderers commit their money or goods, when, according to the custom prevalent in wild insecure countries, they concealed them in the earth. Some form of incantation was practised on the occasion, of which I can only learn one part—the dropping upon the treasure the blood of a slaughtered animal, or burying the slain animal with it.

The Brownie is believed in Berwickshire to be the ordained helper of mankind in the drudgery entailed by sin: hence he is forbidden to receive wages.[1] He is allowed his little treats, however, and the chief of these are knuckled cakes made of meal warm from the mill, toasted over the embers and spread with honey. The housewife will prepare these, and lay them carefully where he may find them by chance. When a titbit is given to a child, parents will still say to him, "There's a piece wad please a Brownie." A bowl of cream was also a favourite dish. If a family desired to get rid of their inmate, they had only to lay out for him a new hood and cloak, and he would take leave of them, singing—

> "A new mantle and a new hood,
> Poor Brownie! ye'll ne'er do mair good."

---

and mentions that he has been informed of some families of the name of Dobie, who carried in their armorial bearings a phantom or spectre passant.—*Demonology and Witchcraft*, letter iii. In a note to canto ii. of *Rokeby* he tells of the Dobie of Mortham, who haunts Greta Dell, but calls it a female spectre, the ghost of a lady formerly murdered in the wood.

[1] Danish tradition goes so far back as to state the origin of the different kinds of sprites. It is said in Jutland that, when our Lord cast the fallen angels out of heaven, some of them fell down on the mounds or barrows, and became Barrow-folk, or (as they are also called) Mount-folk or Hill-folk; others fell into the Elf-moors, and became the progenitors of the Elf-folk; while others fell into dwellings, from whom descend the domestic sprites or Nissir—the Brownies, in fact. Another Danish legend is as follows: While Eve was one day washing her children by a spring our Lord unexpectedly appeared before her. She was terrified, and concealed those of her children which were not yet washed. Our Lord asked her if all her children were there, and to avoid his anger, in case He should see that all her children were not washed, she answered, "Yes." Then our Lord declared that what she had concealed from Him should thenceforth be concealed from mankind, and at the same moment the unclean children disappeared, and were buried under the hills. From these descend all the underground folk—Trolls, Elfs, &c.—Thorpe's *Mythology*, vol. ii p. 115.

Thus the goodman of the parish of Glendevon left out some clothes one night for the Brownie, and heard him take his departure during the night, saying, in a highly offended tone—

> "Gie Brownie coat, gie Brownie sark,
> Ye'se get nae mair o' Brownie's wark."

A lady of Scottish extraction, Mrs. M——, writes thus to me: "It is curious what dislike Brownies have to clothing. There was one in the old peelhouse where I was born. The servants, out of gratitude for his assistance, gave him what they deemed an indispensable portion of man's attire. Unfortunately it was part of a suit of livery, and he vanished crying—

> "Red breeks and a ruffled sark!
> Ye'll no get me to do yer wark."

The story dates from my great grandfather's time; but the old dark closet where Brownie dwelt still exists, though dark no longer."

But not the Brownie alone, with his kindred Northern sprites, is driven away by gifts of clothing. Devonshire Pixies are equally sensitive on this point. It is recorded that one of them on receiving a new suit vanished, exclaiming—

> "Pixy fine, Pixy gay,
> Pixy now will run away."

Nay, a simple word of praise will drive them away, as we learn from the following tale. A farmer at Washington, in Sussex, who had often been surprised in the morning at the large heaps of corn threshed for him during the night, determined at last to sit up and watch what went on. Creeping at midnight to the barn-door and looking through a little chink in it he saw two little "Piskies" working away with their fairie flails, and only stopping now and then for an instant to say to each other "See how I sweat! see how I sweat!" the very thing that befell the "lubbar fiend" in L'Allegro. The farmer in his delight cried out "Well done, my little men," on which the sprites uttered a loud cry and vanished, never to work again in that barn.

The little Swedish Tomte, though he will receive donations of bread, cheese, and even tobacco, is spoiled for work by new clothes; and when a housewife, in gratitude for the meal he sifted in her meal-tub, placed a suit for him on the edge of the tub, he did nothing more for her. He found that the meal damaged his new kirtle, so he cast the sieve away and repeated—

> "The young spark is fine,
> He dusts himself!
> Never more will he sift."[1]

And the Dutch Kaboutermannekin, or Redcap, on receiving new clothes vanishes never to return. A miller in Kempnerland thus rewarded his Redcap for a good deal of hard work expeditiously got through; but the goblin, having put on the clothes and strutted about proudly in them, disappeared. The miller, missing his drudge, laid wait for him on a little bridge over a brook, which the Kaboutermannekin used to cross every evening. He watched the sprites as they passed, some clothed, some naked, and last of all came his household sprite in his new suite. "Haha!" said the miller, "have I got thee?" and was about to seize little Redcap, when a voice like that of his wife was heard from the rivulet, crying for help. The miller turned and jumped into the water, and in a moment all the mannekins were gone.[2]

Cranshaws, in Berwickshire, was once the abode of an industrious Brownie, who both saved the corn and thrashed it for several seasons. At length, after one harvest, some person thoughtlessly remarked, that the corn was not well mowed or piled up in the barn. The sprite took offence at this, and the next night threw the whole of the corn over the Raven Crag, a precipice about two miles off, muttering—

> "It's no weel mowed! It's no weel mowed!
> Then its ne'er be mowed by me again;
> I'll scatter it owre the Raven stane,
> And they'll hae some wark e'er it's mowed again."

This little story is taken from Mr. George Henderson's *Popular Rhymes of Berwickshire*. It reminds us of the

[1] Thorpe's *Mythology*, vol. ii. p. 94. [2] Ibid. vol. iii. p. 191.

Manx Phynnoderee, who, when the farmer complained of his not cutting the grass sufficiently close to the ground, left the grumbler to cut it himself next year, but went after him stubbing up the roots so fast as almost to cut off the man's legs. The Phynnoderee liked clothing as little as the Brownie, and once, when rewarded for special service by the present of a few articles of dress, he lifted them up one by one exclaming,—

> "Cap for the head! alas, poor head!
> Coat for the back! alas, poor back!"

and so on, till, with a melancholy wail, he departed, never to return. Both sprites, like Milton's "drudging goblin," delighted in the "cream-bowl duly set," but the Brownie at least would have resented the charge of labouring to "earn" it. Sir Walter Scott relates how the last Brownie in Ettrick Forest, the Brownie of Bodsbeck, vanished when the mistress of the house placed a porringer of milk and a piece of money in his haunts. He was heard to howl, and cry all night, "Farewell bonnie Bodsbeck!" and in the morning disappeared for ever.[1] The Ettrick Shepherd has given the title of the "Brownie of Bodsbeck" to a tale, in which an exiled Cameronian assumes the character of this mysterious being, and thereby gains shelter and support.

If the Scottish homesteads have their attendant sprites, the wild moorlands are not without their mysterious denizens. In a letter from Mr. Surtees to Sir W. Scott, given in the memoir prefixed to vol. iv. of Surtees's *History of Durham*, we read, on the authority of an old dame named Elizabeth Cockburn, how in the year before the Great Rebellion two young men from Newcastle were sporting on the high moors above Elsdon, and at last sat down to refresh themselves in a green glen near a mountain stream. The younger lad went to drink at the brook, and raising his head again saw the "Brown man of the Muirs," a dwarf very strong and stoutly built, his dress brown like withered bracken, his head covered with frizzled red hair, his countenance ferocious, and his eyes glowing like those of a bull. After some parley, in which the stranger reproved the hunter for trespassing on his demesnes and slaying the creatures who were

[1] *Border Minstrelsy*, vol. i. p. 205.

his subjects, and informed him how he himself lived only on whortleberries, nuts, and apples, he invited him home. The youth was on the point of accepting the invitation and springing across the brook, when he was arrested by the voice of his companion, who thought he had tarried long, and looking round again "the wee brown man was fled." It was thought that had the young man crossed the water the dwarf would have torn him to pieces. As it was he died within the year, in consequence, it was supposed, of his slighting the dwarf's admonition, and continuing his sport on the way home.

Killmoulis is a peculiar species of Brownie, who haunts the mill, and resides in the killogee, or space before the fireplace in the kiln. One would suppose that he took his name from the kiln, but Mr. Wilkie considers "kill" to be a corruption of "gill," and "killmoulis" to mean the miller's servant. This sprite is a singular creature, for he appears to have no mouth; yet the following rhymes testify to his taste for swine's-flesh:—

Auld Killmoulis wanting the mow,
Come to me now, come to me now!
Where war ye yestreen when I killed the sow?
Had ye come ye'd hae gotten yer belly fou.

Killmoulis takes the liveliest interest in the miller and his mill. Should any misfortune threaten them he will wail piteously. At the same time he often torments the goodman sorely by throwing "isles" or ashes out when sheelin or shelled oats are spread out to dry; nor will he leave off his mischievous tricks till the miller calls out,

"Auld Killmoulis wanting the mow,
Come to me now,"

on which he appears, puffing and blowing, in the shape of an old man, the mouth wanting, but with an enormous nose.

Killmoulis will never quit the "logie," his favourite corner, except to thrash the corn in great emergency, or to ride for the howdie, when the miller's wife needs her services—an errand he will fulfil expeditiously enough, though with some rough usage of the horse.

Every mill was haunted by its own Killmoulis; hence the number of wild stories which linger round these secluded spots. In Roxburghshire Killmoulis is thus drawn into the spell of the "blue clue," a divination practised on All-hallowe'en and at other times. You must throw the clue into a pot alone in the gloaming, and wind the worsted on a new clue. Towards the end of the winding Killmoulis will hold the thread. You must ask "Wha holds?" and he will snort out the name of your future spouse.

It appears from Thorpe's *Mythology* (vol. iii. p. 187), that the mills of Holland are haunted too, but by sprites of a more friendly character, bearing the unwieldly name of Kaboutermannekins. In the village of Gelrode, when the millstone was worn, the miller had only to lay it before his mill at night, together with a slice of bread and butter and a glass of beer, and he was sure to find it in the morning beautifully set.

Redcap, Redcomb, or Bloody Cap, is a sprite of another sort from the friendly Brownie. He is cruel and malignant of mood, and resides in spots which were once the scene of tyranny—such as Border castles, towers, and peelhouses. He is depicted as a short thickset old man, with long prominent teeth, skinny fingers armed with talons like eagles, large eyes of a fiery-red colour, grisly hair streaming down his shoulders, iron boots, a pikestaff in his left hand, and a red cap on his head. When benighted or shelterless travellers take refuge in his haunts, he flings huge stones at them; nay, unless he is much maligned, he murders them outright, and catches their blood in his cap, which thus acquires its crimson hue.

This ill-conditioned goblin may, however, be driven away by repeating Scripture words, or holding up the Cross; he will then yell dismally, or vanish in a flame of fire, leaving behind him a large tooth on the spot where he was last seen.

Now here we plainly have the "Redcap sly" who sat in Hermitage Castle with the evil Lord Soulis, sorcerer and tyrant alike, and Warden of the South and West Marshes. To him Redcap said:

" While thou shalt hear a charmèd life,
And hold that life of me,
'Gainst lance and arrow, sword and knife,
I shall thy warrant be.

" Nor forgèd steel nor hempen band
Shall e'er thy limbs confine ;
Till threefold ropes of sifted sand
Around thy body twine."

And when the evil lord was taken, and by the aid of Michael Scott's book, " True Thomas," shaped the ropes "sae curiously," we are told, that—

Redcap sly unseen was by,
And the ropes would neither twist nor turn.

It was, however, beyond Redcap's power to save his lord from his final doom, and, as the spae-book directed, Lord Soulis was boiled to death in a brazen cauldron on the Nine-stane Rig.

I find this goblin referred to in an old proverb given in the *Denham Tracts:* " He caps Bogie, Bogie capt Redcap, and Redcap capt Old Nick," corresponding with the Lancashire saying, " He caps Wryneck, and Wryneck caps the Dule," *i.e.* the Devil. And Sir Walter Scott says of him: " Redcap is a popular appellation of that class of spirits which haunt old castles. Every ruined tower in the South of Scotland is supposed to have an inhabitant of this species." [1]

Mr. Wilkie has recorded the following lines, which he calls " a common song about Redcap":—

Now Redcap he was there,
And he was there indeed;
And grimly he girned and glowed,
Wi' his red cowl on his head.

Then Redcap gave a yell,
It was a yell indeed ;
That the flesh neath my oxter grew cauld,
It grew as cauld as lead.

---

[1] *Minstrelsy of the Scottish Border*, vol. iv. p. 243.

Auld Bluidie-cowl ga'ed a girn,
  It was a girn indeed;
Syne my flesh it grew mizzled for fear,
  And I stood like a thing that is dead.

Last Redcowl gave a laugh,
  It was a laugh indeed;
'Twas mair like a hoarse, hoarse scrough,
  Syne a tooth fell out o' his head.

In East Lancashire stands a public-house called Mother Redcap, doubtless in allusion to some local tradition of a witch.

There are Redcaps in Holland too, but they have little in common with the Scottish Redcap, except the name. They are nearer akin to the Brownie, whom they resemble in their attachment to certain homesteads, in the diligence with which they perform manual labour, and in their abrupt departure on receiving a guerdon in the form of clothing. The Dutch Redcaps light fires during the night, which are invisible save to themselves, but warm the house; and the few sticks they leave of the Hausfrau's stock of brushwood serve her as long as a great bundle, and give double the warmth. They are clad in red from head to foot, and have green hands and faces. A Redcap once made the fortune of a poor man by doing all the work of his little farm, and especially by churning at night more butter than any one else could get from the milk. The man became possessor of a whole herd of cows, and laid up a stocking-full of shining dollars. But, prosperity corrupting him, he grew idle and dissolute, and finally abused Redcap, and threw the bundle of firewood prepared for him by the gudewife into the well. On this the sprite disappeared: the wife was seized with illness, the stocking was only filled with coals, the cows died, and all went to ruin. The peasant begged and prayed that Redcap would return, but to no purpose; he was only answered by the laughs and jeers of the goblin outside the cottage.[1]

Powries, or Dunters, are also sprites who inhabit forts, old castles, peel-towers, or dungeons; and they constantly make a noise there as of beating flax, or bruising barley in the hollow of a stone. If this sound is longer or louder than usual, it portends

[1] Thorpe's *Mythology*, vol. iii. p. 181.

a death or misfortune. Popular tradition reports that the foundation-stones of these old Border castles were bathed with human blood by their builders the Picts; no wonder then that they were haunted in some way or other.

Wag-at-the-wa', another Border sprite, is mentioned in the following verses, which Mr. Wilkie took down from the recitation of an old lady in the village of Bowden, Roxburghshire:—

Wag-at-the-wa' went out i' the night,
To see that the moon was shining bricht,
The moon she was at the latter fa',
" 'Gang hame to yer beds!" cried Wag-at-the-Wa'.

" Why d'ye wag the witch nickit crook,
When the pyet's asleep where the corbies rook?
Hell's e'en shimmert on ye i' the moon's latter fa',
And ruin's fell couter will harry ye a'."

" I maun gae fra' ye, tak' tent what I say,
Gae tear frae the sowie an armfu' o' hay,
Fling wisps i' the fire till it mak' a red low,
Frae the eizels will rise up a dead man's pow.

" The pow will stare ugsome, but dinna heed that,
Thud fast o' the wisps, and beware o' the cat,
For she will yer fae be, wi' teeth and wi' claw,
An' her mewing will soon warn auld Wag-at-the-wa'.

" Whenever the e'en holes wi' low sall be fou,
Then is the time that we maun dread the pow,
For Hell's e'en are firelike and fearfu' to view,
And they oft change their colour fra' dark red to blue.

" They pierce like an elf, prick ilk ane that they see,
Then beware o' their shimmer, if yer seen ye will dee,
Your heart's pulse will riot, your flesh will grow cauld,
Oh, how happy the wight that draws breath till he's auld!

" Then fly frae the house, to the green quick repair,
And Wag-at-the-wa' will full soon meet ye there,
As ye kneel 'neath the Rood and mutter yer prayer. . . ."

These obscure lines do not give us much information respecting Wag-at-the-wa'. We are told elsewhere, however, that he is a sort of Brownie, who presided over the Border kitchen, where he acted family monitor, but was a torment to the servants, especially to the kitchen-maid. His seat was by the hearth, or on the crook or bar of iron, terminating in a large hook, which may be seen in old houses hanging by a swivel from a beam in the chimney to hold pots and kettles. Whenever the crook was empty, Wag-at-the-wa' would take possession of it, and swing there with great complacency, only absenting himself when there was a death in the family. He was fond of children and of household mirth, and hence his attachment to the ingle. When droll stories were told his laugh might be heard distinctly; but if he heard of any liquor being drunk, except home-brewed ale, he would cough and be displeased.

His general appearance was that of a grisly old man, with short crooked legs, while a long tail assisted him in keeping his seat on the crook. Sometimes he appeared in a grey mantle, with the remains of an old "pirnicap" on his head, drawn down over that side of the face which was troubled with toothache, a constant grievance of his; but he commonly wore a red coat and blue breeches, both garments being made of "familie woo."

Altogether there is something uncannie about this ancient sprite, and the mode of his disappearance (for he has passed away from the Scottish ingle) does not speak well for him. A deep cut is now invariably made in the iron of the crook in the form of a cross, and is called the witches' mark, because it warns witches from the fire. This sign also scares away auld Wag-at-the-wa', and keeps him from touching the crook. Still it is deemed wrong and foolish ever to wag the crook, since it is a sort of invitation to the sprite to return. Mr. Wilkie says that he has seen a visitor rise up and leave the house, because one of the boys of the family idly swung the crook: she was so horrified at this "invokerie" that she declared "she wad na abide in the house where it was practised."

Mr. Wilkie says the sign of the cross was in like manner marked on many tools and utensils, down to the "torwoodie" of the harrow, as a protection against sprites of doubtful character—a singular preservative in Presbyterian Scotland! In many parts of England, however, we find an analogous use of this sign. The Durham butchers mark it on the shoulder of a sheep or lamb after taking off the skin, probably because in the peace-offerings of old it was the priest's portion; the housewives mark it on their loaves of bread before placing them in the oven. In the West of England, I believe, the cross is more commonly made on the dough when set to rise.

In the old days, when spinning was the constant employment of women, the spinning-wheel had its presiding genius or fairy. Her Border name was Habetrot, and Mr. Wilkie tells the following legend about her:—

A Selkirkshire matron had one fair daughter, who loved play better than work, wandering in the meadows and lanes better than the spinning-wheel and distaff. The mother was heartily vexed at this taste, for in those days no lassie had any chance of a good husband unless she was an industrious spinster. So she cajoled, threatened, even beat her daughter, but all to no purpose; the girl remained what her mother called her, "an idle cuttie."

At last, one spring morning, the gudewife gave her seven heads of lint, saying she would take no excuse; they must be returned in three days spun into yarn. The girl saw her mother was in earnest, so she plied her distaff as well as she could; but her little hands were all untaught, and by the evening of the second day a very small part of her task was accomplished. She cried herself to sleep that night, and in the morning, throwing aside her work in despair, she strolled out into the fields, all sparkling with dew. At last she reached a flowery knoll, at whose feet ran a little burn, shaded with woodbine and wild roses; and there she sat down, burying her face in her hands. When she looked up, she was surprised to see by the margin of the stream an old woman, quite unknown to her, "drawing out the thread" as she basked in the sun. There was nothing very remarkable in her appearance, except the length and thickness of her lips, only she was seated on a self-bored stone. The girl rose, went to the good dame, and gave her a friendly greeting, but could not help inquiring what made her so "lang lipit." "Spinning thread, ma hinnie," said the old woman, pleased with her friendliness, and by no means resenting the personal remark. It must be noticed that spinners used constantly to wet their fingers with their lips as they drew the thread from the rock or distaff. "Ah!" said the girl, "I should be spinning too, but it's a' to no purpose, I sall ne'er do my task;" on which the old woman proposed to do it for her. Overjoyed, the maiden ran to fetch her lint, and placed it in her new friend's hand, asking her name, and where she could call for the yarn in the evening; but she received no reply; the old woman's form passed away from her among the trees and bushes, and disappeared. The girl, much bewildered, wandered about a little, set down to rest, and finally fell asleep by the little knoll.

When she awoke she was surprised to find that it was evening. The glories of the western sky were passing into twilight grey. Causleen, or the evening star, was beaming with silvery light, soon to be lost in the moon's increasing splendour. While watching these changes, the maiden was startled by the sound of an uncouth voice, which seemed to issue from below a self-bored stone, close beside her. She laid her ear to the stone, and distinctly heard these words: "Little kens the wee lassie on the brae-head that ma name's Habetrot." Then looking down the hole she saw her friend, the old dame, walking backwards and forwards in a deep cavern among a group of spinsters all seated on colludie stones (a kind of white pebble found in rivers), and busy with distaff and spindle. An unsightly company they were, with lips more or less disfigured by their employment, as were old Habetrot's. The same peculiarity extended to another of the sisterhood, who sat in a distant corner reeling the yarn; and she was marked, in addition, by grey eyes, which seemed starting from her head, and a long hooked nose.

While the girl was still watching, she heard Habetrot address this singular being by the name of Scantlie Mab, and tell her to bundle up the yarn, for it was time the young lassie should give it to her mother. Delighted to hear this, our listener got up and turned homewards, nor was she long kept in suspense. Habetrot soon overtook her, and placed the yarn in her hands. "Oh, what can I do for ye in return?" exclaimed she, in delight. "Naething—naething," replied the dame; "but dinna tell yer mither whae spun the yarn."

Scarcely crediting her good fortune, our heroine went home, where she found her mother had been busy making sausters, or black puddings, and hanging them up in the lum to dry, and then, tired out, had retired to rest. Finding herself very hungry after her long day on the knoll, the girl took down pudding after pudding, fried and ate them, and at last went to bed too. The mother was up first the next morning, and when she came into the kitchen and found her sausters all gone, and the seven hanks of yarn lying beautifully smooth and bright upon the table, her mingled feelings of vexation and delight were too much for her. She ran out of the house wildly crying out—

> "Ma daughter's spun se'en, se'en, se'en,
> Ma daughter's eaten se'en, se'en, se'en
> And all before daylight!"

A laird, who chanced to be riding by, heard the exclamation but could not understand it; so he rode up and asked the gudewife what was the matter, on which she broke out again—

> "Ma daughter's spun se'en, se'en, se'en,
> Ma daughter's eaten se'en, se'en, se'en

before daylight; and, if ye dinna believe me, why come in and see it." The laird's curiosity was roused; he alighted and went into the cottage, where he saw the yarn, and admired it so much, he begged to see the spinner.

The mother dragged in the blushing girl. Her rustic grace soon won his heart, and he avowed he was lonely without a wife, and had long been in search of one who was a good spinner. So their troth was plighted, and the wedding took place soon afterwards, the bride stifling her apprehensions that she should not prove so deft at her spinning-wheel as her lover expected. And once more old Habetrot came to her aid. Whether the good dame, herself so notable, was as indulgent to all idle damsels does not appear—certainly she did not fail this little pet of hers. "Bring your bonnie bridegroom to my cell," said she to the young bride soon after her marriage; "he shall see what comes o' spinning, and never will he tie you to the spinning wheel."

Accordingly the bride led her husband the next day to the flowery knoll, and bade him look through the self-bored stone. Great was his his surprise to behold Habetrot dancing and jumping over her rock, singing all the time this ditty to her sisterhood, while they kept time with their spindles:—

> We who live in dreary den,
> Are both rank and foul to see,
> Hidden frae the glorious sun,
> That teems the fair earth's canopie:
> Ever must our evenings lone
> Be spent on the colludie stone.
>
> Cheerless is the evening grey,
> When Causleen hath died away,
> But ever bright and ever fair,
> Are they who breathe this evening air;
> And lean upon the self-bored stone
> Unseen by all but me alone.

The song ended, Scantlie Mab asked Habetrot what she meant by her last line, "Unseen by all but me alone." "There is ane," replied Habetrot, "whom I bid to come here at this hour, and he has heard my song through the self-bored stone." So saying she rose, opened another door, which was concealed by the roots of an old tree, and invited the bridal pair to come in and see her family.

The laird was astonished at the weird-looking company, as he well might be, and inquired of one after another the cause of the strange distortion of their lips. In a different tone of voice, and with a different twist of the mouth, each answered that it was occasioned by spinning. At least they tried to say so, but one grunted out "Nakasind," and other "Owkasaand," while a third murmured "O-a-o-send." All, however, conveyed the fact to the bridegroom's understanding; while Habetrot slily hinted, that, if his wife were allowed to spin, her pretty lips would grow out of shape too, and her pretty face get an ugsome look. So before he left the cave he protested his little wife should never touch a spinning-wheel, and he kept his word. She used to wander in the meadows by his side, or ride behind him over the hills, and all the flax grown on his land was sent to old Habetrot to be converted into yarn.[1]

Such are the tales of Border sprites which Mr. Wilkie has collected. He adds that the villages of Bowden and Gateside had a strange belief that on a certain night in the year (thence called "Cowlug e'en") a number of sprites were abroad with ears resembling those of cows; but he could not discover the origin of the belief, nor which night was thus distinguished.

He mentions also that in the South of Scotland every person was supposed to be attended by a sprite, who had the power of taking away his life—a strange perversion of the doctrine of Guardian Angels. This is called by the old name of "Thrumpin," and is mentioned in these obscure verses:—

When the hullers o' night are loosin',
  When the quakers are crumplin eerie;
When the moon is in the latter fa',
  When the owlets are scraughin drearie;
When the elleried are clumperin,
  When the toweries hard are thrumping,
When the bawkie bird he kisses the yud,
Then, then's the time for thrumpin.
And gif ye miss the mystic hour,
When vengeful sprites are granted power,
  To thrump ilk faithless wight;
The heavens will gloom like a wizard smile,
An' the foremost will dirn his carcase vile
  Fra' all uncannie sight.
For man and beast by the three stones light,
  Hae little chance to thrive;
Till the sixty are past, and not till the last,
  Can man and beast survive.

[1] This story, though not without variations, is radically the same as the three spinners of German household tales—Grimm, K.M. 14; Pretorius' *Gluckstopf*, 404; Peschock's *Nachrichten*, i. 355; *Müllenhoff*, No. 8. In Norway we find the same story (*Asbjörnsen*, p. 69); and again in the collection of *Neapolitan Household Tales* made by Basile in the seventeenth century. We meet with it too in Lithuania (Schleicher, p. 12). The outline of the plot in all is as follows: A poor woman beats her daughter for idleness, and tells a merchant who is passing that she does it to compel her daughter to spin six hanks of yarn. The merchant at once proposes for the daughter, marries her, and then sets her to spin a large quantity of yarn during his absence on a journey. She is assisted by a fairy, who deceives the husband into forbidding his wife to spin any more.—S. B. G.

I have lately heard, from a clerical friend, of a strange Northumbrian sprite, who has been entirely passed over in any accounts of Northern Folk-Lore to which I have had access. This sprite is called the Dunnie; he appears to be of the Brownie type, and is located at Haselrigg, in the parish of Chatton, in Northumberland. Like others of his race, he is much addicted to mischievous, troublesome tricks, such as the following, in which he frequently indulges.

When the midwife is wanted in a farmer's family, and the master goes out to saddle his horse that he may fetch her, the Dunnie will take its form. The false creature carries him safely, receives the midwife also on his back behind the farmer; but on their return, in the muddiest part of the road, he will suddenly vanish, and leave the unhappy pair floundering in the mud. Or, again, when the ploughman has (as he believes) caught his horse in the field, brought him home, and harnessed him, he will, to his dismay, see the harness come "slap to the ground," while the steed kicks up his heels and starts across the country like the wind.

Some years ago, the Dunnie was often seen wandering among the crags of the Cheviots, and heard repeating the following verse again and again, in a melancholy voice:—

> Cocken heugh there's gear enough,
> Collier heugh there's mair,
> For I've lost the key o' the Bounders,
> An' I'm ruined for evermair.

Hence it has been thought that the Dunnie is really the ghost of a "reiver," who had hoarded his ill-gotten pelf in those crags, and therefore haunts them constantly. In Mr. James Hardy's paper on *Legends respecting Huge Stones*, the third line runs, "I've lost the key of the Bowden-door," which corresponds still better with this legend.

Mr. Hardy further informs me that last spring, when passing a quarry at Haselrigg, a friend pointed to the steepest part of the rocks, and said it was there that Dunnie used to hang over his legs when he sat on the crags at night.

In my own county we have a sprite of a more benign character. He bears the homely name of Hob, and resides in Hobhole, a natural cavern in Runswick Bay, which is formed, like the fairy caves near Hartlepool and the recesses near Sunderland, by the action of the tides. He was supposed to cure the whooping-cough, so parents would take children suffering from that complaint into the cave, and in a low voice invoke him thus:—

> Hobhole Hob!
> Ma' bairn's gotten 't kink cough,
> Tak't off! tak't off!

Another sprite, called Hob Headless, infested the road between Hurworth and Neasham, but could not cross the Kent, a little stream flowing into the Tees at the latter place. He has been exorcised, however, and laid under a large stone formerly on the roadside, for ninety-nine years and a day. Should any luckless person sit on that stone, he would be unable to quit it for ever. There is yet a third Hob at Coniscliffe, near Darlington, but I have not been able to gain any information about him. Of a fourth the Vicar of Danby writes: "I have actually unearthed a Hob. He is localised to a farmhouse in the parish, though not in the township of Danby, and the old rhyme turns up among folks that could by no possibility have seen it or heard of it as in print:

> Gin Hob mun hae nowght but Harding hamp,
> He'll come nae mair to berry nor stamp,

A Yorkshire Hob, or Hobthrush, of whom I am informed by Mr. Robinson, of Hill House, Reeth, seems a very Brownie in his powers of work and hatred of clothing. He was attached to the family residing at Sturfit Hall, near Reeth, and used to churn, make up fires, and so on, till the mistress, pitying his forlorn condition, provided him with hat and cloak. He exclaimed—

> Ha! a cap and a hood,
> Hob 'll never do mair good!

and has not been seen since.

The river Tees has its sprite, called Peg Powler, a sort of Lorelei, with green tresses, and an insatiable desire for human life, as has the Jenny Greenteeth of Lancashire streams. Both are said to lure people to their subaqueous haunts, and then drown or devour them. The foam or froth, which is often seen floating on the higher portion of the Tees in large masses, is called "Peg Powler's suds;" the finer less sponge-like froth is called "Peg Powler's cream." Mr. Denham tells us that children are still warned from playing on the banks of the river, especially on Sundays, by threats that Peg Powler will drag them into the water; and he pleads guilty to having experienced great terror whenever, as a boy, he found himself alone by the haunted stream. The river Skerne too has a goblin or sprite, but of what character I have not learned. That of the Ribble is a Peg too, Peg o' Nell. A spring in the grounds of Waddow bears her name, and is graced by a stone image, now headless, which is said to represent her.

Tradition avers that in days of old Peg o' Nell was a servant at Waddow Hall. Before starting one morning to fetch water from the well, the girl offended her mistress the lady of Waddow, who thereupon expressed a wish that she might fall and break her neck. It was winter, and the ground was coated with ice. Peggy fell, and the malediction was fulfilled. But she had her revenge. Waddow Hall now became possessed of an evil genius. When the chickens were stolen, the cow died, the sheep strayed, or the children fell sick, all was due to Peg o' Nell. And further she was inexorable in demanding every seven years a life to be quenched in the waters of the Ribble. When "Peg's night," the closing night of the period, came round, unless a bird, a cat, or a dog was drowned in the stream, some human being was certain to fall a victim there. Accordingly on one anniversary of the fatal evening a young man rode down to an adjoining inn on the way from Waddington to Clitheroe. No bridge then spanned the river at Brangerley; passengers crossed it at the ford, but it was so swollen on this occasion as to be unsafe. The young man was told of this, but he said he had business at Clitheroe, and must go on. The host and hostess tried hard to dissuade him from his purpose, while the maid added, "And its Peg 'o Nell's night, and she has not had her life." The traveller laughed and set off, but neither horse nor rider reached the opposite bank.

The stone image is probably that of some saint brought from either Whalley or Salley Abbey, neither of which are very far off.[1]

The counties of Northumberland and Durham are certainly peculiarly rich in tricksy sprites. There is the Cauld Lad of Hilton, who haunted Hilton Castle in the Valley of the Wear. Seldom seen, he was heard night after night by the servants. If they left the kitchen in order, he would amuse himself by hurling everything widely about; if they left it in confusion, he would arrange everything with the greatest care. Harmless as he seemed, the servants got tired of him; so they laid a green cloak and hood before the kitchen fire, and set themselves to watch the result. At midnight the "Cauld Lad" glided in, surveyed the garments, put them on, frisked about, and, when the cock crew, disappeared, saying:

"Here's a cloak and there's a hood,
The Cauld Lad of Hilton will do no more good.

All this bespeaks him a sprite of the Brownie type; still he is in the neighbourhood deemed the ghost of a servant-boy, slain by an old baron of Hilton in a moment of passion. The baron had ordered his horse to be ready at a certain time, but waited for it in vain, so he went to the stable, found the lad asleep, and struck him a blow with a hay-fork, which killed him. The baron, it is added, covered the victim with straw till night, and then threw him into a pond, where indeed the skeleton of a boy was discovered years afterwards. Some verses, said to be sung by the Cauld Lad at dead of night, certainly accord well with the notion of his being a ghost:

Wae's me, wae's me,
The acorn's not yet
Fallen from the tree,
That's to grow the wood,

[1] From *Rambles on the Ribble*, by W. Dobson, p. 135.

That's to make the cradle,
That's to rock the bairn,
That's to grow to a man,
That's to lay me!

The late Canon Humble once told me how a friend of his was startled during a midnight walk from Hilton to Sunderland on a dark night after an evening spent in conversation about the Cauld Lad. In the loneliest part of the road a blast was blown into the traveller's face, not icy, indeed, but very warm. He leaped into the middle of the road, and his first impulse was to fly, but curiosity got the better of fear, and going back he found a cow with her head thrust into the path through a gap in the hedge.

Mrs. Murray, a lady born and brought up in the Borders, tells me of another Cauld Lad, of whom she heard in her childhood, during a visit to Gilsland, in Cumberland. He perished from cold, at the behest of some cruel uncle or stepdame; and ever after his ghost haunted the family, coming shivering to their bedsides before any one was stricken by illness, his teeth audibly chattering; and, if it were to be fatal, he laid his icy hand upon the part which would be the seat of disease, saying,

"Cauld, cauld, aye cauld,
An' ye'se be cauld for evermair!"

From Mr. Baring-Gould I learn of "a Radiant Boy, a spirit quite *sui generis;*" a boy with shining face, who has been seen in certain houses in Lincolnshire and elsewhere, but who was described more in detail by an old Yorkshire farmer bearing the nickname of John Mealyface. The account given by him to Mr. Baring-Gould runs thus: "John M. was riding one night to Thirsk, when he suddenly saw pass him a Radiant Boy on a white horse. There was no sound of footfall as he drew nigh. Old John was first aware of the approach of the mysterious rider by seeing the shadow of himself and his horse flung before him on the high road. Thinking there might be a carriage with lamps, he was not alarmed till by the shortening of the shadow he knew that the light must be near him, and then he was surprised to hear no sound. He thereupon turned in his saddle, and at the same moment the Radiant Boy passed him. He was a child of about eleven, with a fresh bright face. 'Had he any clothes on, and if so what were they like?' I asked; but John was unable to tell me. His astonishment was so great that he took no notice of particulars. The boy rode on till he came to a gate which led into a field; he stooped as if to open the gate, rode through, and all was instantly dark."[1]

About eighty or ninety years ago, the quiet village of Black Heddon, near Stamfordham, in Northumberland, was greatly disturbed by a supernatural being, popularly called Silky, from the nature of her robes. She was remarkable for the suddenness with which she would appear to benighted travellers, breaking forth upon them, in dazzling splendour, in the darkest and most lonely parts of the road. If he were on horseback, she would seat herself behind him, "rustling in her silks," accompany him a certain distance, and then as suddenly disappear, leaving the bewildered countryman in blank amazement.

Silky had a favourite resort at Belsay, two or three miles from Black Heddon, on a romantic crag beautifully studded with trees, under whose shadow she would wander all night. The bottom of this crag is washed by a picturesque little lake, at whose outlet is a waterfall, over which a fine old tree spreads its waving branches, forming by their intersection a sort of chair. In this Silky loved to sit, rocked to repose by the wild winds, and it is still called Silky's Chair; Sir Charles M. L. Monck, the present proprietor of the place, preserving the tree carefully, on account of the legend.

This sprite exercised a marvellous power over the brute creation, arresting horses in their daily work, and keeping them still as long as she was so minded. Once she waylaid a waggon bringing coals to a farm near Black Heddon, and fixed the team upon a bridge, since called, after her, "Silky's Brig." Do what he would, the driver could not make the horses move a step, and there they would have stood all night had not another farm-servant fortunately come up with some "witch-wood" (mountain-ash) about him. He went to the horses, and

[1] *Yorkshire Oddities*, vol. ii. p. 105.

they moved on at once, but never did their driver dare to go abroad again without being well armed with witchwood.

In some respects Silky showed a family likeness to the Brownies. Like them she would, during the night, tidy a disorderly house; but if cannie decent people had cleaned their rooms, and arranged them neatly, especially on a Saturday afternoon, the wayward sprite would disarrange everything as soon as they were gone to bed, so that on Sunday morning all would be in the wildest confusion.

Silky disappeared from her haunts very suddenly. One day a female servant, being alone in one of the rooms of a house at Black Heddon, was terribly frightened by the ceiling above suddenly giving way, and a black mass falling through it with a crash upon the floor. She instantly fled out of the room, screaming at the pitch of her voice, "The devil's in the house!—the devil's in the house! He's come through the ceiling!" The family collected around her in some alarm, and at first no one dared enter the room; when the mistress at last ventured to go in, she found on the floor a large rough skin filled with gold. From this time Silky was never more heard or seen, so it was believed that she was the troubled phantom of some person who had died miserable because she owned treasure, and was overtaken by her mortal agony before she had disclosed its hiding-place. The Rev. J. F. Bigge relates, however, that an old woman named Pearson, of Welton Mill, whom he visited on her death-bed, told him, a few days before her death, that she had seen Silky the night before, sittting at the bottom of her bed, all dressed in silk.

Mr. James Hardy, Silky's historian, to whom I am indebted for these particulars respecting the wayward sprite, tells me of three sister spirits, also clad in silk attire. One is the family apparition of the mansion of Houndwood, in Berwickshire, and bears the quaint name of "Chappie." A knocking was repeatedly heard at the front-door of this house, but only on one occasion was any one seen. Then a grand lady swept in, and went up the staircase, but was never seen again in or out of the house. Denton Hall, near Newcastle, was also haunted by a female form, clad in rustling silks, and so was a shady avenue near North Shields. This last Silky was thought to be the ghost of a lady who was mistress to the profligate Duke of Argyle in the reign of William III., and died suddenly, not without suspicion of murder, at Chirton, near Shields, one of his residences. The Banshee of Loch Nigdal, too, was arrayed in a silk dress, green in colour. All these traditions date from a period when silk was not in common use, and therefore attracted notice in country places.

Sir Cuthbert Sharpe, in his *Bishoprick Garland,* tells us of the Picktree Brag, a spirit as mischievous and uncannie as the Dunnie, who appeared in widely different shapes on different occasions. Sometimes it was like a calf, with a white handkerchief round its neck, and a bushy tail; sometimes, in form of a coach-horse, it trotted "along the lonin afore folk, settin' up a great nicker and a whinny now and then." Again it appeared as a "dick-ass," as four men holding up a white sheet, or as a naked man without a head. Sir Cuthbert's informant, an ancient dame, told him how her uncle had a white suit of clothes, and the first time he ever put them on he met the Brag, and never did he put them on again but some misfortune befel him. Once, in that very suit, returning from a christening, he encountered the Brag, and being a bold man, he leapt upon its back; "but, when he came to the four lonin ends, the Brag joggled him so sore, that he could hardly keep his seat; and at last it threw him into the middle o' the pond, and ran away, setting up a great nicker and laugh, just for all the world like a Christian."

The Hedley Kow was a bogie, mischievous rather than malignant, which haunted the village of Hedley, near Ebchester. His appearance was never very alarming, and he used to end his frolics with a horse-laugh at the expense of his victims. He would present himself to some old dame gathering sticks, in the form of a truss of straw, which she would be sure to take up and carry away. Then it would become so heavy she would have to lay her burden down, on which the straw would become "quick," rise upright, and shuffle away before her, till at last it vanished from her sight with a laugh and shout. Again, in the shape of a favourite cow, the sprite would lead the milkmaid a long chase round the field, and after kicking and routing during milking-time would upset the pail, slip clear of the tie, and vanish with a loud laugh. Indeed the "Kow" must have been a great nuisance in a farmhouse, for it is said to have constantly imitated the voice of the servant-girl's lovers, overturned the kail-pot, given the cream to the cats, unravelled the knitting, or put the spinning-wheel out of order. But the sprite made himself most obnoxious at the birth of a child. He would torment the man who rode for the howdie, frightening the horse, and often making him upset both messenger and howdie, and leave them in the road. Then he would mock the gudewife, and, when her angry husband rushed out with a stick to drive away the "Kow" from the door or window, the stick would be snatched from him, and lustily applied to his own shoulders.

Two adventures with the Hedley Kow are thus related. A farmer named Forster, who lived near Hedley, went out into the field one morning, and caught, as he believed, his own grey horse. After putting the harness on, and yoking him to the cart, Forster was about to drive off, when the creature slipped away from the limmers "like a knotless thread," and set up a great nicker as he flung up his heels and scoured away, revealing himself clearly as the Hedley Kow. Again, two young men of Newlands, near Ebchester, went out one evening to meet their sweethearts; and arriving at the trysting-place, saw them, as it appeared, a short distance before them. The girls walked on for two or three miles; the lads followed, quite unable to overtake them, till at last they found themselves up to the knees in a bog, and their beguilers vanished, with a loud Ha! ha! The young men got clear of the mire and ran homewards, as fast as they could, the bogie at their heels hooting and mocking them. In crossing the Derwent they fell into the water, mistook each other for the sprite, and finally reached home separately, each telling a fearful tale of having been chased by the Hedley Kow, and nearly drowned in the Derwent.

Surely this Northern sprite is closely akin to Robin Goodfellow, whom Ben Jonson introduced to us as speaking thus:—

Sometimes I meete them like a man,
Sometimes an ox, sometimes a hound,
And to a horse I turn me can,
To trip and trot about them round.

But if to ride
My backe they stride,
More swift than wind away I go:
O'er hedge and lands,
Through pools and ponds,
I whirry laughing, Ho! ho! ho![1]

The Kludde of Brabant and Flanders, an evil spirit of a Proteus-like character, a good deal resembles the Hedley Kow, though, perhaps, he is of a yet more alarming and dreadful character. In fact, he inspires such fear among the peasants, that they will on no account venture into a forest, field, or road which is haunted by him.

[1] The Dunnie, Brag, and Hedley Kow are probably the same as the Nick or Nippen. The Irish Phooka takes the shape of a horse, and induces children to mount him, then plunges with them over a precipice. The Scotch Water Kelpie (Sir W. Scott's *Minstrelsy of the Scottish Border*, p. 3) performs the same pranks. (Motherwell's *Minstrelsy*, p. 93; Buchan's *Ancient Ballads*, vol. i. p. 214.) The Icelanders have a lay to this effect. A damsel (Elen) goes to the waterside and is carried off on the grey Nykknr-horse, which she foolishly mounts. The Nykk claims her as his bride, but she escapes by saying that she will marry *Nobody;* and, as nobody is the Nykk's name, the spell is broken and she escapes.

This is a widespread legend. It exists as a ballad in Faroese, as *Nikurs Visa*, hitherto unpublished.

In Norwegian it is found in *Lanstad*, No. 39, and in Fayes's *Norske Folksagn*, second edition, p. 49.

In Swedish it is contained in *Afzel*, Nos. 11 and 89, and also in *Sagohafder*, vol. ii. p. 154.

In Danish we find it in *Syv*, No. 91; and in Danmarkes gamte *Folke Viser*, No. 39.

There are numerous German versions of the same: Meinert's *Altdeut. Volkslieder*, i. 6, No. 4; Wunderhorn, iv. p. 77; Zuccalmaglio's *Deut. Volkslieder*, No. 29; *Deutsches Museum für* 1852, ii. p. 164, &c.

A Wendish version occurs in *Haup tu Schmaler*, i. No. 34: a Slovakian ballad to the same effect in *Achacel og Korytko*, i. p. 30; Grimm's *Deutsche Sagen*, No. 51; a Bohemian form of the same in Ida v. Dürengsfeld's *Bohmische Rosen*, p. 183.

There is also a Breton popular ballad, very similar, in Villemarqué's *Barzaz Breiz*, fourth edition, vol. i. p. 259.

The Icelandic version is in *Islenzk fornkvæde ved Svend Grundtvig*, pt. i. No. 2.—S. B. G.

Kludde often transforms himself into a tree, small and delicate at first, but rapidly shooting into the clouds, while everything it shadows is thrown into confusion. Again, he presents himself as a black dog, running on its hind-legs, with a chain round its throat; and will spring at the throat of the first person he meets, fling him to the ground, and vanish. Occasionally Kludde will assume the form of a cat, frog, or bat, in which disguises he may always be known by two little blue flames fluttering or dancing before him; but most commonly he appears as an old half-starved horse, and so presents himself to stable-boys and grooms, who mount on it by mistake, instead of on their own horse or mare. Kludde sets off at full speed, the frightened lad clinging on as best he may, till they reach water, into which he rushes and laughs wildly, till his victim, sullen and angry, has worked his way to dry land again.

Oschaert, a sprite which haunted the town of Hamme, near Dendermonde, was of much the same character. On one occasion it appeared to a young man who went out courting—first as an enormous horse, then like a huge dog, then as a rabbit springing backwards and forwards before his path; and finally like a gigantic ass, with fiery eyes as large as plates. It does not appear that Oschaert ever received travellers on his back; but he used sometimes to leap on theirs, and cling on with outspread claws, till the poor victim came either to a cross-road or to an image of the Virgin, when his burden would fall off. On those who were troubled in conscience Oschaert used to press very heavily, striking his claws deep into their flesh, and scorching their necks with his breath. But all is past now. A good priest has exorcised the sprite, and banished him to the seashore for ninety-nine years, and there he wanders now.

Then, in Yorkshire, the villages around Leeds have a nocturnal terror called the Padfoot. He is described as about the size of a small donkey, black, with shaggy hair and large eyes like saucers; and he follows people by night, or waylays them in the road which they have to pass.

A certain Yorkshire woman, called Old Sally Dransfield, the carrier from Leeds to Swillington, is a firm believer in the Padfoot. She declares that she has often seen it—sometimes rolling along the ground before her, like a woolpack—sometimes vanishing suddenly through a hedge. My friend, the Rev. J. C. Atkinson, of Danby, speaks of the Padfoot as a precursor of death; as sometimes visible, sometimes invisible, but ever and anon padding lightly in the rear of people, then again before them or at their side, and uttering a roar totally unlike the voice of any known animal. Sometimes the trail of a chain would be heard, accompanying the light quick pad of the feet. In size it was somewhat larger than a sheep, with long smooth hair. It was certainly safer to leave the creature alone, for a word or a blow gave it power over you; and a story is told of a man, whose way being obstructed again and again by the Padfoot, kicked the thing, and was forthwith dragged along through hedge and ditch to his home, and left under his own window.[1]

These creations of Northern fancy have, together with some individualisms, a good many attributes in common. I imagine that the Padfoot is the same with the Barguest, Bahrgeist, or Boguest of Northumberland, Durham, and Yorkshire, and the

[1] A man in Horbury has lately seen "the Padfooit." He was going home by Jenkin, and he saw a white dog in the hedge. He struck at it, and the stick passed through it. Then the white dog looked at him, and it had "great saucer e'en;" and he was so "flayed" that he ran home trembling and went to bed, when he fell ill and died. The "Padfooit" in this neighbourhood is a white dog like a "flay-craw." It goes sometimes on two legs, sometimes it runs on three. To see it is a prognostication of death. I have no doubt that "the Padfooit" is akin to the two white sows yoked together with a silver chain which ran down the church lane in Lew Trenchard, Devon. It was the custom in ancient times to bury a dog or a boar alive under the cornerstone of a church, that its ghost might haunt the churchyard, and drive off any who would profane it, *i. e.* witches or warlocks.

In Sweden the beast which haunts churchyards is called the Kyrkogrim. It is there said that the first founders of Christian churches used to bury a lamb under the altar. When anyone enters a church out of service-time he may chance to see a little lamb spring across the quire, and vanish. That is the church lamb. Its appearance in the graveyard, especially to the gravedigger, is held to betoken the death of a child. In Denmark the animal is called the Kirkegrim.

A grave-sow is often seen in the streets of Kroskjoberg. This is said to be the apparition of a sow once buried alive, and to forebode death. In building a new bridge at Halle, which was completed in 1843, the people wanted to have a child immured in the foundation to secure its stability.—S. B. G.

Boggart of Lancashire.[1] The proverbial expression, "To roar like a Barguest," attests to the hold he has had on the popular mind. His vocation appears to have been that of a presage of death; and, bearing this in mind, Sir Walter Scott's derivation of his name from the German "bahrgeist," spirit of the bier, seems the most probable among the many suggested. A friend informs me that Glassensikes, near Darlington, is haunted by a Barguest, which assumes at will the form of a headless man (who disappears in flame), a headless lady, a white cat, rabbit, or dog, or a black dog. There is a Barguest, too, in a most uncannie-looking glen, between Darlington and Houghton, near Throstle-nest, and a circumstantial account has been supplied to me of one which haunts or haunted a piece of waste land above a spring called the Oxwells, between Wreghorn and Headingly Hill near Leeds. On the death of any person of local importance in the neighbourhood, the creature would come forth, a large black dog with flaming eyes as big as saucers, followed by all the dogs of the place howling and barking. If any one came in its way the Barguest would strike out with its paw and inflict on man or beast a wound which would never heal. My informant, a Yorkshire gentleman, lately deceased, said he perfectly remembered the terror he experienced when a child at beholding this procession before the death of a certain Squire Wade, of New Grange.

In the county of Westmoreland and some adjacent parts of Yorkshire there was formerly a belief in the existence of a similar being, called the Capelthwaite. He had the power of appearing in the form of any quadruped, but usually chose that of a large black dog. Fifty years ago there was, perhaps still is, in the parish of Beetham, near the town of Milnthorpe, a barn called Capelthwaite barn, as having been the residence of such a being. He was very well disposed towards the occupants of the barn, who suffered him to haunt it unmolested. For them he performed various kind acts, especially helping them in driving home their sheep. On one occasion he is said, after a hard

[1] I am informed by Mr. Dodson that there are several "boggart barns" in the neighbourhood of Preston—in fact, that almost every village contains one,

chase, to have driven a hare by mistake into the barn, observing, "How quickly that sheep runs."

Towards all other persons he appears to have been very spiteful and mischievous, so much so that tradition tells of a Vicar of Beetham in former days going out in his ecclesiastical vestments and saying some prayers or forms of exorcism with intent to "lay" this troublesome sprite in the river Bela. Accordingly the Capelthwaite does not seem to have appeared in later times, except that a man of the neighbourhood who returned home late at night, tipsy, much bruised, and without coat or hat, persistently assured his wife that he had met the Capelthwaite, who threw him over a hedge and deprived him of those articles of dress.

There was also a farm in Yorkshire, not far from the town of Sedbergh, called Capelthwaite farm, and said to be haunted by such a being. Of his reputed doings I can give no account, further than that the stuffed skins of five calves were preserved there, which calves were born at a birth—a fact ascribed to the influence of the Capelthwaite. These particulars were communicated to me by the Rev. W. De Lancey Lawson.

Remarkable as are the points of resemblance between the Folk-Lore of the North and the West of England, the dissimilarity on certain subjects is equally remarkable. How widely do these grotesque and churlish goblins differ from the light and frolicsome Devonshire pixy! The pixy is mischievous too, but graceful and gay in his mischief. I have received from Mr. Baring Gould a very interesting description of a curious oil-painting preserved at Lew Trenchard House, Devon, representing the merry-making of pixies, or elves perhaps, which may be inserted here:—

"In the background is an elfin city, illumined by the moon. Before the gates is a ring of tiny beings, dancing merrily around what is probably a corpse candle: it is a candle-stump, standing on the ground, and the flame diffuses a pallid white light.

"In the foreground is water, on which floats a pumpkin, with a quarter cut out of it, so as to turn it into a boat with a hood. In this the pixy king and his consort are enthroned, while round the sides of the boat sit the court, dressed in the costume of the period of William of Orange, which is the probable date of the painting. On the hood sits a little elf, with a red toadstool as an umbrella over the head of king and queen. In the bow sits Jack-o'-lanthorn, with a cresset in his hands, dressed in a red jacket. Beside him is an elf playing on a jew's-harp, which is as large as himself; and another mischievous red-coated sprite is touching the vibrating tongue of the harp, with a large extinguisher, so as to stop the music.

"The water all round the royal barge is full of little old women and red-jacketed hobgoblins, in egg-shells and crab-shells; whilst some of the imps who have been making a ladder of an iron boat-chain have missed their footing, and are splashing about in the water. In another part of the picture the sprites appear to be illuminating the window of a crumbling tower."

The word fairy, so little in use now in the North of England, is however retained at Caldbeck, in Cumberland, where a curious excavation in a rock is called the Fairy's Kettle, a neighbouring cavern twenty yards in length the Fairy Kirk, and other spots around bear similar appellations. The historian of Cumberland tells us that this place is "the scene of sundry superstitious notions and stories,"[1] but unfortunately he did not think it worth while to preserve them. In a Shropshire village, near Coalbrookdale, it is still said that fairies dance in a ring in an adjoining field, and that any unlucky wight who stepped within the ring would be kept there and never allowed to leave the spot.

Respecting the Evil Spirit, the veritable Satan, I have collected but a few notices, though it must have struck my readers that Redcap and Wag-at-the-wa' were suspiciously like him. Border tradition maintains that he has been known to assume the form of a black ram with fiery eyes and long horns, or of a sow, a bull, a goat or horse, a very large dog, or a brindled cat. It is impossible for him to take that of the lamb. Of birds he can only simulate the crow and the drake. The farmyard cock and hen, and the pigeon, are too pure for him to have anything to do with—the former from their watchfulness, the latter because

[1] Hutchinson's *History of Cumberland*, vol. ii. pp. 388-9.

it has no gall-bladder. It is curious to compare this piece of Border Folk-lore with that of Devonshire, where it is said that the devil can assume all shapes except those of the lamb and the dove. A little girl, on the borders of Dartmoor, told this to one of my relations, adding, "He can't make himself look like *they*, because of Jesus Christ and the Holy Spirit."[1]

Mr. G. Henderson's *Popular Rhymes of Berwickshire* tells us of a remarkable piece of service formerly done to the Evil One. "Cloutie's croft," he says, "or the gudeman's field, consisted of a small portion of the best land, set apart by the inhabitants of most Scottish villages as a propitiatory gift to the devil, on which property they never ventured to intrude. It was dedicated to the devil's service alone, being left untilled and uncropped, and it was reckoned highly dangerous to break up by tillage such pieces of ground."[2]

A little anecdote has been related to me by the minister of ——, on the Tweedside, which shows that the Evil Spirit is held to have power of molesting good Christians in wild lonely places. A country minister, after attending a meeting of his presbytery, had to return home alone, and very late, on a dark evening. While riding in a gloomy part of the road, his horse stumbled, and the good man was suddenly flung to the ground. A loud laugh followed, so scornful and so weird, that the minister felt no doubt of the quarter whence it proceeded. However, with a stout heart, he remounted without delay, and continued his journey, crying out, "Ay, Satan, *ye* may laugh; but, when I fall, I can get up again; when *ye* fell, *ye* never rose"—on which a deep groan was heard. This was firmly believed to have been

[1] A Sussex boy once told me, that, if a letter were placed under the pillow at night offering to the devil to sell one's soul, the letter would be gone in the morning, and half-a-crown found in its place.—S. B. G.

[2] In several parishes in Devonshire is a patch of land hedged in, which is called Gallitrap (*i. e.* Gallows-trap), and considered uncannie. There is such a piece in the parish of Lew Trenchard. The superstition connected with it is that it is a gallows-trap, for if anyone "feyed" to be hung enters the field, he cannot leave it again, but must wander round and round it, without power to find the gate, or climb the fence, till the parson and the magistrate are sent for; the first to take the spell off him, the second to see to his being hung.—S. B. G.

an encounter with the Evil Spirit, and a great triumph for the dauntless minister.

In his *Rambles on the Ribble* Mr. Dobson records what professes to be a genuine Lancashire tale which has been told for generations by many a fireside on the banks of that river. There stood till recently in the town of Clitheroe a public-house bearing the strange name of Dule upon Dun, on the signboard of which the devil was depicted riding off at full speed upon a dun horse, while a tailor, scissors in hand, looked on with delight.

It appears that in former days, when the Evil One used to visit the earth in bodily form and enter into contracts with mortals, giving them material prosperity now in exchange for the soul at a future time, a tailor of Clitheroe entered into some such agreement with him. At the expiration of the term, however, the tailor having failed to receive any benefit at all from the agreement, asked from his Satanic Majesty the boon of "one wish more." It was granted. A dun horse was grazing hard by, and the ready-witted tailor, pointing to the animal, wished that the devil might ride straight to his own quarters upon it and never come back to earth to plague mortal. Instantly the horse was bestridden by the Evil One, who speedily rode out of sight never to return in a bodily shape. People came from far and near to see the man who had outwitted the devil, and soon it occurred to the tailor to set up an alehouse for the entertainment of his visitors, taking for a sign the devil riding a dun horse, or as the neighbours called it for brevity "the Dule upon Dun."

A strange story is told by Scottish firesides, how the devil desired to learn one trade after another, but failed in all. First, he would be a weaver, but he pricked his fingers with the pins of the temples, and threw up that occupation. A scrap of an old song speaks of his weaving days—

The weaver de'il gaed out at night
To see the new, new moon,
Wi' a' the traddles at his back,
An' the sowin' bag aboon.

Next he tried his fortune as a tailor, but first he sewed his fingers to the cloth, and then spoiled the sleeve of the coat he was making by cutting the curve of the elbow wrong; on which his master, out of all patience, ran the bodkin into his side and knocked him over the board with the goose. After this he took service with a blacksmith, and attempted to shoe a horse, but he only pricked the horse, and drove the nails into his own finger. As a farrier he maltreated the horse; as a tinker he split the caldrons he should have mended; as a carpenter he wounded himself with the chopper, bruised his hands with the plane, fell over the logs of wood he should have sawn, and got the toothache from the noise produced by filing the tools. Lastly, as a shoemaker, he took wrong measures, and lost the rubsticks which were under his care, till his master gave him a severe "yocking," and disgusted him for ever with the awl and the last. Nothing remained to him but to start verse-maker, and wander from alehouse to alehouse, singing the drinking-songs he composed.

The honest Yorkshiremen under the Hambleton hills bring in the devil's name when they account for their custom of saying their prayers aloud—a most praiseworthy one, though Margaret, in *Much Ado About Nothing*, reckons it among her "ill qualities." They say that the devil hears them, and lets them alone for that night at least. Now it is remarkable that Sir Richard Baker, in his *Meditations and Disquisitions upon the Lord's Prayer* (1638, p. 7), after recommending vocal prayer as pleasing to God, and giving cause of joy to the angels, proceeds: "We shall doe well to use vocall prayers if it be only to fright the devill. For he sees not our hearts, but he heares our tongues: and when hee heares our words, because he knowes not our hearts, hee feares they come from our hearts, and in that feare hee trembles: and we shall doe well, as much as we can, to keepe him under our feare, seeing he endeavours as much as he can to bring us under his power."

CHAPTER VIII.

WORMS OR DRAGONS.

Probable Origin of these Legends—Worm of Sockburn—The Pollard Worm or Brawn—The Lambton Worm—The Laidley Worm of Spindleston Heugh—The Linton Worm—Dragons at S. Osyth's—Deerhurst—Mordeford—Chipping Norton—Denbigh—S. Leonard and the Worm.—The Helstone Dragon.—Review of the Subject.

MONG the rich and varied Folk-Lore of the North of England and the Scottish Lowlands it is imposible not to remark how numerous and characteristic are the legends respecting dragons, or, as we locally call them, worms—a name taken from the Norse *Ormr*, a serpent or dragon. These tales are sometimes enshrined in ballads, sometimes bound up with the tenure of property, sometimes sculptured as part of church decorations; but all live yet upon the lips of the people, though of course we cannot presume to guess how long they will maintain their ground against the combined forces of railroads and collieries.

Sir Walter Scott, in his *Minstrelsy of the Scottish Border*, accounts for these legends by suggesting that in bygone days, before our country was drained and cleared of wood, large serpents may have infested British woods or morasses, and taxed the prowess of British champions. I believe that Mr. Surtees held the same opinion, and Lord Lindsay, in his *Sketches of Christian Art*, writes as follows: " The dragons of early tradition, whether aquatic or terrestrial, are not perhaps wholly to be regarded as fabulous. In the case of the former, the race may be supposed to have been perpetuated till the marshes or inland seas left by the Deluge were dried up. Hence probably the legends of the Lernæan hydra, &c. As respects their terrestrial brethren (among whom the serpent, which checked the army of Regulus for three days near the River Bagradus in Numidia, will be remembered), their existence, testified as it is by the universal credence of antiquity, is not absolutely incredible. Lines of descent are constantly becoming extinct in animal genealogy."

The opinion half avowed by Sir Walter Scott and Lord Lindsay has now taken possession of other thoughtful minds. Mr. Henry Lee avows his belief in the existence of the sea-serpent, a monster as terrible as was ever confronted by champion or knight; while our great astronomer, Mr. Proctor, after long and patient research, has arrived at the conclusion that there do still linger in the ocean depths creatures of strange form and gigantic size, closely allied to the mighty Saurians of pre-Adamite times, creatures which are nocturnal in their habits and therefore seldom seen by man, but which do occasionally rise to the surface in daylight. And Mr. Waterhouse Hawkins, in a recent lecture at the London Institution on the age of dragons, boldly condemns the careless habit of treating such creatures as mere products of the human fancy in the childhood of the world, and bids us look for the prototype of the medieval dragon in the gigantic monsters of early days, with which man had to make war in his first struggles for existence on the earth which was given him to subdue.

In truth they have but gradually disappeared before him. It is well known that within the last century at the mouth of one of the Siberian rivers the remains of a colossal mammoth were hewn out of an iceberg in perfect preservation, while the Moa, if not actually surviving in the interior of New Zealand, has but recently become extinct. Captain Hope describes a strange sea-monster which he saw from the "Fly" in the Gulf of California, lying at the bottom of the ocean. It had the head and general appearance of an alligator, with a long neck and four paddles instead of legs. And in the vaults of the British Museum is preserved the arm of a gigantic cuttle-fish, from the measurement of which we may calculate that the total length of the animal must have been fifty feet.

Such strange misshapen monsters were the dread of man when yet a new inhabitant of our globe. To the Egyptian the crocodile was his dragon, to the dweller on the coast the leviathan or sea-monster, to the Arabian in the desert the poisonous snake. But there has been a period in the history of the world when it was tenanted not only by serpents huge and terrible, but by creatures which still more closely resemble the ideal dragon as pictured by medieval painters or described by our poets and balladmongers.

> This dragon had two furious wings,
> Each one upou each shoulder;
> With a sting in his tail as long as a flail,
> Which made him bolder and bolder.
> He had long claws, and in his jaws
> Four-and-forty teeth of iron,
> With a hide as tough as any buff
> Which did him round environ.[1]

Such an animal was the Pterodactyle, one of those huge saurians or lizards whose fossilized bones lay hidden in the earth for centuries, till a Cuvier or a Buckland with penetrating eye and patient hand should piece them together and lay before an astonished world the perfect skeleton. The Pterodactyle as thus revealed to us is a winged reptile, with a long neck, a large head and eyes, a body covered with scales, and two feet on which to stand like a bird. Well might Dr. Buckland see in so extraordinary a creature a resemblance to Milton's fiend, who—

> O'er bog, or steep, through strait, rough, dense, or rare,
> With head, hands, wings or feet pursues his way,
> And swims, or sinks, or wades, or creeps, or flies.

The "baby thought" of the human race having been moulded by such strange and terrible creatures, we cannot wonder that the earliest traditions of almost every nation tell of monsters of sea or land—the foes of man. The Folk-Lore of China teems with tales of dragons and serpents. In the Grecian mythology we find the many-headed Hydra destroyed by Hercules, the boar of Calydon by Meleager, the Cretan Minotaur by Theseus, as well as the sea-monster from whom Perseus saved Andromeda, the horses of Diomede who were fed on human flesh, and the Cyclop Polypheme blinded by Ulysses; while Norse mythology tells of the Jormangaund, a sea-serpent surrounding the globe and defying the mighty Thor to do more than move it slightly,

[1] *Dragon of Wantley.*

and the Kraken, which buries its vast bulk in the muddy ooze of ocean's depths, only rising from time to time to engulf some unhappy ship beneath the waves.

That our entire country has been pervaded by a belief in such terrible creatures we learn from the names of Wormshead, Great Orme's Head, Ormesleigh, Ormeskirk, Wormigill, Wormelow, and Wormeslea, with others of a similar character scattered over the land, but in the main we must look to the North of England for legends of any remarkable vigour or beauty respecting them.

Let us begin with the Worm of Sockburn, whose story is interesting from its extreme antiquity, and its connection with an old tenure of land. The manor of Sockburn was for generations held by the presentation of a falchion to the Bishop of Durham on his first entrance into his diocese. This service is said to date from the time of Bishop Pudsey, who purchased from Richard I. for himself and his successors the title of Earl of Sadberge. And from the time of this "jolye Bishop of Durham" (as Hugh Pudsey is called in an old record) to that of Van Mildert, the last of her Palatines, each bishop, as he entered his diocese, was met on Croft Bridge, or in the middle of the River Tees, by the lord of the manor of Sockburn, who, after hailing him Count Palatine and Earl of Sadberge, presented him with the falchion, and said these words:

"My Lord Bishop, I here present you with the falchion wherewith the champion Conyers slew the worm, dragon, or fiery flying serpent, which destroyed man, woman, and child; in memory of which the king then reigning gave him the manor of Sockburn, to hold by this tenure, that upon the first entrance of every bishop into the county this falchion should be presented."

The Bishop then took the falchion into his hand, and immediately returning it, wished the lord of Sockburn health and a long enjoyment of the manor.

A fragment of verse, which I think we may safely ascribe to Mr. Surtees, the historian of the Palatinate, tells of—

Sockburn, where Conyers so trusty
A huge serpent did dish up
That had else ate the Bishop,
But now his old falchion's grown rusty, grown rusty.

There is mention made of this tenure in the inquest held on the death of Sir John Conyers in A.D. 1396. The falchion also appears in painted glass in a window of Sockburn church, and together with the worm is sculptured in marble on the tomb of the ancestor of the Conyers family. In April 1826 the steward of Sir Edward Blackett, then lord of Sockburn manor, presented the falchion on Croft Bridge to Dr. Van Mildert, the last Prince-Bishop of Durham. I regret to say that the Palatinate Act has provided for the extinction of this service.

As to the Pollard Worm it appears to have been in fact a wild boar or brawn, akin to the boar or brawn of Brancepeth, which in former days was lord of the forest from the Wear to the Gaunless, till Hodge of Ferry, marking its track, dug a pitfall into which he lured it to its destruction. The following communication, which I have received through the kindness of Colonel Johnson, whose family have long been owners of a portion of the Pollard lands, gives fuller particulars of the Pollard worm or brawn than have hitherto been published.

Long long ago, when extensive forests covered the greater part of Durham and adjoining counties, and wild animals of all sorts abounded in them, a huge and very savage wild boar inhabited the woods of Bishop Auckland. The injury it did in the neighbourhood was very great. All attempts to kill or drive away the creature were in vain. Several knights and others who went out to encounter it were killed, and at last both the King and the Bishop of Durham thought it needful to come forward in the matter. The King issued a proclamation to the effect that whoever should bring the boar's head to Westminster should receive a reward, while the Bishop Count Palatine, who resided a great part of the year at Auckland Castle, and whose tenants and retainers suffered most from the beast's depredations, declared that he would give a princely guerdon to any champion who was bold and skilful enough to rid him of the monster.

A member of the Pollard family, even at that time an honourable and ancient one, armed himself and rode out to the boar's lair or den in Etherley Dene. After ascertaining its usual track, he secured his horse in a place of safety and ascended a large beech tree which overshadowed a glade through which the monster was accustomed to pass. He shook down a quantity of ripe beechmast and patiently awaited the creature's approach. As he foresaw, the boar was arrested by the rich repast, and began at once to gorge itself with its favourite food.

After eating voraciously for a long time the boar moved away drowsily and heavily. The Pollard descended rapidly from his hiding-place and attacked the retreating animal. It turned, and though not in good plight for fighting made a fierce resistance, so that the champion did not kill it till after a desperate struggle, which must have occupied the greater part of the night, for the sun rose just as Pollard severed the boar's head from the trunk, cut out the tongue, and placed it in his wallet. Worn out with fatigue, the conqueror stretched himself at the foot of the beech-tree and fell into a deep sleep, which lasted some hours. On awaking he turned to take up the boar's head, which he was to bear to the King in proof of his victory, but to his dismay it was gone, and with it all hopes of the royal reward. So nothing remained for the Pollard but to mount his horse and ride to Auckland Castle, there to tell his tale and make the best use he could of the boar's tongue, which happily lay in his wallet, and of its carcase, which was stretched under the beech-tree. He arrived before the castle-gate at an unseasonable moment, just as the Bishop was sitting down to dinner. However, his lordship sent the champion word that he might take for his guerdon as much land as he could ride round during the hour of dinner. Weary as he was, Pollard had all his wits about him. He turned his horse's head and rode round Auckland Castle, thus making it and all it contained his own. The Bishop could not but acknowledge his claim, and gladly redeemed castle, goods, and chattels on the best terms he could. He granted the champion a freehold estate, still known as the Pollard's lands, with this condition annexed. The possessor was to meet every Bishop of Durham on his first coming to Auckland Castle, and to present him with a falchion, saying, "My Lord, I, on behalf of myself, as well as several others, possessors of Pollard's lands, do humbly present your lordship with this falchion at your first coming here, wherewith as the tradition goeth he slew of old a mighty boar which did much harm to man and beast. And by performing this service we hold our lands." It may be added that the crest of the Pollard family is an arm holding a falchion.

But to return to the boar's head which disappeared so strangely. While our hero, worn out with the conflict, lay sleeping under the shade of the beech-tree, the lord of Mitford Castle near Morpeth rode up, being then on his way to London. He took in the state of things at a glance, and, knowing of the reward the King had promised, he stealthily dismounted from his horse, took up the head, slung it at his saddlebow, remounted, and resumed his journey with all speed. On arriving in London he went straight to the royal palace, showed the head, and obtained the reward.

It is added that Pollard too went to London afterwards, and urged his claims, pleading that the head Mitford had brought was without a tongue, but to no purpose.

The Lambton Worm, partly from the romantic character of its history, partly because it relates to a family of note in the county, seems to have taken deep hold of the popular mind in Durham, and it is peculiarly fortunate in a chronicler. About thirty years ago, Sir Cuthbert Sharpe, the friend of Mr. Surtees, and his assistant in the History of the Palatinate, collected every particular respecting this Worm from old residents in the neighbourhood of Lambton, and placed the whole in the *Bishoprick Garland*, a collection of legends, songs, ballads, &c., relating to the county of Durham. As only one hundred and fifty copies of this little work were printed, and it is now extremely scarce, free use has been made of it in the following account of the Worm of Lambton:—

The park and manor-house of Lambton, belonging to a family of the same name, lie on the banks of the Wear, to the north of Lumley. The family is a very ancient one, much older, it is believed, than the twelfth century, to which date its pedigree extends. The old castle was dismantled in 1797, when a site was adopted for the present mansion on the north bank of the swiftly-flowing Wear, in a situation of exceeding beauty. The park also contains the ruins of a chapel, called Brugeford or Bridgeford, close to one of the bridges which span the Wear.

Long, long ago, some say about the fourteenth century, the young heir of Lambton led a careless profane life, regardless alike of his duties to God and man, and in particular neglecting to attend mass, that he might spend his Sunday mornings in fishing. One Sunday, while thus engaged, having cast his line into the Wear many times without success, he vented his disappointment in curses loud and deep, to the great scandal of the servants and tenantry as they passed by to the chapel at Brugeford.

Soon afterwards he felt something tugging at his line, and trusting he had at last secured a fine fish, he exerted all his skill and strength to bring his prey to land. But what were his horror and dismay on finding that, instead of a fish, he had only caught a worm of most unsightly appearance! He hastily tore the thing from his hook, and flung it into a well close by, which is still known by the name of the Worm Well.

The young heir had scarcely thrown his line again into the stream when a stranger of venerable appearance, passing by, asked him what sport he had met with. To which he replied, "Why, truly, I think I have caught the devil himself. Look in and judge." The stranger looked, and remarked that he had never seen the like of it before; that it resembled an eft, only it had nine holes on each side of its mouth; and, finally, that he thought it boded no good.

The worm remained unheeded in the well till it outgrew so confined a dwelling-place. It then emerged, and betook itself by day to the river, where it lay coiled round a rock in the middle of the stream, and by night to a neighbouring hill, round whose base it would twine itself; while it continued to grow so fast, that it soon could encircle the hill three times. This eminence is still called the Worm Hill. It is oval in shape, on the north side of the Wear, and about a mile and a half from old Lambton Hall.

The monster now became the terror of the whole country side. It sucked the cows' milk, worried the cattle, devoured the lambs, and committed every sort of depredation on the helpless peasantry. Having laid waste the district on the north side of the river it crossed the stream and approached Lambton Hall, where the old lord was living alone and desolate. His son had repented of his evil life, and had gone to the wars in a distant country. Some authorities tell us he had embarked as a crusader for the Holy Land.

On hearing of their enemy's approach, the terrified household assembled in council. Much was said, but to little purpose, till the steward, a man of age and experience, advised that the large trough which stood in the courtyard should immediately be filled with milk. This was done without delay; the monster approached, drank the milk, and, without doing further harm, returned across the Wear to wrap his giant form around his favourite hill. The next day he was seen recrossing the river; the trough was hastily filled again, and with the same results. It was found that the milk of "nine kye" was needed to fill the trough; and if this quantity was not placed there every day, regularly and in full measure, the worm would break out into a violent rage, lashing its tail round the trees in the park, and tearing them up by the roots.

The Lambton Worm was now, in fact, the terror of the North Country. It had not been left altogether unopposed. Many a gallant knight had come out to fight with the monster, but all to no purpose; for it possessed the marvellous power of reuniting itself after being cut asunder, and thus was more than a match for the chivalry of the North. So, after many conflicts, and much loss of life and limb, the creature was left in possession of its favourite hill.

After seven long years, however, the heir of Lambton returned home, a sadder and a wiser man: returned to find the broad lands of his ancestors waste and desolate, his people oppressed and wellnigh exterminated, his father sinking into the grave overwhelmed with care and anxiety. He took no rest, we are told, till he had crossed the river and surveyed the Worm as it lay coiled round the foot of the hill; then, hearing how its former opponents had failed, he took counsel in the matter from a sybil or wise woman.

At first the sybil did nothing but upbraid him for having brought this scourge upon his house and neighbourhood; but when she perceived that he was indeed penitent, and desirous at any cost to remove the evil he had caused, she gave him her advice and instructions. He was to get his best suit of mail studded thickly with spear-heads, to put it on, and thus armed to take his stand on the rock in the middle of the river, there to meet his enemy, trusting the issue to Providence and his good sword. But she charged him before going to the encounter to take a vow that, if successful, he would slay the first living thing that met him on his way homewards. Should he fail to fulfil this vow, she warned him that for nine generations no lord of Lambton would die in his bed.

The heir, now a belted knight, made the vow in Brugeford chapel; he studded his armour with the sharpest spear-heads, and unsheathing his trusty sword took his stand on the rock in the middle of the Wear. At the accustomed hour the Worm uncoiled its "snaky twine," and wound its way towards the hall, crossing the river close by the rock on which the knight was standing eager for the combat. He struck a violent blow upon the monster's head as it passed, on which the creature, "irritated and vexed," though apparently not injured, flung its tail round him, as if to strangle him in its coils.

In the words of a local poet:

> The worm shot down the middle stream
>   Like a flash of living light,
> And the waters kindled round his path
>   In rainbow colours bright.
> But when he saw the armed knight
>   He gathered all his pride,
> And coiled in many a radiant spire
>   Rode buoyant o'er the tide.
> When he darted at length his dragon strength
>   An earthquake shook the rock,
> And the fireflakes bright fell round the knight
>   As unmoved he met the shock.
> Though his heart was stout it quailed no doubt,
>   His very life-blood ran cold,
> As round and round the wild Worm wound
>   In many a grappling fold.

Now was seen the value of the sybil's advice. The closer the Worm wrapped him in its folds the more deadly were its self-inflicted wounds, till at last the river ran crimson with its gore. Its strength thus diminished, the knight was able at last with his good sword to cut the serpent in two; the severed part was immediately borne away by the swiftness of the current, and the Worm, unable to reunite itself, was utterly destroyed.

During this long and desperate conflict the household of Lambton had shut themselves within-doors to pray for their young lord, he having promised that when it was over he would, if conqueror, blow a blast on his bugle. This would assure his father of his safety, and warn them to let loose the favourite hound, which they had destined as the sacrifice on the occasion, according to the sybil's requirements and the young lord's vow. When, however, the bugle-notes were heard within the hall, the old man forgot everything but his son's safety, and rushing out of doors, ran to meet the hero and embrace him.

The heir of Lambton was thunderstruck; what could he do? It was impossible to lift his hand against his father; yet how else to fulfil his vow? In his perplexity he blew another blast; the hound was let loose, it bounded to its master; the sword, yet reeking with the monster's gore, was plunged into its heart; but all in vain. The vow was broken, the sybil's prediction fulfilled, and the curse lay upon the house of Lambton for nine generations.

The exact date of the story is of course uncertain. Sir Cuthbert Sharpe appends to it the following entry from an old manuscript pedigree, lately in the possession of the family of Middleton, of Offerton: "John Lambton, that slewe ye worme, was knight of Rhodes and lord of Lambton, after ye dethe of fower brothers—'*sans eschew malle.*'" Now nine ascending generations, from a certain Henry Lambton, Esq. M.P. would exactly reach to Sir John Lambton, knight of Rhodes; and it was to that Henry Lambton that the old people of the neighbourhood used to look with great curiosity, marvelling whether the curse would "hold good to the end." He died in his carriage, crossing the new bridge of Lambton, on the 26th of June, 1761;[1] and popular tradition is clear and unanimous in maintaining that, during the period of the curse, no lord of Lambton ever died in his bed. I have frequently heard my mother relate how her mother used to speak of the deep and wide-spreading anxiety which prevailed during the latter years of Henry Lambton, and when tidings reached Durham of his death and the fulfilment of the prophecy the universal feeling was one of deep awe, not unmingled with a certain satisfaction in the final accomplishment of what had been looked forward to so long and so earnestly. The violent deaths of some of this fated family are recorded in history. Sir William Lambton, a colonel of a regiment of foot in the service of Charles I. was slain at Marston Moor; and his son William, as gallant a Royalist as his father, received his death-wound at Wakefield, at the head of a troop of dragoons, A.D. 1643. Surely such deaths as these show how a curse may pass into a blessing!

It may be added that two stone figures of some antiquity and tolerable workmanship existed lately at Lambton Castle. One of these was apparently an effigy of our hero—studded armour, sword, and vanquished monster, all as described in the legend, except that the Worm is endowed with ears, legs, and even a pair of wings. The other figure was a female one, and marked by no very characteristic features. It might, however, have been meant for the sybil. The trough from which the Worm took its daily tribute of milk is still to be seen at Lambton Hall; and Mr. Surtees mentions that in his young days he saw there a piece of some tough substance, resembling bull's hide, which was shown him as part of the Worm's skin.

From the green banks of the Wear we must pass to the stern and rock-bound coast of Northumberland if we would make acquaintance with the Laidley (*i. e.* loathly, or loathsome) Worm of Spindleston Heugh. Its history is exceedingly popular on the

[1] The parish registers record that Henry Lambton was baptized at Bishops Wearmouth, November 9, 1697, obiit cæl. et intest. June 26, 1761, and was buried on July 4 of the same year.

Borders, as Sir Walter Scott remarks in his *Minstrelsy of the Scottish Border*, though he refrains from transcribing it on account of its resemblance to "Kempion." The legend was put into verse—very unequal, however, in character—by a former vicar of Norham.

It opens with a parting between a king and his daughter. He goes out to win a second bride, and leaves his child, the Lady Margaret, in charge of Bamborough Castle. We see her, during her father's absence, arranging everything against his return, tripping out and tripping in, with the keys hanging over her left shoulder. At last the day arrives; the chieftains of the Border are all assembled to receive the king and queen. They come; the Lady Margaret welcomes them to hall and bower, and then, turning sweetly to her stepmother, reminds her that everything now is hers. One of the chieftains, struck by the young girl's beauty and simplicity, praises her loudly in the queen's hearing, as

Excelling all of woman kind
In beauty and in worth.

The jealous queen mutters, "You might have excepted me;" and from that hour Margaret's fate was sealed. The next morning the maiden was standing at her bower-door, laughing for joy of heart; but before nightfall her stepdame had witched her to a loathsome Worm, so to abide till her brother, the Childe of Wynde, should come to her rescue from beyond seas. The cave is still shown at Spindleston Heugh where the Worm hid itself by day; during the night it would wander on the coast. We do not hear of any depredations it committed beyond the exaction of a tribute of milk (that favourite beverage of northern worms!); but so poisonous was the creature that for seven long miles in every direction the country was laid waste—no green thing would grow.

At last, word went over the sea to the Childe of Wynde, that his native land was desolated by a Laidley Worm on Spindleston Heugh; and, fearing lest any harm should befall his sister, he summoned his merry men, thirty-and-three in number:

They built a ship without delay,
  With masts of the rowan-tree,
With fluttering sails of silk so fine,
  And set her on the sea.

They went on board, the wind with speed
  Blew them along the deep;
At length they spied a huge square tower
  On a rock so high and steep.

The sailors recognised the Northumbrian coast and King Ida's Castle, and made towards shore.

Meanwhile, the queen looked out of her bower-window, and spying the gallant ship with its silken sails, sent out her evil companions, the "witch wives," to sink it in the waters; but they returned baffled and sullen, murmuring that there must be rowan-wood about the ship, for all their spells were powerless. Next she dispatched a boat with armed men to withstand the landing of the vessel; but the gallant Childe speedily put them to the rout. Lastly, it would seem that the Worm itself withstood its deliverer, for we are told that

The Worme lept up, the Worme lept down,
  She plaited round the stone,
And aye, as the ship came close to land,
  She banged it off again.

However, the Childe of Wynde steered the ship out of her reach, ran ashore on the sands of Budle, a small village near Bamborough, and, drawing his sword, went boldly towards the monster, as if to do battle at once. But the creature submitted, exclaiming,—

"O quit thy sword, and bend thy bow,
  And give me kisses three;
For though I be a poisonous Worme,
  No hurt I'll do to thee.

O quit thy sword, and bend thy bow,
  And give me kisses three;
If I'm not won ere set of sun,
  Won shall I never be."

He quitted his sword, and bent his bow,
  He gave her kisses three;
She crept into her hole a Worme,
  But out stept a ladye.

Our hero folded his recovered sister in his mantle, and bore her with him to Bamborough Castle, where he found his father inconsolable for her loss, though, through the queen's witcheries, he had tamely submitted to it. However, the queen's power was over now, and the Childe pronounced her unalterable doom. Changed into a toad, she was to wander till doomsday round Bamborough Castle, and the fair maidens of that neighbourhood believe that she still vents her malice against them by spitting venom at them.

Crossing the Border into Roxburghshire, we approach the haunts of the Wormē of Linton, and very romantic they are. There is the mountain-stream of the Cale, bursting in brightness from the Cheviot Hills, and hurrying into the plain below, where it pauses ere it wends its way to join the Tweed. There is the low irregular mound, marking where stood the tower of Linton, the stronghold of the Somervilles; there is the old village church, standing on its remarkable knoll of sand; there are the stately woods of Clifton, and, above all, the lofty heights of Cheviot crowning the distance.

Such is the fair scene which tradition avers was once laid waste by a fierce and voracious monster. His den, still named the "Worm's Hole," lay in a hollow to the east of the hill of Linton; and small need had he to leave it, for from this retreat he could with his sweeping and venomous breath draw the neighbouring flocks and herds within reach of his fangs. Still he did occasionally emerge and coil himself round an eminence of some height, at no great distance, still bearing the name of Wormington or Wormistonne. Liberal guerdons were offered to any champion who would rid the country of such a scourge, but in vain—such was the dread inspired by the monster's poisonous breath. Not only were the neighbouring villagers beside themselves with terror, but the inhabitants of Jedburgh, full ten miles off, were struck with such a panic that they were ready to desert their town.

At last, however, the laird of Lariston, a man of reckless bravery, came forward to the rescue of this distressed district; and, as the Linton cottagers testify to this day, having once failed in an attack with ordinary weapons, he resorted to the expedient of thrusting down its throat a peat dipped in scalding pitch and fixed on his lance. The device proved perfectly successful. The aromatic quality of the burning pitch, while it suffocated and choked the monster, preserved the champion from the effects of its poison-laden breath. While dying, the worm is said to have contracted its folds with such violent muscular energy that the sides of Wormington Hill are still marked with their spiral impressions. In requital of his service, the laird of Lariston received the gift of extensive lands in the neighbourhood.

The Somerville family (for nearly four hundred years lords of Linton) claim the merit of this exploit for the John Somerville who received the barony of Linton in 1174, and built its tower. They maintain that it was conferred on him by William the Lion as a reward for slaying the Worm, and they bear a dragon for their crest in memorial of it. Unfortunately, however, in their hands the Worm loses much of its grandeur and importance. The monster encircling the hillock with its snaky coils becomes "in length three Scots' yards, and somewhat bigger than an ordinary man's leg, with a head more proportionable to its length than greatness, in form and colour like to our common muir-edders." In this disparaging way at least is the Linton Worm described by the author of *The Memoirs of the Somervilles*, A.D. 1680.

The sculptured effigy of the monster, which may still be seen with the champion who slew it, at the south-western extremity of Linton church, differs from both accounts. A stone, evidently of great antiquity, is there built into the wall. It is covered with sculpture in low relief, and bears figures which, though defaced by time, can yet be made out pretty clearly. A knight on horseback, clad in a tunic or hauberk, with a round helmet, urges his horse against two large animals, the foreparts of which only are visible, and plunges his lance into the throat of one. Behind him is the outline of another creature, apparently of a lamb. The heads of the monsters are strong and powerful, but more like those of quadrupeds than of serpents. It is perplexing also to see two of them, but not the less does popular tradition connect the representation with the Linton Worm, and aver that the inscription below it, now quite defaced, ran thus:—

> The wode laird of Larristone
> Slew the Worme of Wormestone,
> And wan a' Linton parochine.

It should be added, that, though the present church appears to have been rebuilt at no very distant date, it stands on the site of the former one, and is formed from its materials; this sculptured stone having stood, it is said, above the door of the old church. Whether it really represents some doughty deed by which the first Somerville won the favour of William the Lion, or visibly embodies the great conflict between Christianity and Paganism, has been much disputed by antiquaries. The figure, resembling a lamb behind the victorious knight, is certainly suggestive of a mythical interpretation, and reminds us of the banner of St. Eric, so treasured by the ancient Swedes, and stored in the cathedral at Upsala, which bore on one side, in gold embroidery, a lamb and a dragon.

There is another legend connected with Linton, of exceeding interest. It is sometimes interwoven with that of the Worm, and, though I am informed that in its more correct form it stands alone,[1] I may perhaps be pardoned for a little discursiveness if I pause to relate it. The church is built on a little knoll of fine compact sand, without any admixture of stone, or even pebbles, and widely different from the soil of the neighbouring heights, The sand has nowhere hardened into stone, yet the particles are so coherent, that the sides of newly-opened graves appear smooth as a wall, and this to the depth of fifteen feet. This singular phenomenon is thus accounted for on the spot.

Many ages ago a young man killed a priest in this place, and was condemned to suffer death for murder and sacrilege. His doom seemed inevitable, but powerful intercession was made for him, especially by his two sisters, who were fondly attached to their brother. At last his life was granted him, on condition that the sisters should sift as much sand as would form a mound on which to build a church. The maidens joyfully undertook the task, and their patience did not fail. They completed it, and the church was built, though it is added that one of the sisters died immediately after her brother's liberation, either from the effects of past fatigue or overpowering joy. Such is the version of the legend, deemed the correct one at Linton. The villagers point to the sandy knoll in confirmation of its truth, and show a hollow place a short distance to the westward as that from which the sand was taken.

The legends of serpents and dragons rife in other parts of England are, on the whole, but meagre when compared with these Northern tales. A few are enumerated by a contributor to *The Folk-Lore Record* of 1878. At St. Osythes, in Essex, appeared, A D. 1170, a dragon of marvellous bigness, which, by moving, set fire to houses. At Deerhurst, near Tewkesbury, a serpent of prodigious size was once a great grievance to the place, poisoning the inhabitants, and devouring their cattle, till the king proclaimed that any one who destroyed the serpent should receive an estate in the parish belonging to the crown. One John Smith placed a quantity of milk near the creature's lair, which it drank and then lay down to sleep. Smith cut off its head with an axe and received the estate, which still continued in his family when Sir Robert Atkyns wrote this account. The axe also was carefully preserved. At Mordiford, in Herefordshire, the tradition yet survives of a furious combat between a dragon and a condemned malefactor, who was promised pardon on the condition of his destroying his antagonist. He did kill it, but fell a victim to the poison of its breath. The contest is said to have taken place in the river Lug, and the dragon is represented in a painting in Mordiford church as a winged serpent, about twelve feet long, with a large head and open mouth. Near Chipping Norton, in Oxfordshire, A.D. 1349, was a serpent with two heads, faces like women, and great wings after the manner of a bat.

In Wright's *History of Ludlow* we meet with a legend relating to the village of Bromfield, near that town, which has been preserved by Thomas of Walsingham, a historian of the fourteenth century: "In the year 1344 a certain Saracen physician came to Earl Warren to ask permission to kill a serpent or dragon which had its den at Bromfield, and was committing great ravages in the Earl's lands on the borders of Wales. The Earl consented, and the dragon was overcome by the incantations of the Arab; but certain words which he had dropped led to the belief that large treasure lay hid in the dragon's den. Some men of Herefordshire, hearing of this, went by night, at the instigation of a Lombard, named Peter Picard, to dig for the gold; and they had just reached it when the retainers of the Earl Warren, having discovered what was going on, fell suddenly upon them, and threw them into prison. The treasure, which the Earl took possession of, was very great."[1]

A town in Wales is said to have derived its present name from a dragon or winged serpent. Long ago such a creature haunted the precincts of the castle of Caledfryn-yn-Rhos, now called Denbigh Castle, attacking man and beast till everyone was scared from approaching its den, and the town was left desolate. At last a member of the noble family of Salisbury, of Lleweni, known among his countrymen as Sir John of the Thumbs, because he had eight fingers and two thumbs on each hand, volunteered to attack the monstrous reptile. A desperate conflict ensued, and Sir John succeeded at last in thrusting his sword deep under the dragon's wing, on which, with a horrible yell, it expired. Sir John cut off its head and bore it in triumph to the spot where his friends and the townspeople were awaiting his return. When he came in sight of them he shouted out "Dim Bych," "no more dragon," words which have passed into the name of the place. This curious narration was translated from the Welsh by Mr. James Jones.

One legend, however, from the South of England vies in poetic beauty with those of the North. It is that of St. Leonard and the Dragon, which I subjoin as it was related to my fellow-worker in the very forest with which the tale is connected. Leonard, first a courtier of the Frank-king Clovis, afterwards a disciple of S. Remigius and a hermit saint, dwelt at one time in

[1] Page 28.

the beautiful forest in Sussex which bears his name, as afterwards in a wood near Limoges, in France. At first he found nothing to molest him there except the nightingales, whose constant singing disturbed him when he said his offices. He simply bade them to depart, and they went, never to return. While year by year every other copse and thicket in the county resounds through the days and nights of spring with the song of countless nightingales, St. Leonard's Forest continues silent to the present time.

But the saint soon became aware that the forest contained another denizen, a dragon of great strength and malignity, the dread of all the villages around. Fierce encounters soon took place between the two, the saint, though often sorely wounded, driving his antagonist further and further into the inmost recesses of the forest, till at last the creature disappeared in the underwood and was thought to be slain. The scenes of these successive combats are revealed afresh every year, when beds of fragrant lilies of the valley spring up wherever the earth was sprinkled by the blood of the warrior saint.

In later days, however, the monster would seem to have reappeared. We read in an account written A.D. 1614,[1] that such a serpent "was oft-times seen at a place called Faygate, and it hath been seen within a mile of Horsham, a wonder, no doubt most terrible and noisome to the inhabitants thereof. It was reported to be nine feet in length, with a quantity of thickness about the middest, and somewhat smaller at both ends. It rid away as fast as a man could run, was very proud of countenance, and had on either side of him two great bunches as big as a large football, which some thought would soon grow to be wings, but God, I hope, will defend the poor people in the neighbourhood that he shall be destroyed before he grow so fledged. One man did set out with two mastiff dogs to chase it, as yet not knowing the great danger of it, but his dogs were both killed,

[1] The full title of this account is "*True and Wonderful.—A Discourse relating a strange and monstrous Serpent or Dragon, lately discovered and yet living to the great annoyance and divers slaughters, both men and cattell, by his strong and violent poyson. In Sussex, two miles from Horsham, in a woode called St. Leonard's Forrest, and thirty miles from London, this present month of August,* 1614. *Printed at London by John Trundle* 1614." Quoted from Mrs. Latham's "West Sussex Superstitions,"—*Folk-Lore Record*, vol.

and he himself was glad to return with haste to preserve his own life."

The memory of St. Leonard's antagonist has never died out in Sussex. Stories of monstrous serpents have been repeated there from that day to this. A few years back "an oudacious large one" is said to have appeared in the west of that county. Its lair was near a bye-path which it suffered nobody to traverse, but would rush out and drive back any traveller with a terrible hissing, and what Queen Elizabeth would have called "an ill smell."

I will only add that the late Dr. Mantell, the geologist, used to quote the legend of St. Leonard's dragon as one possibly to be traced to the saurians, whose fossil remains are still to be found abundantly in the neighbouring beds of Tilgate Forest.

Nor are the legends connected with Helston, a remote Cornish town between the Lizard and Land's End, without a certain interest. I give them as they are kindly communicated to me by Miss E. Phillips, a lady who formerly resided in that place.

Many years ago Helston was threatened with destruction by a fiery dragon who appeared in the sky and hovered for some days over the place, bearing in his claws a red-hot ball. The terrified inhabitants escaped to the neighbouring villages, leaving behind them, sad to say, the old and weak to perish. At last, however, the dragon passed over Helston and dropped the fiery ball upon the downs more than half a mile away, at a spot still pointed out. Thus the town was saved, and this deliverance is commemorated every year on the 8th of May by a festivity called the Flora Day. Flowers are cultivated diligently for this fête, the maidens of Helston being specially adorned with lilies of the valley, while every youth should wear a tulip in his hat.

All assemble in the market-house, the young men bringing bouquets of flowers for their partners, and on the band striking up the Flora, or Furry tune, a lively and rather pretty melody, the dance begins. Down the street, through the public buildings, and all the principal shops and dwelling-houses, the dancers take their way, the master and mistress standing at the entrance of many a granite house to receive them and speed them onwards through the back door and out into the street again. One party of dancers was sent off to the moor soon after dawn to begin the dance from the very spot on which the dragon had cast down the dread instrument of destruction, but all meet at last in the assembly rooms, where they go through a country dance to the same gay Flora tune. Nothing can be more picturesque than the whole scene.

The ball flung down by the dragon is shown in the yard of the principal hotel; but another tale is sometimes told respecting it, which runs as follows:—There was once a fearful contest for the possession of the town between St. Michael, the patron saint of its church, and the arch fiend. Satan was vanquished, and as he suddenly fled away he hurled at the archangel this great stone, from whence the town derived its name, once spelt Hellestone. The hotel, which is called the Angel, claims to stand on the site of the conflict.

The whole subject is one of very great interest. These stories of hero and dragon—victorious hero and defeated dragon—are clearly but the reflex, with a little local colouring, of earlier tales of the same character, which have been rife in the world from very remote times. Such tales come before us in widely separated countries, among people of different races, interwoven with almost every form of religion. They are the inheritance of every branch of the human family, and the question recurs again and again to the thoughtful mind, how are we to account for the firm hold they possess over the heart of man.

It is considered by some authors that these legends are figurative; that they grow up around the memory of such monsters of cruelty as Attila or the infamous Baron de Retz, who are accordingly handed down to posterity with the outward lineaments of dragons and such like monsters. This theory is however plainly insufficient to cover the whole question, though it may be that in certain localities connected with such tyrants the circumstances of their barbarities may have been introduced into the old mythical stories. Indeed it is well known that in the ballad of the Dragon of Wantley we find portrayed in a covert manner the tyrannical acts of a certain Yorkshire squire, who, in order to make a chase for deer, pulled down a whole village near Sheffield and utterly ruined many of its inhabitants. Other writers see in the dragon only the huge serpent, the gigantic saurian, or other enormous creature such as formerly disputed with man the mastery of the world, only by degrees disappearing before him. To others again all is pure allegory. In every tale of champion and dragon they simply see "the ceaseless universal strife" between good and evil, once shown in all its intensity upon Mount Calvary, and since repeated wherever the good soldiers of the Cross have in their turn fought the same fight and won the same victory.

For myself I would only ask whether the last two points of view may not be held together. Believing as I do that the ancient dragon myth embodies and has helped to uphold in the world a belief in truth victorious over error, holiness triumphant over sin, it yet does appear to me perfectly clear that the outward form and presentment of evil as thus set before us is borrowed from those monstrous forms of animal life which were more familiar to our ancestors than happily they are to their descendants.

That the dragon has been from the beginning a world-wide type and embodiment of the Spirit of Evil is clear, and this even when it was the object of direct worship, which it soon became. And in this manner:—the children of Eve, smarting under the curse which her disobedience entailed upon them, feared the power that had over-mastered her, and went on to offer prayers and sacrifices to a being they dreaded though they could not love. Thus a religion of terror sprang up, and "that old serpent, which is the Devil and Satan," has since received the adoration of countless votaries in the very form wherein he tempted their first mother. He was thus worshipped as the evil Deity of the ancient Egyptians and Persians, and is figured under the same form in the hieroglyphics of Mexico and of China. So proud, indeed, are the Chinese to this day of their dreadful king, that they call their country "the land of the Dragon Throne."

Alongside, however, of the practice of dragon-worship, we do meet on the stream of history with tales of maiden innocence self-offered for the redemption of parents, friends, or country, and of heroic courage assailing the monster and setting the devoted one free. In China, the fair damsel, Ki, was herself both victim and champion, while in such beautiful Greek myths as that of Perseus and Andromeda the grand Christian legend of St. George and the Dragon is more perfectly foreshadowed—a grand legend, indeed, whether we take the hero to represent Christianity triumphant over Paganism, or Holiness over Sin; nor can we, at the present day, fully estimate the vast power it exercised for good over half-instructed people when it met their eyes in painting or sculpture, or stirred their spirits when sung or recited in ballads. The dullest mind and hardest heart could not fail to learn from it something of the hatefulness of evil, the beauty of self-sacrifice, and the all-conquering might of truth.

Whether the legend was founded on a true history, or was called into existence to meet the cravings of a recently Christianized world, may be open to doubt, but certain it is, that, presented as was its subject in so attractive a form, it exactly met the wants of men who in those days of ignorance needed some material embodiment which should forcibly impress upon them the great contest between good and evil.

And when this was done, so vigorously yet with so much beauty, we cannot be surprised at the influence it has exercised. It is no wonder that St. George has been adopted as the patron saint of Sicily, Arragon, Valencia, Genoa, Malta, and Barcelona, as well as of our own country, or that orders of knighthood should have been instituted in his honour and bearing his name in Venice, Spain, Austria, Genoa, Rome, Bavaria, Russia, Hanover, and, above all, in England, whose "ancient word of courage" has long been "fair St. George."

CHAPTER IX.

OCCULT POWERS AND SYMPATHIES.

Seventh Sons or "Marcoux"—Twins—Aërial Appearances—The Schoolboy and Neville's Cross – Sympathy between Bees and their Owners—Sacred character of Bees—The Old Woman and Spider—Marks on the Leg of the Pig—The Presbyterian Minister and the Fisher Folk.

AMONG occult powers exercised, or thought to be exercised, by certain members of the human race, none have been more widely credited than those supposed to reside in seventh sons. The seventh of a family of sons, no daughters intervening, has the reputation of healing scrofula and other kindred complaints with the touch. This belief has been universal in Great Britain as well as in France, and it still crops out here and there. In the village of Ideford, in South Devon, lived (perhaps still lives) a respectable farmer, who claimed to heal as a seventh son, and patients resorted to him from Exeter, Torquay, and other places at some little distance.

Persons thus gifted are called in France *marcoux*, after St. Marcoul, a holy man who died A.D. 658. His reputation for sanctity rests on his performance of many miracles in the cure of this disease, which is named after him St. Marcoul's Evil. Louis IX. and other French kings his successors, who be it remembered used like our English monarchs to touch for the evil, were accustomed after their coronation to go on pilgrimage to Corbigny, 120 miles from Rheims, to perform a nine days' devotion at the shrine of St. Marcoul. The Painted Chamber in the Palace at Westminster, which appears to have been the place where our sovereigns touched for the evil, was formerly called the chamber of St. Marcoul.[1]

[1] See No. 39, *Archæological Journal.*

The Orléannais is the district where the belief in the powers of the *marcou* is the strongest. "If a man is the seventh son of his father, no female intervening, he is a *marcou;* he has on some part of his body the mark of a fleur-de-lis, and, like the King of France, he has the power of curing the king's-evil. All that is necessary to effect a cure is that the *marcou* should breathe upon the part affected, or that the sufferer should touch the mark of the fleur-de-lis. Of all the *marcoux* of the Orléannais, he of Ormes is the best known and most celebrated. Every year, from twenty, thirty, forty leagues around, crowds of patients come to visit him . . . . The *marcou* of Ormes is a cooper in easy circumstances, being the possessor of a horse and carriage. His name is Foulon, and in this country he is known by the appellation of '*Le beau marcou.*' He has the fleur-de-lis on his left side."[1]

On the Borders the sign of the seven stars marks the seventh son to be a channel of healing. If seventh sons thus marked are brought up as doctors they are in great requisition; in any case, people resort to them to be touched for the king's-evil. The belief in their powers holds its ground firmly in the Western Highlands. There the seventh son lays his hand on the party affected, commonly, but not always, uttering an invocation to the Trinity. In the island of Lewis he gives the patient a six-penny-piece with a hole in it, through which a string is passed to wear round the neck. Should this be taken off a return of the malady may be looked for. Dr. Mitchell adds, that when seven sons are born in succession the parents consider themselves bound, if possible, to bring up the seventh for a doctor. Seventh sons are also seers, having the privilege, if such it be, of second-sight. Their healing powers are, on the Borders, shared with twins and children born with cauls; but in all these cases the virtue is held to be so much subtracted from their own vital energy, and if much drawn upon they pine away and die of exhaustion. The Portuguese belief is widely different. A seventh son is declared in Portugal to be changed every Saturday night into an ass, and to be chased by dogs till morning light.[2]

[1] *Choice Notes.*—Folk-Lore, p. 59. [2] Communicated by Professor Marecco.

As to twins, a strong sympathy is believed to exist between them, so that what gives pain or pleasure to the one is suffered or enjoyed by the other as well. Should one die, however, the other, though weakly before, will at once improve in health and strength, the life and vital energy of his fellow being added to his own.

This curious belief recalls to the memory how, in Spenser's "Faerie Queene," Agapé, the mother of three brave knights,

> Borne of one mother in one happie mold,
> Borne at one burden in one happie morne,

visits the three Fates that she may learn the length of her sons' lives, and finding the thread of their existence

> So thin as spiders' frame,
> And eke so short that seemed their ends out shortly came,

finding also that no prayer of hers could avail to lengthen their allotted span, she asked and obtained the following request:

> "Then since," quoth she, the "terme of each man's life,
> For nought may lessened or enlarged be;
> Grant this: that when ye shred with fatall knife
> His life, which is the eldest of the three,
> Which is of them the shortest, as I see,
> Eft soones his life may pass into the next;
> And when the next shall likewise ended bee,
> That both their lives may likewise be annext
> Unto the third, that his may so be trebly wext."[1]

While speaking of twins, I may perhaps mention that in Sussex a "left twin," that is a child who has outlived its fellow twin, is thought to have the power of curing the thrush by blowing three times successively into the patient's mouth, provided this same patient be of opposite sex to the operator.

There is a strong tendency in the "North Countrie" to connect the past and the present, external nature and the history and destiny of man. Thus the aurora borealis is still well known there as "the Derwentwater Lights," in consequence of having been particularly red and vivid at the time of that unfortunate nobleman's execution. The death of Louis XVI. was fore-

[1] Book iv. Canto 2.

shadowed, too, by the aurora borealis; and myriads of fighting men were seen in the sky night after night, all through the county of Durham, before the French Revolution. The late Canon Humble informed me that he had heard people declare they had distinctly heard the cries of the combatants and groans of the wounded. Again, before the rising of either 1715 or 1745, appearances were seen in the sky as of encountering armies, which were, however, subsequently explained by a refraction in the atmosphere, causing something like the Fata Morgana. A few Jacobite gentlemen raised certain troops of horse, and exercised them on some of the high ground in Lancashire, and, these being seen reflected in the clouds, formed the apparition. Still, without doubt, wars have been ushered in by such aërial appearances. Armies were seen contending in the clouds before the destruction of Jerusalem, as well as before the battle of Ivry and the persecutions of the Waldenses in the seventeenth century.

But further: Our great battles have left an abiding impress on the imagination and heart of the Northern.

Thus to this day "a Nevell" means in Durham a knock-down blow, doubtless from the battle of Neville's Cross.

The following incident, which occurred to my fellow-worker, is a further witness of this. She was teaching in a Sunday-school in the city of Durham, and the chapter (from the first book of Samuel) having been duly read in class, one of the pupils observed that he did not like that chapter as well as last Sunday's, because there were no battles in it. On this the teacher thought fit to dilate on the blessings of peace and the horrors of war; to all which, like a truculent young northern as he was, the boy turned a deaf ear, only observing that there had been a great battle close to Durham once. "And where was it fought?" asked she. "At Neville's Cross," answered the lad, promptly. "I go there very often of an evening to see the place; and if you walk nine times round the Cross, and then stoop down and lay your head on the turf, you'll hear the noise of the battle and the clash of the armour." These were the young fellow's exact words. The walking round the Cross I believe to be purely local; but the sites of other great battles of the world are in like manner haunted by echoes of the fight; and the Northamptonshire peasant on Naseby field, and the Greek shepherd on the plains of Marathon, alike listen for them with thrilling heart.

I may, perhaps, allude here to the sympathy supposed to exist between bees and their owners, a belief in which seems to have extended over every part of our island. It is said here and there that bees will not thrive in a quarrelsome family; that if a swarm alight on a dead tree there will be a death in the owner's house within a year—

> Swarmed on a rotten stick the bees I spied,
> Which erst I saw when Goody Dobson died.—*Gay.*

but that a strange swarm settling in one's garden brings good fortune; that stolen bees never thrive; that bees love children, "Bees have for thee no sting" (*Lyra Innocentium*); that if they make their nest in the roof of a house none of the girls born in it will marry; that bees must not be bought, they would thrive as ill as if they were stolen; they should be exchanged for another swarm in the following year, or bartered for something in kind; on the borders of Dartmoor the ordinary equivalent is a bag, *i. e.* half-a-sack of wheat; and, above all, that on the death of the master, or indeed of any member of his family, the bees will desert their hives, unless some one takes the house-key, raps with it three times on the board that supports the hives, informs the bees what has taken place, and fastens a bit of black crape to the hive. This last belief I know to be prevalent in Northumberland, Lincolnshire, Oxfordshire, Surrey, and Sussex, as well as Devonshire, and a Yorkshire lady speaks of it as follows: "When I came to F——, in 1847, everything was much as it had been when my husband's mother was living. She had not then been dead a year. In the garden I noticed a row of bee *skeps*, to which were attached one or two pieces of black crape. The hives were empty. On inquiry, one of the servants said, 'Ah! the bees are all flown, ma'am; they are offended because none of the family went to tell them of mistress's death. I suppose the young ladies did not think of such things, and, though I put the bits of mourning on them, they all went away.'"

Precisely the same belief holds in North Germany, where they also maintain that when the master of the house dies some one must go into the garden and shake the trees, saying, "The master is dead,—the master is dead," else they will all decay.

From the same Yorkshire friend I learn that bees further require a taste of every thing served at the funeral feast, and that an instance has lately come before her in which this had been done, and a small portion of each dish laid before the hives. In Lancashire the bees demand an announcement of marriage also, on pain of misfortune to the bridal pair. The same thing is done in Brittany, where a piece of red cloth is tied to the hives while imparting the information.

Bees have in many parts of France been regarded with religious reverence as the instruments for fabricating wax for the altar-lights, and it was considered a sacrilegious act to kill them. The same feeling existed in Wales. Thus the Gevantian code says: "The origin of bees is from Paradise; God conferred this blessing upon them, therefore mass cannot be said without the wax;" and it was once held in that country that bees were created white, but turned brown at the Fall. That strange writer, Charles Butler, in his *Feminine Monarchie*, A.D. 1634, tells how "A certain woman, having some stalls of bees which yielded not unto her her desired profit, but did consume and die of the murrain, made her moan to another woman, more simple than herself, who gave her counsel to get a consecrated host and put it among them. According to whose advice she went to the priest to receive the host, which, when she had done, she kept it in her mouth, and, being come home again, she took it out and put it into one of her hives, whereupon the murrain ceased and the honey abounded. The woman, therefore, lifting up the hive at the due time to take out the honey, saw therein (most strange to be seen) a chapel built by the bees, with an altar in it, the walls adorned by marvellous skill of architecture, with windows conveniently set in their places, also a door, and a steeple with bells. And, the host being set on the altar, the bees, making a sweet noise, flew round about it." And, further, he relates that some thieves having stolen a pyx and cast the wafer under a hive of bees, the bees that night made another pyx of "whitest wax," round which they sang most sweetly, as the owner of the hive found at midnight. Both these stories he takes from Bosius de Signis Ecclesiæ.

Mr. Hawker, of Morwenstowe, in his *Echoes of Old Cornwall*, versifies a legend of the same character, and connects it with Cornwall. Somewhat different is a narration given in an old French book by the Jesuit Father Toupain Bridoul, on "The miraculous respects and acknowledgments which birds, beasts, and insects, upon several occasions, have rendered to the Holy Sacrament of the altar." It runs thus: "Bees honour the Holy Host divers ways, by lifting it from the earth and carrying it in their hives as it were in procession. A certain peasant of Auvergne, a province in France, perceiving that his bees were likely to die, to prevent this misfortune was advised, after he had received the communion, to reserve the host, and to blow it into one of the hives. As he tried to do it the host fell on the ground. Behold now a wonder! On a sudden all the bees came forth out of their hives, and, ranging themselves in good order, lifted the host from the ground, and carrying it in upon their wings placed it among the combs. After this the man went out upon his business, and at his return found this advice had succeeded ill, for all his bees were dead."

Again, bees are said at Christmas to hum a Christmas hymn. Thus the Rev. Hugh Taylor writes: "A man of the name of Murray died about the age of ninety, in the parish of Earsdon, Northumberland. He told a sister of mine that on Christmas Eve the bees assemble and hum a Christmas hymn, and that his mother had distinctly heard them do this on one occasion when she had gone out to listen for her husband's return. Murray was a shrewd man, yet he seemed to believe this implicitly." It is mentioned by Hutchinson[1] that, in the parish of Whitbeck, in Cumberland, bees are said to sing at midnight as soon as the day of the Nativity begins, and also that oxen kneel in their stalls at the same day and hour.

[1] *History of Cumberland*, vol. i. p. 555.

One or two instances, in which popular belief glorifies the world around us with light borrowed from the days when Our Saviour walked on earth, have been given already. I add another of exceeding beauty which has come before me. In the little town of Malton, in Yorkshire, a few years ago, my friend the late Dr. Dykes, while visiting an old woman during her last illness, observed a spider near her bed, and attempted to destroy it. She at once interfered, and told him with much earnestness that spiders ought not to be killed; for we should remember how, when our Blessed Lord lay in the manger at Bethlehem, the spider came and spun a beautiful web, which protected the innocent Babe from all the dangers which surrounded Him. The old woman was about ninety years of age. I have never met with the legend elsewhere, but it may have originated the Kentish proverb—

He who would wish to thrive,
Must let spiders run alive.

The spider is curiously connected with the history of Mahomet. He is said during his flight from Mecca to have been saved by a spider and a pigeon. While he was concealed in a cave his enemies came up in pursuit of him, but, perceiving a spider's web across the cave's mouth and a pigeon in her nest just above, they concluded the place to have been undisturbed and did not enter it. There is a Hebrew tradition to the same effect concerning King David. While flying from Saul in the desert of Ziph, a web, it is said, was spun over a cave in which he rested, and thus the band in search of him were led to believe that no one could be concealed there. Accordingly in the Chaldaic paraphrase of Psalm lvii. instead of "I will cry unto the Most High God, even unto the God that shall perform the cause which I have in hand," we find "I will cry unto the Most High and Mighty God, which sent the spider that she should spin her web in the mouth of the cave to preserve me."[1]

It is well known that the Italian peasant maintains the John Dorée to have been the fish captured by St. Peter at our Lord's

[1] Neale and Littledale on the Psalms, vol. ii. p. 14.

bidding, and that he sees within its mouth the impress of the tribute-money, and on its sides the marks of the Apostle's thumb and finger. I learn from Professor Marecco that on the inside of the foreleg of the pig six small rings are to be found apparently burned in, and that these are said to be the marks of the Devil's fingers, made when he entered the herd of swine. The Professor confesses himself unable to assign the exact locality of this belief, but the following verse respecting the flounder and other fish comes from the county of Durham :

> Haddock, cod, turbot, and ling,
> Of all the fish i' the sea herring's the king.
> Up started the flowk and said " Here am I,"
> And ever since that his mouth stands awry.

Let me conclude this chapter with an incident related to me by the late Canon Humble, and which is remarkable as evincing in North Britain a tone of mind rather medieval than modern. When the Rev. G. J. first went to officiate in the remote seaside village of M———, where almost all his congregation were fisherfolk, he was far from popular among them. However, it happened that he was invited to go out to sea for a night during the fishing season. He went, and on the return home in the morning the number of fishes in that boat was found to be one hundred and fifty-three, the same as at the miraculous draught of fishes recorded in St. John xxi. 2. From that hour the people's feeling towards their pastor changed. They one and all bowed to the will of Heaven thus made known in his favour, and acknowledged him to be a true fisherman in the bark of St. Peter.

CHAPTER X.

HAUNTED SPOTS.

The Willington Ghost—Maiden's Castle—Kirkstall Abbey—The Sexhow Farmer and Old Nannie—Mines Haunted—The Old Lady of Littledean—The Bowbrig Ladies—Apparition in Fifeshire—Haunted Spots in Durham—In Yorkshire—Sir Walter Calverley—Dalton Hill Head—Haunted Houses—Appearance at Ripon—Canon Humble's Narration—Madame Gould—Devon Legends—Sussex Ghosts.

THE universal voice of mankind has ever pointed out certain places as the borderland between the material and the spiritual world—has, truly or falsely, indicated deserted houses, marshy wastes, lonely roads, spots where enormous crimes have been perpetrated, and so forth, as haunted. In general, places which once were closely connected with man, but are now deserted by him, are thus distinguished in the popular mind, rather than those which have always been barren and desolate. It is natural then that with a past rich in historic incidents of the wildest kind haunted spots should abound in the North. Time would fail me to count them, nor could I by isolated instances give my readers a notion of the extent to which my native county is crowded by these shadowy beings. Almost every ancient barn, every cross road, every county mansion, is or has been haunted. Not many years back our squirearchy would have evinced some sense of shame had not every old family its ancestral ghost, nay, many of our yeomen claimed the same distinction.

Thus we have one haunted house at Willington Dene, another at North Shields, and a third at Chester-le-Street; Crook Hall, near Durham, has its "White Ladie," South Biddick Hall its shadowy tenant Madam Lambton, and Netherby Hall a rustling lady who walks along a retired passage in that mansion, her dress rustling as she moves on. But the Willington ghost is perhaps the most remarkable among them, and I am disposed to give its history somewhat at length. It attracted much notice at the time, hundreds of people crowding day after day to visit the place of its appearance. And a good deal of information respecting it has been kindly supplied to me by a son of the owner of the property, who permits me to state that he corroborates the following facts, his family being at the time they lived in the haunted house too young to perceive the supernatural character of what they saw and heard.

The steam corn-mill at Willington with its adjacent dwelling-house were built A.D. 1800. In 1806 the premises were purchased by Messrs. Unthank and Procter, the latter gentleman being father to the present owner; and in 1831 Mr. Joseph Procter, the present owner, a member of the Society of Friends, went to reside in the house with his wife. It was not till three years after this that they began to be molested by what is popularly called the Willington Ghost. I may observe at the outset that the house and mill are detached and that there is no cellaring under the former. Both stand on a little promontory bordered on three sides by a watercourse in full view of the Willington viaduct on the Newcastle and Tynemouth Railway.

The first annoyance was from strange and unaccountable sounds. When the servants went in the evening to fasten the garden gate they heard footsteps behind them, but could see no one. Then the master used to hear a noise as of something heavy descending from the roof and falling through floor after floor, with a heavy thump upon each till it reached the bottom of the house. Again there would be a commotion in the kitchen, as if the things in it were moved and thrown about, but on going down stairs the master would be relieved on finding it was "only the ghost," as the disturber of their peace began to be familiarly called.

One night the peculiar creak and squeaking of a certain water-cart was heard by Thomas Mann, the foreman at the mill, so that he felt sure it was being dragged out of the yard, but on following the noise he saw nothing, and when he returned to the yard the water-cart was standing in its usual place. Again, one day when Mrs. Procter called her nurse a voice answered her from the nursery in the tone too well known in the house, but the room was found to be empty and the woman out of doors. My informant also distinctly remembers, when a child, hearing what he thought to be his nurse moving about in the room, but on entering it no one was there, and the nurse not even in the house. All this reminds us of "Old Jeffrey," the sprite which haunted Epworth Vicarage during the residence of the Wesley family, and who, like his brother of Willington, has never been satisfactorily accounted for.

On the 2nd of June, 1835, Mr. Joseph Procter detailed the several circumstances I have related to Mr. Parker, of Halifax, by letter, adding, "The disturbances came to our knowledge in the beginning of first month, but had existed some time previously. There were several credible witnesses to the apparition of a woman in her grave-clothes at four separate times outside the house." Later in the same month, the family being from home, a gentleman from Sunderland, Edward Drury by name, asked and obtained leave to spend a night in the haunted house, which was then left in charge of an old servant. Mr. Drury seems to have had a good deal of curiosity on the subject, though he was sceptical as to anything supernatural in what had taken place. The history of the night is best given in his own words, merely premising that Mr. Procter returned home alone on account of business on the 3rd of July, the very day on which Mr. Drury and his companion, a medical man, arrived in the evening, also unexpectedly. After the house was locked up the two friends examined every corner of it minutely. The rooms on the third story were unfurnished, and the closet whence the apparition issued was too shallow to contain a person. Mr. Drury's letter to Mr. Procter is as follows:—

Sunderland, July 13, 1840.

DEAR SIR,—I hereby, according to promise in my last letter, forward you a true account of what I heard and saw at your house, in which I was led to pass the night from various rumours circulated by most respectable parties, particularly from an account by my esteemed friend Mr. Davisôn, whose name I mentioned to you in a former letter. Having received your sanction to visit your mysterious dwelling, I went on the 3rd of July, accompanied by a friend of mine, named T. Hudson. This was not according to promise, nor in accordance with my first intent, as I wrote you I would come alone, but I felt gratified at your kindness in not alluding to the liberty I had taken, as it ultimately proved for the best. I must here mention, that, not expecting you at home, I had in my pocket a brace of pistols, determining in my mind to let one of them drop, as if by accident, before the miller, for fear he should presume to play tricks upon me, but after my interview with you I felt there was no occasion for weapons, and did not load them, after you had allowed us to inspect as minutely as we pleased every portion of the house. I sat down on the third story landing, fully expecting to account for any noises I might hear in a most philosophical manner; this was about 11 o'clock p.m. About 10 minutes to 12 we both heard a noise, as if a number of people were pattering with their bare feet upon the floor; and yet so singular was the noise that I could not minutely determine from whence it proceeded. A few minutes afterwards we heard a noise as if some one was knocking with his knuckles among our feet; this was immediately followed by a hollow cough from the very room from which the apparition proceeded. The only noise after this was as if a person was rustling against the wall in coming up stairs. At a quarter to one I told my friend that, feeling a little cold, I would like to go to bed, as we might hear the noises equally well there. He replied that he would not go to bed till daylight. I took up a note which I had accidentally dropped and began to read it; after which I took out my watch to ascertain the time, and found that it wanted ten minutes to one. In taking my eyes from the watch, they became rivetted upon a closet door, which I distinctly saw open, and also saw the figure of a female, attired in greyish garments, with the head inclined downwards, and one hand pressed upon the chest as if in pain, and the other, that is the right hand, extended towards the floor, with the index finger pointing downwards. It advanced with an apparently cautious step across the floor towards me; immediately as it approached my friend, who was slumbering, its right hand was extended toward him. I then rushed at it, giving at the time, as Mr. Procter states, a most awful yell, but instead of grasping it I fell upon my friend, and I recollected nothing distinctly for nearly three hours afterwards. I have since learnt that I was carried downstairs in an agony of fear and terror.

I hereby certify that the above account is strictly true and correct in every respect.

EDWARD DRURY.

A brother of Mrs. Procter's, Mr. Dodgson, was also molested. The following narration of his experiences, taken from Howett's *Journal*, is attested by the family as perfectly correct. "One of Mrs. Procter's brothers, a gentleman in middle life, and of a peculiarly sensible, sedate, and candid disposition, a person apparently most unlikely to be imposed upon by fictitious alarms or tricks, assured me that he himself had on a visit there been disturbed by the strangest noises, that he had resolved before going that if any such noises occurred he would speak and demand of the invisible actor who he was and why he came thither; but the occasion came, and he found himself unable to fulfil his intention.

"As he lay in bed one night he heard a heavy step ascend the stairs towards his room, and some one striking as it were with a thick stick the balusters as he went along. It came to his door, he essayed to call, but his voice died away in his throat. He then sprang from his bed, and opening the door found no one there, but now heard the same heavy steps deliberately descending (though perfectly invisible) the steps before his face, and accompanying the descent with the same loud blows on the balusters. He proceeded to the room of Mr. Procter, who he found had heard the sounds, and who also now arose, and with a light they made a speedy descent below, and a thorough search there, but without discovering anything that could account for the occurrence."

Two sisters of this gentleman, visitors at Willington in the summer of ——, told of their bed being lifted up under them and shaken, and of its curtains being drawn up, after which they saw a female figure emerge from the wall, bend over them, and re-enter the wall. Their terror was great and they refused to sleep in that room again. One sister was moved to a distant part of the house, the other went to the foreman's house, which was not far off. There she beheld another apparition outside the mill-house, which was also seen by Thomas Mann, the foreman, and his wife and daughter. Mr. Mann, a most respectable person, who had been long employed at the mill, saw it first, and called the others to view it.

The appearance it presented was that of a bare-headed man in a flowing robe like a surplice, who glided backwards and forwards about three feet from the floor, or level with the bottom of the second-story window, seeming to enter the wall on each side and thus present a side view in passing: it then stood still in the window, and a part of the body came through both the blind (which was close down) and the window, as its luminous body intercepted the view of the framework of the window. It was semi-transparent and as bright as a star, diffusing a radiance all around. As it grew more dim it assumed a blue tinge and gradually faded away from the head downwards. The foreman passed twice close to the house under the window, and also went to inform the family, but found the house locked up. There was no moonlight nor a ray of light visible anywhere about, and no person near. Had any magic lantern been used it could not possibly have escaped detection, and it is obvious that nothing of that kind could have been employed in the inside, as in that case the light could only have been thrown upon the blind, and not so as to interrupt the view both of the blind and window from without. The owner of the house slept in that room, and must have entered it shortly after the figure disappeared.

The lifting up of the bed at night as though by some one under it occurred several times. Investigations were made but to no purpose. On one occasion Mrs. Procter felt it when alone with her little infant and nurse. She told no one but her husband. The next night another person, who had not been told of it, felt the same thing and reported it to Mr. Procter privately. About this time Mrs. Procter was aware one night of a cold hand placed on her chest, though nothing was visible. She was greatly alarmed, and cannot think of it to this day without shuddering. A son of the family, then very young, repeatedly felt his bed raised under him and used to complain that a large dog got under his bed and lifted him up. All this time the constant pattering of little feet was kept up on the floor of the upper room. The servants were in constant terror of strange sights and sounds, and in consequence were often changed.

The family quitted the house altogether in 1847, but for some time previously the disturbances had become less frequent. They passed away altogether during the subsequent occupation of the premises by the clerk and foreman with their wives and children.

I would remind my readers that veracity is a characteristic quality of the Society of Friends, to which Mr. Procter and his family belonged, and will only add that Mr. Procter stated at the time that he could bring forty witnesses to attest the supernatural visitations which marked his residence at Willington.

There was a wild legend in my native city of a subterranean passage between Finchale Abbey and the cathedral of Durham, and of an attempt to penetrate it. One man succeeded up to a certain point where there was a strong door which barred progress. He returned scared by the horrors he had witnessed and refused to brave them again. Another, more desperate, declared he would succeed or perish in the attempt. He took with him a horn which he blew from time to time, so that those in the upper air might know of his whereabouts. The horn was heard at intervals till the crowd above reached Gilesgate Moor, when a shrill and hasty blast alarmed them--it was the last they could distinguish—the man had succumbed to the horrors of the place.

Respecting Cleveland, Mr. G. M. Tweddell says that every old castle and ruined monastery there has its legend of a subterranean passage leading therefrom, which some one has penetrated to a certain distance till he came to an iron chest supposed to be full of gold, on which was perched a raven. This raven points out, he considers, the Scandinavian origin of the legend. A cock or hen, however, sometimes takes the place of the raven.

I learn from Mr. Robinson, of Hill House, Reeth, Yorkshire, that in his neighbourhood as in many others is a place called Maiden's Castle, in which tradition avers a chest of gold is buried. "Many attempts," he says, "have been made to gain possession of the treasure, and one party of adventurers actually came up to the chest and laid hold of it, when a hen appeared, flapped her wings, and put out the light. This occurred three times, and the men were obliged to desist. The next day was Sunday, still they returned to the place. A violent storm of thunder and rain came on, however, and the 'drift,' in miners' phrase, 'ran.' My informant, an old man of the place, knew this, he said, for a fact."

A somewhat similar tale is told of Kirkstall Abbey, near Leeds. I give it in the genuine vernacular as it was told to my informant fifty years ago by the last survivor of the family of

Ellis, who had lived for generations at a house now called the Abbey House, Kirkstall, but the proper name of which is the Bar Grange. "Th' man war thrashing i th' Abba lair, and at nooning a thocht he'd streckin his back, an when he gat out he saw a hoile under th' Abba, an he crept in, and he fun an entry and he went doon it, and at bottom there was a gert house place. There were a gert fire blazing on t' hart-stone, an in ae corner war tied up a fine black horse. And when it seed him it whinnied. An behind the horse was a gert black oak kist, and at top o' t' kist a gert black cock, an cock crawed. Th'man said to hissel 'Brass in t' kist, I'll hae sum on't.' An as he went up to't, t' horse whinnied higher and higher, and cock crawed louder and louder, an when he laid his hand on t' kist t' horse made such a din, an t' cock crawed and flapped his wings, an summat fetched him such a flap on t' side o' his head as felled him flat, an he knowed nowt more till he came to hissel an he war lying on't common in t' lair, and never could he find the hoile under the Abba again."

Mr. G. M. Tweddell thus relates the history of an apparition which with fitting retributive justice haunted a certain Yorkshire farmer.

An old woman of Sexhow, near Stokesley, appeared after her death to a farmer of the place, and informed him that, beneath a certain tree in his apple orchard, he would find a hoard of gold and silver which she had buried there. He was to take a spade and dig it up, keep the silver for his trouble, but give the gold to a niece of hers who was then living in great poverty, and whose place of abode she pointed out. At daybreak after his dream or vision, the farmer went to the spot indicated, dug and found the treasure, but kept it all to himself, though the sum allotted to him was considerable, and might have satisfied him. From that day, however, he never knew rest or happiness. Though a sober man before, he took to drinking, but all in vain —his conscience gave him no rest. Every night, at home or abroad, old Nanny's ghost failed not to dog his steps, and reproach him with his faithlessness. At last, one Saturday evening, the neighbours heard him returning from Stokesley Market very late; his horse was galloping furiously, and as he left the high road to go into the lane which led to his own house he never stopped to open the gate at the entrance of the lane but cleared it with a bound. As he passed a neighbour's house, its inmates heard him screaming out, " I will—I will—I will!" and looking out they saw a little old woman in black, with a large straw hat on her head, whom they recognised as old Nannie, seated behind the terrified man on the runaway nag, and clinging to him closely. The farmer's hat was off, his hair stood on end, as he fled past them, uttering his fearful cry, " I will—I will—I will!" But when the horse reached the farm all was still, for the rider was a corpse!

Mines have ever been supposed to be haunted; nor can we wonder at it considering the many unearthly sounds constantly to be heard there—" the dripping of water down the shafts, the tunnelling of distant passages, the rumbling of trains from some freshly-explored lode," and all received upon the ear in gloom and often in solitude. The following instance, told by a miner on his sick-bed to his clergyman, is recorded in *Communications with the Unseen World* (page 121): " The overseer of the mine he had been used to work in (at Whitehaven) for many years, was a Cumberland man; but being found guilty of some unfair proceedings he was dismissed by the proprietors from his post, though employed in an inferior situation. The new overseer was a Northumberland man, who had the burr that distinguishes that county very strongly. To this person the degraded overseer bore the strongest hatred, and was heard to say that some day he would be his ruin. He lived, however, in apparent friendship with him, but one day they were both destroyed together by the firedamp. It was believed in the mine that, preferring revenge to life, the ex-overseer had taken his successor, less acquainted than himself with the localities of the mine, into a place where he knew the firedamp to exist, and that without a safety-lamp; and had thus contrived his destruction. But ever after that time, in the place where the two men perished, their voices might be heard high in dispute, the Northumbrian burr being distinctly audible, and also the well-known pronunciation of the treacherous murderer." Compare with this incident the following communication from the Rev. S. Baring-Gould: "I know a man who is haunted by two spectres. He has shaking fits, during which his eyes wander about the room; then he sees the ghosts. He was a miner, and is said to have half-cut through the rope when some men against whom he bore a grudge were going down the pit; the rope broke, and they were dashed to pieces. Their ghosts haunt him night and day, and he can never remain long in one house, or endure to be alone night or day."

Mr. Wilkie relates a story somewhat similar to that given above from Cleveland, but with a happier termination. It runs as follows: "The ancient tower of Littledean, on the Tweedside, had long been haunted by the spirit of an old lady, once its mistress, who had been a covetous, grasping woman, and oppressive to the poor. Tradition averred that she had amassed a large sum of money by thrift or extortion, and now could not rest in her grave because of it. Still, in spite of its ghost, Littledean Tower was inhabited by a laird and his family, who found no fault with their place of abode, and were not much troubled by thoughts of the supernatural world. One Saturday evening, however, a servant-girl, who was cleaning shoes in the kitchen by herself, suddenly observed an elf-light shining on the floor. While she gazed on it, it disappeared, and in its place stood an old woman wrapped in a brown cloak, who muttered something about being cold, and asked to warm herself at the fire. The girl readily consented, and seeing that her visitor's shoes were wet, and her toes peeping out blue and cold from their tips, she good-naturedly offered to dry and clean the shoes, and did so. The old lady, touched by this attention, confessed herself frankly to be the apparition that haunted the house. 'My gold wud na let me rest,' said she, 'but I'll tell ye where it lies; 'tis 'neath the lowest step o' the Tower stairs. Take the laird there an' tell him what I now tell ye; then dig up the treasure, and put it in his hands. An' tell him to part it in two shares: one share let him keep, for he's master here now; the other share he maun part again, and gie half to you, for ye are a kind lassie and a true, and half he maun gie to the poor o' Maxton, the old folk and the fatherless bairns, and them that need it most. Do this and I sall rest in my grave, where I've no rested yet, and never will I trouble the house mair till the day o' doom.' The girl rubbed her eyes, looked again, and behold the old woman was gone!

"Next morning the young servant took her master to the spot which had been indicated to her, and told him what had taken place. The stone was removed, and the treasure discovered, and divided according to the instructions given. The laird, being blessed with a goodly family of sturdy lads and smiling maidens, found no difficulty in disposing of his share. The servant-girl, so richly endowed, found a good husband ere the year had passed. The poor of Maxton for the first time in their lives blessed the old lady of Littledean, and never was the ancient tower troubled again by ghost or apparition."

The same locality supplies us with another legend. About half-a mile to the east of Maxton, a small rivulet runs across the turnpike-road, at a spot called Bow-brig-syke. Near this bridge lies a triangular field, in which, for nearly a century, it was averred that the forms of two ladies, dressed in white, might be seen pacing up and down. Night after night the people of the neighbourhood used to come and watch them, and curiosity brought many from a great distance. The figures were always to be seen at dusk; they walked arm-in-arm over precisely the same spot of ground till morning light. Mr. Wilkie adds, that, about twelve years before the time of his noting down the story, while some workmen were repairing the road, they took up the large flat stones upon which foot-passengers crossed the burn, and found beneath them the skeletons of two women lying side by side. After this discovery, the Bow-brig ladies were never again seen to walk in the Three-corner field.

Mr. Wilkie says further, that he received this account from a gentleman who saw and examined the skeletons, and who added that they were believed to be those of two ladies, sisters to a former laird of Littledean. Their brother is said to have killed them in a fit of passion, because they interfered to protect from ill-usage a young lady whom he had met at Bow-brig-syke.

He placed their bodies upon the bridge, and lowered the flat stones upon them to prevent discovery. Some years later he met with his own death near the same fatal spot. While riding with his dogs he fell over the brae opposite to the bridge, and was found lying dead by the Tweedside. Tradition identifies him with the laird Harry Gilles, whose adventure in hunting has already been related.

The following narration was communicated to one of my clerical friends by a lady of Perth. One of her friends went to stay at a country house in Fifeshire, where she arrived just in time to dress for dinner, and was shown straight to her room. Her toilet completed, she was on her way downstairs, when something wrong in the lower part of her dress made her stoop down. As she looked up again she saw a lady richly dressed and very handsome emerge from a short staircase which had its exit on the principal landing, and move hastily towards the staircase she was descending. She stood aside and the form passed her without any acknowledgment of the courtesy. There was a cold sneer on her face which particularly attracted the visitor's attention. She walked on, however, to the drawing-room, spoke to her host and hostess, and having been introduced to the rest of the party turned to look round for the beauty who had passed her on the stairs, but she was not there. Next morning she mentioned the circumstance to the lady of the house, but she turned off the subject with some trivial remark. However, during her stay the visitor was shown over the house, and among other rooms was taken into one at the top of the short staircase mentioned before. It was evidently disused, and a number of old family portraits were hanging on its walls. Among these there was one vacant place, and the picture that should have filled it was on the floor with its face to the wall. When the visitor noticed this her hostess said, "It is the portrait of one who brought disgrace upon the family. This used to be her room." She turned the picture round, and the visitor started. It was the very form and face she had beheld on the staircase. She was then told it was by no means the first time the apparition had been seen, but she believed always by strangers, not by members of the family.

I believe that there is firm faith in ghosts, and their power of revisiting the earth, throughout the entire county of Durham; and it is thought that a Romish priest is the proper person to lay them. The great season for their appearance is St. Thomas's eve and day, and they haunt the earth till Christmas eve, when the approaching festival, of course, puts them to flight. We of the North believe firmly in the benign influences of Christmas-tide as described by Shakespeare:—

> Some say that ever gainst that season comes
> Wherein our Saviour's birth is celebrate,
> The bird of dawning singeth all night long;
> And then they say no spirit dares stir abroad;
> The nights are wholesome; then no planets strike,
> No fairy takes, nor witch hath power to charm,
> So hallowed and so gracious is the time.

It was on one of the unlucky days (between St. Thomas's and Christmas eve), which happened also to be a Friday, that one of the waits disappeared at the foot of Elvet Bridge, Durham, not to be seen again; since which event the waits have never played in that city on Friday nights. On St. Thomas's eve and day, too, have carriers and waggoners been most alarmed by the ghost of the murdered woman, who was wont to haunt the path or lane between the Cradle Well and Neville's Cross. With her child dangling at her side, she used to join parties coming in or going out of Durham in carriers' carts or waggons, would enter the vehicles, and there seat herself; but would always disappear when they reached the limits of her hopeless pilgrimage.

Night after night, too, when it is sufficiently dark, the Headless Coach whirls along the rough approach to Langley Hall, near Durham, drawn by black and fiery steeds. We hear of this apparition, too, in Northumberland. "When the death-hearse, drawn by headless horses, and driven by a headless driver, is seen about midnight, proceeding rapidly, but without noise, towards the churchyard, the death of some considerable person in the parish is sure to happen at no distant period."[1] And it is recorded in Bee's Diary, that the death of one John Borrow, of Durham, was presaged by a vision of a coach drawn by six black swine, and driven by a black driver.

The Headless Coach, or more correctly coach with headless coachman, appears again in Norfolk. Mr. Henry Denny writes thus of it: "I remember well my mother talking about a certain person, whose name I have forgotten, but who formerly lived in what is called Pockthorp, a part of the city near the river Wensam, a man of some substance. He used to be seen by people late at night driving a coach and four horses over the tops of the houses, the coachman and horses all without heads. The crack of the whip was heard and then the carriage and horses were seen in the air. He was always seen going in the direction of Pockthorp, or the old bridge which leads to Monshold Heath. The belief was a common one fifty or sixty years ago."

Beverley, in Yorkshire, has also a like apparition. The headless ghost of Sir Josceline Percy drives four headless horses nightly above its streets, pausing over a certain house, of which I can say nothing more by way of identification than that it was tenanted a few years back by a Mr. Gilbey. This house was said to contain a chest with 100 nails in it, one of which dropped out every year. Tradition avers that this nocturnal disturbance is connected with Sir Josceline once riding on horseback into Beverley Minster. There is in the Minster a Percy shrine.[2]

"At Dalton, near Thirsk," writes Mr. Baring-Gould, "is an old barn, which is haunted by a headless woman. One night a tramp went into it to sleep. At midnight he was awakened by a light, and sitting up he saw a woman coming towards him from the end of the barn, holding her head in her hands like a lantern, with light streaming out of the eyes, nostrils, and mouth. He sprang out of the barn in a fright, breaking a hole in the wall to escape. This hole I was shown six years ago. Whether the barn still stands I cannot say."

As for Yorkshire, indeed, the Rev. J. Barmby assures me that

[1] *Rambles in Northumberland.*

[2] Communicated by the Rev. W. De Lancey Lawson.

there were plenty of ghosts or bogles about the village of Melsonby, a district with which he used to be well acquainted. A well there, called the Lady Well, was haunted by a lady without a head, and Berry Well by a bogle in the form of a white goose. Not far off was a conical hill, called Diddersley Hill, on Gatherley Moor, where an old farmer declares the fairies used to dance in his young days. And near this hill an arch spanned the road, not of any great antiquity, certainly; still a mounted horseman was to be seen upon it in the early morning light, to the great terror of the farmers' lads who had to pass beneath, starting before dawn with carts for coals into "Bishoprig," *i. e.* the county of Durham.

The village of Calverley, near Bradford, in Yorkshire, has been haunted since the time of Queen Elizabeth by the apparition of Master Walter Calverley, now popularly called Sir Walter. It is averred that this man murdered his wife and children, and, refusing to plead, was subjected to the "*peine forte et dure.*" In his last agony he is said to have exclaimed, "Them that love Sir Walter, loup on, loup on!" which accordingly became the watchword of the apparition, which frequented a lane near the village of Calverley. There is no fear, however, of meeting it at present; the ghost has been laid, and cannot reappear as long as green holly grows on the manor. My friend, Mr. Barmby, however, informs me that his grandfather, when a child, and riding behind his father on horseback, saw the apparition, and was terrified by it; while the father, to allay his boy's fears, said "It's only Sir Walter." This Master Walter Calverley is the hero of "The Yorkshire Tragedy," one of the plays attributed by some to Shakespeare.

The late Canon Humble informed me that a house at Perth, let in tenements, was considered haunted on account of the strange and unaccountable sounds heard there. Sometimes music was heard, proceeding apparently from a fixed spot in the wall. It was always heard in the same place and the same time, *i. e.* between seven and eight in the evening and one and two in the early morning, but sometimes for a longer, sometimes for a shorter, period of time. Again, there were unaccountable rappings and knockings by unknown hands. The only thing alleged in explanation was, that a former proprietor and inhabitant of the house was a very wicked man.

From the Rev. J. F. Bigge I learn a few particulars respecting another haunted house—Dalton Hill Head, once belonging to the family of Hedley, of Newcastle, but purchased from them by Mr. Collingwood, of Dissington. Some years ago a woman, named Mary Henderson (a connection, it appears, of George Stephenson, the engineer), had sole charge of the house; but the gardener lived close by, and kept a mastiff, called "Ball." Against the advice of the gardener, she pried into a hidden closet, and discovered in it a quantity of children's bones, some in hat-boxes, some wrapped in articles of clothing. She begged for the dog as a companion through the night, closed the house, and went to bed, but was soon awakened by strange sounds of dancing and singing up stairs. Being a bold woman, she got up to investigate into the matter, but the dog was terrified, and unwilling to accompany her. She took him in her arms, and went round the house. All was still and empty, but an attic window stood open. We are not informed whether the disturbances continued after this investigation.

One of my clerical friends, an incumbent in Yorkshire, has been good enough to communicate to me a family legend of an apparition witnessed by one of his aunts, and often told by her. This lady used, when a girl, to visit at the house of a gentleman near Ripon, and on one occasion, when about thirteen or fourteen years old, was spending the afternoon there. She was playing in the garden with his children, young people of about her own age, when one of them exclaimed, "Why, there is brother —— walking at the bottom of the garden." She looked up, and recognised the form and features of the young man, who was then in India. His figure appeared with perfect distinctness upon a gravel path which led round the garden, but not to any other place. One of the children, a young girl, ran into the house and told her father what they had seen. He bade her run away and go on playing—it must be a mistake. However, he took out his watch, noted the time, and wrote down the day and hour. When the next Indian mail arrived it brought intelligence of his son's death, at the very time when the children had seen his "eidolon" in the garden.

A story of the same character and as remarkable was thus related to me by the late Canon Humble: "I do not recollect whether I told you a very curious circumstance which occurred to a man I knew very well named S——, then a curate of St. A——, Newcastle. He had, when in his previous curacy of L—— B——, been paying his addresses to a young lady who resided at F—— Hall, near B——, but a coolness had taken place between them. One summer evening he was riding in the neighbourhood and saw the lady standing at the end of the drive which led to her house, without her bonnet, and dressed in light blue muslin. He thought at once that she had seen him in the distance and come out to have a word of explanation, so he attempted to direct his steed towards her. The animal would not go, but snorted and turned away. He brought its head round, but it began to kick and plunge so violently as to endanger his seat. He could do nothing with it, and was obliged at last to follow its wishes instead of his own. The next morning, feeling that some explanation was due, he determined to go and tell the young lady how her dress had startled his horse and how impossible he had found it in consequence to approach her. On reaching F—— Hall he found it closed, and was informed that Miss M——, the lady in question, had died the evening before, at the very time he had seen her form on the road."

Through the kindness of the Rev. S. Baring-Gould I am enabled to conclude my series of apparitions and haunted houses with the account of one which, though from another part of England, is of such exceeding interest that I am much gratified with the permission to record it in these pages as I received it from his pen:—

"Lew Trenchard House is haunted by a White Lady, who goes by the name of Madame Gould, and is supposed to be the spirit of a lady who died there—like Queen Elizabeth, seated in her chair—April 10, 1795. Her maiden name was Belfield; she was born in 1711, and she married William Drake Gould, son of Henry Gould, of Lew Trenchard, and Elizabeth, daughter of Philip Drake of Littleham.

"At Lew House there is a corridor extending the whole length of the upper story of the house; along this the lady is supposed to walk at night, and her step has been frequently heard.

"My mother has often told me how she has heard the step at night, as though proceeding from high-heeled shoes, walking slowly up the corridor, and thinking it might be my father coming to bed she has opened the door to admit him; but on looking out she has seen the moon streaming in through the windows on an empty passage, down which she still heard the measured tread. My sister often expressed her desire to hear the steps of the spectral lady, but was still disappointed, though she sat up on purpose.

"One summer night, however, she was sitting in her room, with window and door open, writing a letter, and thinking of anything but the old Madame, when she heard steps along the corridor. At the moment she thought it might be my father, and she rose, took up her candle, and went to the door to speak to him. To her surprise she saw no one, but the steps passed her, and went on into the lumber-room at the end of the passage. Being a resolute and courageous young lady she followed the sound into the room, but could see no one. She also opened the only other door beyond her own, and which gave admittance to one of the servants' rooms, to ascertain whether the noise could have proceeded thence, but she found the two maids fast asleep.

"At the end of the house is a long oak-tree avenue; the White Lady is said to have been seen pacing up and down this, gleaming in and out among the gnarled tree-trunks, as she passed into the moonlight or disappeared in the shade.

"About three miles off is a quaint old granite mansion, half pulled down by my grandfather, and turned into a substantial farmhouse. This ancient house belonged originally to the Woods, and there was a standing feud between that family and my own, till they were ruined, and Madame Gould bought the land and house from them; after which she declared she should die happy.

"On the confines of this property, called Orchard, is a deep gloomy valley, through which trickles a rill of dark water, under the shadow of the thick fir plantations which clothe the sides of the glen. It goes by the name of the Black Valley, and the Bratton-Clovelly road plunges down into it, crosses a little bridge, and scrambles up the opposite side through the gloom of the overhanging trees. On the side of the road is an old mine-shaft, long abandoned. It is confidently asserted by Lew and Bratton people that, on dark nights, Madame Gould is to be seen, dressed all in white, standing by the side of the stream, with a phosphorescent light streaming from her face and her clothes; and that she stoops and takes up handfuls of water, which she allows to trickle down in sparkling drops through her fingers. Sometimes she combs her long brown floating hair with a silver comb; and many a Bratton man, returning from market, has seen her and been nearly frightened out of his wits. Not many years ago a man of that village had his leg broken by falling over a hedge, in his attempt to escape from the apparition as it issued from the old mining-shaft and made towards him.

"A young man, named Symmonds, living at Galford, a farm in the parish, left home for America during the old Madame's lifetime. After some years he returned, and hiring a horse at Tavistock he rode home, a distance of twelve miles. It was a clear moonlight night, and as he passed through the Lew Valley, with the white rime lying thick on the grass, he noticed a newly-ploughed field, in which the plough had been left. On this was seated a lady in white satin, with long brown hair floating down her shoulders. Her face was uplifted, and her eyes directed towards the moon, so that Mr. Symmonds had a full view of it. He recognised her at once, and taking off his hat he called out, 'I wish you a very good night, Madame.' She bowed in return, and waved her hand, the man noticing the sparkle of her diamond rings as she did so. On reaching home, after the first greetings and congratulations, he said to his aged parents, 'What do you think now? I have seen that strange Madame Gould sitting on a plough, this time o' night, and with frost on the ground, looking at the moon.' All who heard him started, and a blank expression passed over their countenances. The young man, seeing that he had surprised them more than he anticipated, asked what was the matter. The reply was, 'Madame was buried three days ago in Lew church.'

"It must be noticed that a belief connected with the appearance of spirits, up to the third day after death or burial, is very ancient. S. Macarius the Younger, of Alexandria (A.D. 373), thus speaks: 'On the third day, the oblation having been made in the church, the alleviation of its pain, which it underwent through separation from the body, the departed soul . . . . . receives good hope. For two days it was permitted to the soul to wander about on the earth at its will. Wherefore the soul, enthralled with love to its body, sometimes haunts the mansion wherein it had dwelt, sometimes the sepulchre in which its body is laid, and thus for two days it seeks, as it were, its part, in seeking its corpse.'

"But to return to the subject under consideration.

"An old woman once entered the orchard near Lew church, and seeing the trees laden with apples she shook some down and filled her pockets, keeping one in her hand to eat. She then turned to the gate into the road, but suddenly there flashed before her in the way the figure of the old Madame in white, pointing to the apple. The poor woman in an agony of terror cast it away, and fled across the orchard to a gap in the hedge on the opposite side; but at the moment she reached it the figure of the White Lady appeared standing in the gap, looking at her sternly, and pointing to her pocket. It was not till the old goody had emptied it of the stolen apples that the spectre vanished.

"Old Lew Trenchard church was handsomely furnished with a carved oak screen and bench-ends. Some of these ends alone remain. They are of excellent workmanship: one representing St. Michael weighing souls, one a lady's portrait in a medallion, with a jester in cap and bells in a niche beneath it, another a gentleman's portrait with an old battlemented gateway beneath it. The other bench-ends bear shields with the emblems of the Passion upon them. The screen has wholly disappeared.

"The carpenter who was employed in 1832 to replace these old benches with neat deal pews, before leaving his work one evening, out of curiosity, opened the vault in which lay William Drake Gould and his lady. Finding the lady's coffin-lid loose, he proceeded to raise it, that he might take a look at the redoubted Madame. Immediately she opened her eyes, sat up, and rose to her feet. The carpenter, who was an elderly man, frightened out of his senses, rushed from the church, which was filled with light from the body of the risen lady. As the man dashed down the churchyard avenue he turned his head back, and saw her over his shoulder gleaming in the porch, and preparing to sail down the path after him.

"From the church to his house was a good mile and a quarter, and the road passes nearly all the way through woods. He ran as he never ran before, and as he ran his shadow went before him, cast by the light which shone from the spectral lady who followed him. On reaching his house he burst the door open, and dashed into bed beside his wife, who was infirm and bed-ridden. Both then saw the figure standing in the doorway, and the light from it was so intense that, to use the old woman's words, she could see by it a pin lying on the floor.

"There is a stone shown on the 'ramps' of Lew Slate Quarry where seven parsons met to lay the old Madame. Opinions differ as to what took place—whether she was laid in part or not at all. Some say that the white owl, which nightly flits to and fro in front of Lew House, is the spirit of the lady conjured by the parsons into a bird; others doubt this; but I believe all agree that the parsons failed because one of the number was 'a bit fresh' when he came, and had forgotten the right words to be used.

"I have not the smallest doubt in my own mind that this history is in its essentials of very great antiquity; that the apparition is really an ancient white lady, who has suffered anthropomorphosis, and become Madame Gould; the same stories and the same superstitions having been rife ages before the birth of the lady to whom they have now been applied.

"In many points Madame Gould strongly resembles the German Dame Holle: such as her connection with water and her silver comb, as well as the appearance to the apple-picker. Holle or Holdar, in Germany, is a very beautiful white lady with long flowing hair of a golden hue; she haunts fountains and streams, and is often engaged in washing. She is well disposed, and rebukes bad children, punishing theft and other faults. Her dress is white with a golden girdle, and she is radiant with light. She is an ancient Teutonic goddess. Curiously enough, also, she lives in mountains, and issues luminous from the mouth of caves, just as Madame Gould appeared to the man from the old mine-shaft. In one account of the apparition which I obtained, Madame Gould was expressly said to have appeared with golden hair; whereas her portrait represents her as a very beautiful woman, with long brown hair floating down her back.

"I have given these stories of the old Madame with some fulness because I believe her to be unquestionably an ancient Saxon goddess, who has fallen from her pedestal, and undergone anthropomorphosis and localization; and such instances, though not uncommon in Norway or Germany, are rare in England."

Devonshire is no doubt a land of ghost stories. I remember how racily some of them were told by the late Rev. William Woollcombe, an aged clergyman of that county with whose family my own is connected. One was of a young lady in North Devon, whose father had been carried off by smugglers, kept a prisoner for a "year and a day," and only released on payment of a large sum of money. He did not long survive his restoration to his home, and his daughter, an only child and motherless, soon followed him to the grave, worn out by that year of loneliness and suspense. But she did not rest there; her spirit haunted the neighbouring town, a straggling fishing-place, whose inhabitants were supposed to be implicated in the abduction of her father. Her mode of punishing them was peculiar. She would flit from house to house on Sunday morning while the dinners were cooking, and, laying her cold hand on the meat, would taint it, so that it became absolutely uneatable. Another story, told to account for the peculiar shape of the dining-room in a certain Dartmoor vicarage, was to this effect:—

Some years back a clergyman, on taking possession of a living on the confines of Dartmoor, found it necessary to enlarge the house, which was really little better than the peasants' cottages around it. He lengthened the one sitting-room, and made it into a tolerable dining-room, adding a drawing-room and two or three bedrooms. These improvements satisfied his wife and children; but there was one interested party whom he had left out of consideration—the spirit of his predecessor, an old gentleman who had outlived all his family, and passed many solitary years in the remote parsonage.

And ere long the consequences of this neglect appeared. Sounds were soon heard of an evening as though a figure in a dressing-gown were sweeping in and out of the rooms, and treading with a soft yet heavy tread, and this particularly in the dining-room, where the old Vicar had spent the last years of his life, sitting over the fire, or pacing up and down in his dressing-gown and slippers. The eerie sounds began at nightfall, and continued at intervals till morning. Uneasiness pervaded the household. Servants gave warning and went away; no one applied for their vacant places. The daughters fell ill, and were sent away for change of air; then their mother was anxious about them, and went to see how they were going on; and so the Vicar was left alone, at the mercy of his predecessor's ghost. At first he bore up bravely, but one Saturday night, while he was sitting up late, and wearily going over his Sunday sermons, the "pad, pad" of the measured tread struck so painfully upon his nerves that he could bear it no longer. He started up, opened the window, jumped out, and made the best of his way to the nearest farm, where lived his churchwarden, an honest Dartmoor farmer.

There the Vicar found a kind welcome; and when he told his tale, in a hesitating sort of way, owning his dislike to solitude and apologising for the weakness of nerves which made him fancy he heard the sounds so often described to him, his host broke in with a declaration of his belief that the old Vicar was at the bottom of it, just because of the alterations in the house he had lived in so many years. "He never could abide changes," pursued the farmer, "but he's had his day, and you should have yours now. He must be laid, that's certain; and, if you'll go away next week to your missis and the young ladies, I'll see to it."

And see to it he did. A jury of seven parsons was convoked, and each sat for half-an-hour with a candle in his hand, and it burned out its time with each, showing plainly that none of them could lay the ghost. Nor was this any wonder, for were they not all old acquaintances of his, so that he knew all their tricks? The spirit could afford to defy them; it was not worth his while to blow their candles out. But the seventh parson was a stranger, and a scholar fresh from Oxford. In his hand the light went out at once. He was clearly the man to lay the ghost, and he did not shrink from his task; he laid it at once, and in a beer-barrel.

But now a fresh difficulty arose. What was to be done with the beer-barrel and its mysterious tenant? Where could it be placed secure from the touch of any curious hand, which might be tempted to broach the barrel, and set free the ghost? Nothing occurred to the assembled company but to roll the thing into one corner, and send for the mason to inclose it with stones and mortar. This done, the room looked very odd with one corner cut off. Uniformity would be attained if the other three were filled up as well; and besides, the ghost would be safer if no one knew the very spot in which he was reposing. So the other corners were blocked up, and with success. What matters it if the room be smaller!—the parsonage has never been haunted since.

I will only add one more story, which is well authenticated, at least as far as the laying of the ghost. About fifty years ago the beautiful avenue of C—— Place, Sussex, was haunted by the spirit of Madam S——. There was much excitement in the neighbourhood in consequence, and the vicar of the parish was applied to to lay the ghost. He with two of the neighbouring clergy met in C—— church at midnight, and used some form of prayer calculated to satisfy the popular mind, after which, it is said, she never appeared again. The names of the clergymen are still remembered in the neighbourhood.

Madam S. is said to have haunted the place in consequence of a threat she had uttered when objecting to the marriage of a daughter. The daughter married, and the mother haunted her. This laying of a ghost, however, is not always an easy task. Homersfield, in Suffolk, was a haunted house, and a priest was sent for to lay the unquiet spirit that so tormented the inmates. He came, book in hand, but to no purpose, for the instant he began to read a prayer the ghost got a line ahead of him. At last one of the family hit on this devise. The next time, as soon as the priest began his exorcism, two pigeons were let loose, the spirit stopped to look at them, the priest got before him in his prayer, and the work was accomplished—the ghost has never again been heard of.

CHAPTER XI.

DREAMS.

Dreams presaging Death in the North of England—in Ireland—of the Rev. Jacob Duché—Dead Bodies Discovered through Dreams—Visions at Horhury—in Lincolnshire—The Bodach Glas—Second-sight.

F dreams which convey an intimation, either of what is actually taking place at a great distance or of future events, many instances have been recorded, and many are treasured in the memory of different families through this as well as other countries. Where such dreams and their fulfilment are well accredited we cannot disbelieve them; nor can I see why we should be desirous to do so, since we know from Scripture that dreams have been used as the vehicle of intercourse between the visible and the invisible worlds. Some dreams worthy of note are scattered through these pages; a few others, chiefly warnings of death, remain to be recorded.

The first was related to me by a clerical friend, who knew the persons concerned in it and heard it from them. Three brothers, whom we will call Charles, James, and Edward, lived in different parts of one of the northern counties of England. Edward, on awaking one morning, was surprised to find his wife still in bed, and asked why she was not getting up as usual. She said that she was quite unnerved by a terrblie dream, and must wait a little to recover herself. At first he laughed at her fears, but, seeing that she was really in distress, inquired what the dream had been. His wife told him that she had seen him with his two brothers, Charles and James, standing in earnest conversation on a grass-plot. Meanwhile, a young man then dead, but formerly in the employment of Edward, came towards them with a paper in his hand, much crossed and blotted over. The ground suddenly opened, James fell into the chasm and disappeared. "You and Charles," said the poor wife, "would press to the margin of the dangerous pit to see what had become of him, and I was endeavouring to keep you back." While she was uttering these words the sound of a horse galloping into the courtyard roused her husband. He went to the window, threw it up, and asked what was the matter. The reply was, "Come over directly to ———. Your brother, Mr. James B———, is just dead." It appeared afterwards that Mr. James B——— had been in his usual health till about three o'clock that morning, when he was seized with violent internal pains and died in a few minutes.

The wife, who related this to my informant, dwelt a good deal on the appearance in her dream of the young man lately in her husband's employ, saying he had once before appeared to her in a dream which had been duly fulfilled. During an absence of her husband, she had been much alarmed by a report that the vessel in which he had sailed for London was lost, but she had been reassured by a dream in which this young man had told her he was safe and would write to her within three days, which came to pass accordingly.

A very touching dream, also a portent of death, has been thus reported to me on credible authority. It is said to have occurred some years ago in the family of an Irish bishop. A little boy came downstairs one morning, saying, "Oh, mamma, I have had such a nice dream; somebody gave me such a pretty box, and I am sure it was for me, for there was my name on it. Look, it was just like this," and taking up a slate and pencil the child drew the shape of a coffin. The parents gazed at one another in alarm, not lessened by the gambols of the child, who frolicked about in high health and spirits. The father was obliged to go out that morning, but he begged the mother to keep the child in her sight through the day. She did so, till on dressing to go out in her carriage the little boy slipped away to the stables, where he begged the coachman to take him by his side while he drove to the house-door, a thing he had often done before. On this occasion, however, the horses were restive, the driver lost control over them, and the child was flung off and killed on the spot.

Another dream, which has always appeared to me very remarkable, I give in the words of the late Rev. Dawson Warren, vicar of Edmonton, a clergyman with whose family I am closely connected. He recorded it on the authority of his mother, a lady of considerable sense and talents, who had seen the documents upon which its truth was substantiated, and who fully believed it. The dreamer, the Rev. Jacob Duché, a chaplain in America at the time of the Revolutionary War, was compelled to take refuge in England, but returned to his home and family on the re-establishment of peace. When Mr. Duché was returning to America to rejoin his family, and was about halfway across the Atlantic, he dreamed one night that he had landed, arrived in Philadelphia, and was hastening to his home. His house-door appeared to be open; he thought that he ran into his study, and that he found sitting in his own chair his wife, wringing her hands and lamenting the death of their favourite son. She seemed to tell him the painful particulars, and then his grief awakened him. He related his dream to his fellow-passengers and to the captain of the ship, and was so deeply impressed by the circumstance that he wrote out a full account of it, and got it attested by their signatures. On his arrival at Philadelphia he hastened to his house; he found the door open, he flew to his study, he found his wife sitting in his chair, and in an agony of grief she told him of the death of their beloved son, which had taken place at the very time of the dream.

A remarkable discovery of a dead body by a dream took place in my own county in the year 1848, and was narrated in the papers of the day. Mr. Smith, gardener to Sir Clifford Constable, was supposed to have fallen into the Tees, his hat and stick having been found near the waterside, and the river was dragged for some time but without success. A person named Awde, from Little Newsham, a small village four miles from Wycliffe, then dreamt that poor Smith was lying under the ledge of a certain rock about 300 yards below Whorlton Bridge, and that his right arm was broken. The dream so affected this man that he got up early and set out at once to search the river. He went to the boat-house, told his story to the person in charge there, and asked for the boat. He rowed to the spot he had seen in his dream, and on the first trial he made with the boat-hook he drew up the body of the drowned man, and found the right arm actually broken.

The late Canon Humble paralleled this history with one from Cornwall, which came to his own knowledge. A lady of Truro dreamt the night before a boating-party that the boat was upset, and she herself drowned. She therefore determined not to join it, and sent an excuse. The party returned safely, however, and the lady, after telling a friend what had passed, and describing where she had dreamt the body would be found, ceased to think of the matter. A month or two later the lady had occasion to cross the Truro river at King Harry's Passage—the boat was upset—she was drowned, and they sought for the body in vain. Then the friend to whom she had told her dream came forward and pointed out the spot marked out in that dream as the body's resting-place, and there it was found.

It is remarkable that dreams are dwelt on a good deal in the Talmud and fast enjoined on persons who have been unfortunate in this respect. Among prescribed dreams are those in which the teeth seem to be falling out, or the ceiling of the room coming down.

Of visions or waking-dreams, two very interesting ones have been communicated to me by the gentleman to whom these pages are so largely indebted, the Rev. S. Baring-Gould. I give them in his own words: "An old woman, Widow Freeman, lived at Horbury some years ago, and is there buried. She was a most devout and earnest Churchwoman, a frequent communicant, and regular at daily matins. She often had visions, one of which was as follows: The old woman was sitting in her cottage, reading her Bible or prayer-book, when a sudden blaze of light filled the room, and on looking up the whole chamber was illuminated with dazzling white glory. Numerous white doves were flitting about, flashing in the light, winnowing the air with their wings, and encircling the window. She observed that their beaks (nibbs she called them) were steeped in blood, and they dropped the blood upon her. In another moment they vanished, but the light became painfully dazzling, and in the midst of it stood Our Lord displaying His five wounds. She was left in a state of overwhelming joy, and could not restrain herself from relating what she had seen to some of her neighbours and to the parish priest; but she had a strong aversion to relating it to any one who did not believe in the supernatural, lest, as she termed it, she should be 'giving that which is holy unto dogs, and casting pearls before swine.'

"Another Horbury woman, of a different character from Widow Freeman, and by no means so attentive to her religious duties, had a vision whilst engaged in her work this month (November, 1865). She saw suddenly before her a monstrous and very terrible beast 'summat like a padfoit,' and she was 'right fleyed to see't; it had great goggle e'en and a mouth ravening for blood.' It seemed about to rush upon her and rend her in pieces, when a hand appeared marked with blood, and this hand smote the beast, and it fled with a bellow that shook the house."

The following dream recorded by the same hand is very remarkable: "A man at ——, in Lincolnshire, known for his drunken and disorderly life, had a dream. He thought that he was driving down a winding lane on a dark night. He heard footsteps behind him and turned to look, but could only discern a dark figure approaching, without being able to see the face. The stranger came up with the cart, and the driver saw that he was dressed in a long dark cloak. Suddenly the foot-traveller threw open the cloak, and asked to be received into the cart, and by the wounds in His hands the poor man recognised 'his dear Saviour.' Before he answered the man awoke. For some time he lived a better life, but gradually relapsed, and before the year was out had become worse than ever. Then he dreamt again. He was driving down the same dark lane, but no footstep sounded behind him. He looked round. At that moment the cart was upset, he fell into a ditch full of fire, and awoke with a scream, wafting the flames from his mouth. A few nights after the wretched man left a public-house drunk in his cart, and was found next morning lying under his cart with his neck broken."

The belief in death-omens peculiar to certain families is purely Celtic, and does not, therefore, fall within the province of Border Folk-Lore. Mr. Wilkie indeed mentions the Maug or May Moulach, but calls it a spirit akin to the Killmoulis, whereas it is "the girl with the hairy left-hand" which haunts Tulloch Gorms, and gives warning of a death in the Grant family, like the Banshee in many old houses in Ireland, the Bodca-an-Dun in the family of Rothmarchas, or the spectre of the bloody hand in that of Kinchardines. Such a prophet of death was the Bodach Glas, or dark grey man, of which Sir Walter Scott makes such effective use in Waverley towards the end of Fergus Mac Ivor's history. Its appearance foretold death in the clan of ——, and I have been informed on the most credible testimony of its appearance in our own day. The Earl of E——, a nobleman alike beloved and respected in Scotland, and whose death was truly felt as a national loss, was playing on the day of his decease on the links of St. Andrews at the national game of golf. Suddenly he stopped in the middle of a game, saying, "I can play no longer, there is the Bodach Glas. I have seen it for the third time; something fearful is going to befall me." He died that night at M. M——, as he was handing a candlestick to a lady who was retiring to her room. The clergyman from whom I received this story endorses it as authentic, and names the gentleman to whom Lord E—— spoke.

I learn from another friend the particulars of one of the other two presages of impending doom vouchsafed to this nobleman. It was a warning of his wife's death, and was thus given: Shortly after her confinement, which she had passed through safely, he went from home to attend a wedding, and during his absence dreamt that he read in *The Times* newspaper an announcement of Lady E——'s death on a day not far distant. The dream affected him a good deal, and his dejection the next day was apparent to every one. He returned home, found the Countess doing well, but soon after she caught cold from being moved into a damp room; illness came on, and her husband was roused up one night with tidings of her being in a dangerous state. It was the morning indicated by the dream. The Earl remembered it, and rose up (as he afterwards expressed it) with a yell of agony. Before nightfall she had expired.

Second-sight, again, belongs properly to the Highlands, and accordingly lies beyond the limits I have laid down for myself in this work. Mr. Wilkie says little respecting it, except that the seventh sons of seventh sons are persons marked out to be the possessors of the mysterious gift. He calls the seer an Elleree, a name I only know in his manuscript, but which doubtless means a person skilled in the affairs of Elle or Fairydom, and says that, if he sees sparks of fire falling on a person, that person's death is near at hand. But the more common presage of death is for the Elleree to see the man wrapped in his shroud, and, according as the shroud covers more or less of the figure, will the death be near or remote. Again, should the Elleree see a funeral, and distinguish the persons of any of the attendants, those men are marked for an early grave.

It is to be regretted that this subject of second-sight—which, as Sir Walter Scott asserts, is attested by evidence which neither Bacon, Boyle, nor Johnson were able to resist,—has not arrested the attention of some philosophical thinker qualified to inquire into the matter, and give what explanation may be possible. For myself, I will only relate one incident which has always appeared to me very remarkable, and, professing myself wholly unable to offer any explanation, I will simply detail the circumstances, which for five-and-twenty years have been clearly imprinted on my memory.

About a quarter of a century has passed away since I started from D—— to join a party of tourists near Glasgow. We met, and determined that the gentlemen should take a walking and fishing ramble through Ross-shire and Inverness-shire, while the ladies should remain at the country-house of a friend, who had already gathered round her a merry group of young people, lately set free from the restraints of school, and bent on enjoying the beauty and freedom of the Western Highlands. The walking tour over, all were to spend a few days there together before the party broke up.

Our kind hostess was the widow of a Highland chief, and was descended from a family long celebrated for possessing a more than usual portion of second-sight. She firmly believed that the prophetic mantle had fallen upon her, but her disposition was cheerful and lively, and being herself still young she had a decided preference for the society of young people.

Her residence was situated on the slope of a steep hill, about half-a-mile from the side of a beautiful lake, which it overlooked. The lake was at this point a mile at least in breadth, and on its opposite shore stood a small farmhouse, with a few inclosed fields around it. The lake was several miles long, and had its egress into a river, which in winter, or when swollen by the heavy rains which are common in hilly countries, was of considerable size. The only means of crossing this river was by a stone bridge about half-a-mile from the end of the lake. When I have added, that in the garden of our friend was an inclosure which had for centuries been the burying-place of her husband's clan, and in which his remains were laid, I shall have given every particular necessary for the elucidation of the rest of the tale.

A month quickly passed among the rivers and lakes of Scotland, and we found ourselves at the widow's hospitable residence. Our welcome there was kind; but before an hour had passed we could not help noticing that a gloom hung over the party lately so merry. The conversation was evidently forced. The younger ladies looked anxious and distressed; their hostess sad, almost stern, as they sat apart, speaking little and evidently wrapped in thought. Something unusual had plainly occurred, and we eagerly sought an evening walk with some of the younger ladies, that we might learn what had so completely transformed our hitherto cheerful hostess.

The tale we were told was, in brief, as follows: About a week previously, Mrs. F—— (as we will designate the widow) had appeared at the breakfast table deadly pale, and with bloodshot eyes. She was reluctant to speak, and would not allow that anything was the matter, till towards evening a flood of tears relieved her, and she owned that she was distressed by a dream of the night before, so remarkable and so vivid that she felt convinced it would be realised. She described it thus:—

Looking from the windows of her house she had seen a long funeral procession come up the opposite side of the lake, from the direction of the river-bridge. When they reached the small farmhouse, the horses were taken out of the carriages and turned into an inclosure to graze; the coffin was brought down to the lake-side and placed in one of the boats, while the funeral party crossed in the large ferry-boat, commonly used for conveying cattle. On reaching the shore in front of Mrs. F——'s house, the procession again formed, and proceeded to the graveyard, where the funeral took place; the earth was heaped on the grave, and the mourners departed. Without calling at the house, they recrossed the lake, harnessed their animals, and disappeared by the same road by which they had come.

On hearing this narration, the young people ridiculed the notion of attending to the fancies of a dream, and by their bright cheerful conversation had succeeded at last in restoring Mrs. F—— to something like cheerfulness. But towards evening on the following day a horseman rode up to the door, and delivered a note from the undertaker of an adjacent town. This note announced that Mrs. F——'s mother-in-law had died suddenly at her residence, twenty miles off, and requested that a grave should be prepared for her in the family burying-ground. On inquiry, the messenger stated that the old lady had died at an hour coincident with the remarkable dream of her daughter-in-law, after a very slight indisposition, of which, in consequence of a family disagreement, Mrs. F—— had not heard.

The whole party was struck with awe. The widow quietly observed, "You see it is true," and retired to her own room for the rest of the day. On the fifth day the funeral took place, actually fulfilling, contrary to all likelihood, every circumstance connected with the dream. The old lady had died at her residence, the road from which ran by the same side of the river and lake with Mrs. F——'s house; it was therefore most improbable that the funeral procession should cross the lake. But all was to be accomplished. On the night preceding the burial a dreadful thunderstorm swept away the stone bridge which spanned one of the mountain streams that flowed into the lake about a mile from Mrs. F——'s house. The result was that the funeral party was unable to proceed by the road. They could not pass the stream, now a raging torrent, so they retraced their steps, and crossing the river, continued their journey on the opposite side of the lake. The lady of the house saw all from her windows—the horses turned loose to graze, the boats occupied exactly as foretold, the funeral completed, the last sod heaped on the grave, and the party turning to depart without even calling at the house of the nearest connection of the deceased. For the second time she saw it all; but with what feelings who shall dare to say?

APPENDIX.

The following remarkable story, communicated to me by Mr. Joseph Crawhall, was taken down from the lips of an old inhabitant of Newcastle-on-Tyne. The old man said he had known it all his life, and there can be little doubt that it is an ancient tale of that place. I have never met with the story before, but it bears a resemblance to some of Mr. Ralston's Russian Folk-Lore stories, and, like the nursery tale of *Toads and Diamonds*, it shows the good results of courtesy and kindness:

There was once an old woman who hired a servant-girl to keep her house clean and tidy. She told the girl to rise early and sweep out every corner, but to be sure *not* to sweep the chimney, and every night she went through the same, saying she was never to put her brush up the chimney. One morning, however, the servant thought she would put the brush up the chimney; she did so, and down fell a bag of money. She took it up and ran away.

As she went along she came to a gate, which spoke, and said to her, "Pretty maiden, will you open me, for I have not been opened for many a year?" "Open yourself," said the girl, "I have no time to open you." So she went on, and came to a cow, and the cow said, "Pretty maiden, stop and milk me, for I have not been milked for many a day." "Milk yourself," said the girl, "I have no time to milk you." So she went on, and came to a mill, and the mill said, "Pretty maiden, will you turn me, for I have not been turned for many a day." "Turn yourself," said the girl, "I have no time to turn you." By this time the girl began to get tired, so she hid the bag in the mill-hopper.

When the old woman got up in the morning, and missed the girl, she went straight to the chimney, and found her money was gone. So she set off directly after the girl, and when she came to the gate she said, "Gate o' mine, gate o' mine, have you seen a maid o' mine, with a ji-jaller bag, and a long leather bag, with all the money in that ever I had ?" and the gate said, " Further on."

Then she went on and came to the cow, of whom she asked the same question, and got the same answer. And she went on and came to the mill, and said, " Mill o' mine, mill o' mine, have you seen a maid o' mine, with a ji-jaller bag, and a long leather bag, with all the money in it that e'er I had ?" and the mill said, " Down the mill-hopper." So the old woman got her money again, and soon she hired a new girl, and told her the very same things she had told the first. The new girl did just like the first, and ran away; but when she came to the gate she opened it, and when she came to the cow she milked it, and when she came to the mill she turned it. So when the old woman went after the girl, and asked the gate, the cow, and the mill whether they had seen her, there was no answer, and the girl got away with the bag of money.

INDEX.

with black ribbon, of spinster with white, 58; extinguishing fire where corpse is kept, 59; killing cats and dogs after passing over a corpse, *ib.*; carrying the dead with the sun, 61—case at Stanton, *ib.*; in Wales carried on right hand of way and by north gate, *ib.*

Deazil, the: circling a person thrice with the sun, brings good fortune; the reverse direction or "withershins" evil fortune (Highlands), 61

Deerhurst, near Tewkesbury: a prodigious serpent molested the inhabitants; one John Smith enticed it with milk, cut off its head, and received an estate as a recompense, 298

Deliverance, charm for easy, 169

Deloraine, farmer's witch wife of, 197

Denbigh: a dragon haunted the precincts of the castle; killed by Sir John of the Thumbs, 299

Denham Tracts quoted on Bogie and Redcap, 254

Denny (Mr. H.) on spell with hemp-seed, 104; on Headless Coach at Norwich, 327

Denton Hall, haunted by a silky, 269, 70

Derry, elf shooting in county, 186-7

Derwentwater lights, the aurora-borealis, 307

De Salle's (Eusebe) *Peregrinations en Orient* on divining by Bible and Key at English consulate, 237

Devil: sacrificing black cock to, 147; French receipt for raising him, *ib.*; assumes the form of various quadrupeds, 277; can simulate the crow and duck, but not the lamb, cock, pigeon, or dove, *ib.*; piece of land ("Clontie's Croft") set apart as a propitiatory gift to (Scotland), 278; molesting a minister, *ib.*; selling one's soul to (Sussex), *ib.*; story of the tailor of Clitheroe who outwitted him, 279; his attempt to learn several trades a failure (Scotland), 279-80; praying aloud keeps him away, 280

Devil's bird: the swallow in Ireland; the yellow-hammer in Scotland, 123

Devil's knell: a hundred strokes and then thrice three, rung on Christmas Eve in Cleveland, 66

Dew, washing the face with May; climbing hills to "meet the dew," 85; *see* Witches and May-dew

Dill hinders witches, 227

Diddersley Hill, fairies once danced on, 328

Dishaloof: the rite used in saining a corpse, 53

Disease cured by waters of Loch Monar, 164-5; by the elements in the Eucharist, 146

Dishclout boiled in crock, causes loss of lovers, 116

Dittisham, an incantation at, 224; by "shaping" of a wedding dress, 35

Divination by horse-knot or *Centaurea nigra;* by "kemps" or spikes of ribwort plantain; by water and holly, 99; by nine leaves of she-holly; by knot-weed, 100; by yarrow from a young man's grave; by hanging sark to dry, 101; by sprigs of sage, rose water, and shift; by knotting garter about stocking, 102; by the willow wand; by "hair-snatching" in Germany; by crossed garters and looking-glass in Belgium, 103; by sowing hemp-seed on All Hallowe'en—and on St. Martin's night in Norfolk, 104; by new-laid egg;

2 C

ERRATUM.

In page 4, note [1], line 2, *for* Dæmonium, *read* Dæmonum.

Westminster: Printed by Nichols and Sons, 25, Parliament Street